When I start thinking about a story, it sort of grows in my head... But when I try to tell someone how it's going to go, I often think, "Ack, that won't work..."
Back when *M&R* was just developing, I started telling the story to my editor full of confidence. But sure enough, I was only halfway through when I said, "Forget it... It won't work..." That's when my editor got this real look of concern on his face and said, "Nishi, you're going to have to try not being so hard on yourself."
It's been like running a marathon in the dark since. I have to thank my readers for reaching out a helping hand and keeping me going. You're the only reason I've made it this far... Here's the conclusion to Enchu's story!

– Yoshiyuki Nishi

Yoshiyuki Nishi was born in Tokyo. Two of his favorite manga series are *Dragon Ball* and the robot-cat comedy *Doraemon*. His latest series, *Muhyo & Roji's Bureau of Supernatural Investigation*, debuted in Japan's *Akamaru Jump* magazine in 2004 and went on to be serialized in *Weekly Shonen Jump*.

MUHYO & ROJI'S

BUREAU OF SUPERNATURAL INVESTIGATION

VOL. 15
SHONEN JUMP Manga Edition

STORY AND ART BY
YOSHIYUKI NISHI

Translation & Adaptation/Alexander O. Smith
Touch-up Art & Lettering/Brian Bilter
Design/Yukiko Whitley
Editor/Amy Yu

VP, Production/Alvin Lu
VP, Sales & Product Marketing/Gonzalo Ferreyra
VP, Creative/Linda Espinosa
Publisher/Hyoe Narita

Printed in the U.S.A.

Published by VIZ Media, LLC
P.O. Box 77010
San Francisco, CA 94107

10 9 8 7 6 5 4 3 2 1
First printing, February 2010

www.viz.com

www.shonenjump.com

THE WORLD'S
MOST POPULAR MANGA

SHONEN JUMP MANGA EDITION

Muhyo & Roji's Bureau of Supernatural Investigation BSI

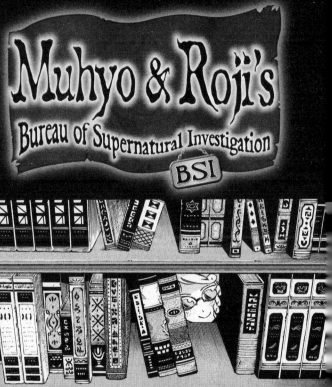

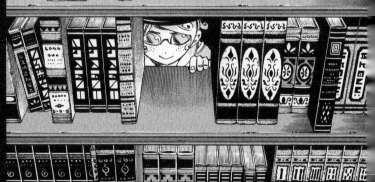

Vol. 15 The Long Nightmare

Story & Art by Yoshiyuki Nishi

Dramatis Personae

Jiro Kusano (Roji)

Assistant at Muhyo's office, recently promoted from the lowest rank of "Second Clerk" to that of (provisional) "First Clerk." Roji has a gentle heart and has been known to freak out in the presence of spirits. Lately, he has been devoting himself to the study of magic law so that he can pull his own weight someday.

Toru Muhyo (Muhyo)

Young, genius magic law practitioner with the highest rank of "Executor." Always calm and collected (though sometimes considered cold), Muhyo possesses a strong sense of justice and even has a kind side. Sleeps a lot to recover from the exhaustion caused by his practice.

Harumi Busujima

Executor and one of the only practitioners in the world capable of "remote magic law."

Yu Abiko (Biko)

Muhyo's classmate and an Artificer. Makes seals, pens, magic law books and other accoutrements of magic law.

Yoichi Himukai (Yoichi)

Judge and Muhyo's former classmate. Expert practitioner of all magic law except execution.

Page Klaus

Chief Investigator for the Magic Law Association, Yoichi's boss, and Muhyo and Enchu's former instructor.

Rio Kurotori (Rio)

Charismatic Artificer who turned traitor when the Magic Law Association stood by and let her mother die.

Soratsugu Madoka (Enchu)

Muhyo's former classmate and Executor-hopeful until one event turned him onto the traitor's path.

Umekichi Sasanoha

First clerk and Busujima's assistant. In his true envoy form, he is called *Unryuso*. "Umekichi" is his human-form alias.

Hanao Ebisu (Ebisu)

Judge and assistant to Goryo. Fired once, but has since been reinstated.

Daranimaru Goryo (Goryo)

Executor and former rival to Muhyo. When Ark captured him, it was Muhyo who came to the rescue.

Seven-Faced Dog

An envoy with the ability to change shape. Specialist at uncovering spectral crimes.

Ginji Sugakiya

Upperclassman at M.L.S. Boasts the rank of Assistant Judge even though he is still enrolled in school.

Reiko Imai

Brave Judge who joined Muhyo and gang during the fight against Face-Ripper Sophie.

Teeki

Dangerous entity marked as a traitor to the Magic Law Association for 800 years.

Nana Takenouchi (Nana)

High school student, spirit medium and amateur photographer. Working as an assistant photographic investigator.

Lili & Maril Mathias

Twin siblings world-renowned for their research in magic law.

Kiriko

A familiar, serving as a go-between for practitioners and their envoys. Fond of Nana, whom she calls "Sis."

Kenji Sato (Kenji)

Muhyo and Roji saved this troublemaker from a ghost, earning his grudging respect.

Yuuri

Favored envoy of Muhyo, summoned during the forming of Muhyo's contract with Pluto.

The Story

Magic law is a newly established practice for judging and punishing the increasing crimes committed by spirits; those who use it are called "practitioners."

While Goryo was successful in driving back Ivy, Muhyo and gang have literally gone underground to escape Buhpu the Puppetmaster's sudden assault. At Yoichi's suggestion, they decide to hold Buhpu off without their executor. They fight with traps, tricks and magic circles, and it works—but at what price? Meanwhile, Muhyo and the rest aren't back on the surface long when Teeki finds them! Busujima uses the highly risky technique of Envoy Possession to hold him off while Muhyo tries to fuse his new Book of Magic Law with the Writ of Passage. Page goes back down to see what's become of Yoichi's team… and finds Enchu waiting for him.

Bobby

Former M.L.S. haunt released by Roji's Dagger of Absolving.

Isabi

A practitioner of forbidden magic law who turned himself into an envoy. He revealed the location of the Writ of Passage to Page.

Muhyo & Roji's Bureau of Supernatural Investigation

BSI

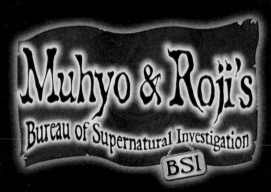

CONTENTS

15

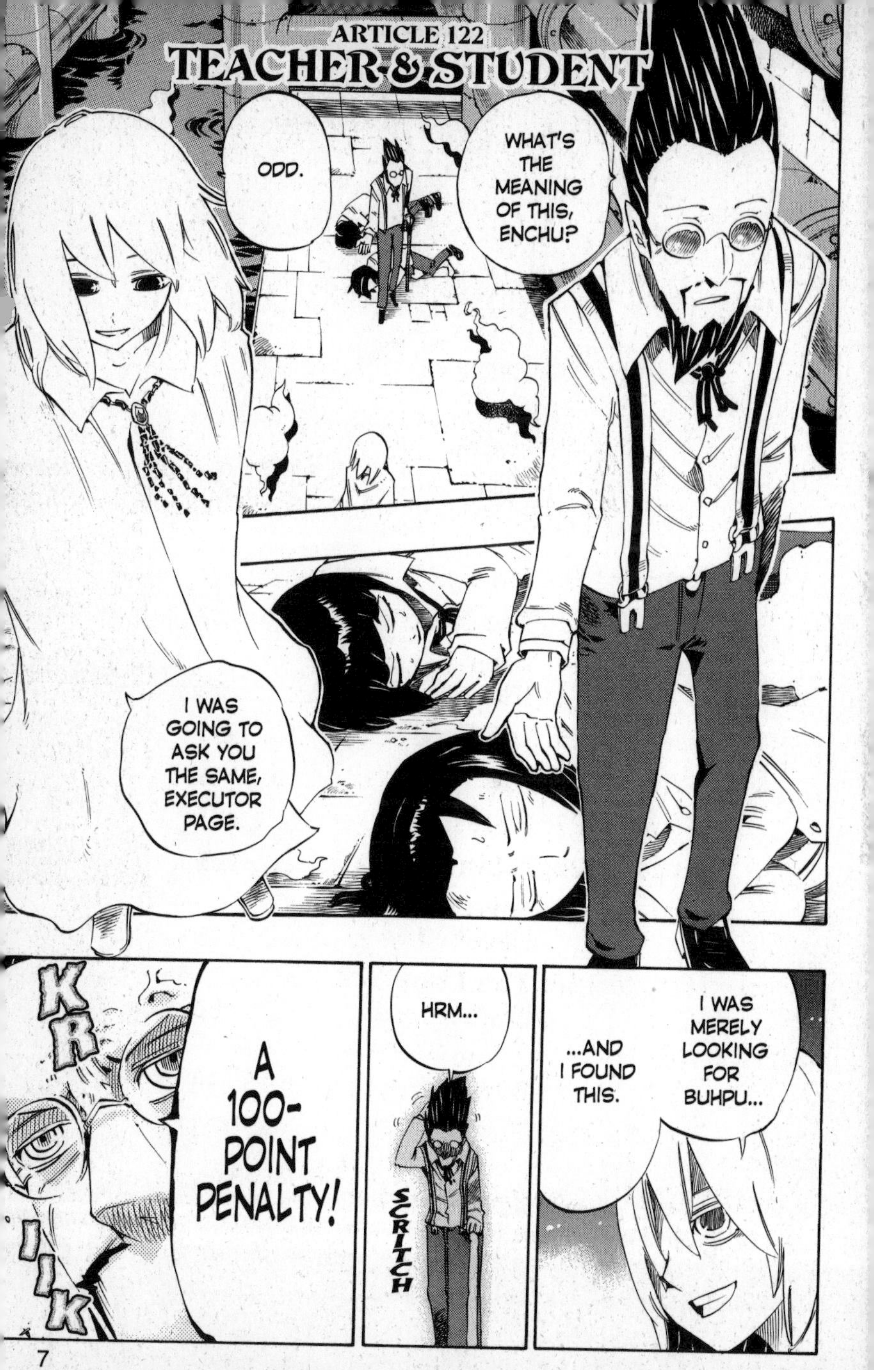
ARTICLE 122
TEACHER & STUDENT
WHAT'S THE MEANING OF THIS, ENCHU?
ODD.
I WAS GOING TO ASK YOU THE SAME, EXECUTOR PAGE.
I WAS MERELY LOOKING FOR BUHPU...
...AND I FOUND THIS.
HRM...
SCRITCH
A 100-POINT PENALTY!
KRIIK

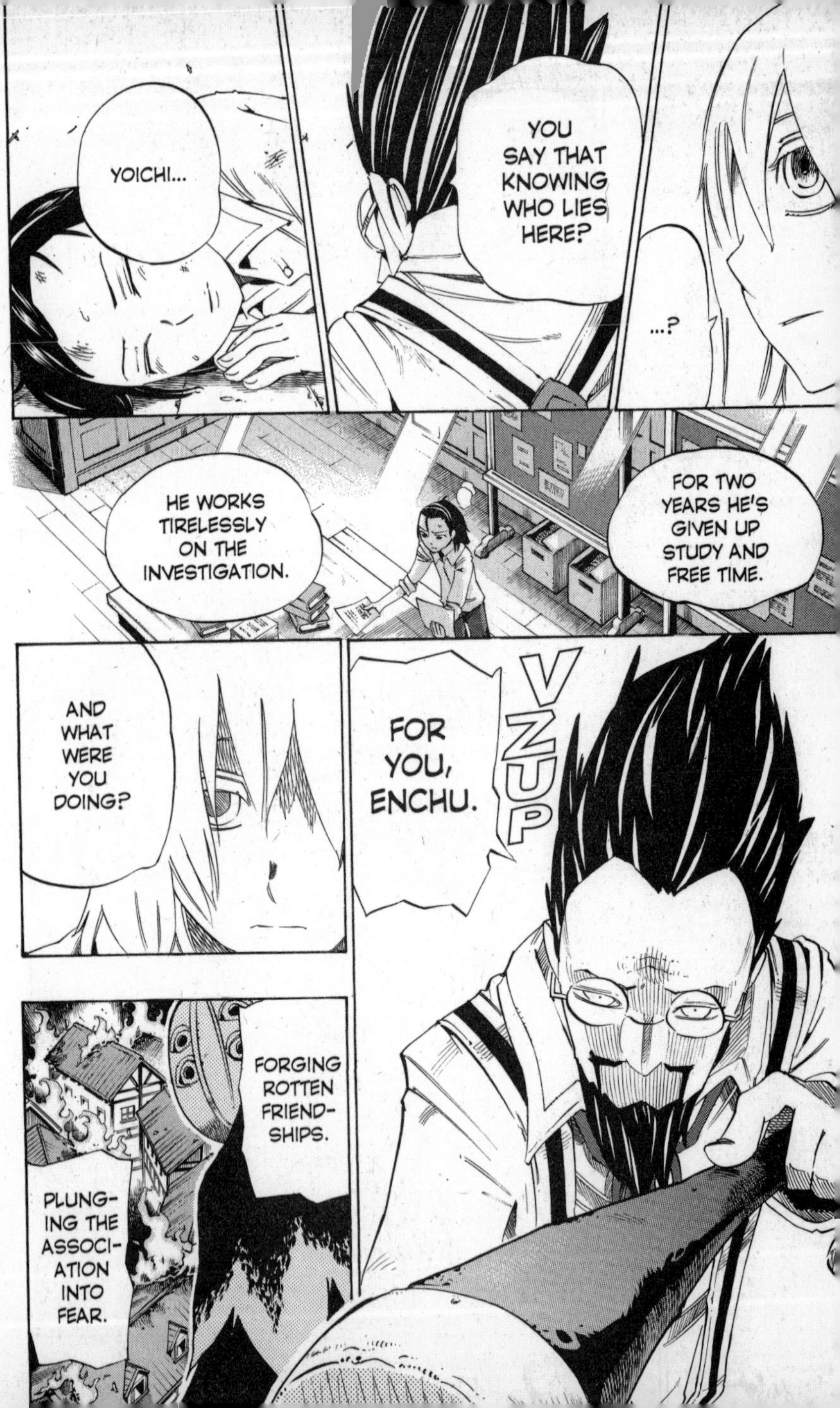
...?
YOU SAY THAT KNOWING WHO LIES HERE?
YOICHI...
FOR TWO YEARS HE'S GIVEN UP STUDY AND FREE TIME.
HE WORKS TIRELESSLY ON THE INVESTIGATION.
VZUP
FOR YOU, ENCHU.
AND WHAT WERE YOU DOING?
FORGING ROTTEN FRIEND-SHIPS.
PLUNG-ING THE ASSOCI-ATION INTO FEAR.

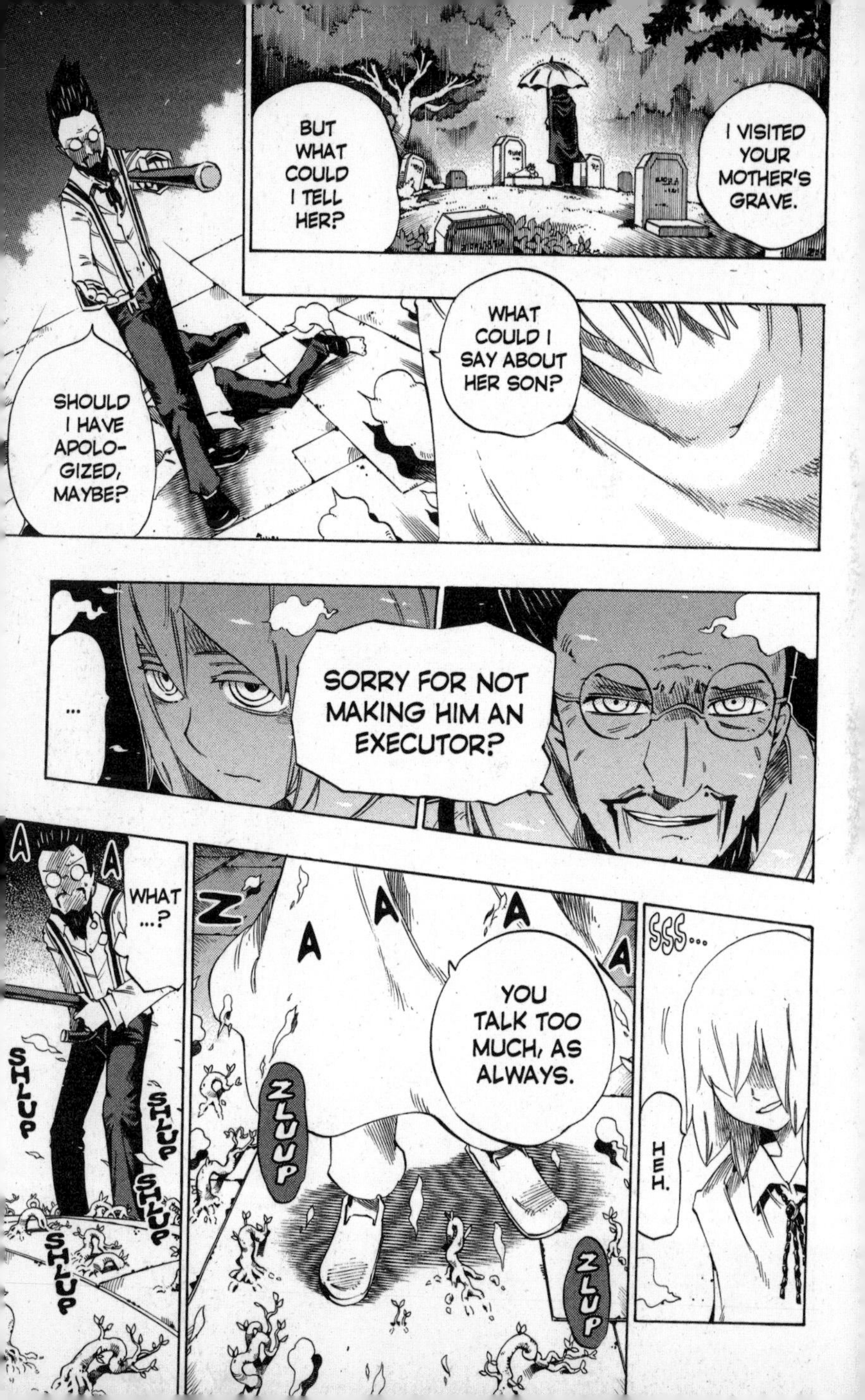
I VISITED YOUR MOTHER'S GRAVE.
BUT WHAT COULD I TELL HER?
WHAT COULD I SAY ABOUT HER SON?
SHOULD I HAVE APOLOGIZED, MAYBE?
SORRY FOR NOT MAKING HIM AN EXECUTOR?
...
SSS...
HEH.
ZAAAAA
YOU TALK TOO MUCH, AS ALWAYS.
ZLUUP
ZLUP
AA
WHAT ...?
SHLUP
SHLUP
SHLUP
SHLUP
SHLUP

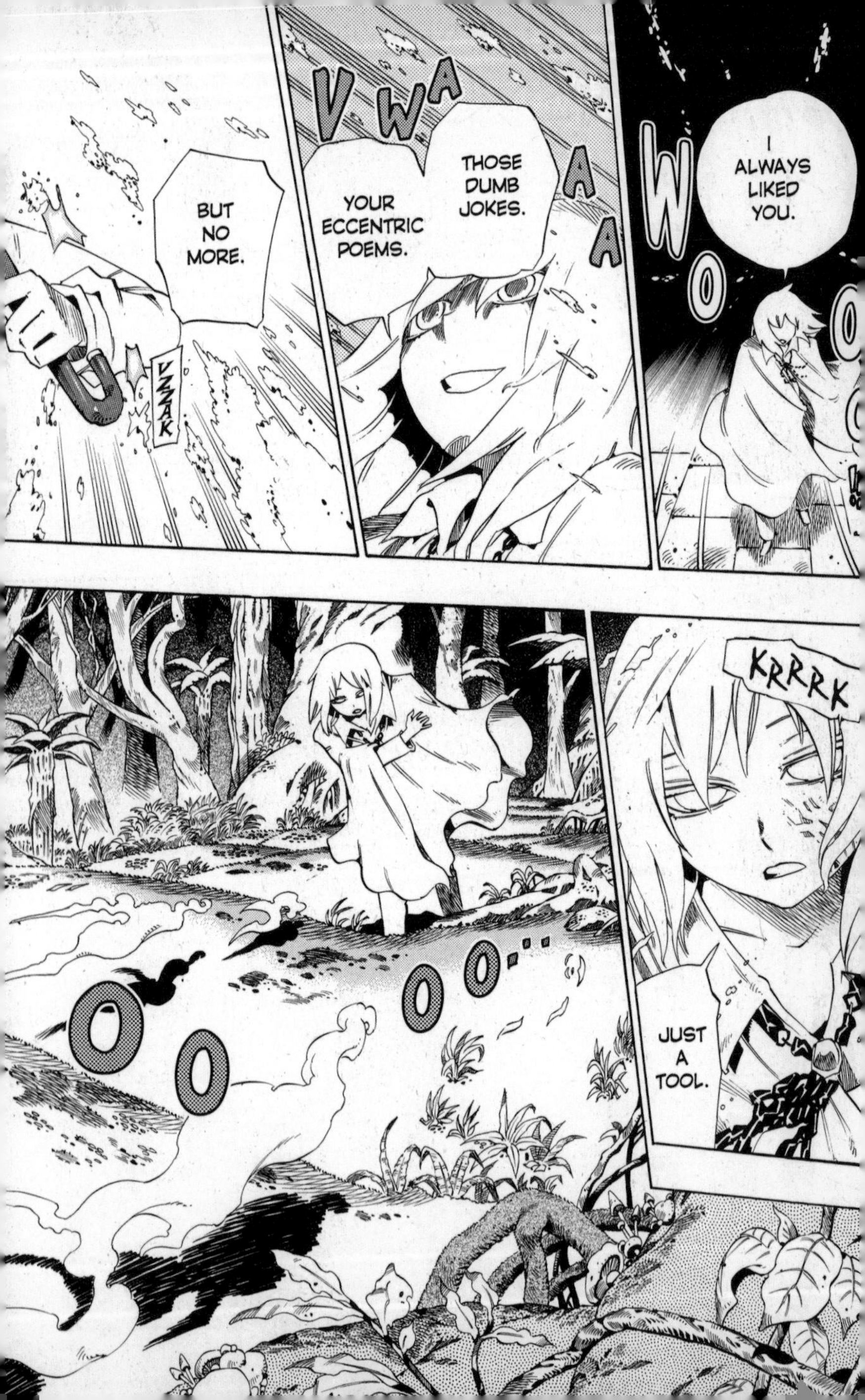
I ALWAYS LIKED YOU.
WOOO
THOSE DUMB JOKES.
YOUR ECCENTRIC POEMS.
VWAAA
BUT NO MORE.
VZZAK
KRRRK
JUST A TOOL.
OOOOO...

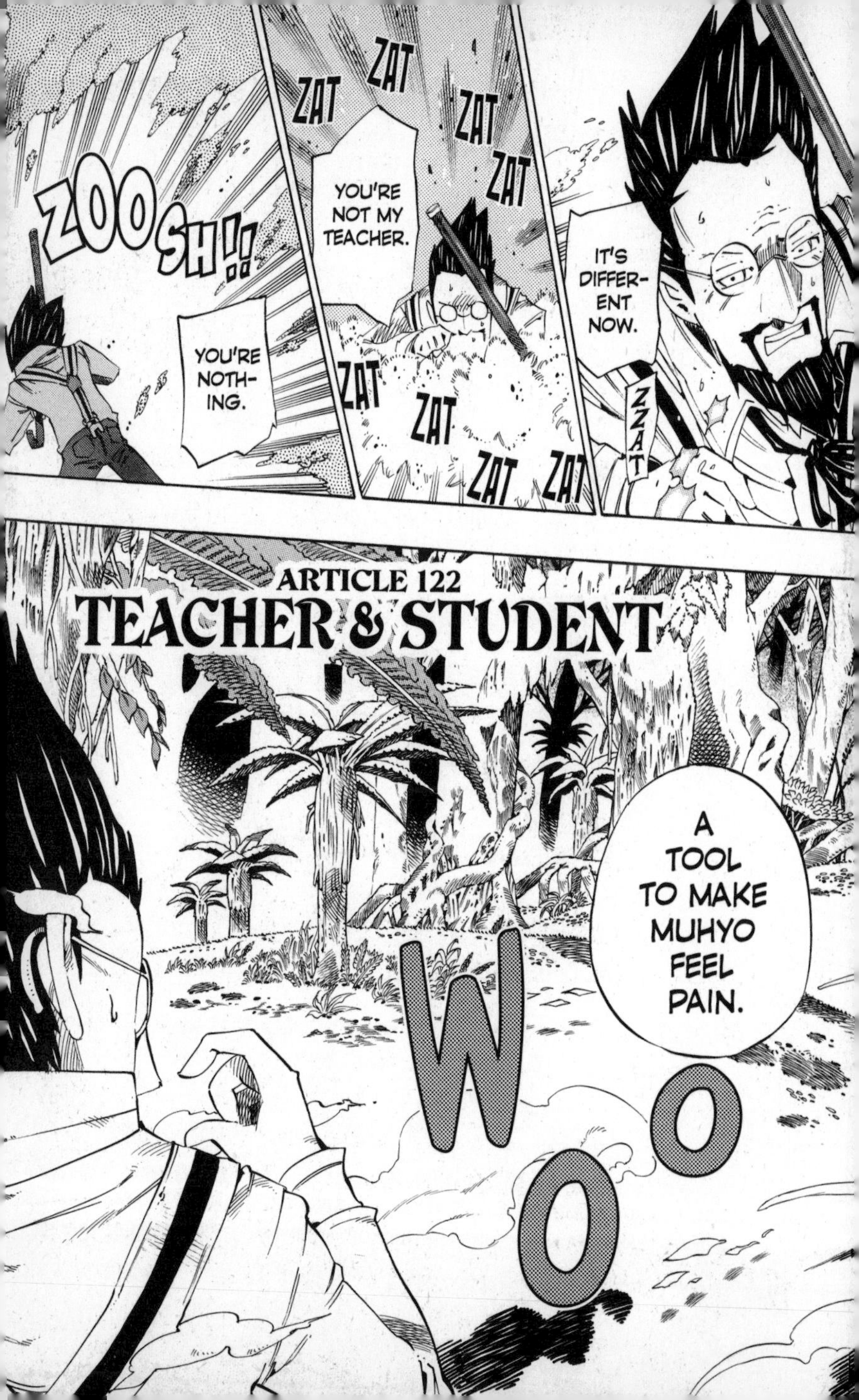
IT'S DIFFERENT NOW.
ZZAT
ZAT ZAT ZAT ZAT
YOU'RE NOT MY TEACHER.
ZAT ZAT ZAT ZAT
ZOOSH!!
YOU'RE NOTHING.
ARTICLE 122
TEACHER & STUDENT
A TOOL TO MAKE MUHYO FEEL PAIN.
WOOO

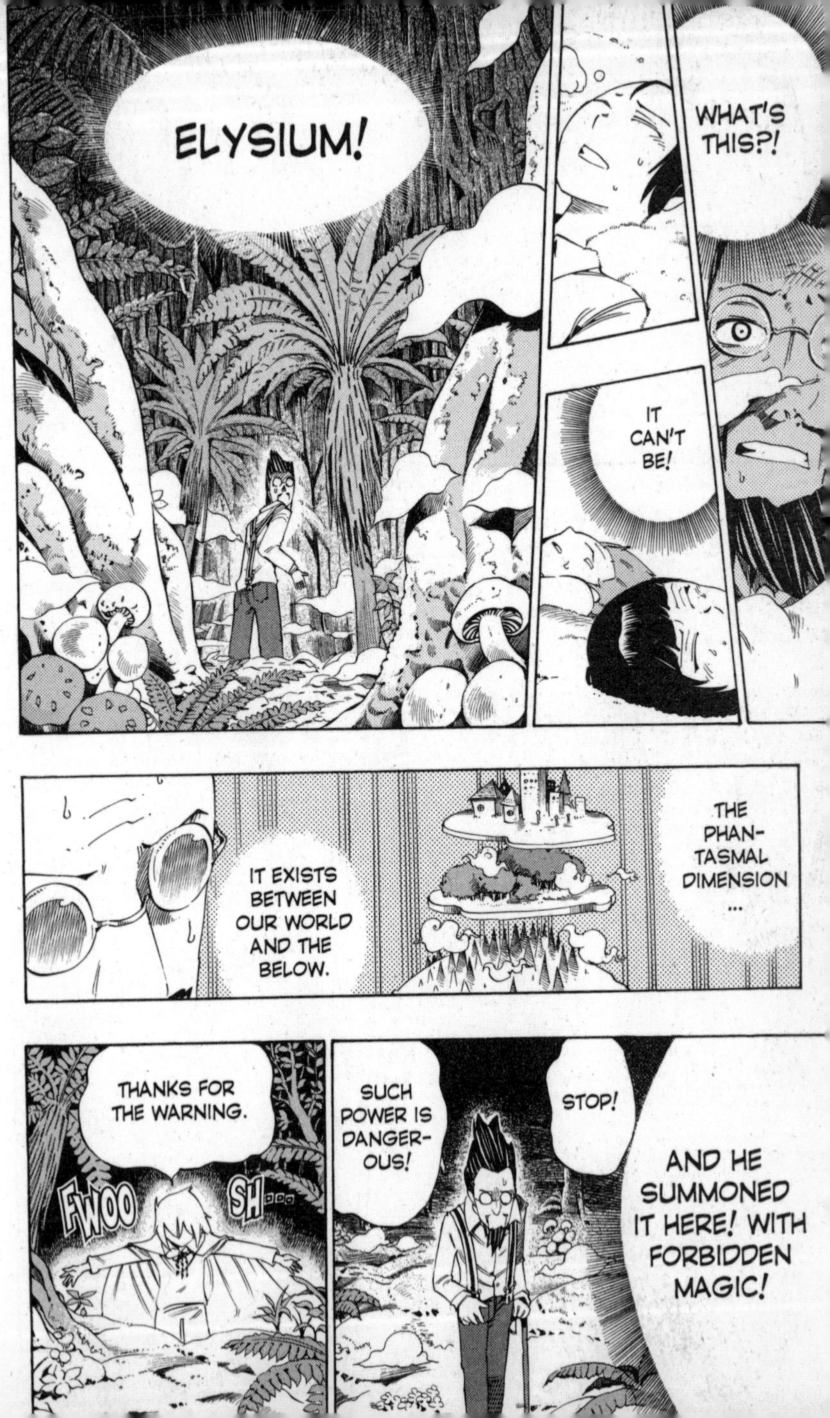
WHAT'S THIS?!
IT CAN'T BE!
ELYSIUM!
THE PHANTASMAL DIMENSION ...
IT EXISTS BETWEEN OUR WORLD AND THE BELOW.
AND HE SUMMONED IT HERE! WITH FORBIDDEN MAGIC!
STOP!
SUCH POWER IS DANGEROUS!
THANKS FOR THE WARNING.
FWOOSH...

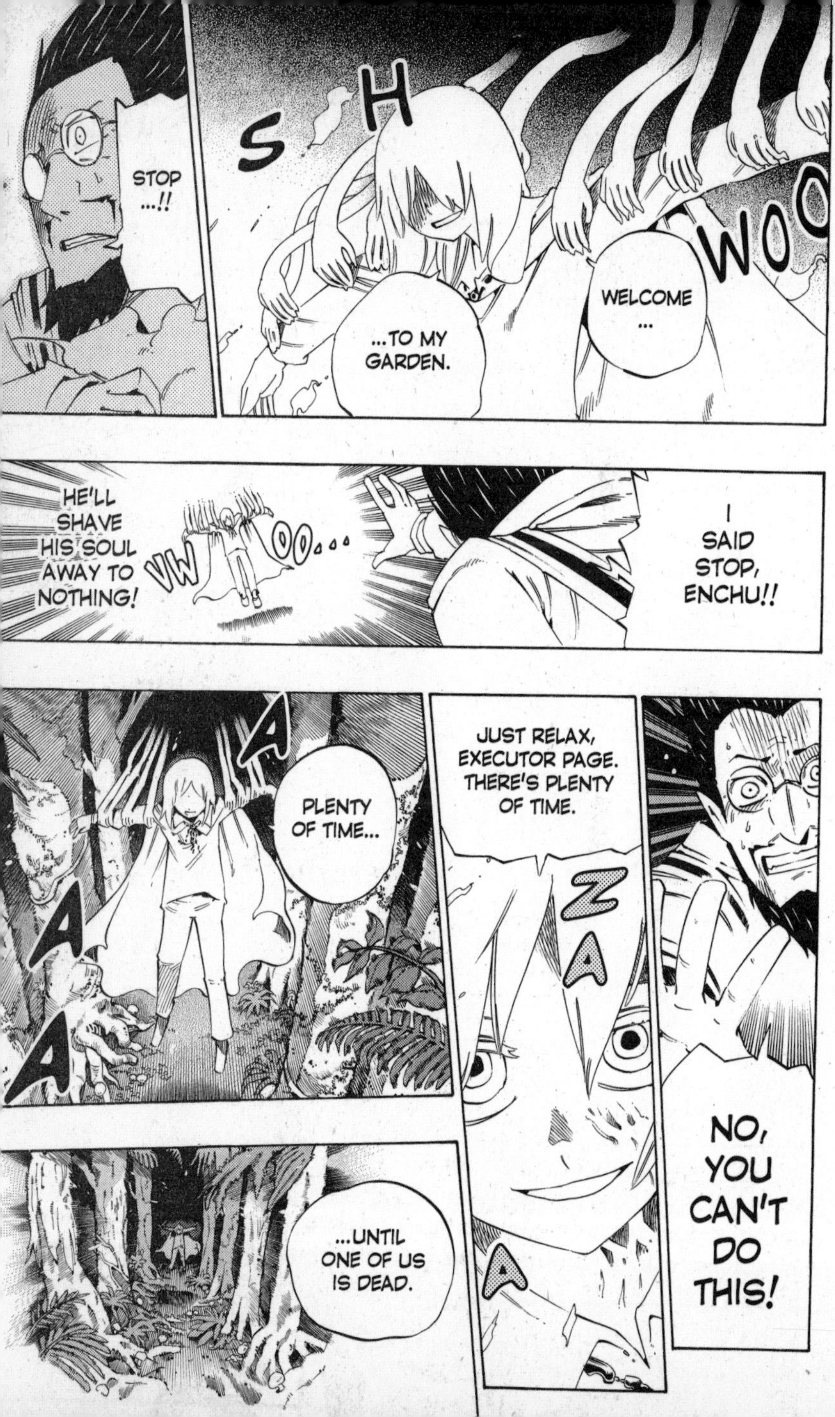
SH
WOO
WELCOME ...
...TO MY GARDEN.
STOP ...!!
I SAID STOP, ENCHU!!
VWOO...
HE'LL SHAVE HIS SOUL AWAY TO NOTHING!
NO, YOU CAN'T DO THIS!
JUST RELAX, EXECUTOR PAGE. THERE'S PLENTY OF TIME.
ZAA
AAA
PLENTY OF TIME...
...UNTIL ONE OF US IS DEAD.

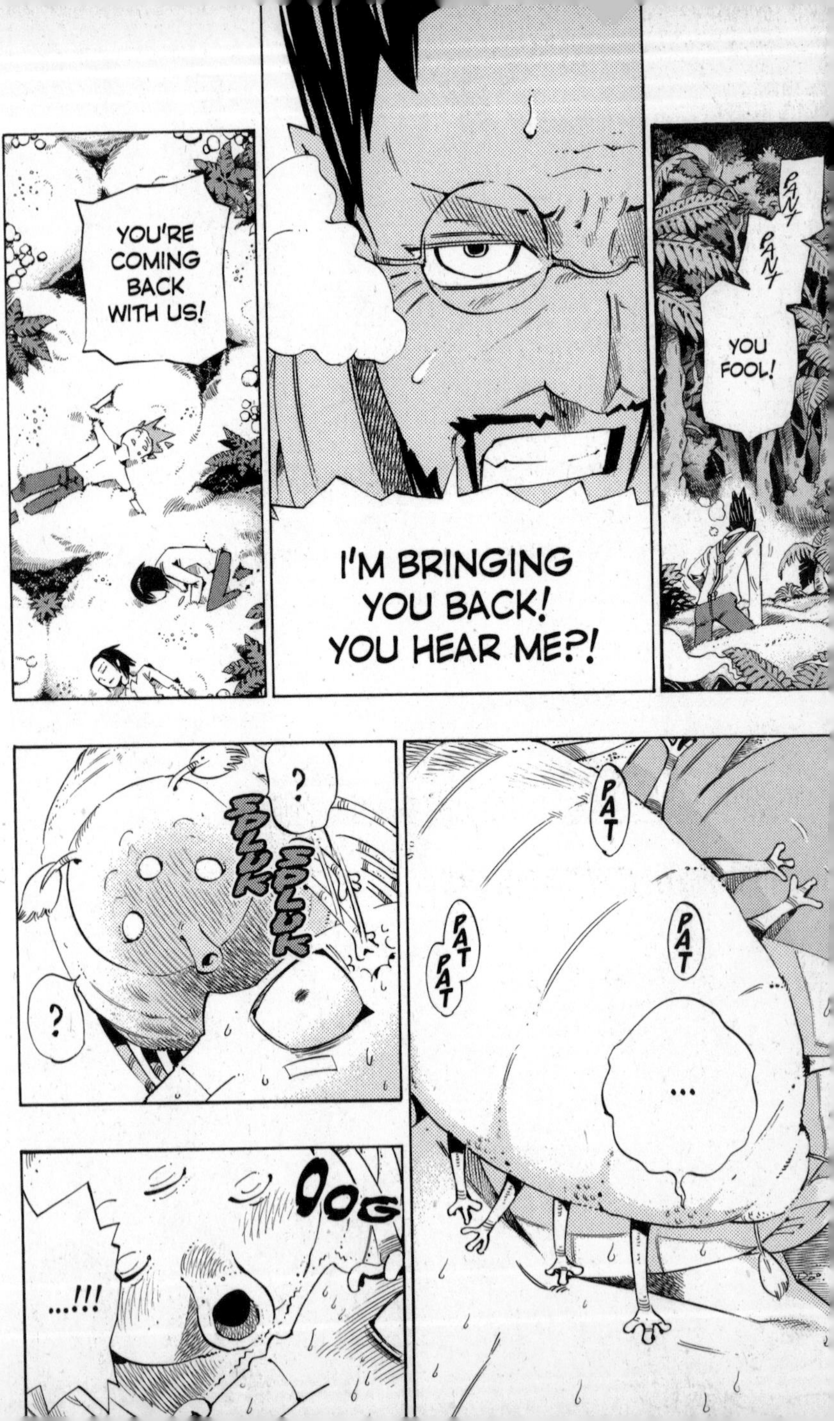
PANT
PANT
YOU FOOL!
I'M BRINGING YOU BACK! YOU HEAR ME?!
YOU'RE COMING BACK WITH US!
PAT
PAT PAT
PAT
...
?
SPLUK
SPLUK
?
OOG
...!!!

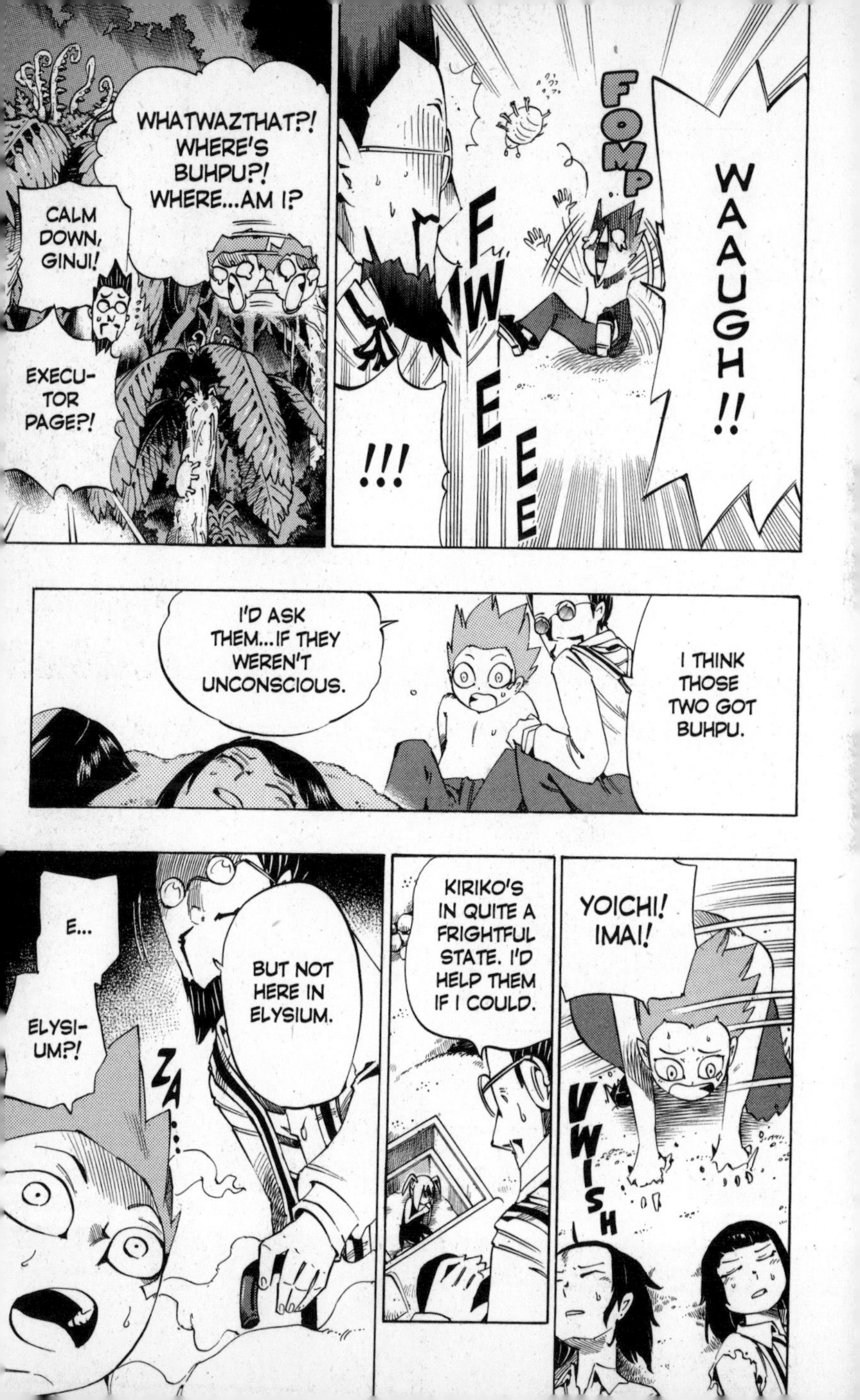
WAAUGH!!
FOMP
FWEEE
!!!
WHATWAZTHAT?! WHERE'S BUHPU?! WHERE...AM I?
CALM DOWN, GINJI!
EXECUTOR PAGE?!
I THINK THOSE TWO GOT BUHPU.
I'D ASK THEM...IF THEY WEREN'T UNCONSCIOUS.
YOICHI! IMAI!
UWISH
KIRIKO'S IN QUITE A FRIGHTFUL STATE. I'D HELP THEM IF I COULD.
BUT NOT HERE IN ELYSIUM.
E... ELYSIUM?!
ZA...

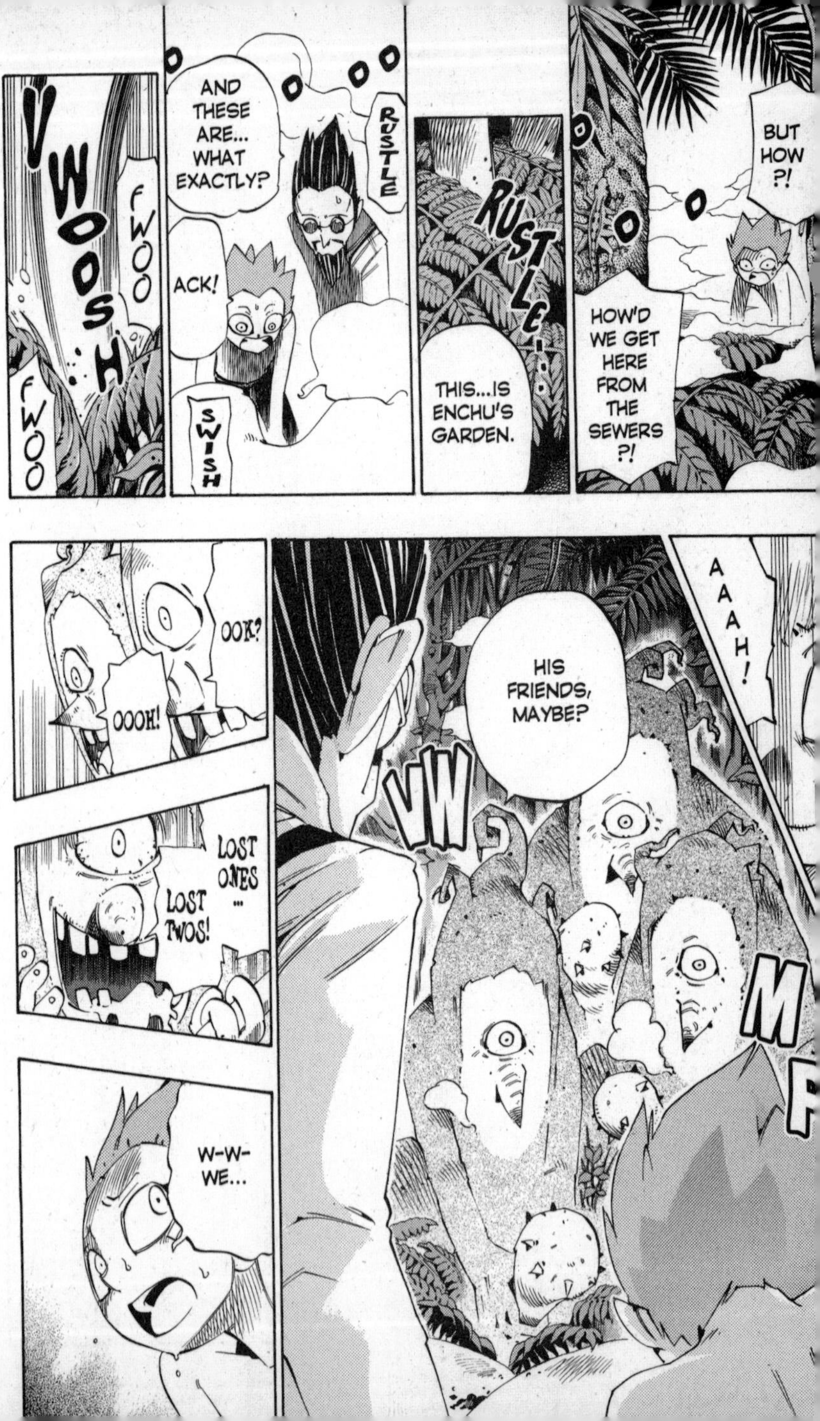
BUT HOW ?!
HOW'D WE GET HERE FROM THE SEWERS ?!
RUSTLE...
THIS...IS ENCHU'S GARDEN.
RUSTLE
AND THESE ARE... WHAT EXACTLY?
ACK!
SWISH
VWOOSH
FWOO
FWOO
AAAH!
HIS FRIENDS, MAYBE?
VW
OOK?
OOOH!
LOST ONES...
LOST TWOS!
W-W-WE...

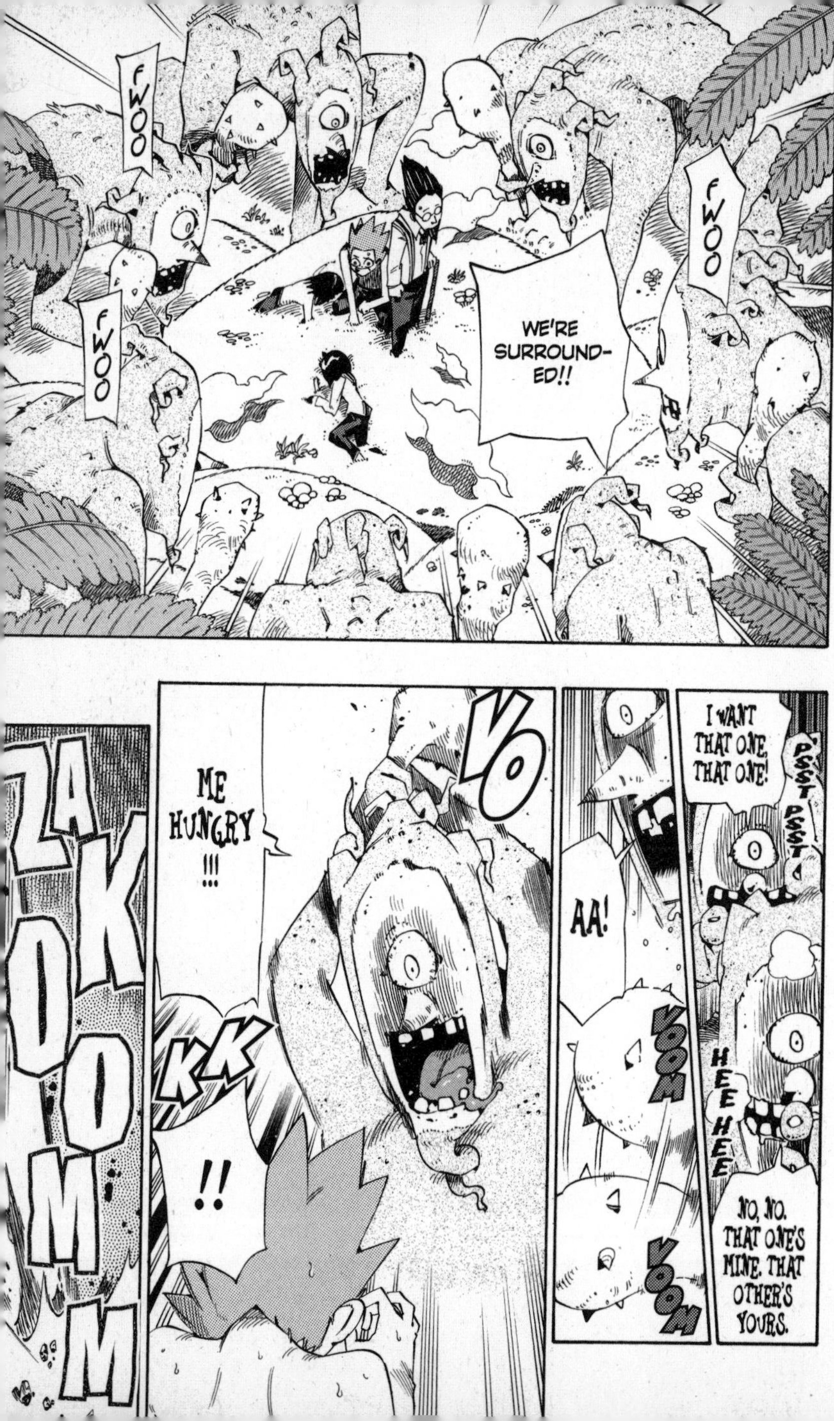
FWOO
FWOO
WE'RE SURROUNDED-ED!!
FWOO
I WANT THAT ONE, THAT ONE!
PSST PSST
HEE HEE
NO, NO. THAT ONE'S MINE. THAT OTHER'S YOURS.
AA!
VOOM
VOOM
VO
ME HUNGRY!!!
KK
!!
ZAKOOOMM

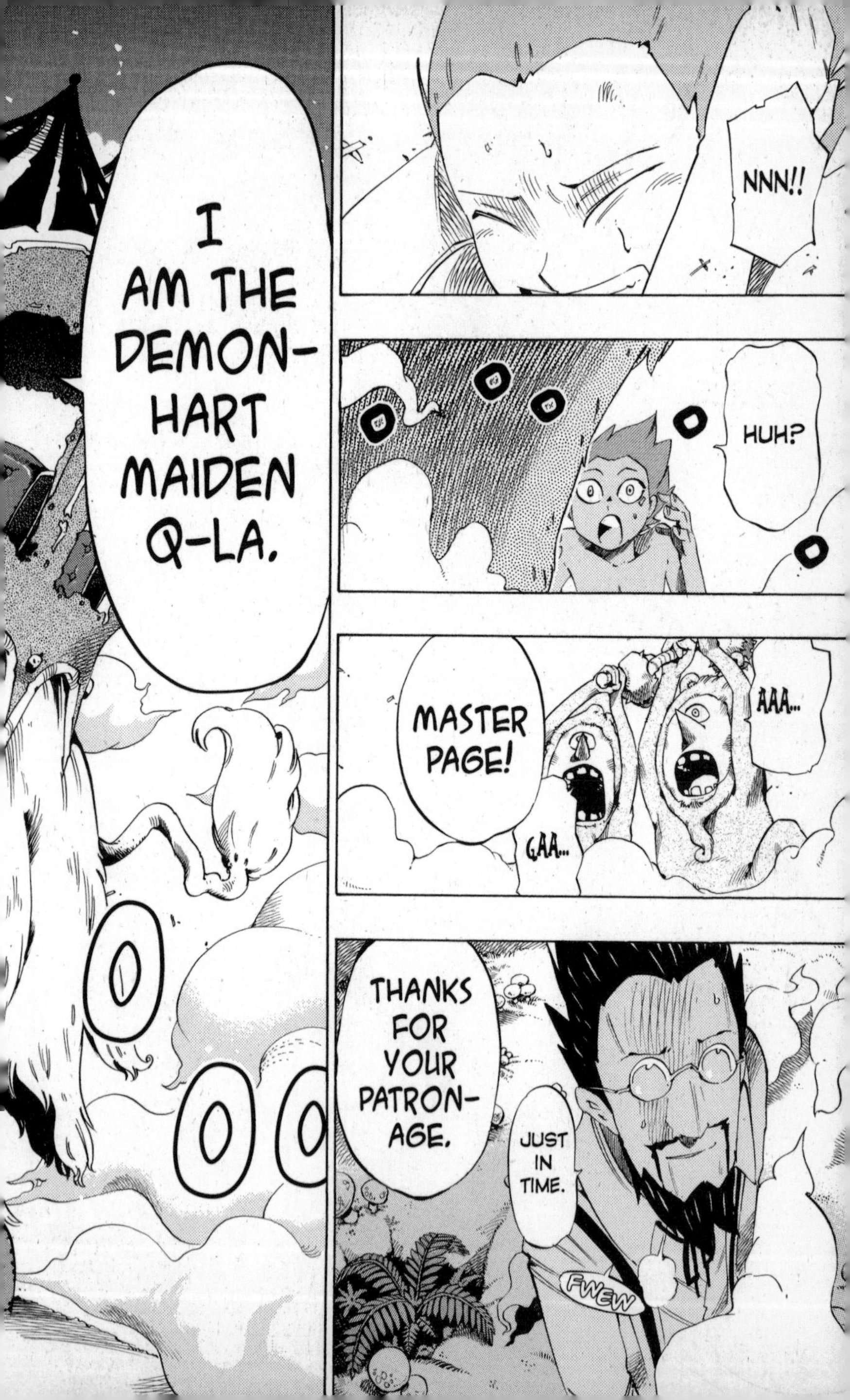
NNN!!
HUH?
AAA...
MASTER PAGE!
GAA...
THANKS FOR YOUR PATRON-AGE.
JUST IN TIME.
FWEW
I AM THE DEMON-HART MAIDEN Q-LA.

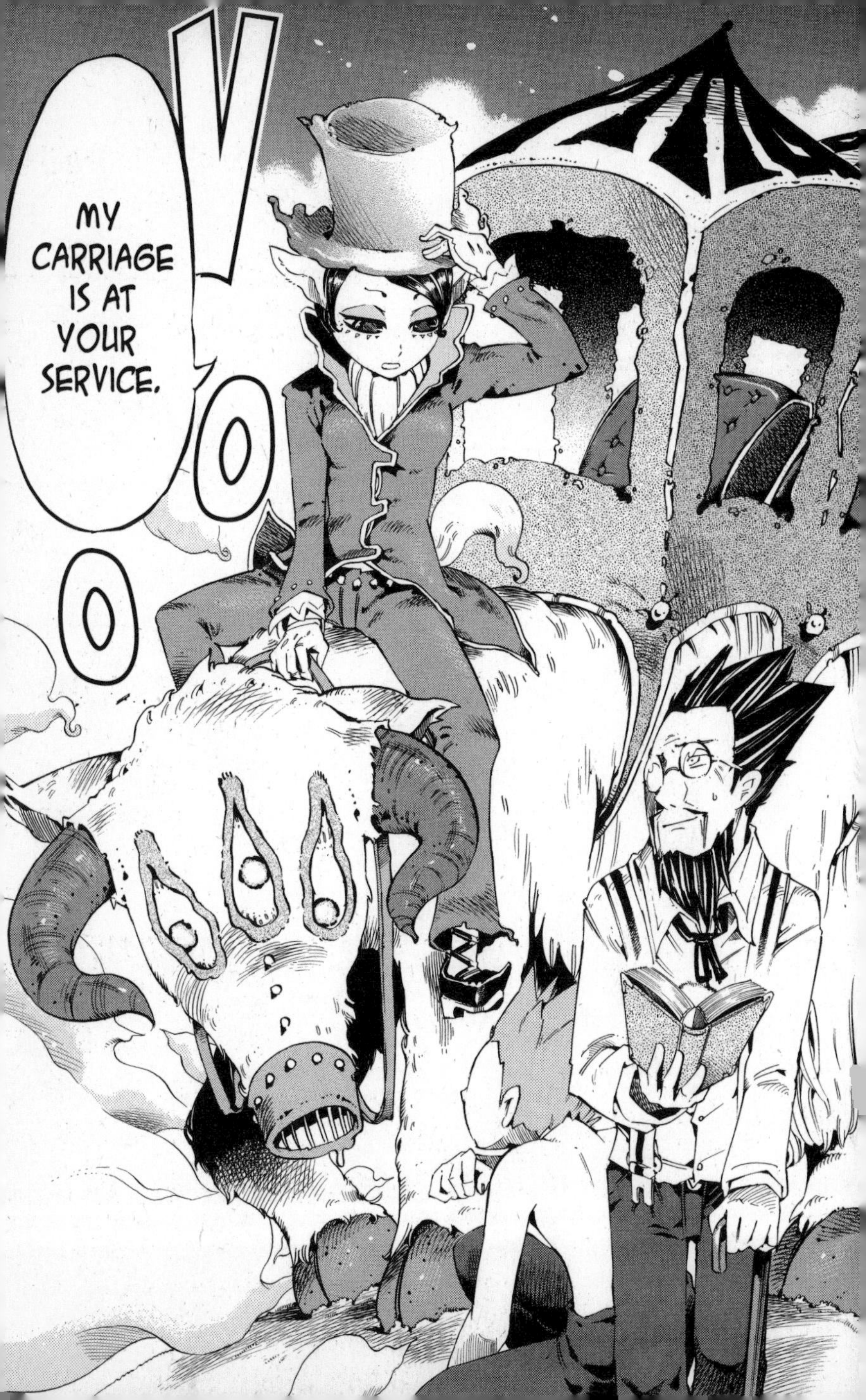
VOOO
MY CARRIAGE IS AT YOUR SERVICE.

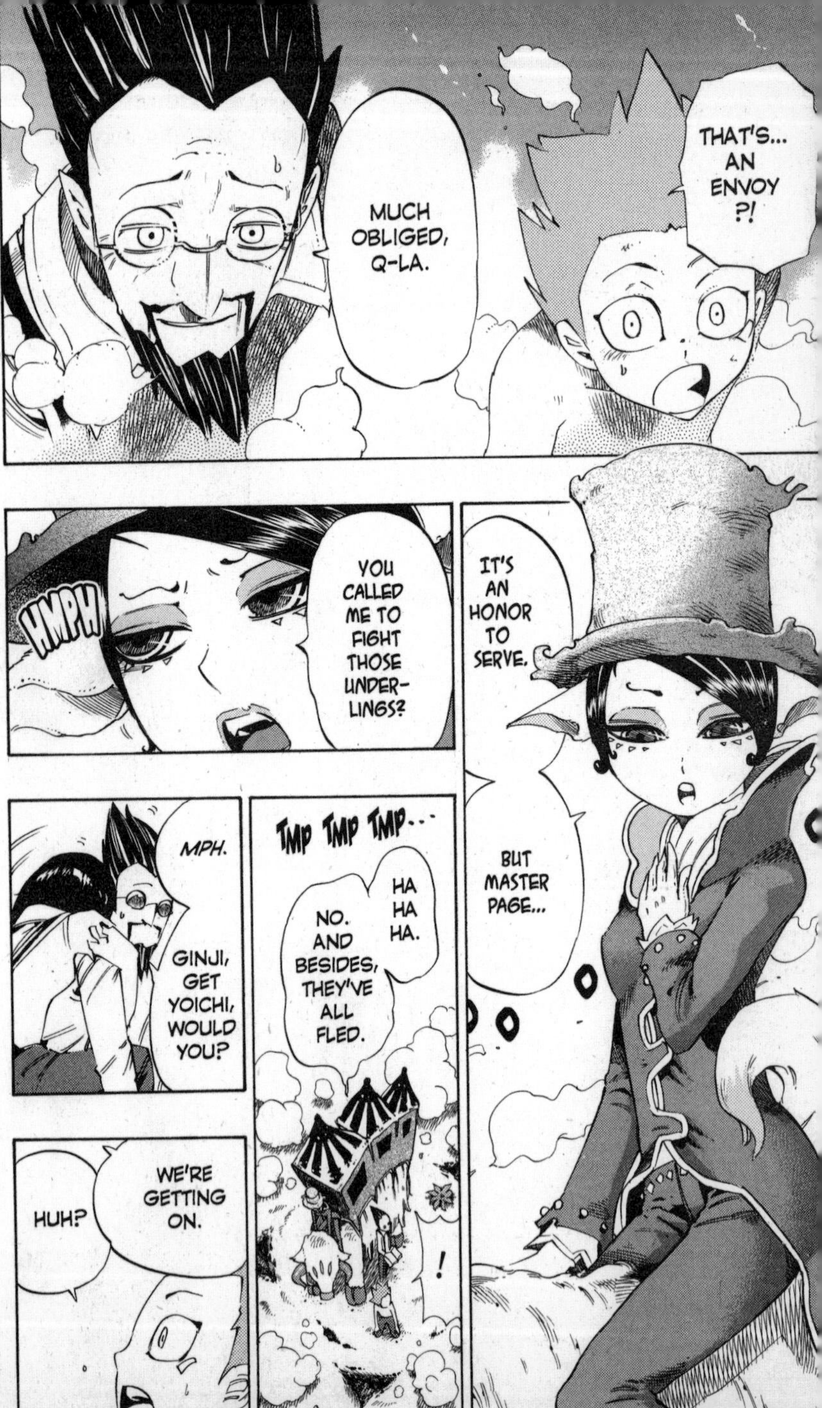
THAT'S... AN ENVOY ?!
MUCH OBLIGED, Q-LA.
IT'S AN HONOR TO SERVE.
BUT MASTER PAGE...
YOU CALLED ME TO FIGHT THOSE UNDER-LINGS?
HMPH
TMP TMP TMP...
HA HA HA.
NO. AND BESIDES, THEY'VE ALL FLED.
MPH.
GINJI, GET YOICHI, WOULD YOU?
WE'RE GETTING ON.
HUH?

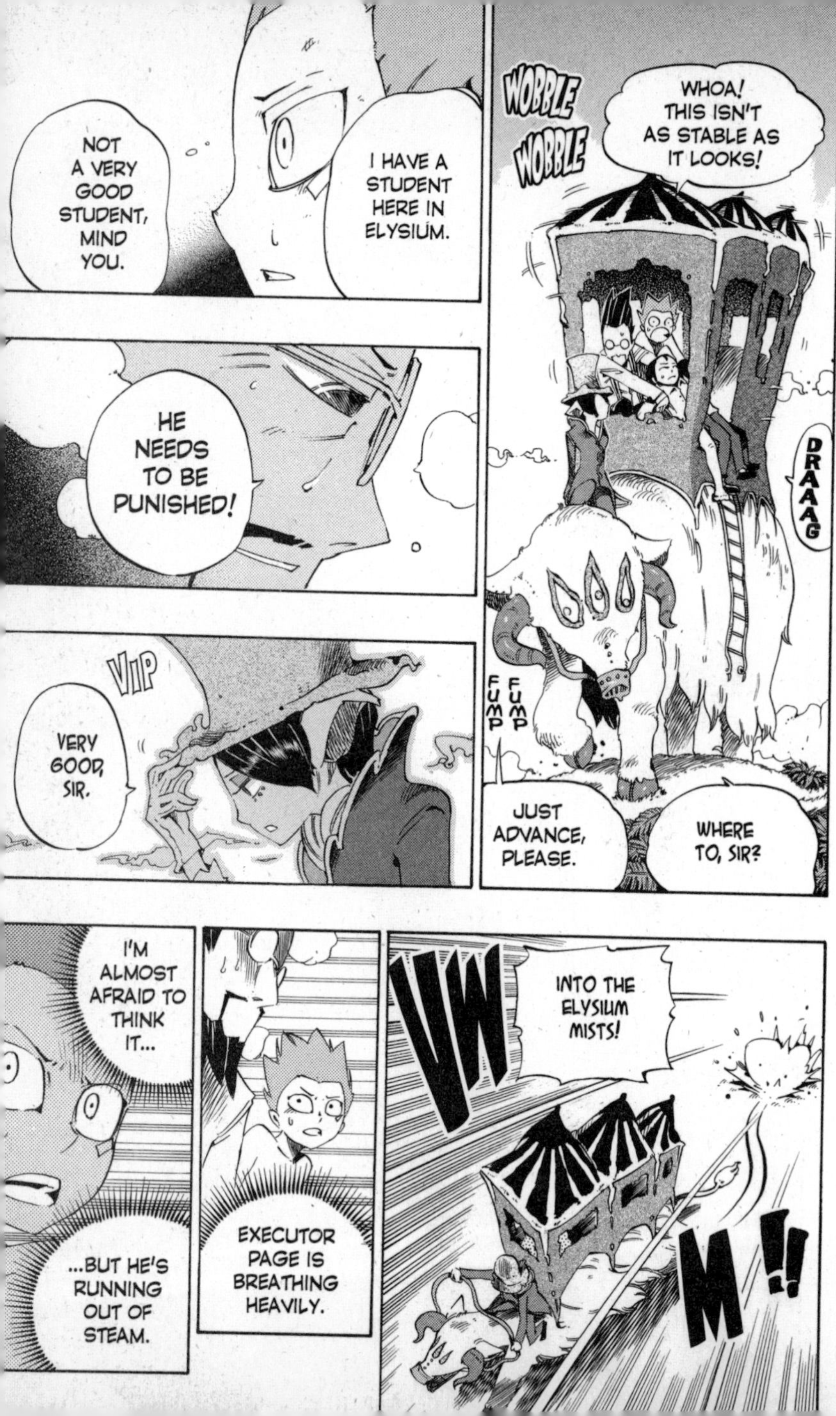
WOBBLE WOBBLE
WHOA! THIS ISN'T AS STABLE AS IT LOOKS!
DRAAAG
FUMP FUMP
WHERE TO, SIR?
JUST ADVANCE, PLEASE.
I HAVE A STUDENT HERE IN ELYSIUM.
NOT A VERY GOOD STUDENT, MIND YOU.
HE NEEDS TO BE PUNISHED!
VIP
VERY GOOD, SIR.
INTO THE ELYSIUM MISTS!
VVM!!
EXECUTOR PAGE IS BREATHING HEAVILY.
I'M ALMOST AFRAID TO THINK IT...
...BUT HE'S RUNNING OUT OF STEAM.

[redacted]

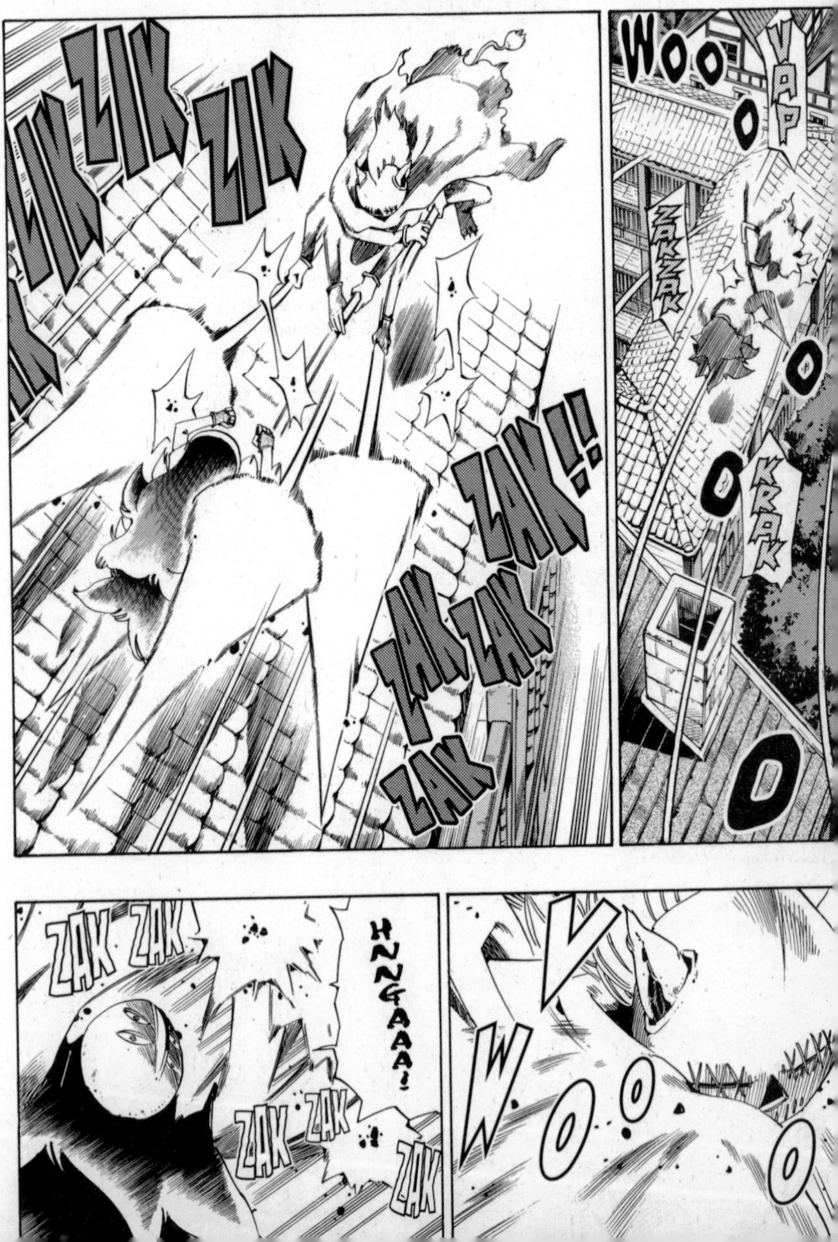
WOOOOOOO
VAP
ZAKZAK
KRAK
ZIK ZIK ZIK
ZAK!!
ZAK ZAK
ZAK
ZAK ZAK
VWOOOO
ZAK ZAK
HNNGAAA!
ZAK ZAK
ZAK

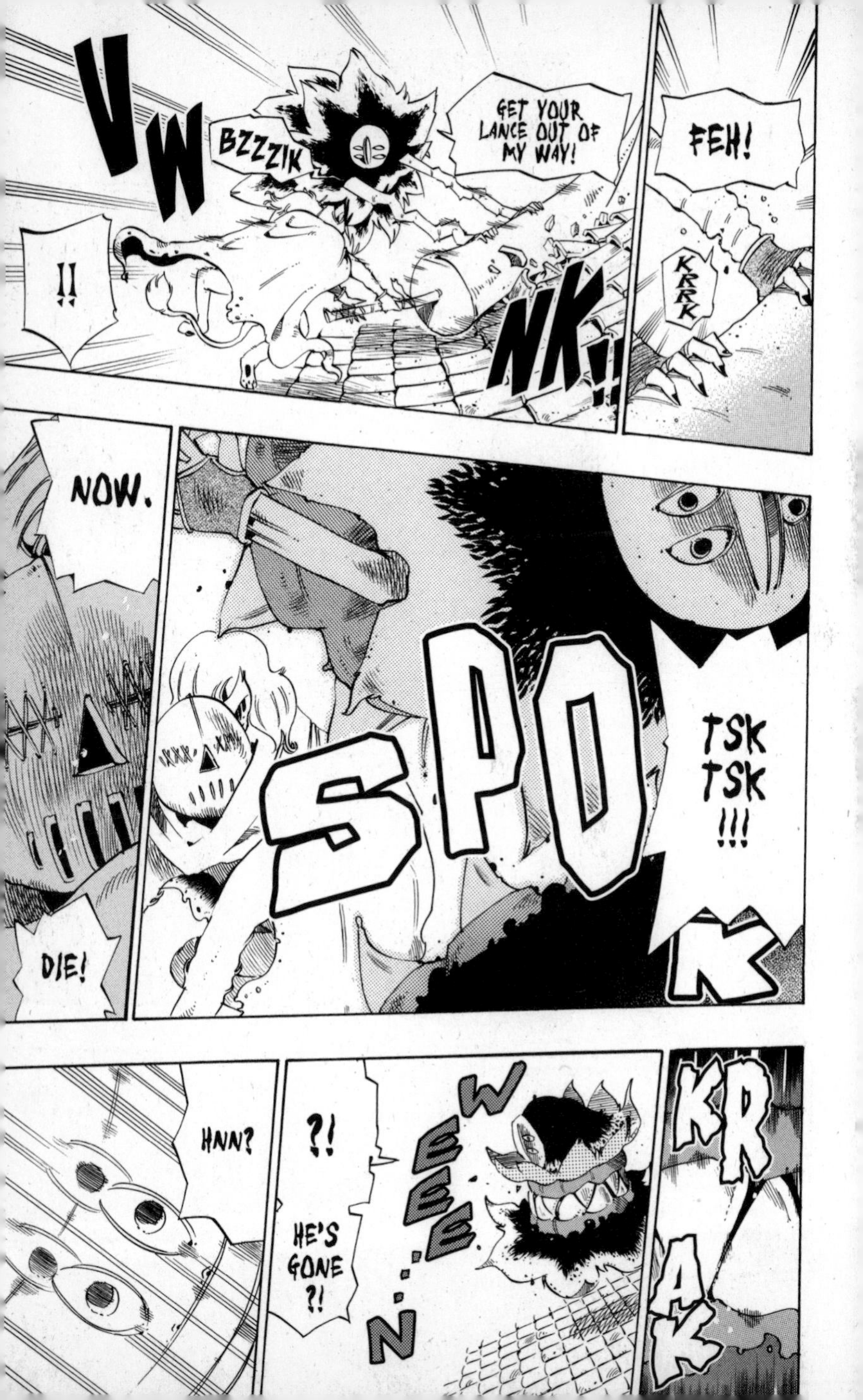
FEH!
KRRK
GET YOUR LANCE OUT OF MY WAY!
BZZZIK
VW
NK!!
!!
TSK TSK !!!
SPOK
NOW.
DIE!
KRAK
WEEEN...
?!
HE'S GONE ?!
HNN?

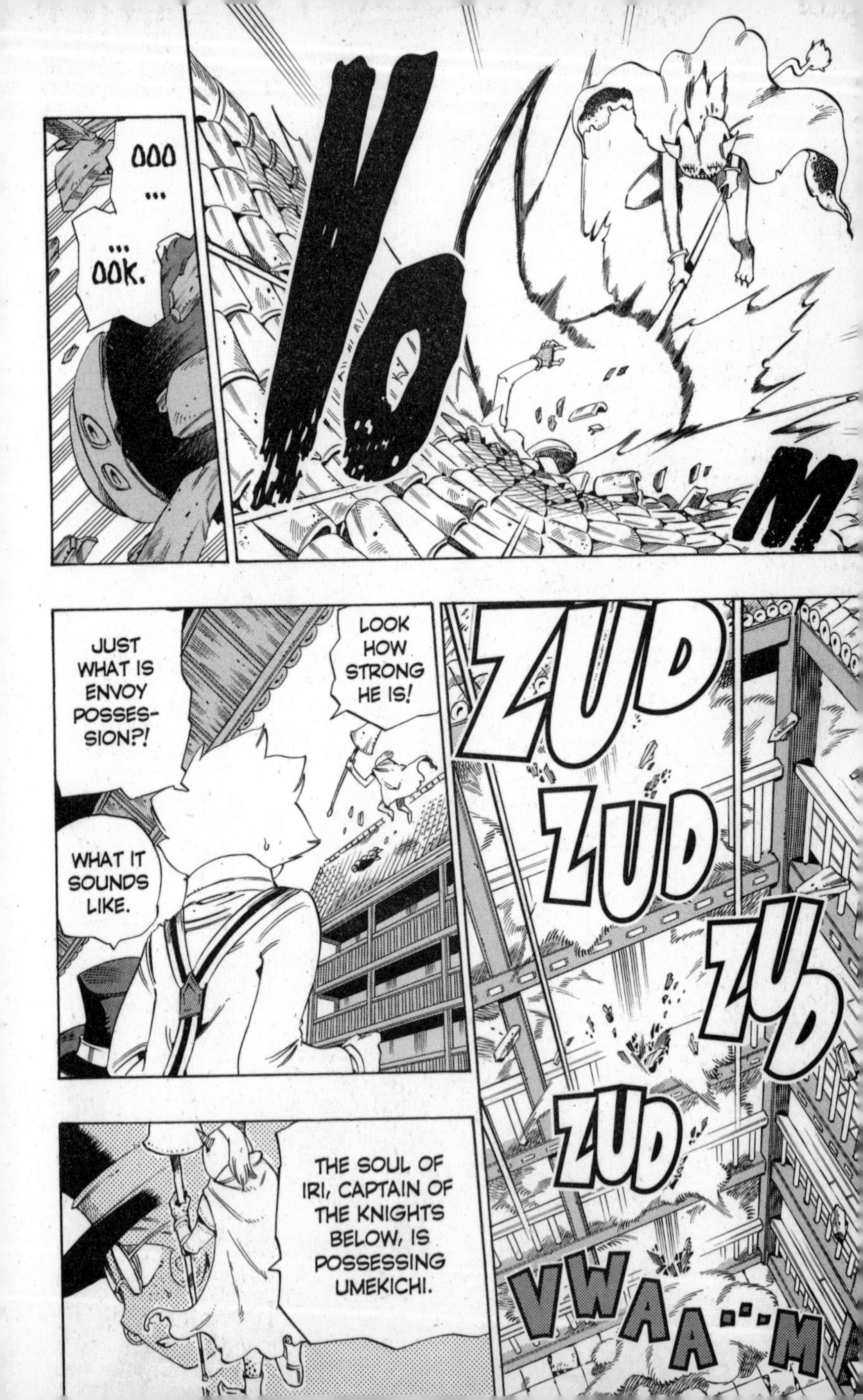
VO..M
OOO...
...OOK.
ZUD
ZUD
ZUD
ZUD
VWAA..M
LOOK HOW STRONG HE IS!
JUST WHAT IS ENVOY POSSESSION?!
WHAT IT SOUNDS LIKE.
THE SOUL OF IRI, CAPTAIN OF THE KNIGHTS BELOW, IS POSSESSING UMEKICHI.

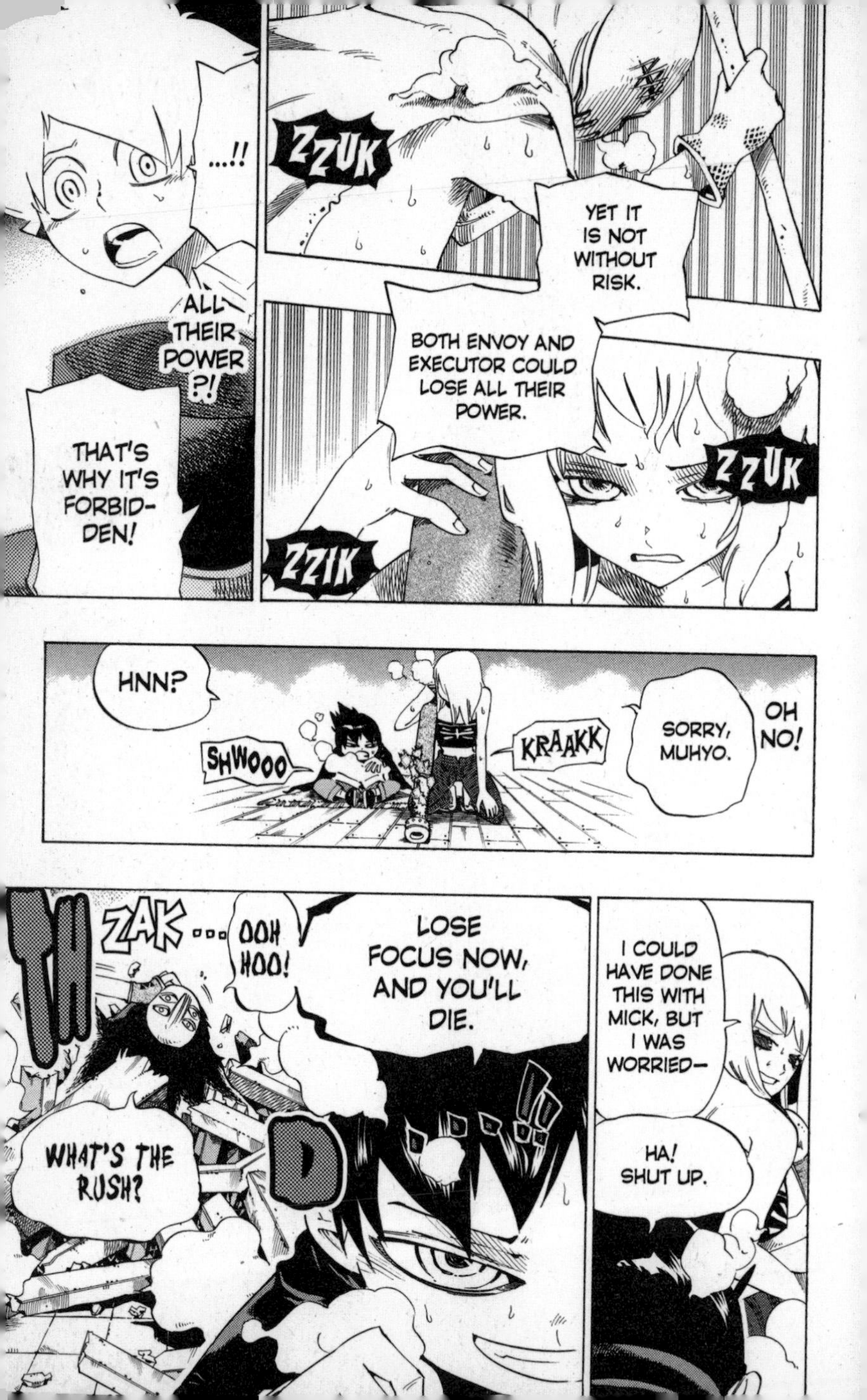
ZZUK
YET IT IS NOT WITHOUT RISK.
BOTH ENVOY AND EXECUTOR COULD LOSE ALL THEIR POWER.
ZZUK
ZZIK
...!!
ALL THEIR POWER?!
THAT'S WHY IT'S FORBID-DEN!
OH NO!
SORRY, MUHYO.
KRAAKK
SHWOOO
HNN?
I COULD HAVE DONE THIS WITH MICK, BUT I WAS WORRIED—
HA! SHUT UP.
LOSE FOCUS NOW, AND YOU'LL DIE.
OOH HOO!
ZAK...
TH
WHAT'S THE RUSH?
D
!!

—AMONGST THE ELYSIUM FLOWERS—

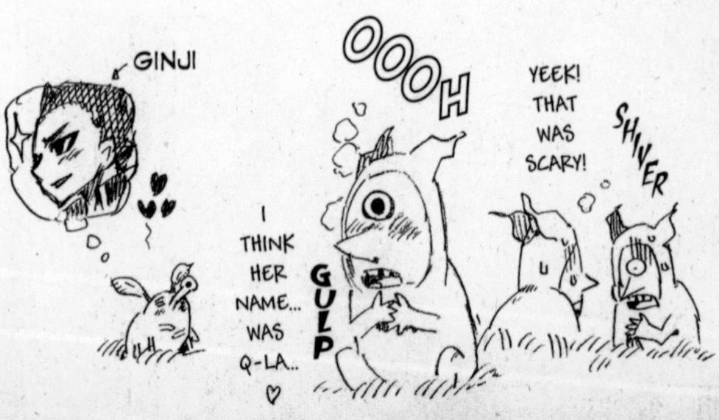
SHIVER
YEEK! THAT WAS SCARY!
OOOH
GULP
I THINK HER NAME... WAS Q-LA.. ♡
GINJI

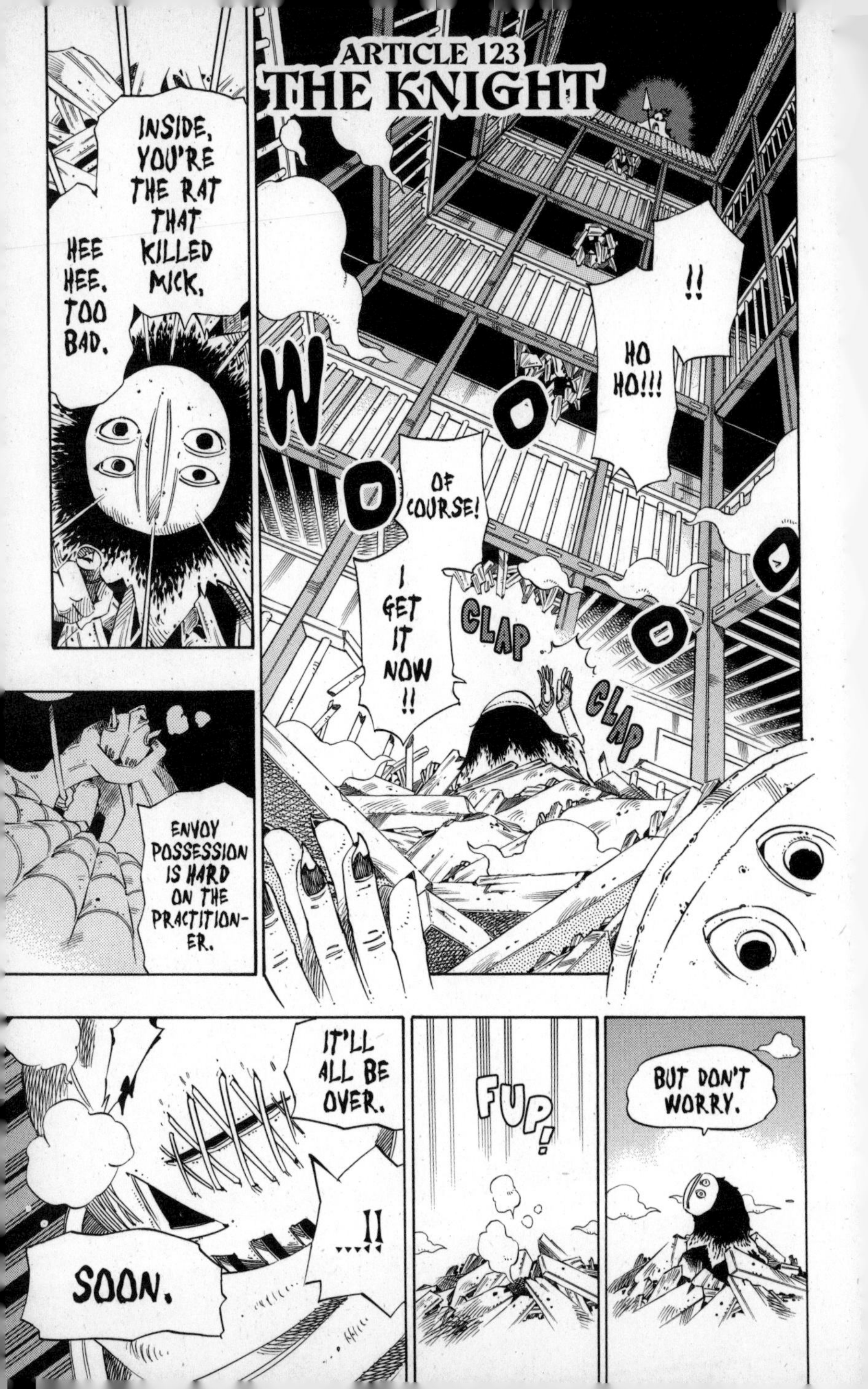
ARTICLE 123
THE KNIGHT
!!
HO HO!!!
WOOOOO
OF COURSE!
I GET IT NOW!!
CLAP
CLAP
INSIDE, YOU'RE THE RAT THAT KILLED MICK.
HEE HEE. TOO BAD.
ENVOY POSSESSION IS HARD ON THE PRACTITIONER.
BUT DON'T WORRY.
FUP!
IT'LL ALL BE OVER.
...!!
SOON.

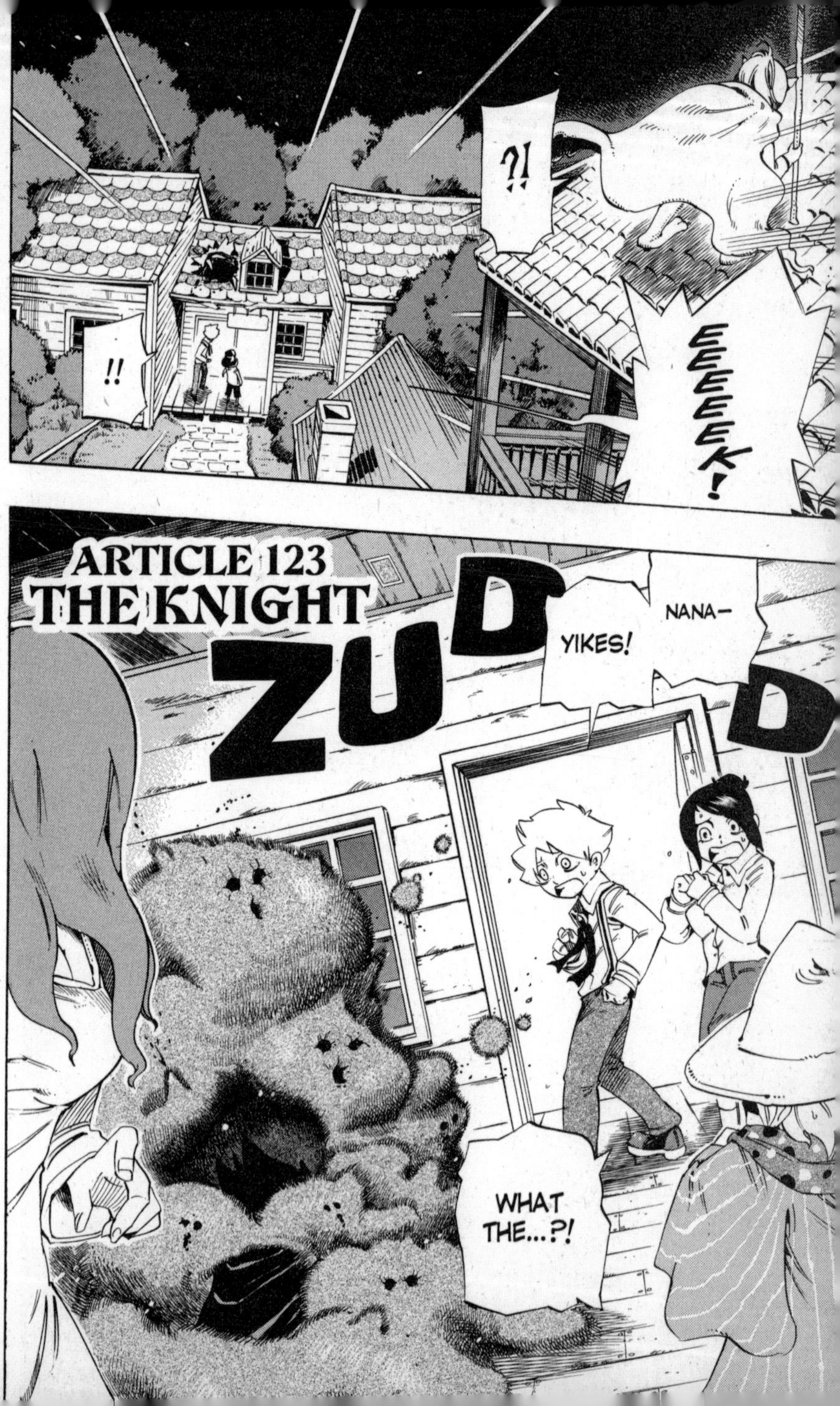
EEEEEK!
?!
!!
ARTICLE 123
THE KNIGHT
NANA-
YIKES!
ZUDD
WHAT THE...?!

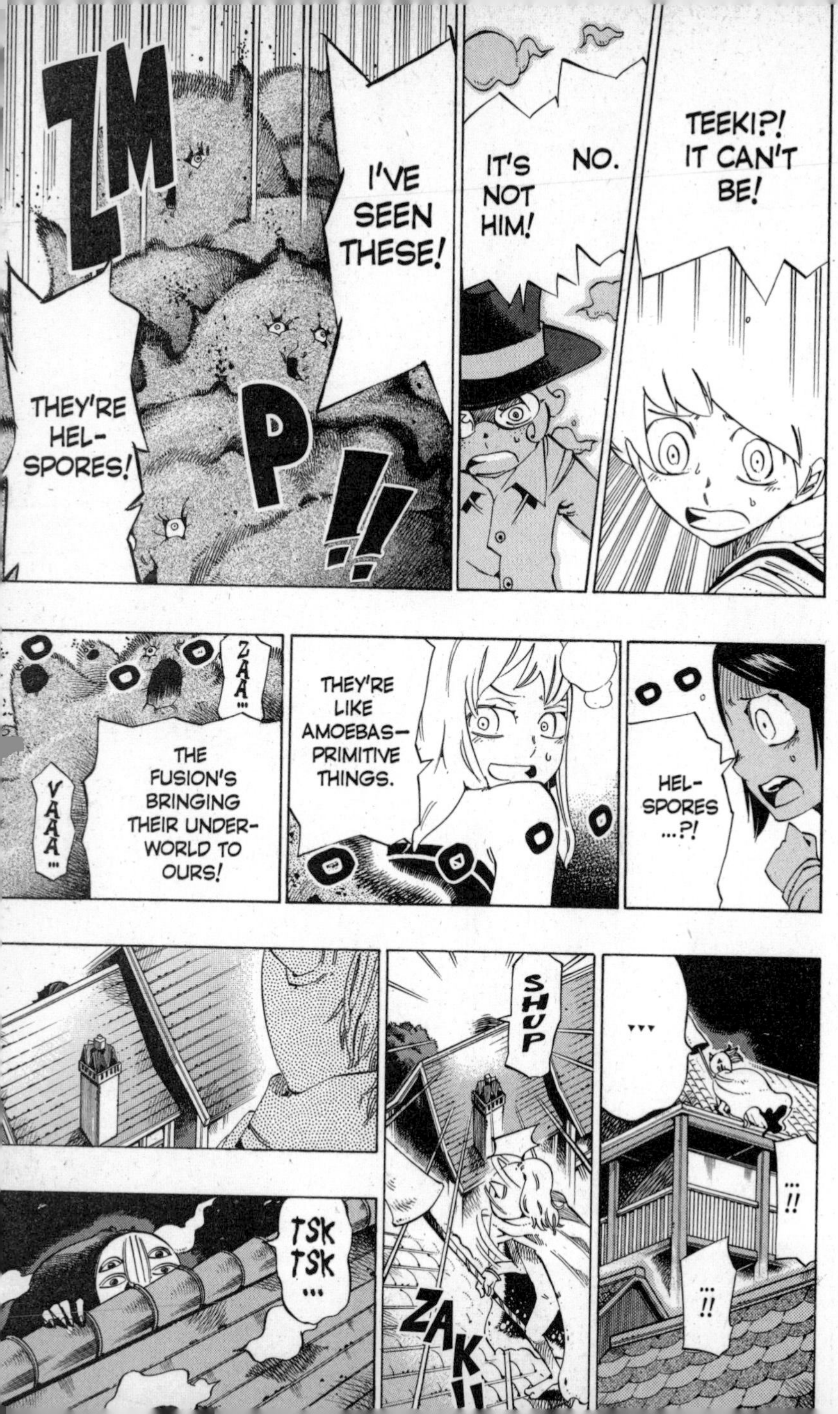
TEEKI?! IT CAN'T BE!
NO.
IT'S NOT HIM!
I'VE SEEN THESE!
ZM
P!!
THEY'RE HEL-SPORES!
HEL-SPORES ...?!
THEY'RE LIKE AMOEBAS—PRIMITIVE THINGS.
ZAA...
THE FUSION'S BRINGING THEIR UNDER-WORLD TO OURS!
VAAA...
...
...!!
...!!
SHUP
ZAK!!
TSK TSK ...

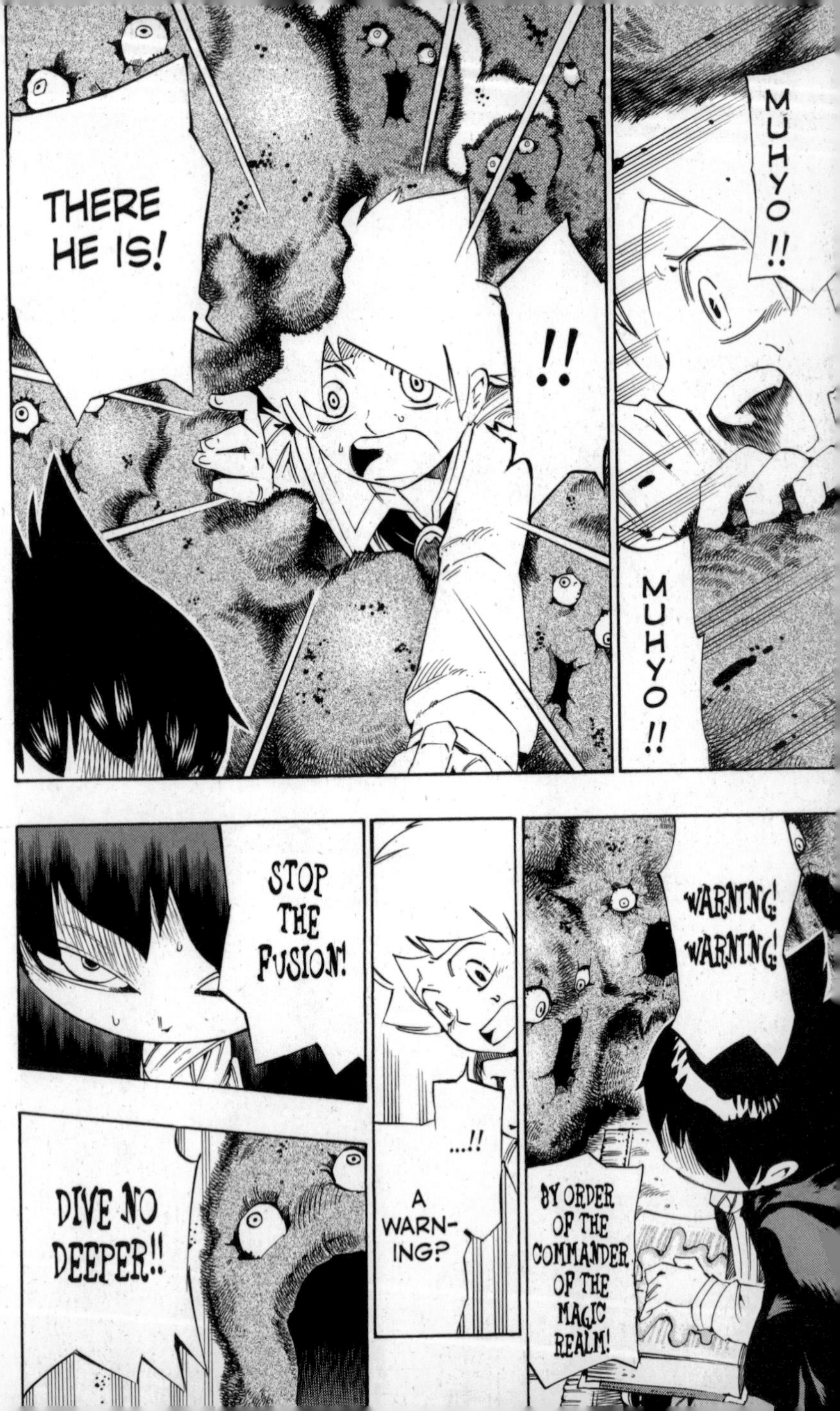

MUHYO!!
MUHYO!!
!!
THERE HE IS!
WARNING! WARNING!
BY ORDER OF THE COMMANDER OF THE MAGIC REALM!
...!!
A WARN-ING?
STOP THE FUSION!
DIVE NO DEEPER!!

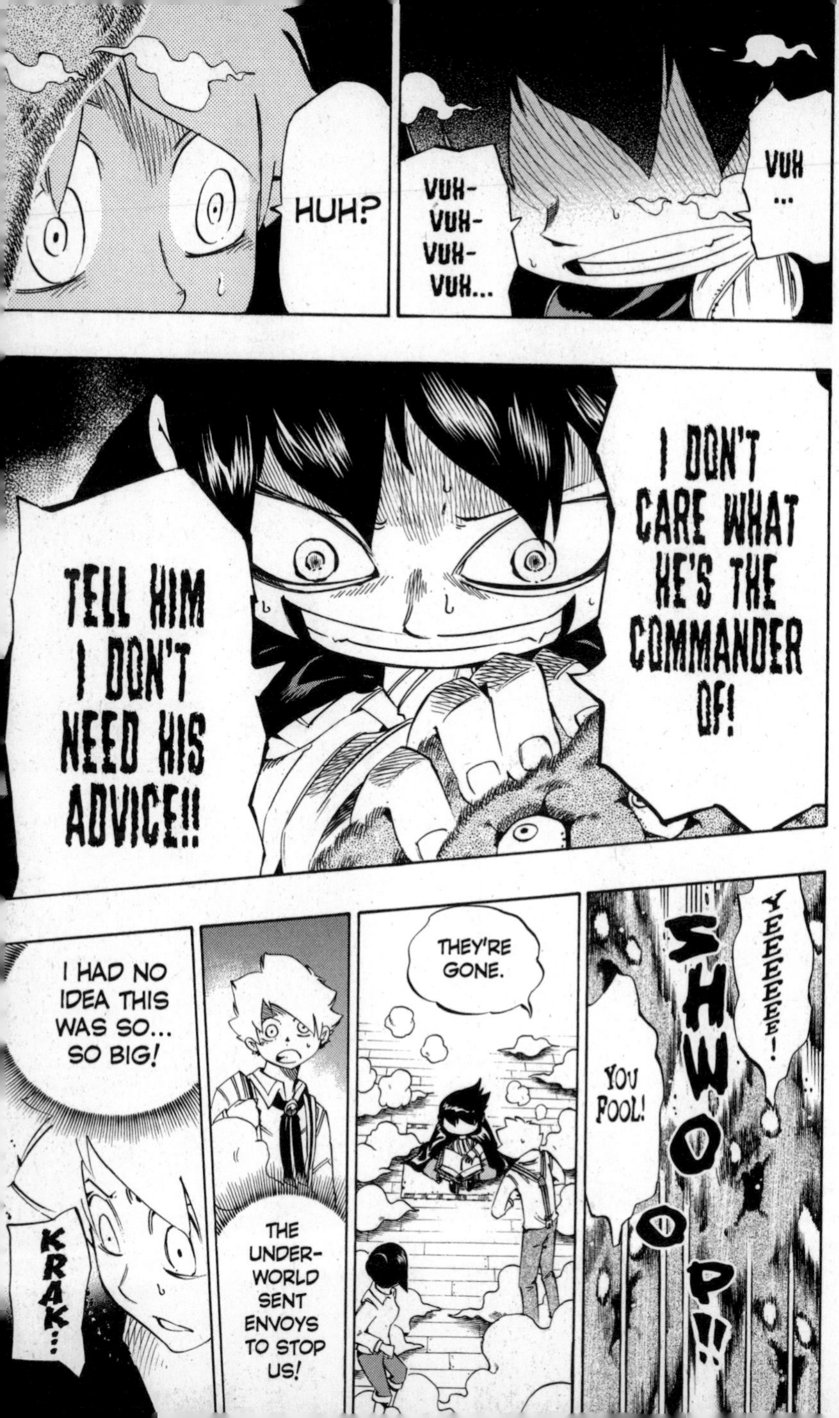
VUH ...
VUH- VUH- VUH- VUH...
HUH?
I DON'T CARE WHAT HE'S THE COMMANDER OF!
TELL HIM I DON'T NEED HIS ADVICE!!
YEEEEEE!
SHWOOOP!!
YOU FOOL!
THEY'RE GONE.
THE UNDER-WORLD SENT ENVOYS TO STOP US!
I HAD NO IDEA THIS WAS SO... SO BIG!
KRAK...

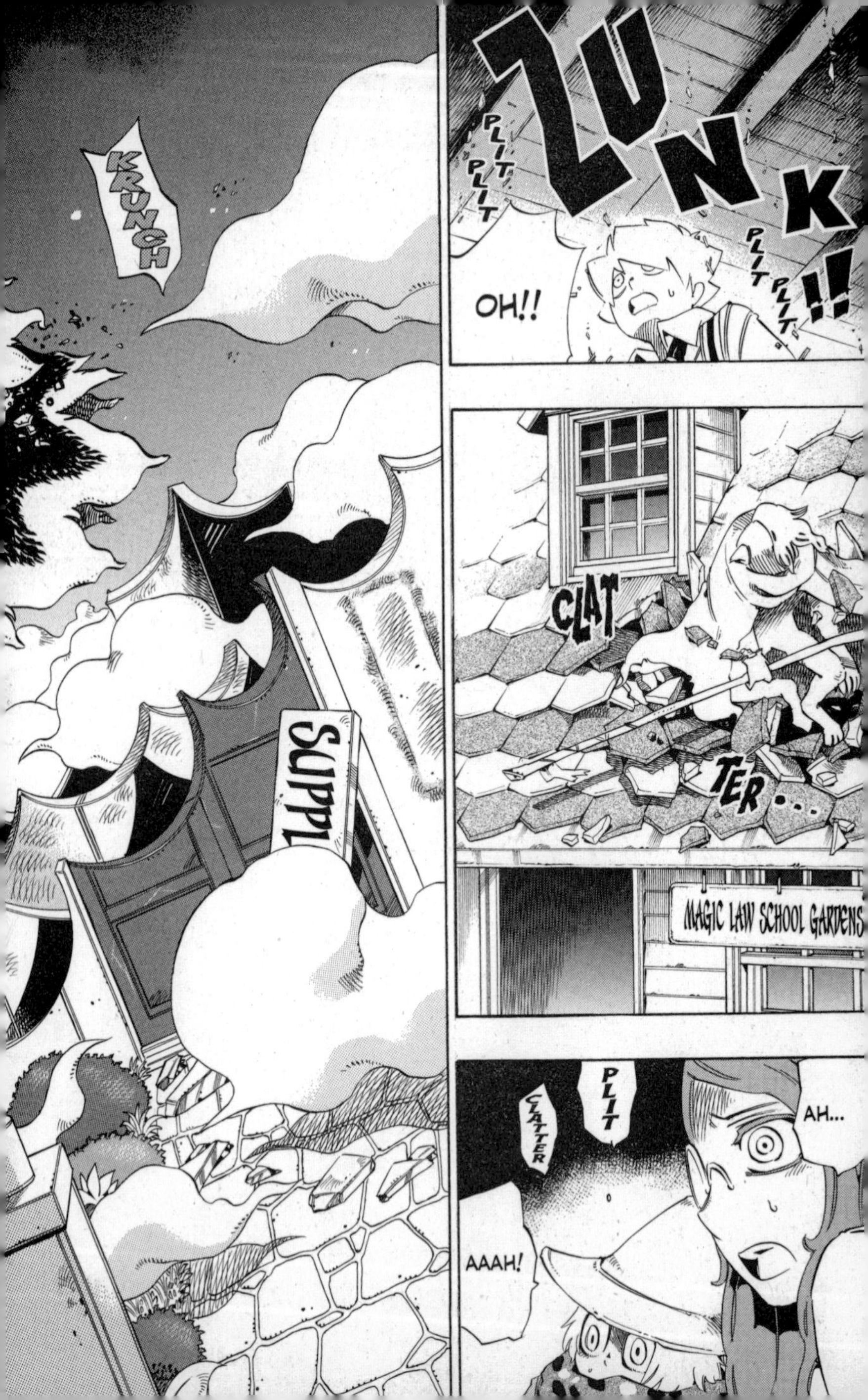
ZUNK!!
PLIT PLIT PLIT
PLIT PLIT
OH!!
CLAT
TER...
MAGIC LAW SCHOOL GARDENS
AH...
PLIT
CLATTER
AAAH!
KRUNCH
SUPPL

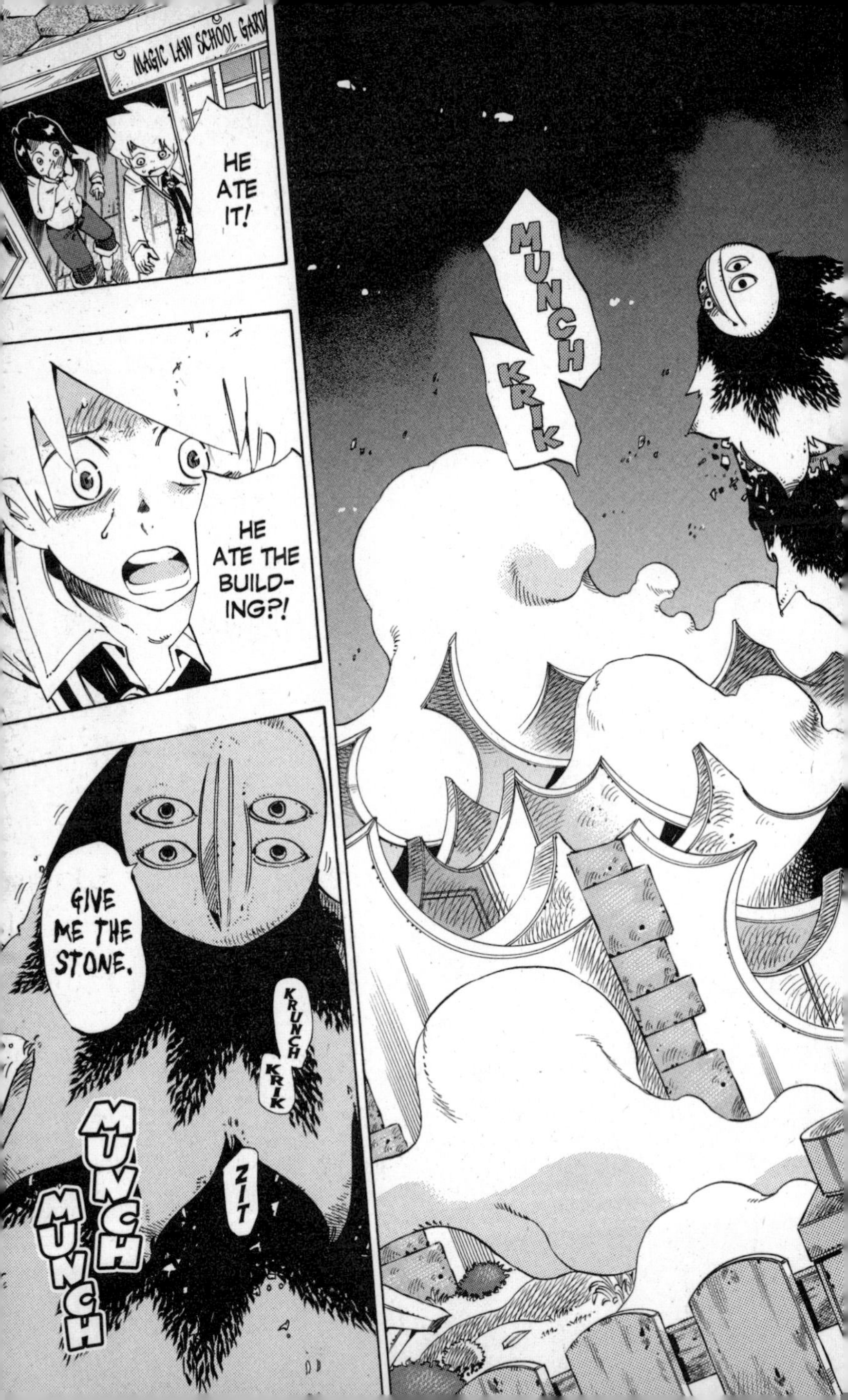
MUNCH
KRIK
MAGIC LAW SCHOOL GARD
HE ATE IT!
HE ATE THE BUILD-ING?!
GIVE ME THE STONE.
KRUNCH
KRIK
ZIT
MUNCH
MUNCH

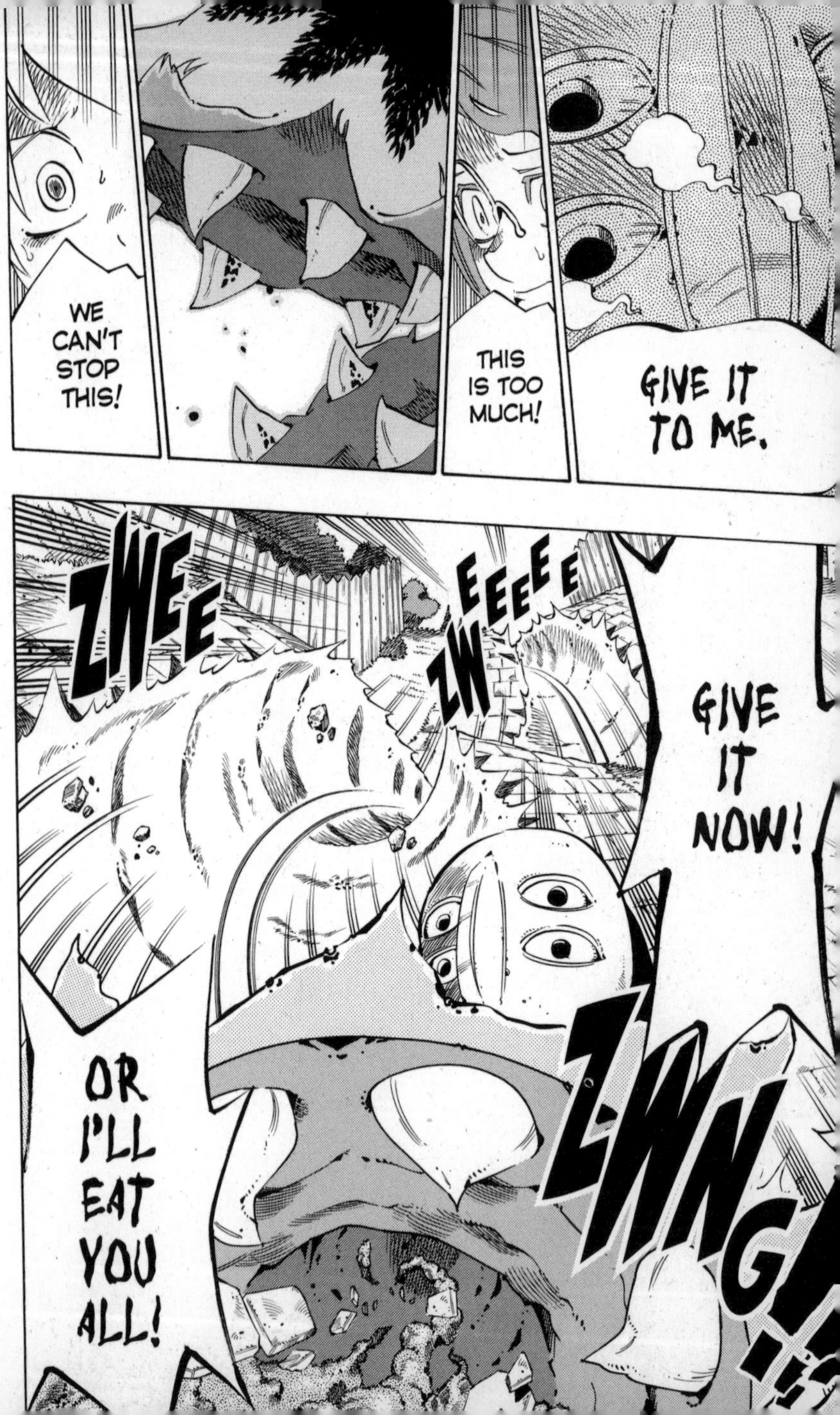
GIVE IT TO ME.
THIS IS TOO MUCH!
WE CAN'T STOP THIS!
GIVE IT NOW!
ZWEEEEE
ZWEE
ZWNG!!
OR I'LL EAT YOU ALL!

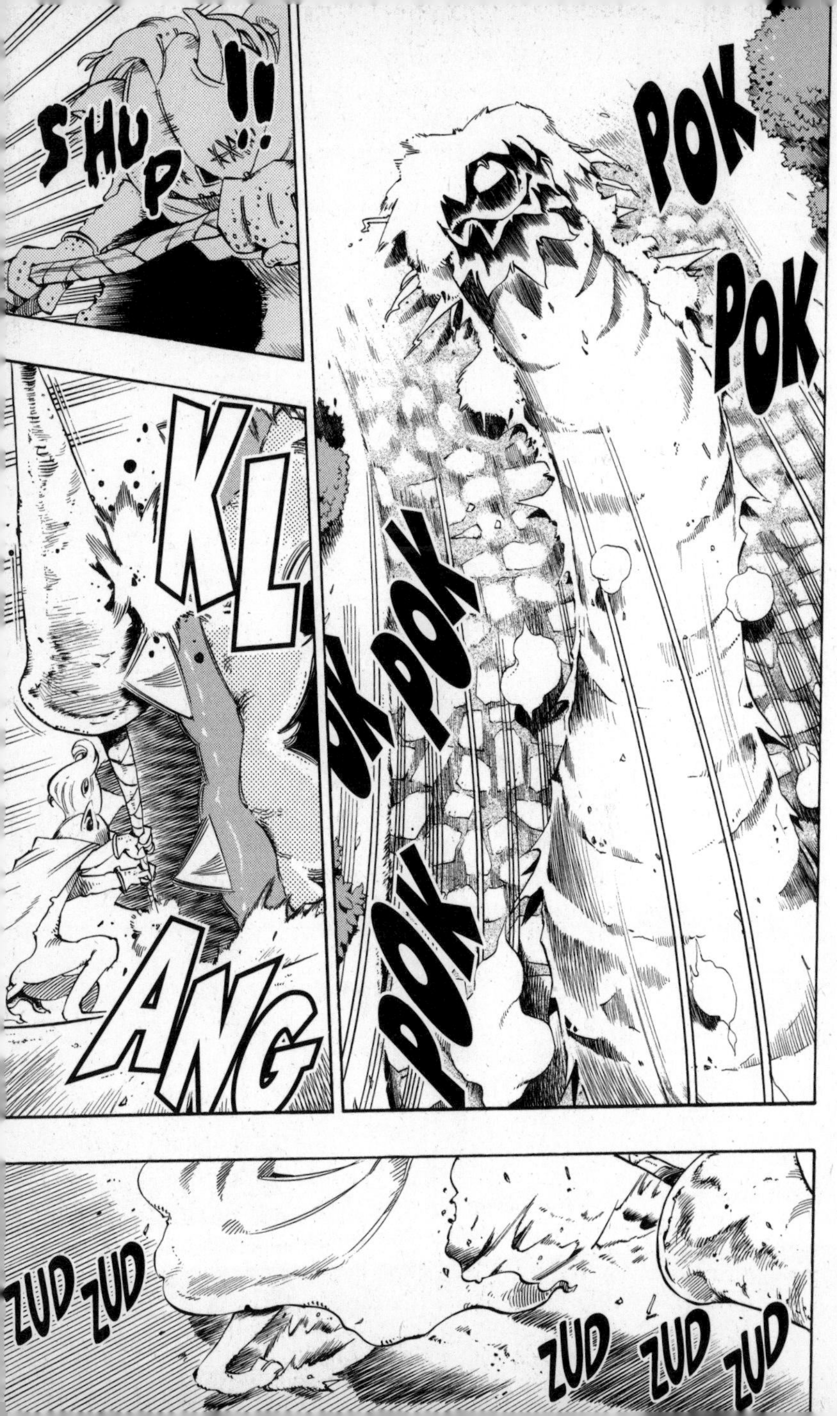
POK
POK
POK POK OK
SHUP!!
KL
ANG
ZUD ZUD ZUD
ZUD ZUD

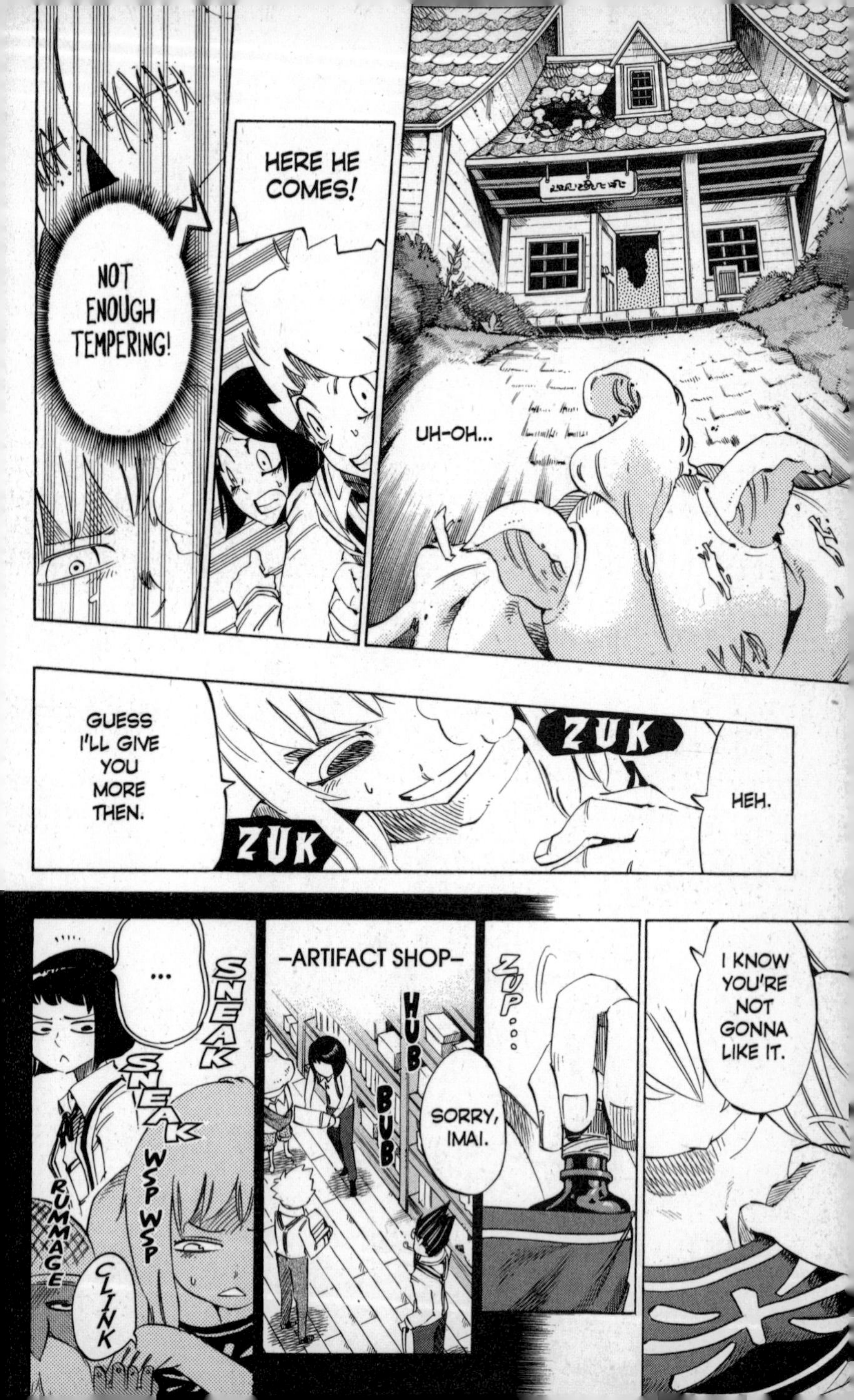
UH-OH...
HERE HE COMES!
NOT ENOUGH TEMPERING!
HEH.
ZUK
GUESS I'LL GIVE YOU MORE THEN.
ZUK
I KNOW YOU'RE NOT GONNA LIKE IT.
ZUP...
-ARTIFACT SHOP-
HUB BUB
SORRY, IMAI.
...
SNEAK SNEAK
WSP WSP
RUMMAGE
CLINK

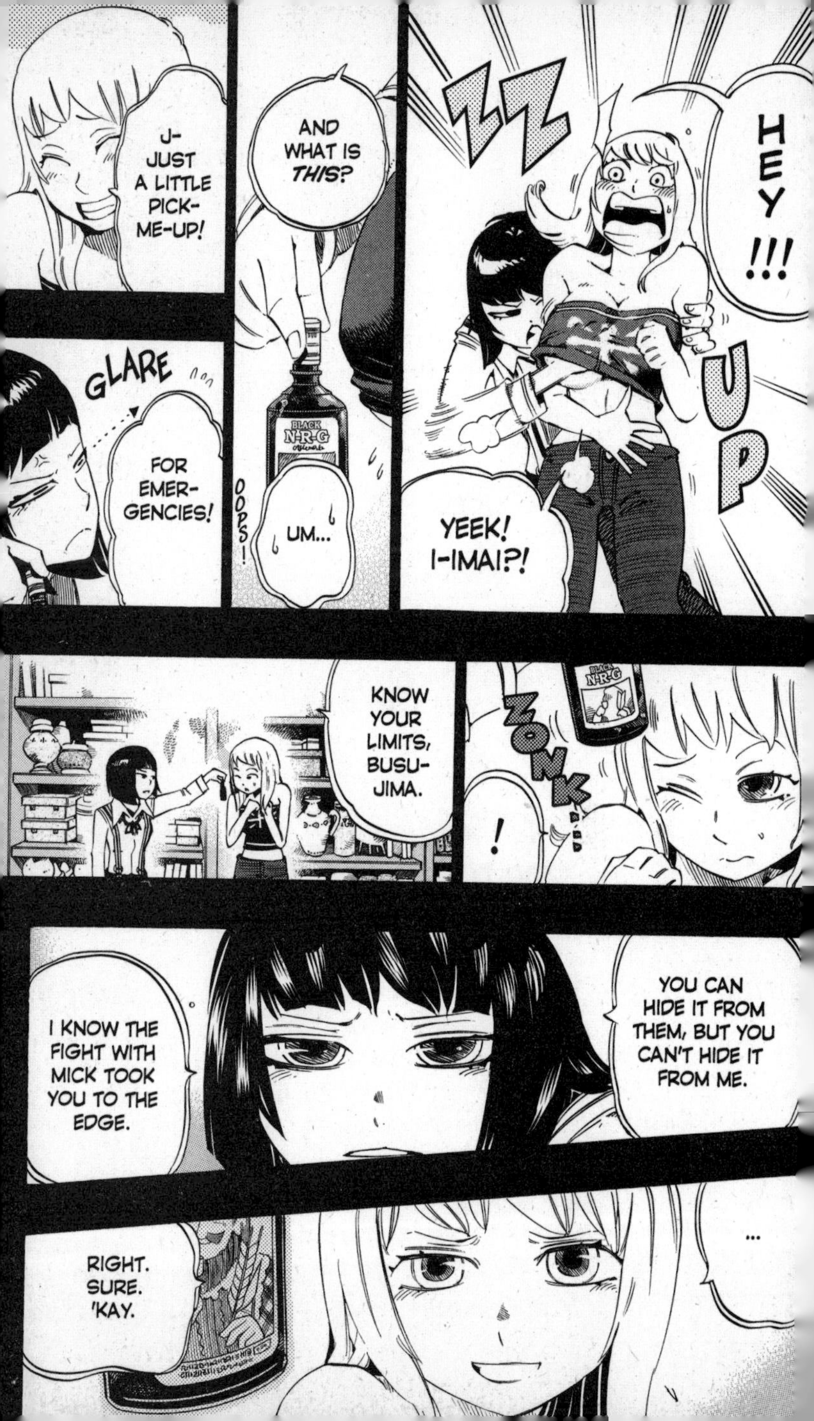
ZZ
HEY!!!
UP
YEEK! I-IMAI?!
AND WHAT IS THIS?
OOPS!
UM...
J- JUST A LITTLE PICK-ME-UP!
GLARE
FOR EMERGENCIES!
BLACK N-R-G
ZONK
!
KNOW YOUR LIMITS, BUSUJIMA.
YOU CAN HIDE IT FROM THEM, BUT YOU CAN'T HIDE IT FROM ME.
I KNOW THE FIGHT WITH MICK TOOK YOU TO THE EDGE.
...
RIGHT. SURE. 'KAY.

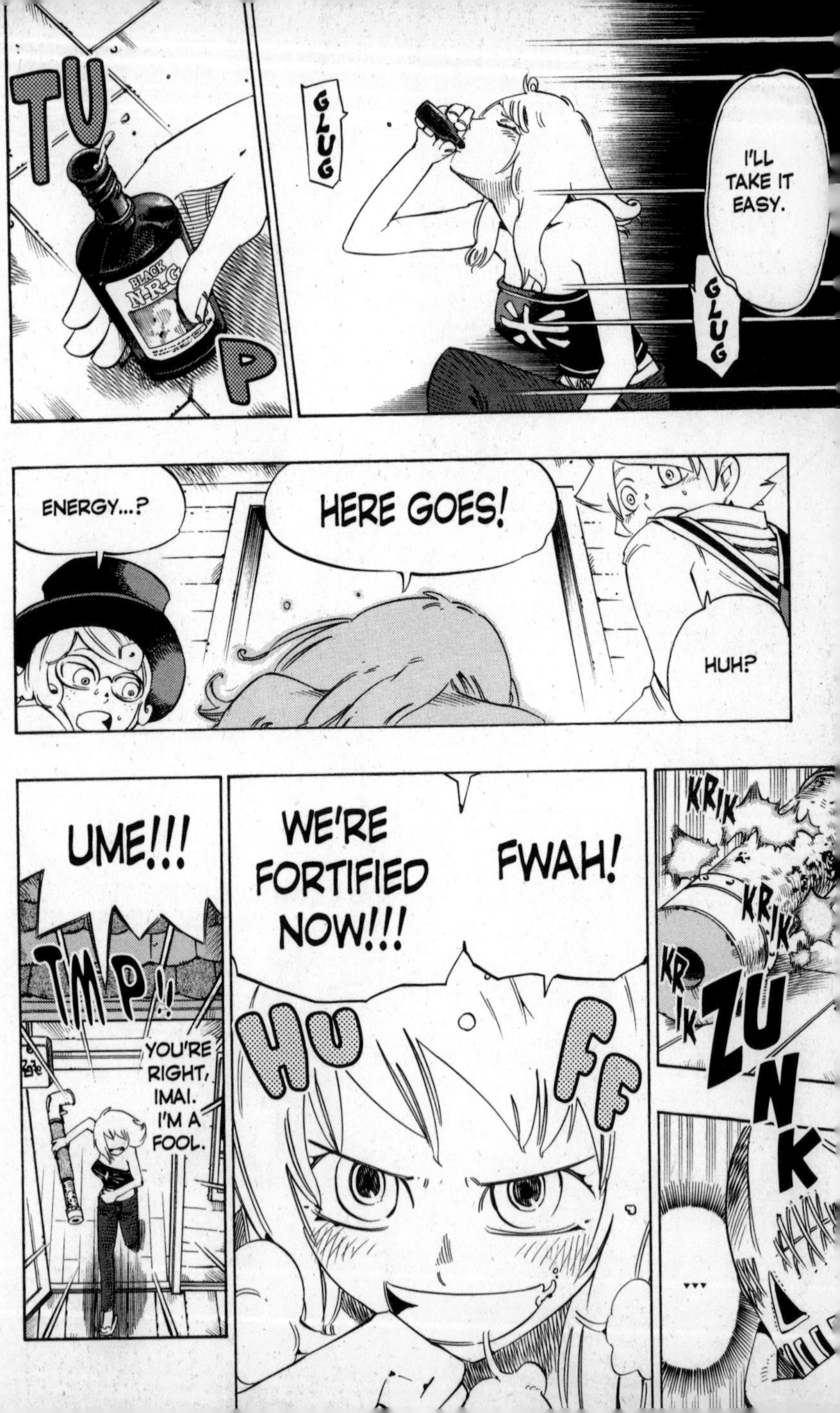
I'LL TAKE IT EASY.
GLUG
GLUG
TUP
HUH?
HERE GOES!
ENERGY...?
KRIK KRIK KRIK
ZUNK
...
FWAH!
WE'RE FORTIFIED NOW!!!
HUFF
UME!!!
TMP!!
YOU'RE RIGHT, IMAI. I'M A FOOL.

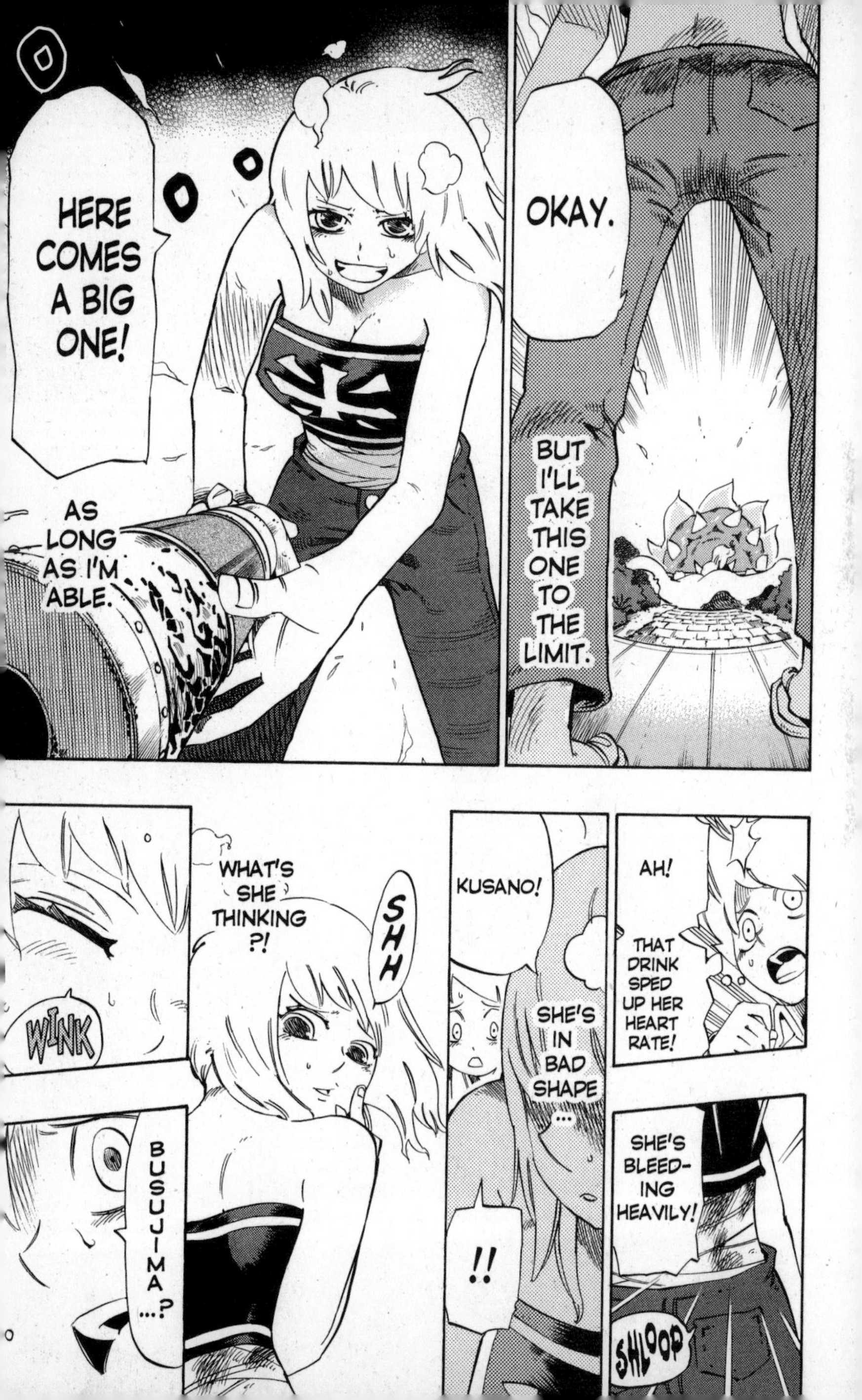
OKAY.
BUT I'LL TAKE THIS ONE TO THE LIMIT.
HERE COMES A BIG ONE!
AS LONG AS I'M ABLE.
AH!
THAT DRINK SPED UP HER HEART RATE!
SHE'S BLEEDING HEAVILY!
SHLOOP
KUSANO!
SHE'S IN BAD SHAPE...
!!
WHAT'S SHE THINKING?!
SHH
WINK
BUSUJIMA...?

NO...!!

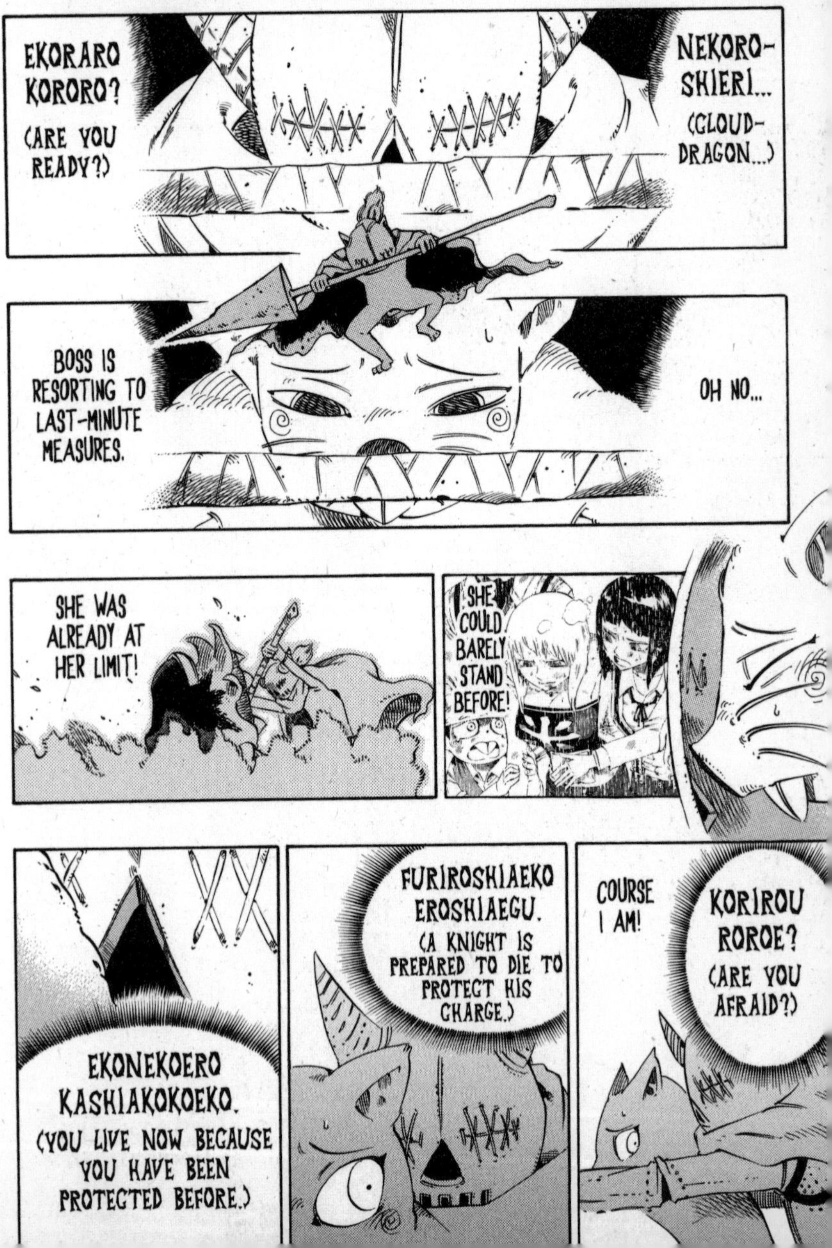

NEKORO-SHIERI...
(CLOUD-DRAGON...)
EKORARO KORORO?
(ARE YOU READY?)
OH NO...
BOSS IS RESORTING TO LAST-MINUTE MEASURES.
SHE COULD BARELY STAND BEFORE!
SHE WAS ALREADY AT HER LIMIT!
KORIROU ROROE?
(ARE YOU AFRAID?)
COURSE I AM!
FURIROSHIAEKO EROSHIAEGU.
(A KNIGHT IS PREPARED TO DIE TO PROTECT HIS CHARGE.)
EKONEKOERO KASHIAKOKOEKO.
(YOU LIVE NOW BECAUSE YOU HAVE BEEN PROTECTED BEFORE.)

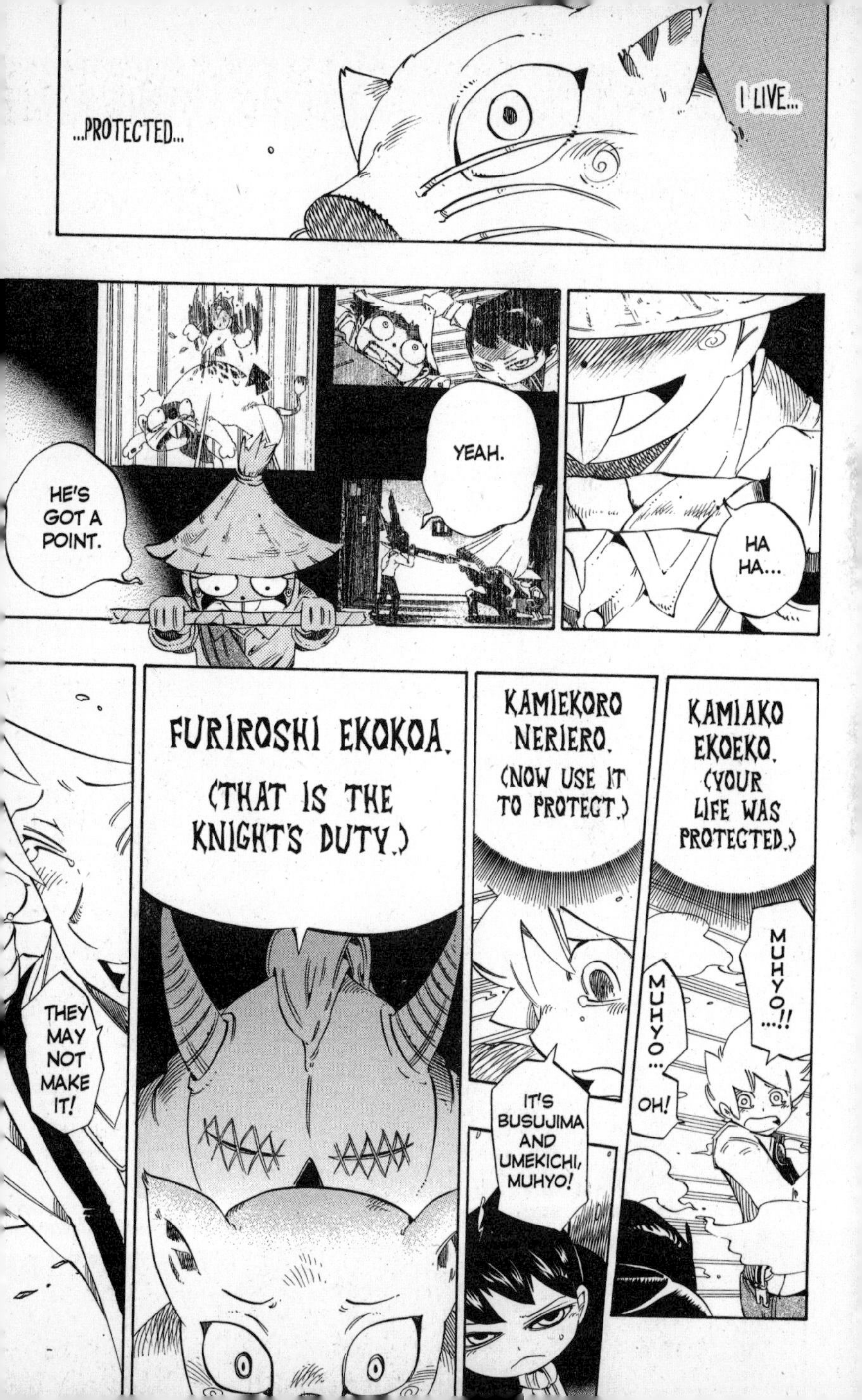
I LIVE...
...PROTECTED...
HA HA...
YEAH.
HE'S GOT A POINT.
KAMIAKO EKOEKO. (YOUR LIFE WAS PROTECTED.)
MUHYO...!!
MUHYO...
OH!
KAMIEKORO NERIERO. (NOW USE IT TO PROTECT.)
IT'S BUSUJIMA AND UMEKICHI, MUHYO!
FURIROSHI EKOKOA. (THAT IS THE KNIGHT'S DUTY.)
THEY MAY NOT MAKE IT!

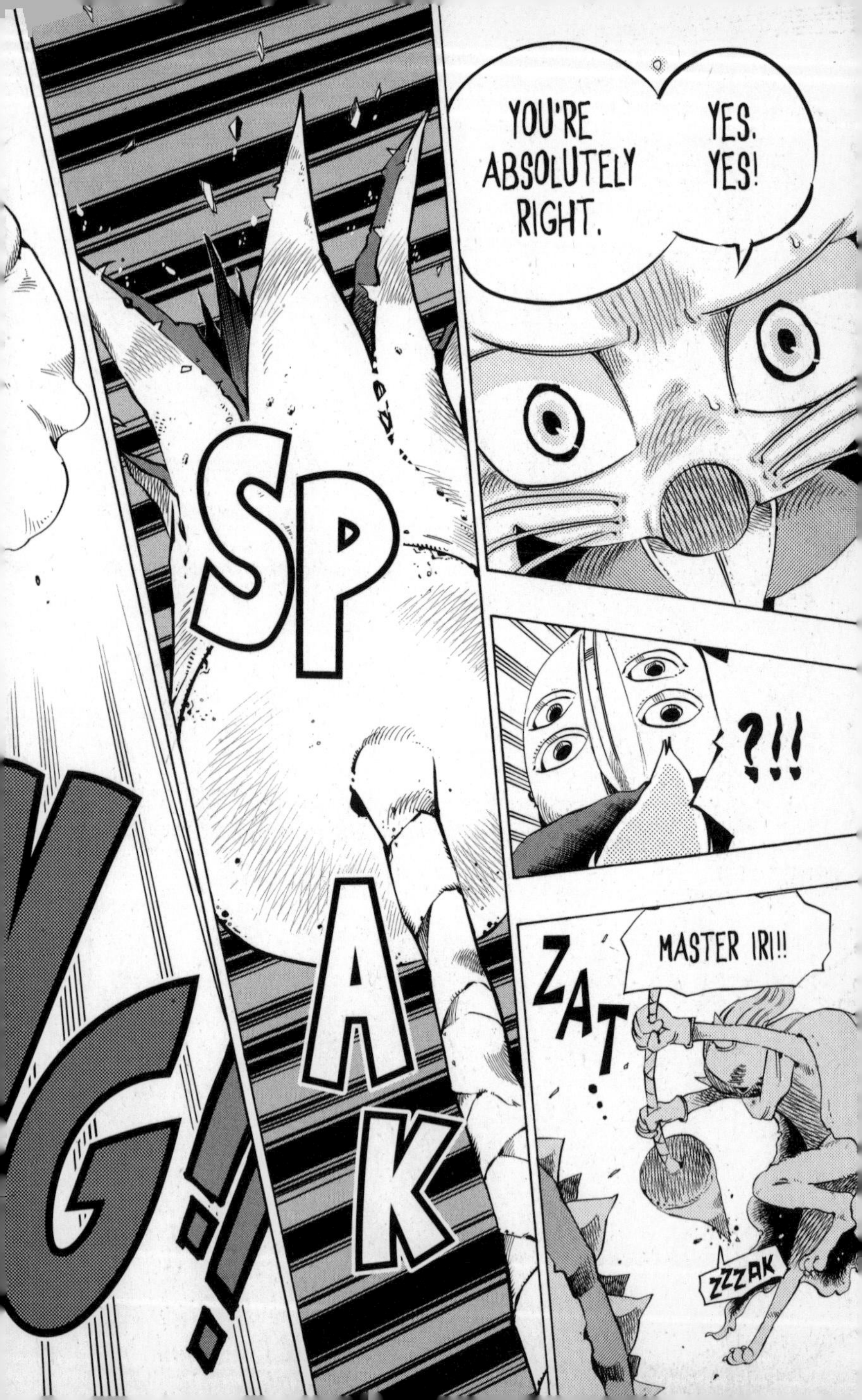
YOU'RE ABSOLUTELY RIGHT.
YES. YES!
?!!
MASTER IRI!!
ZAT
ZZZAK
SPAK
G!!

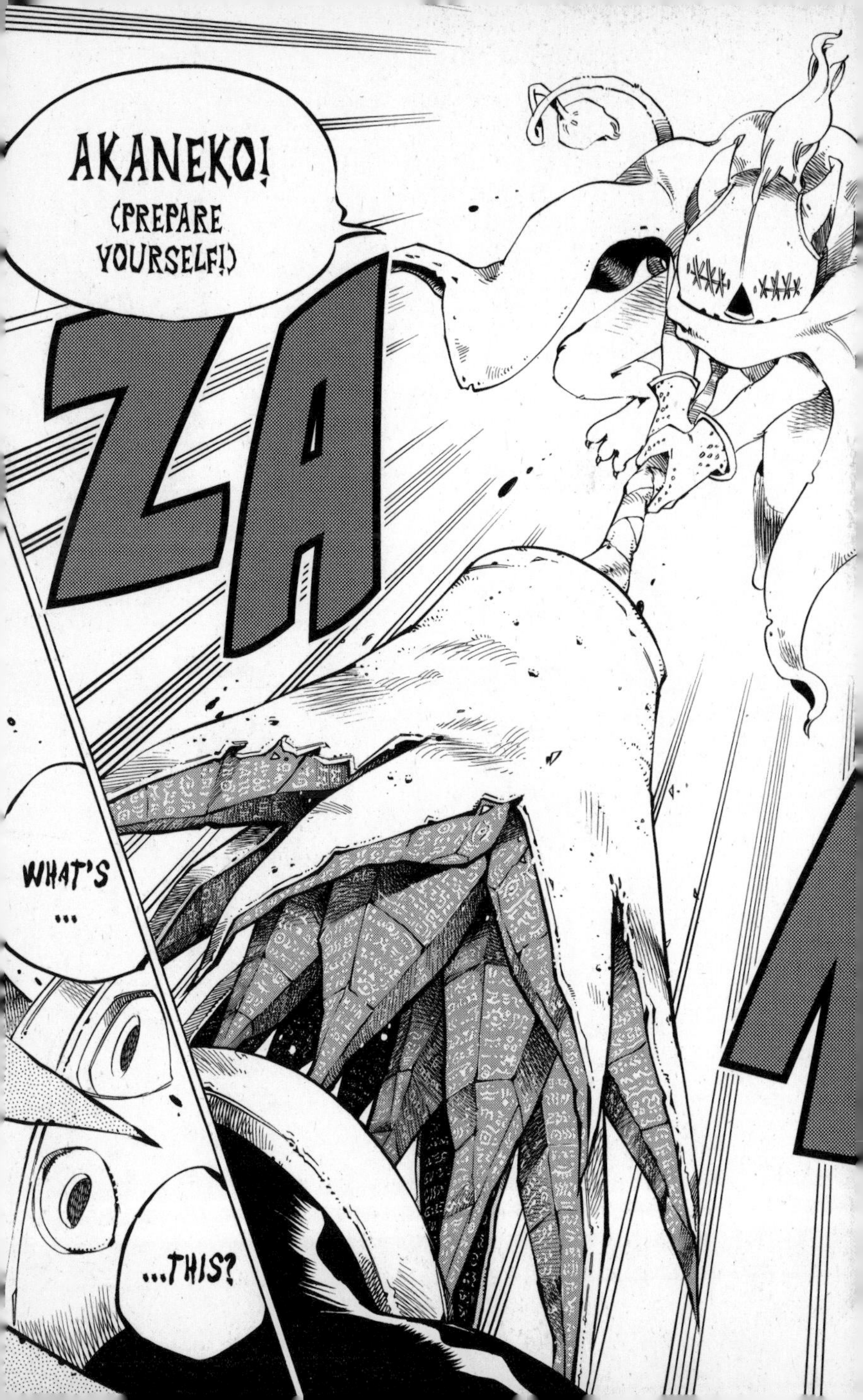
AKANEKO! (PREPARE YOURSELF!)
ZA
WHAT'S ...
...THIS?

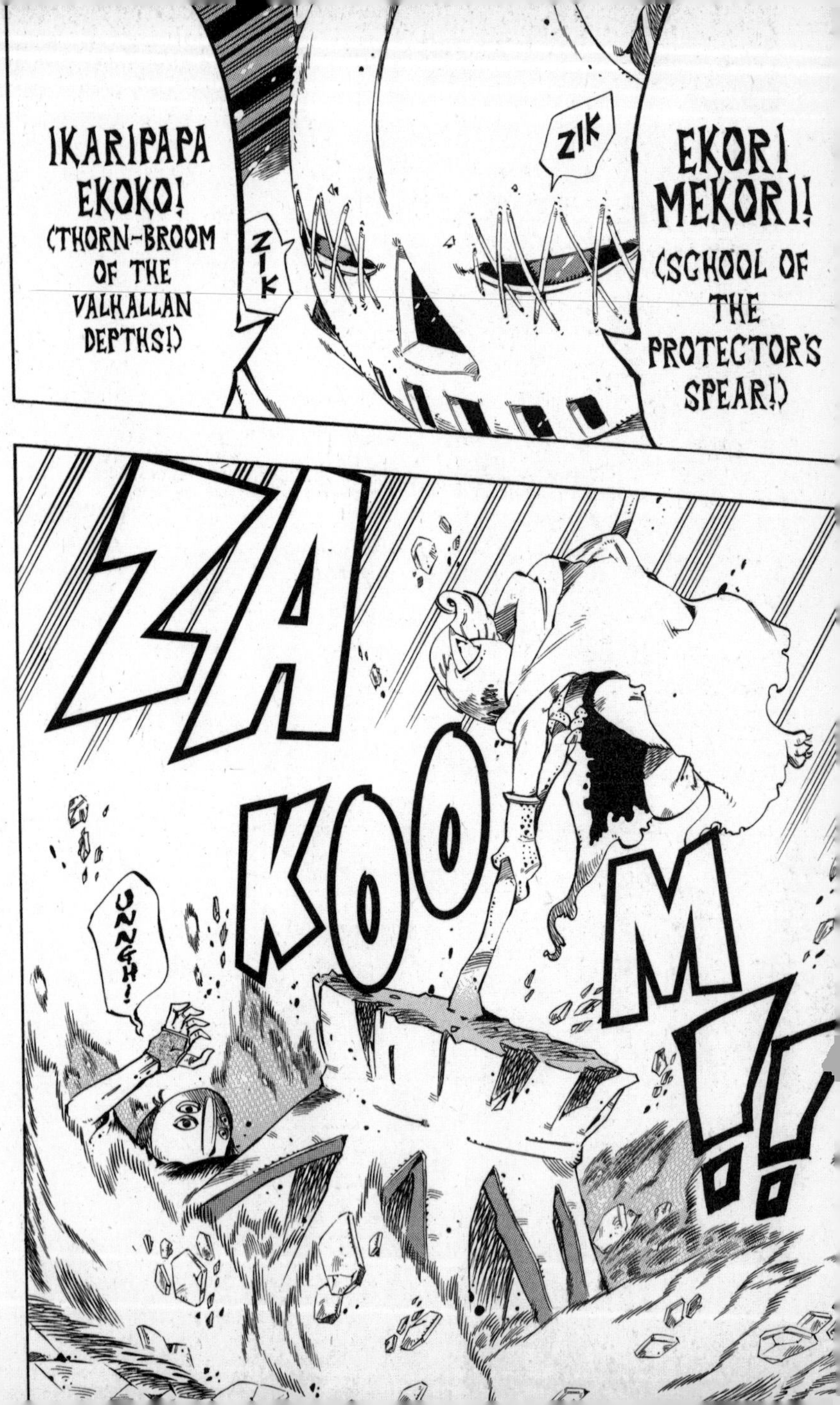
EKORI MEKORI!! (SCHOOL OF THE PROTECTOR'S SPEAR!)
ZIK
ZIK
IKARIPAPA EKOKO! (THORN-BROOM OF THE VALHALLAN DEPTHS!)
ZAKOOOM!!
UNNGH!

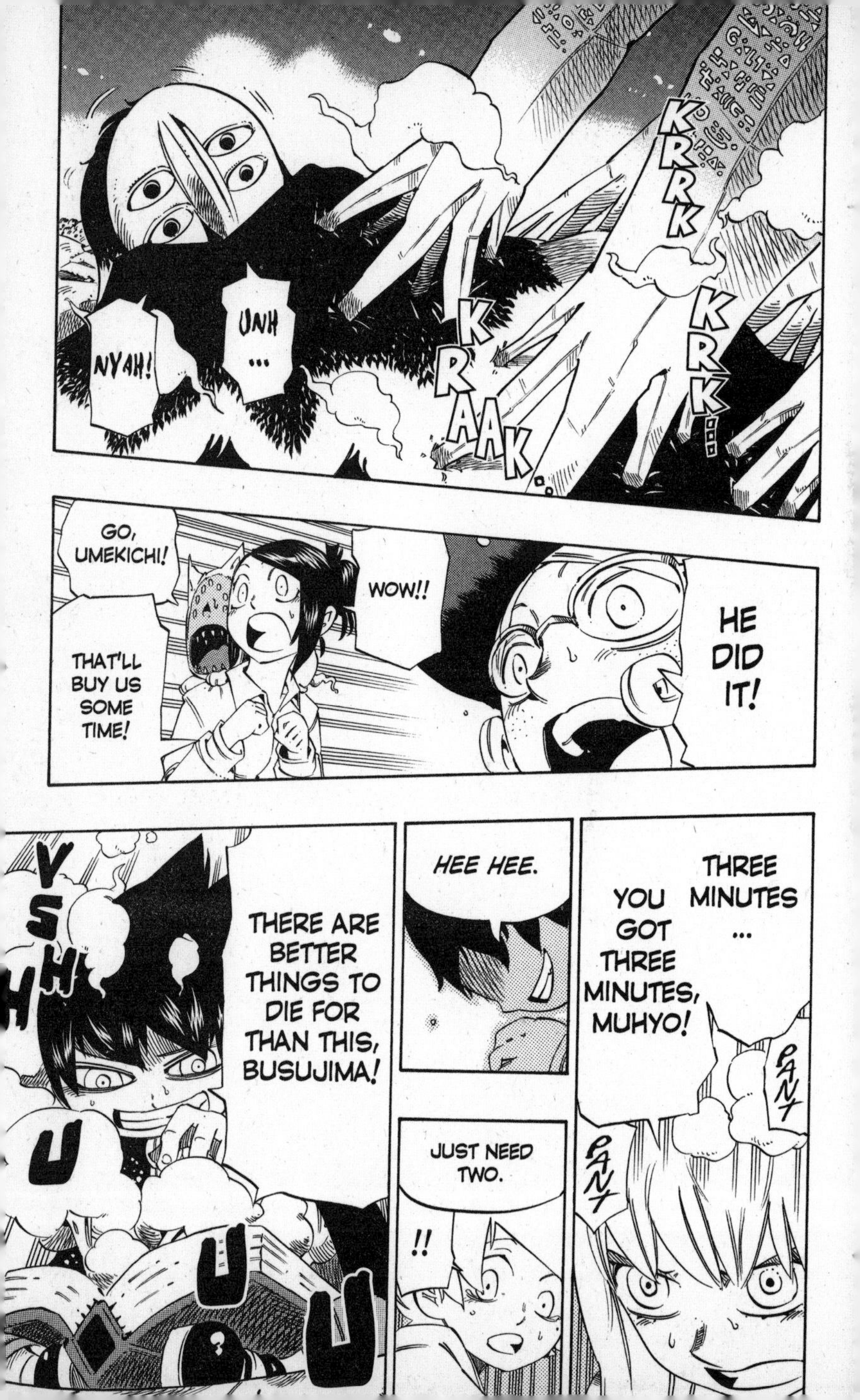
KRRK
KRK...
KRAAK
UNH ...
NYAH!
HE DID IT!
WOW!!
GO, UMEKICHI!
THAT'LL BUY US SOME TIME!
THREE MINUTES ...
YOU GOT THREE MINUTES, MUHYO!
PANT
PANT
HEE HEE.
JUST NEED TWO.
!!
THERE ARE BETTER THINGS TO DIE FOR THAN THIS, BUSUJIMA!
VSHH
UUUU

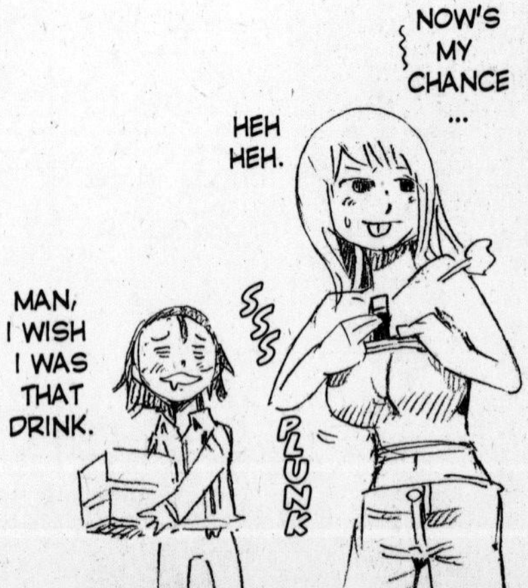
NOW'S MY CHANCE...
HEH HEH.
SSS
PLUNK
MAN, I WISH I WAS THAT DRINK.

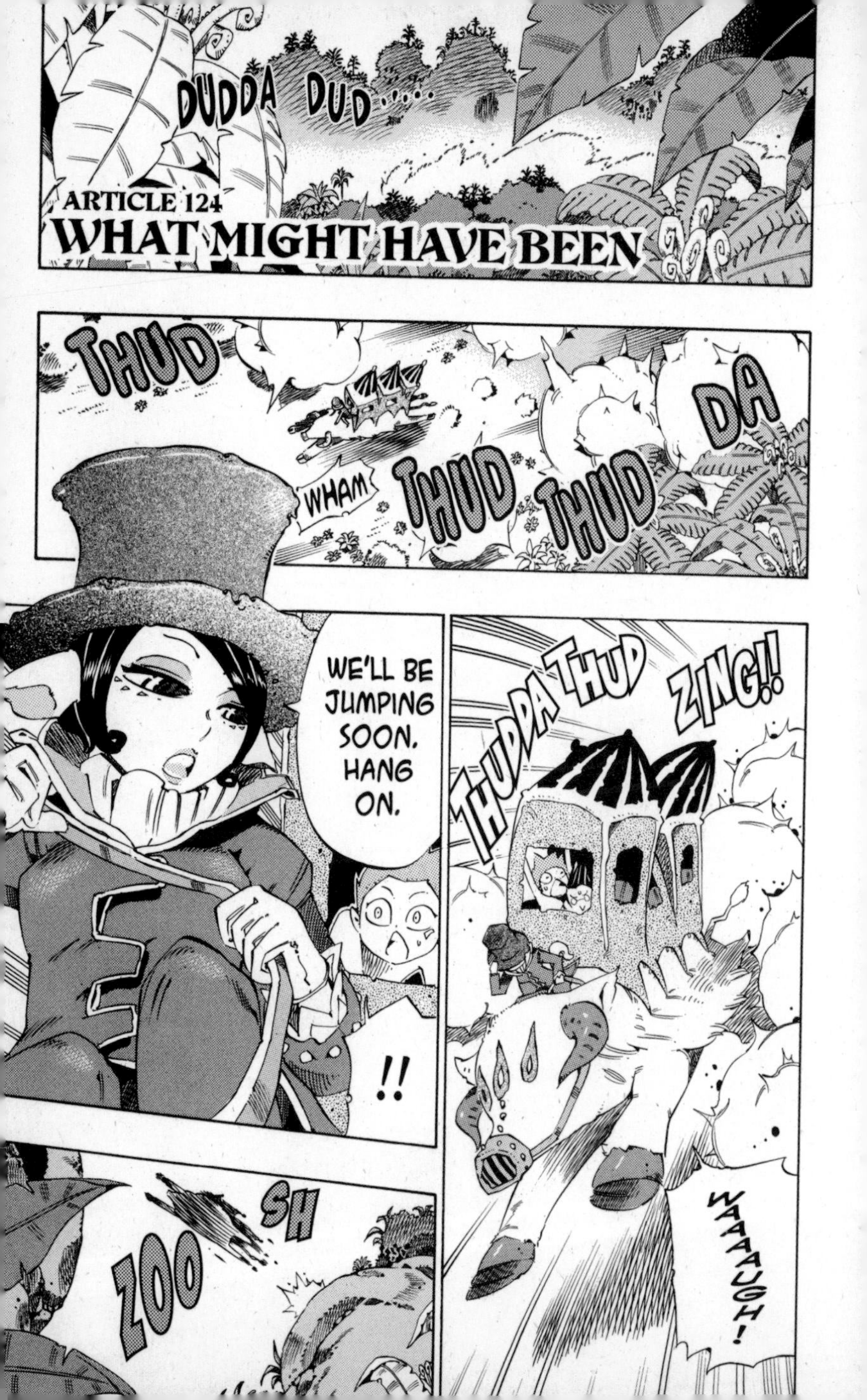
DUDDA DUD....
ARTICLE 124
WHAT MIGHT HAVE BEEN
DA
THUD
THUD
WHAM
THUD
ZING!!
THUDDA THUD
WAAAAUGH!
WE'LL BE JUMPING SOON. HANG ON.
!!
ZOO
SH

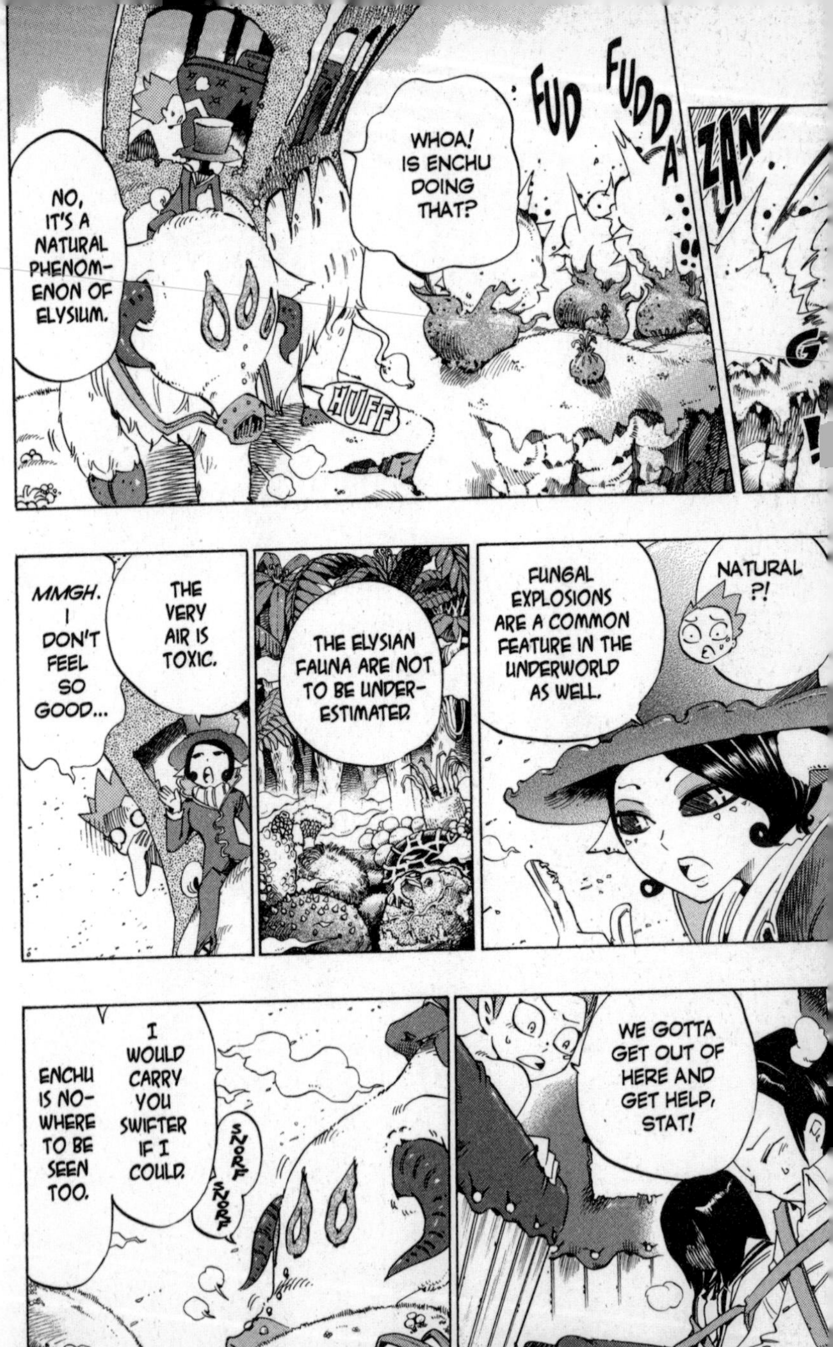
ZAN
G
!
FUDDA
FUD
WHOA! IS ENCHU DOING THAT?
NO, IT'S A NATURAL PHENOM-ENON OF ELYSIUM.
HUFF
NATURAL ?!
FUNGAL EXPLOSIONS ARE A COMMON FEATURE IN THE UNDERWORLD AS WELL.
THE ELYSIAN FAUNA ARE NOT TO BE UNDER-ESTIMATED.
THE VERY AIR IS TOXIC.
MMGH. I DON'T FEEL SO GOOD...
WE GOTTA GET OUT OF HERE AND GET HELP, STAT!
I WOULD CARRY YOU SWIFTER IF I COULD.
SNORF SNORF
ENCHU IS NO-WHERE TO BE SEEN TOO.

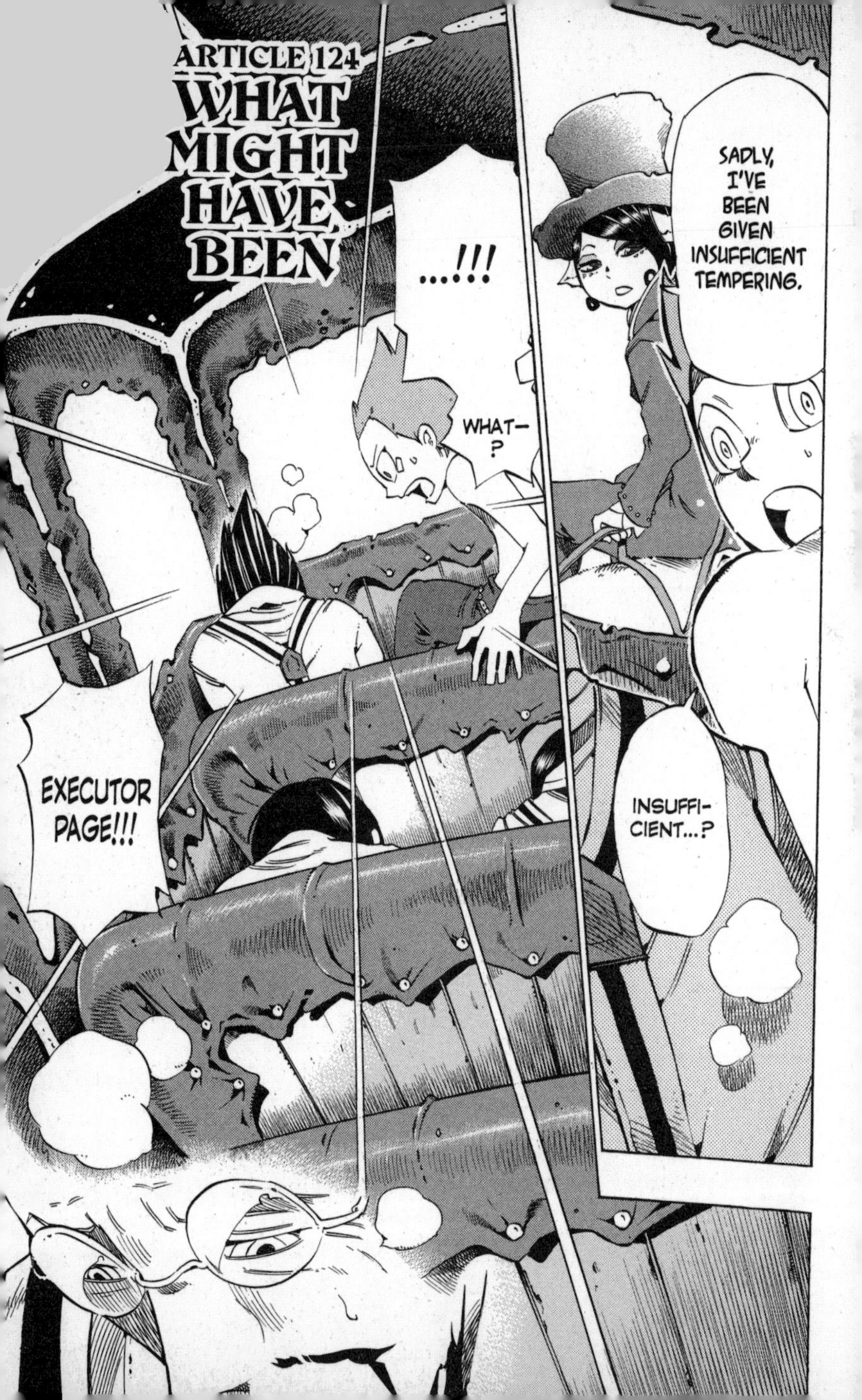
SADLY, I'VE BEEN GIVEN INSUFFICIENT TEMPERING.
INSUFFI-CIENT...?
ARTICLE 124
WHAT MIGHT HAVE BEEN
...!!!
WHAT—?
EXECUTOR PAGE!!!

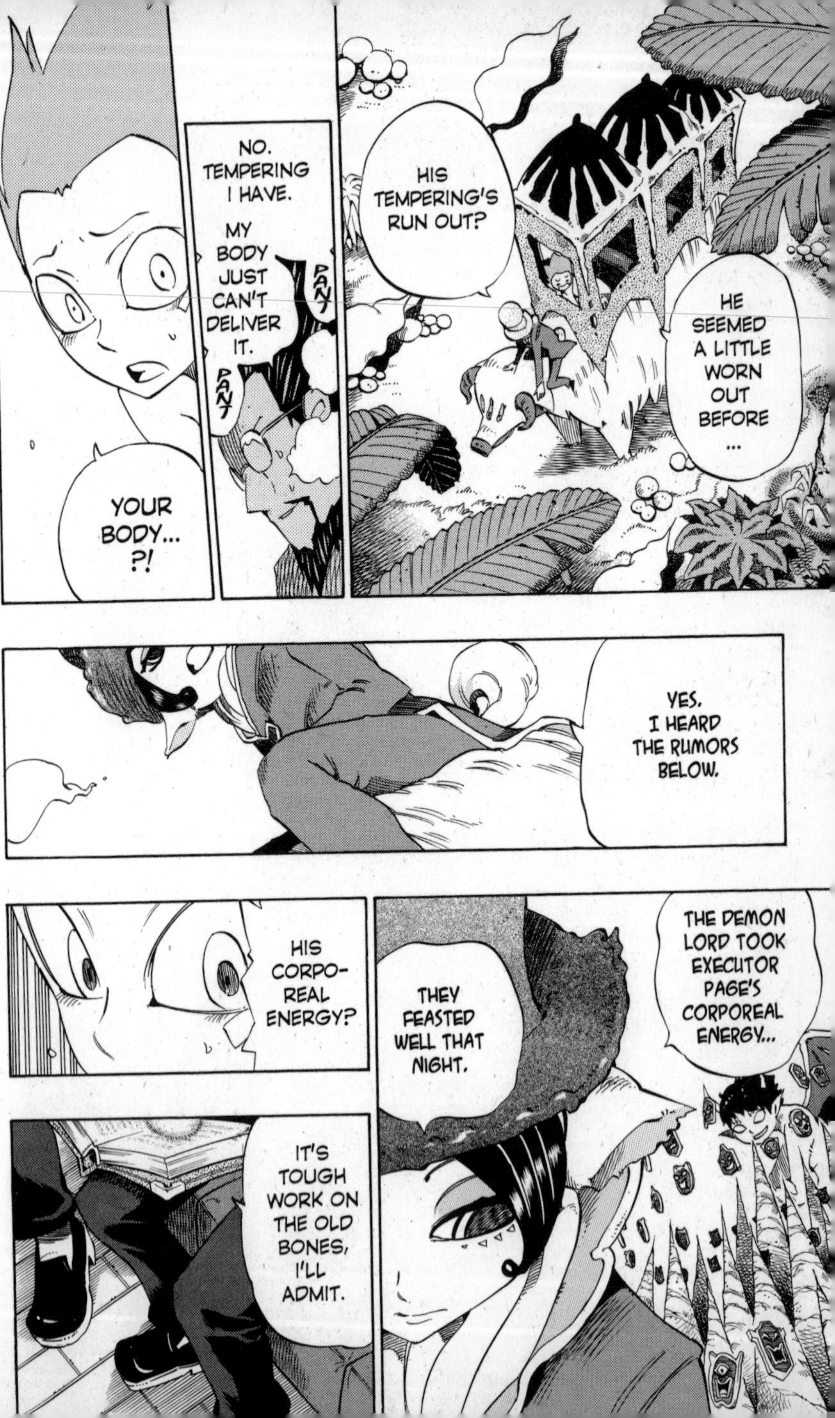
HE SEEMED A LITTLE WORN OUT BEFORE...
HIS TEMPERING'S RUN OUT?
NO. TEMPERING I HAVE.
MY BODY JUST CAN'T DELIVER IT.
PANT
PANT
YOUR BODY...?!
YES. I HEARD THE RUMORS BELOW.
THE DEMON LORD TOOK EXECUTOR PAGE'S CORPOREAL ENERGY...
THEY FEASTED WELL THAT NIGHT.
HIS CORPO-REAL ENERGY?
IT'S TOUGH WORK ON THE OLD BONES, I'LL ADMIT.

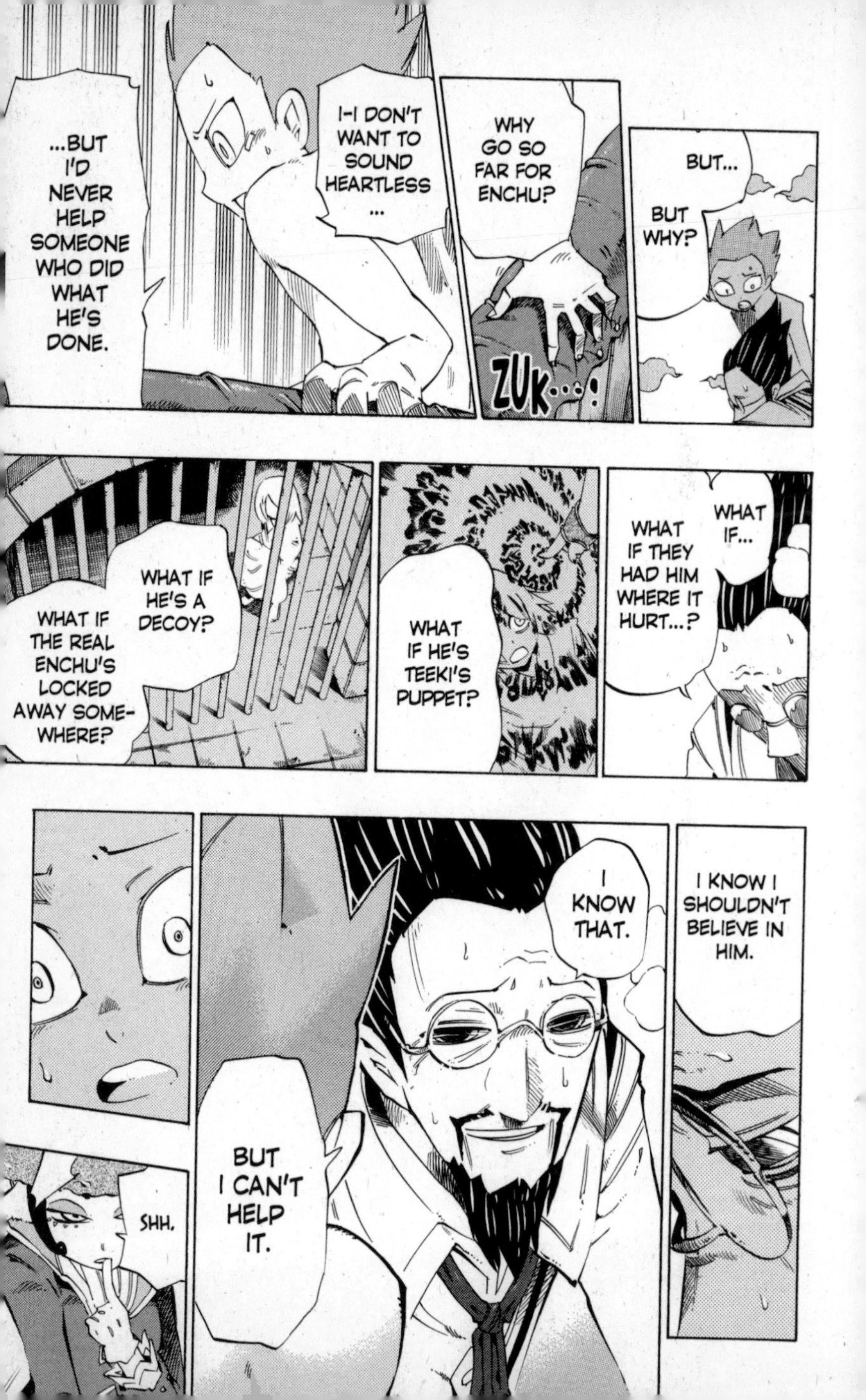
BUT...
BUT WHY?
WHY GO SO FAR FOR ENCHU?
ZUK...!
I-I DON'T WANT TO SOUND HEARTLESS...
...BUT I'D NEVER HELP SOMEONE WHO DID WHAT HE'S DONE.
WHAT IF...
WHAT IF THEY HAD HIM WHERE IT HURT...?
WHAT IF HE'S TEEKI'S PUPPET?
WHAT IF HE'S A DECOY?
WHAT IF THE REAL ENCHU'S LOCKED AWAY SOME-WHERE?
I KNOW I SHOULDN'T BELIEVE IN HIM.
I KNOW THAT.
BUT I CAN'T HELP IT.
SHH.

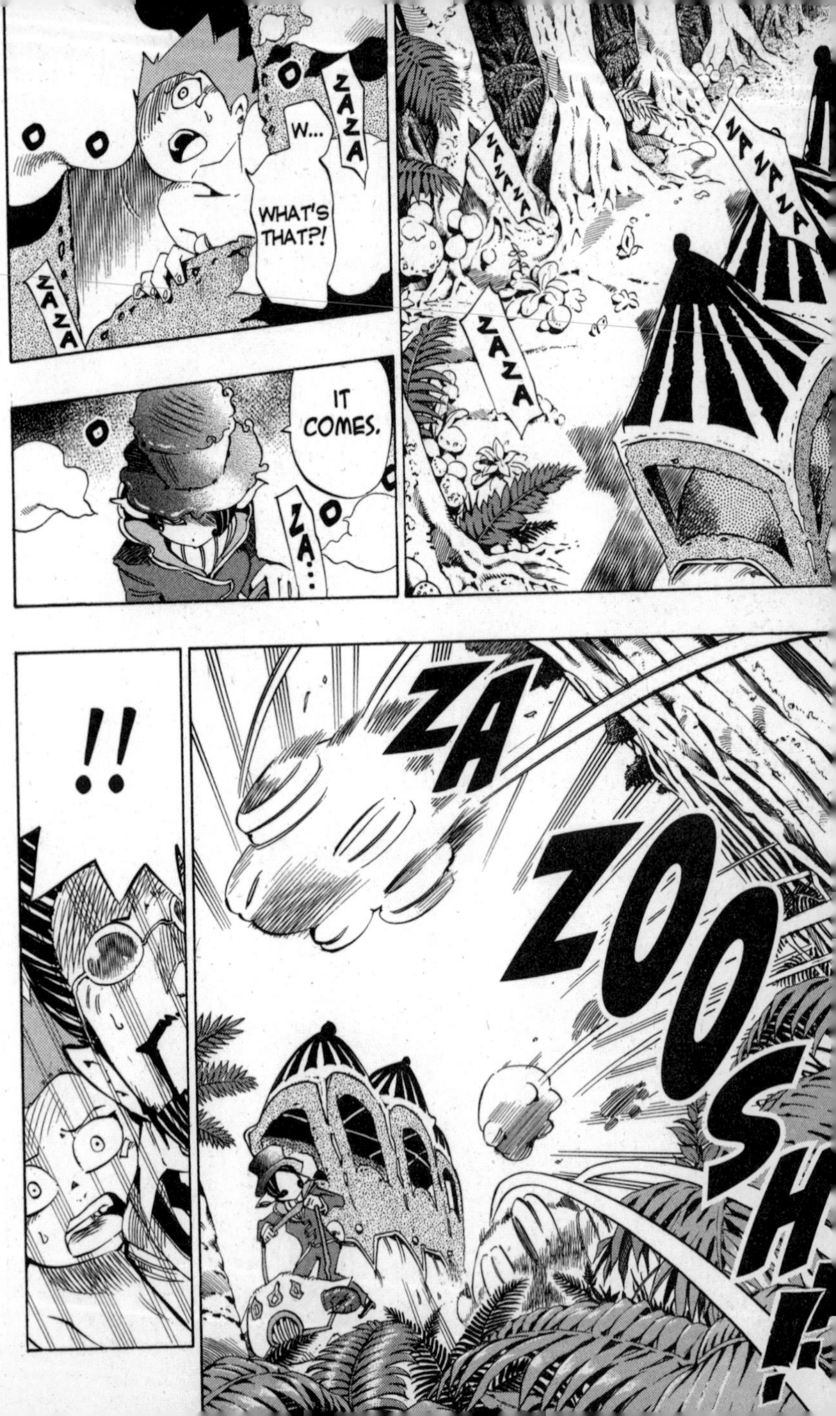
ZAZAZA
ZAZAZA
ZAZA
O
ZAZA
W...
WHAT'S THAT?!
O O
ZAZA
IT COMES.
O
ZA...
O
ZA
ZOOSH!!
!!

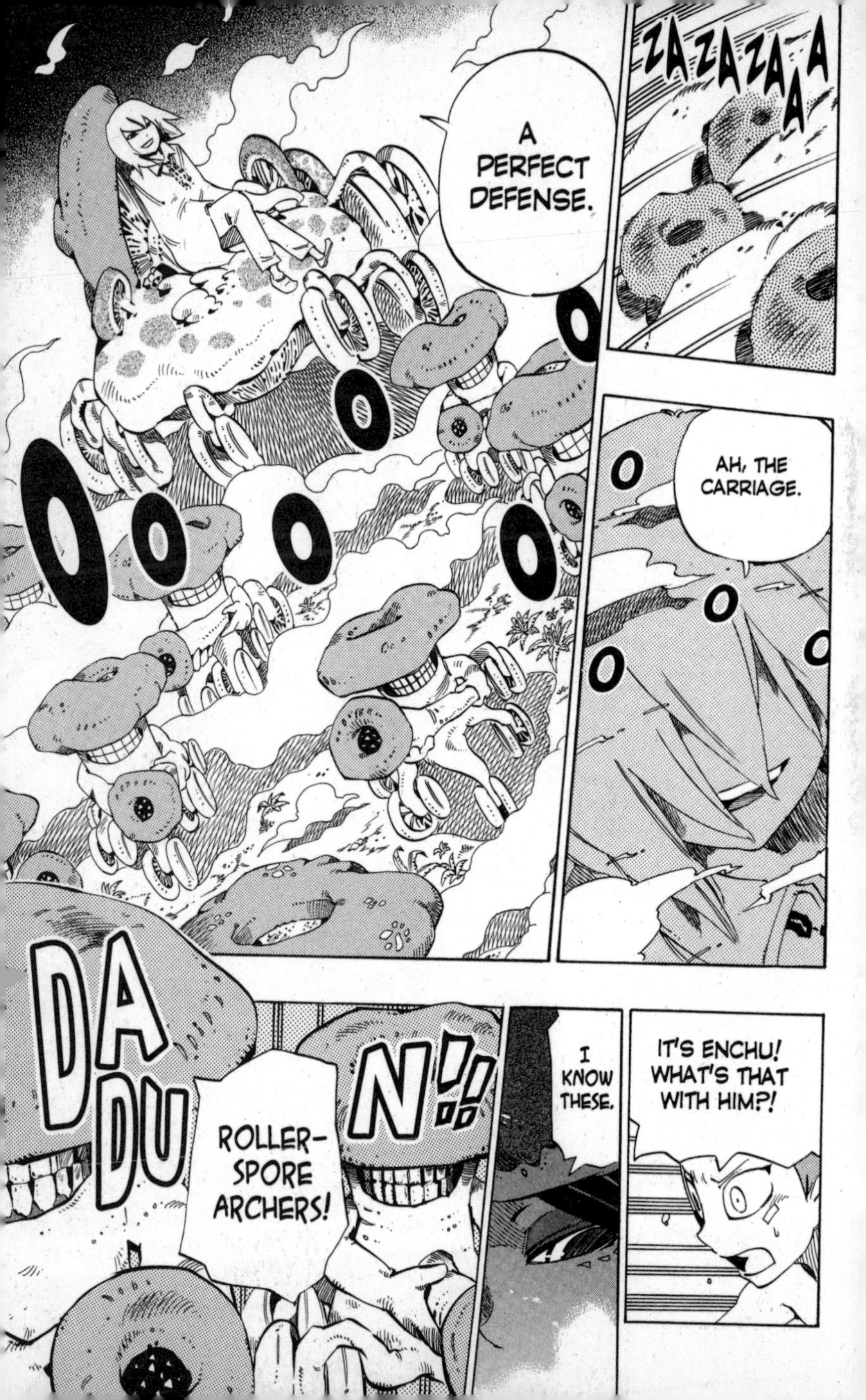
ZAZAZAAA
AH, THE CARRIAGE.
A PERFECT DEFENSE.
IT'S ENCHU! WHAT'S THAT WITH HIM?!
I KNOW THESE.
DADUN!!
ROLLER-SPORE ARCHERS!

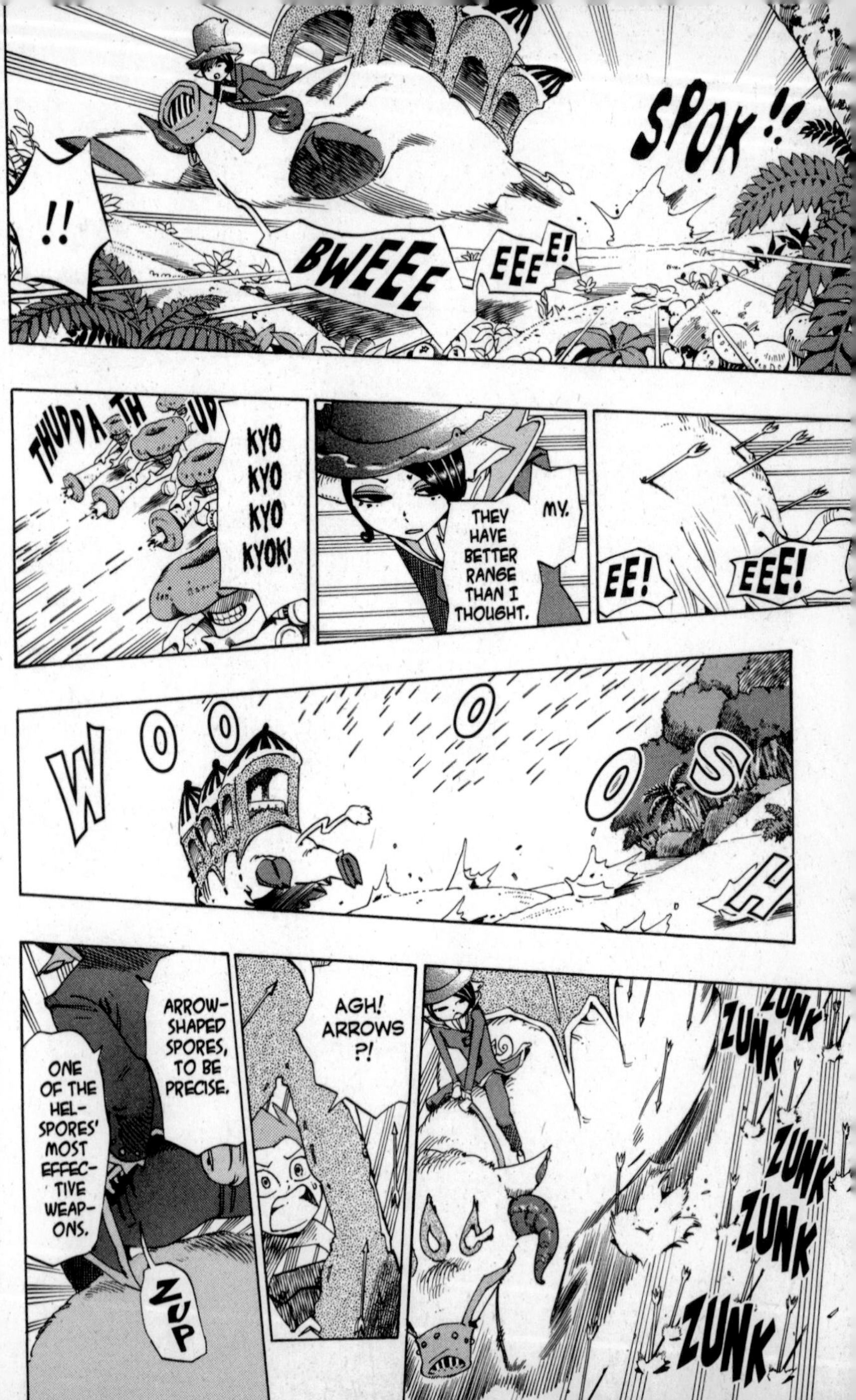
SPOK!!
BWEEE EEEE!
!!
EEE!
EE!
MY.
THEY HAVE BETTER RANGE THAN I THOUGHT.
KYO KYO KYO KYOK!
THUDDA TH UD
WOOOOOOSH
ZUNK ZUNK
ZUNK ZUNK ZUNK ZUNK
AGH! ARROWS?!
ARROW-SHAPED SPORES, TO BE PRECISE.
ONE OF THE HEL-SPORES' MOST EFFECTIVE WEAPONS.
ZUP

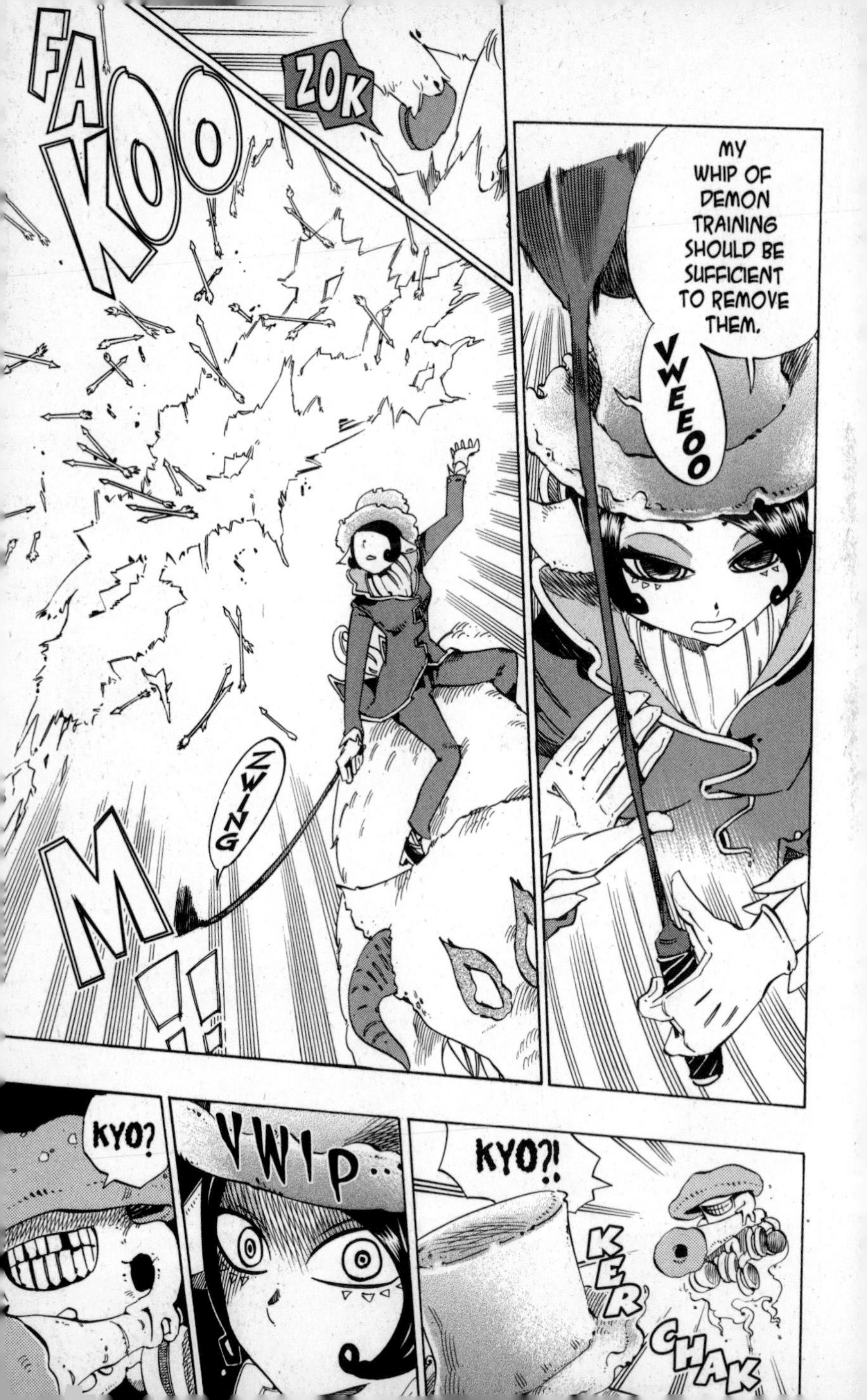
MY WHIP OF DEMON TRAINING SHOULD BE SUFFICIENT TO REMOVE THEM.
VWEEOO
ZOK
FAKOOOM!!
ZWING
KYO?!
KERCHAK
VWIP...
KYO?

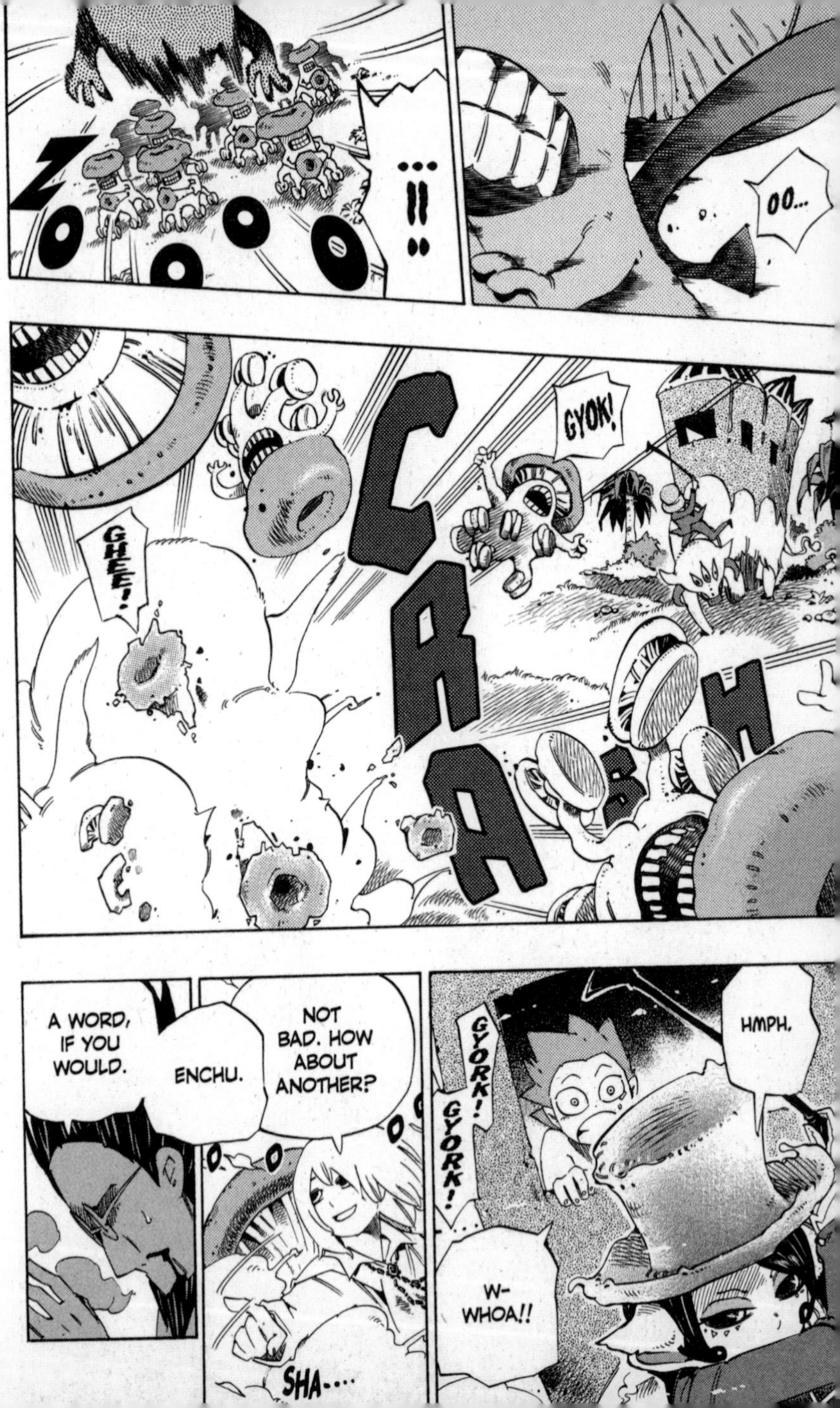

OO...
...!!
ZOOOOO
GYOK!
CRASH
GHEE!
HMPH.
GYORK! GYORK!
W-WHOA!!
NOT BAD. HOW ABOUT ANOTHER?
ENCHU.
SHA....
A WORD, IF YOU WOULD.

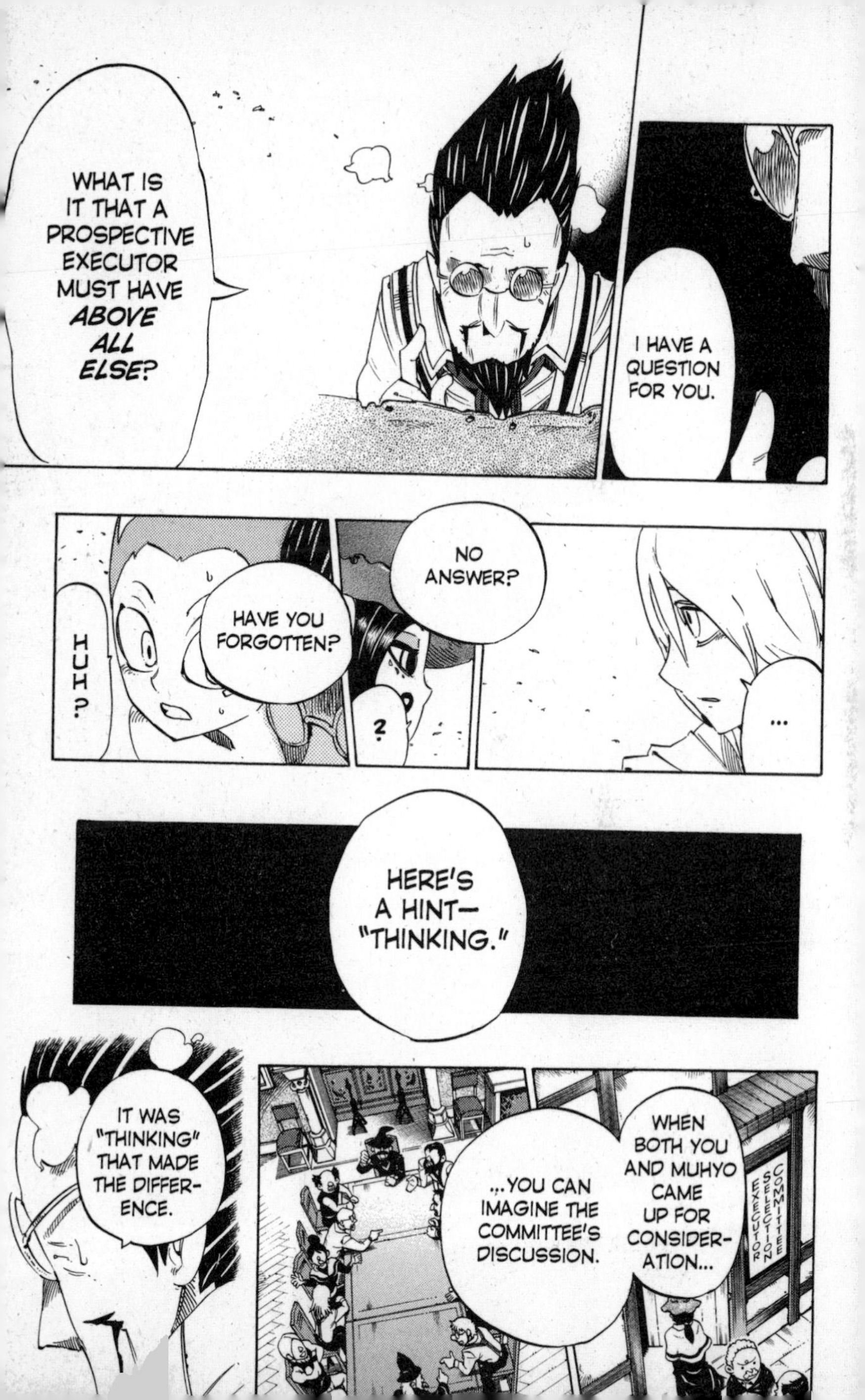
I HAVE A QUESTION FOR YOU.
WHAT IS IT THAT A PROSPECTIVE EXECUTOR MUST HAVE *ABOVE ALL ELSE?*
...
NO ANSWER?
?
HAVE YOU FORGOTTEN?
HUH?
HERE'S A HINT—"THINKING."
EXECUTOR SELECTION COMMITTEE
WHEN BOTH YOU AND MUHYO CAME UP FOR CONSIDER-ATION...
...YOU CAN IMAGINE THE COMMITTEE'S DISCUSSION.
IT WAS "THINKING" THAT MADE THE DIFFER-ENCE.

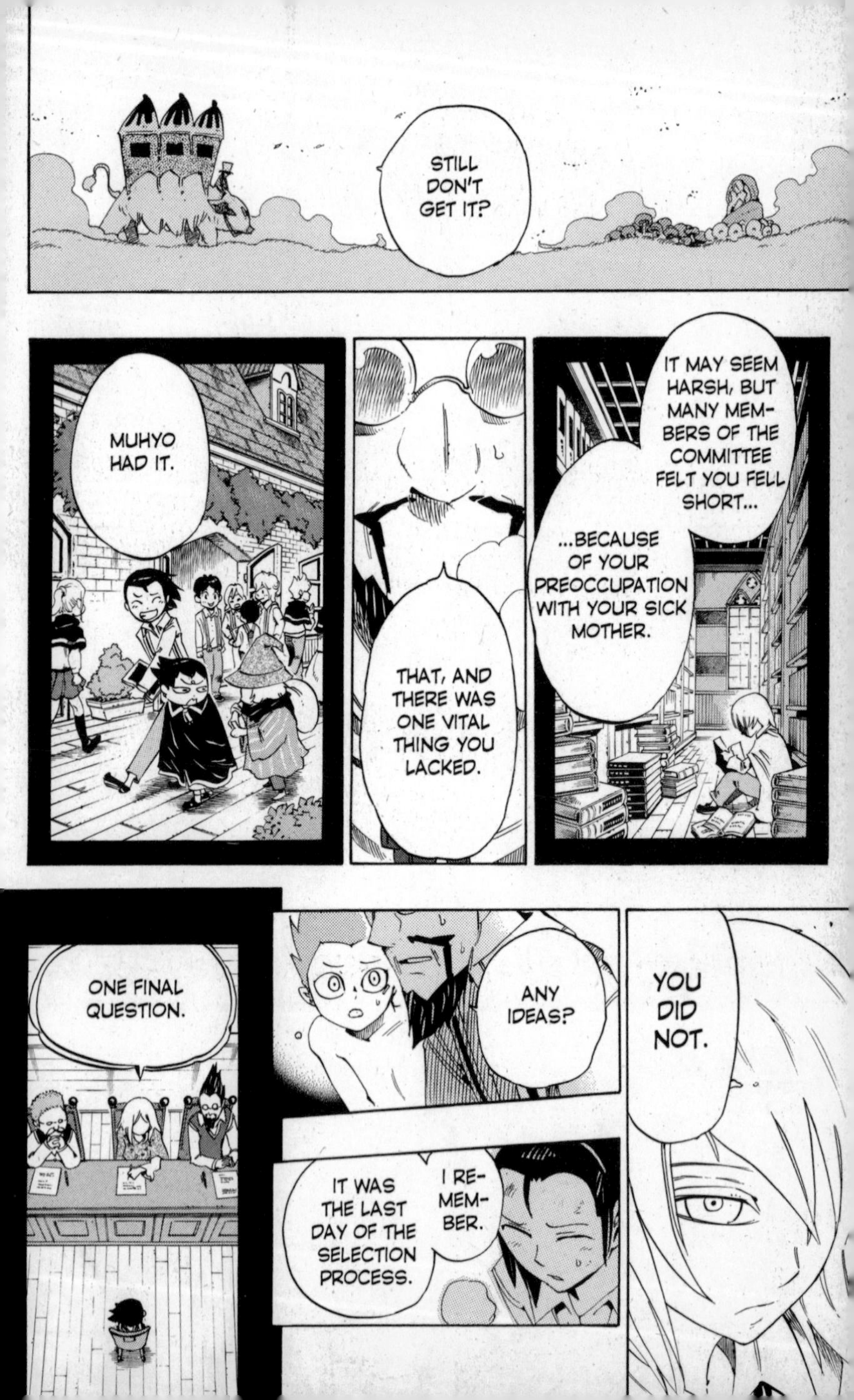
STILL DON'T GET IT?
IT MAY SEEM HARSH, BUT MANY MEM-BERS OF THE COMMITTEE FELT YOU FELL SHORT...
...BECAUSE OF YOUR PREOCCUPATION WITH YOUR SICK MOTHER.
THAT, AND THERE WAS ONE VITAL THING YOU LACKED.
MUHYO HAD IT.
YOU DID NOT.
ANY IDEAS?
I RE-MEM-BER.
IT WAS THE LAST DAY OF THE SELECTION PROCESS.
ONE FINAL QUESTION.

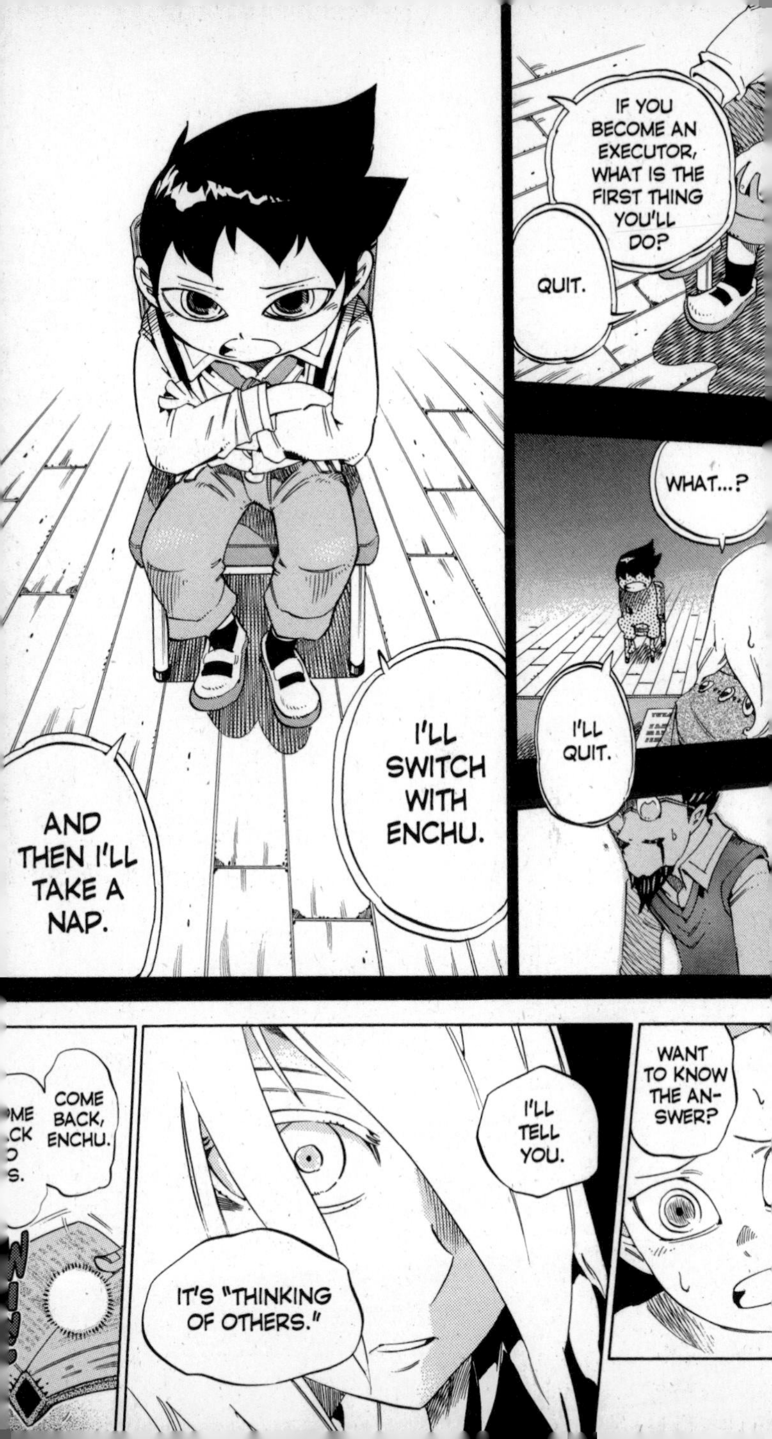
IF YOU BECOME AN EXECUTOR, WHAT IS THE FIRST THING YOU'LL DO?
QUIT.
WHAT...?
I'LL QUIT.
I'LL SWITCH WITH ENCHU.
AND THEN I'LL TAKE A NAP.
WANT TO KNOW THE AN-SWER?
I'LL TELL YOU.
IT'S "THINKING OF OTHERS."
COME BACK, ENCHU.

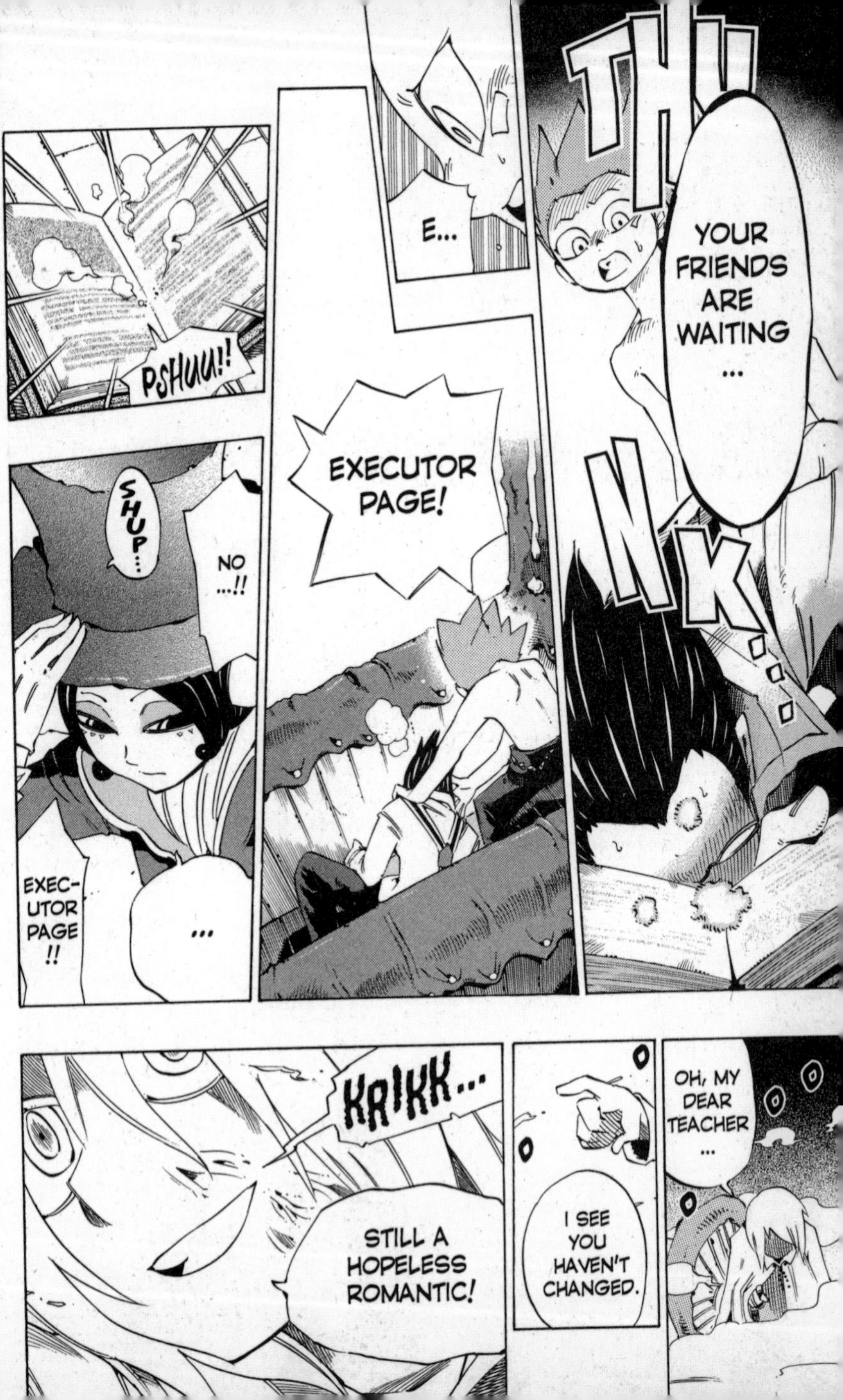
TH
YOUR FRIENDS ARE WAITING ...
NK
E...
EXECUTOR PAGE!
PSHUU!!
SHUP...
NO ...!!
EXEC-UTOR PAGE !!
...
OH, MY DEAR TEACHER ...
I SEE YOU HAVEN'T CHANGED.
KRIKK...
STILL A HOPELESS ROMANTIC!

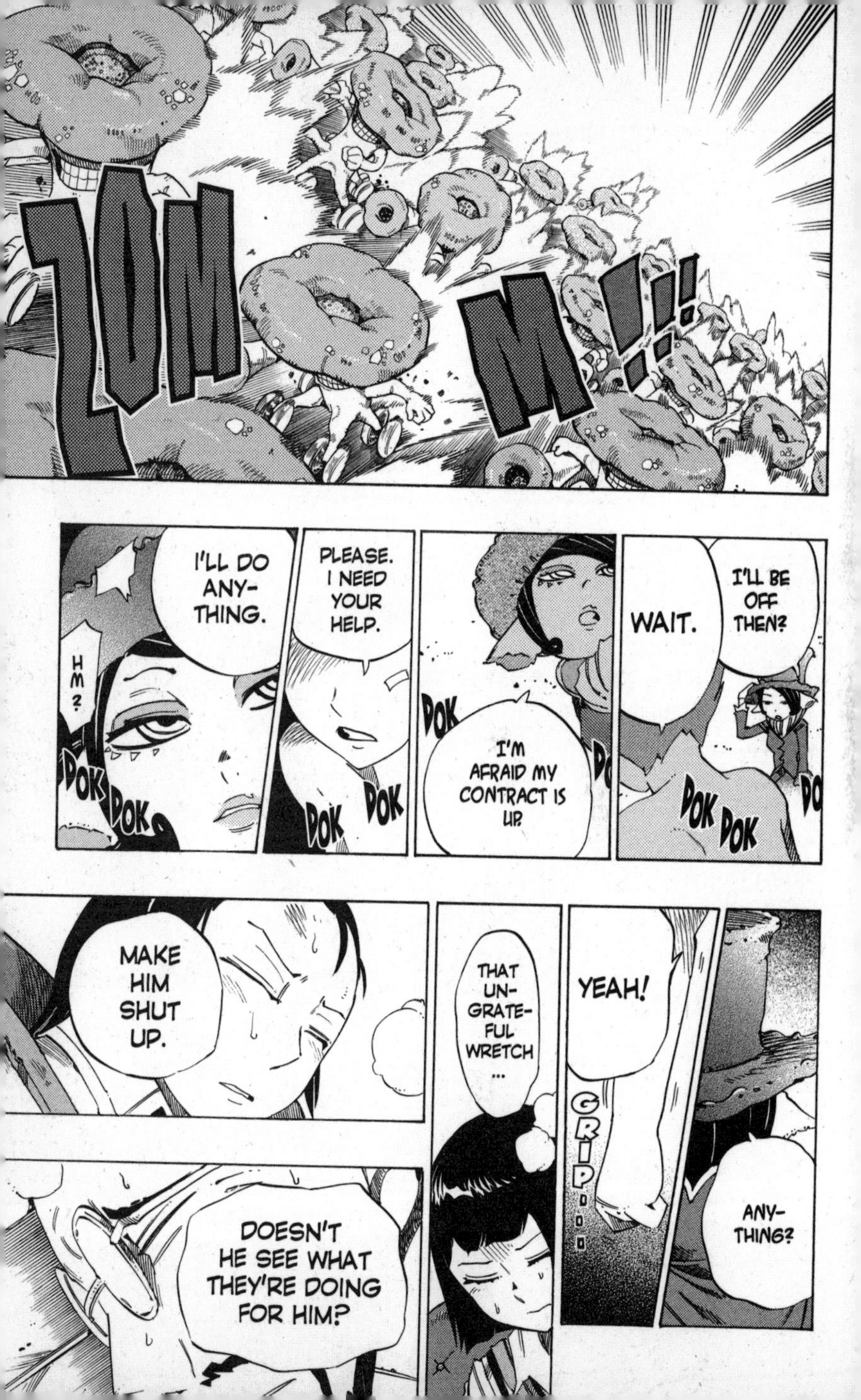
ZOMM!!!
I'LL BE OFF THEN?
WAIT.
DOK DOK
I'M AFRAID MY CONTRACT IS UP.
DOK
PLEASE. I NEED YOUR HELP.
DOK DOK
I'LL DO ANYTHING.
HM?
DOK DOK
ANY-THING?
YEAH!
GRIP...
THAT UN-GRATE-FUL WRETCH...
MAKE HIM SHUT UP.
DOESN'T HE SEE WHAT THEY'RE DOING FOR HIM?

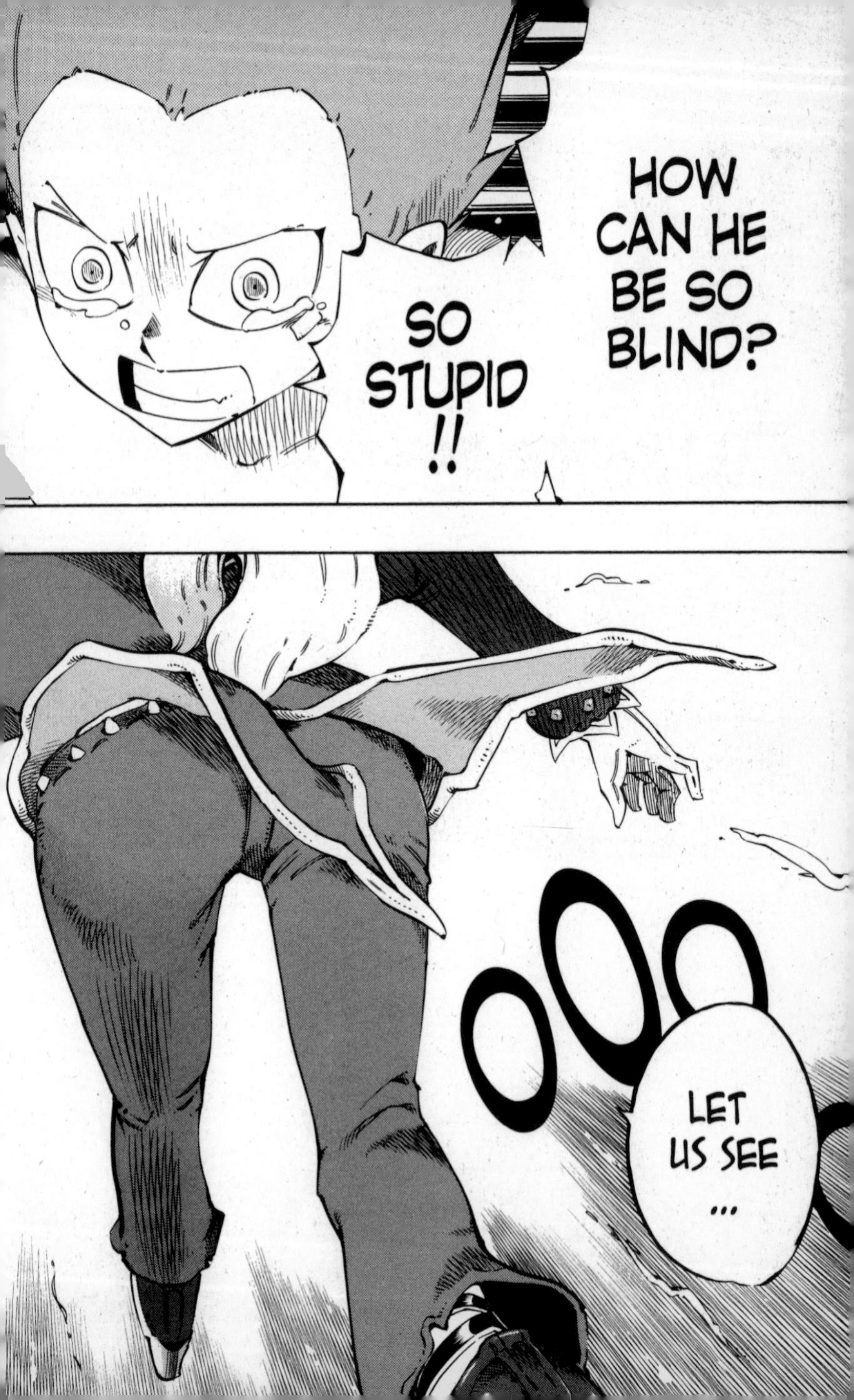
HOW CAN HE BE SO BLIND?
SO STUPID !!
LET US SEE ...

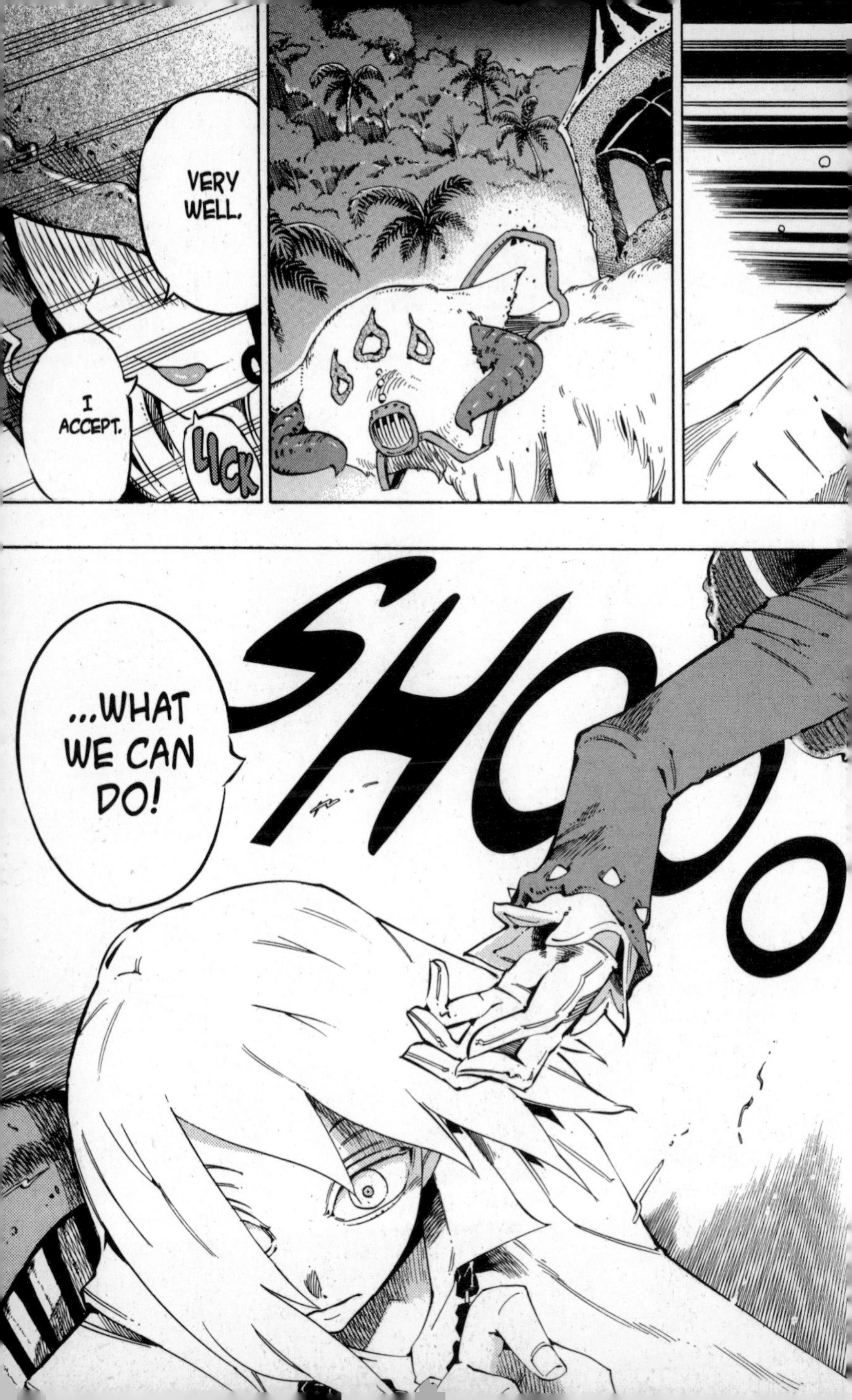
VERY WELL.
I ACCEPT.
LICK
SHOOO
...WHAT WE CAN DO!

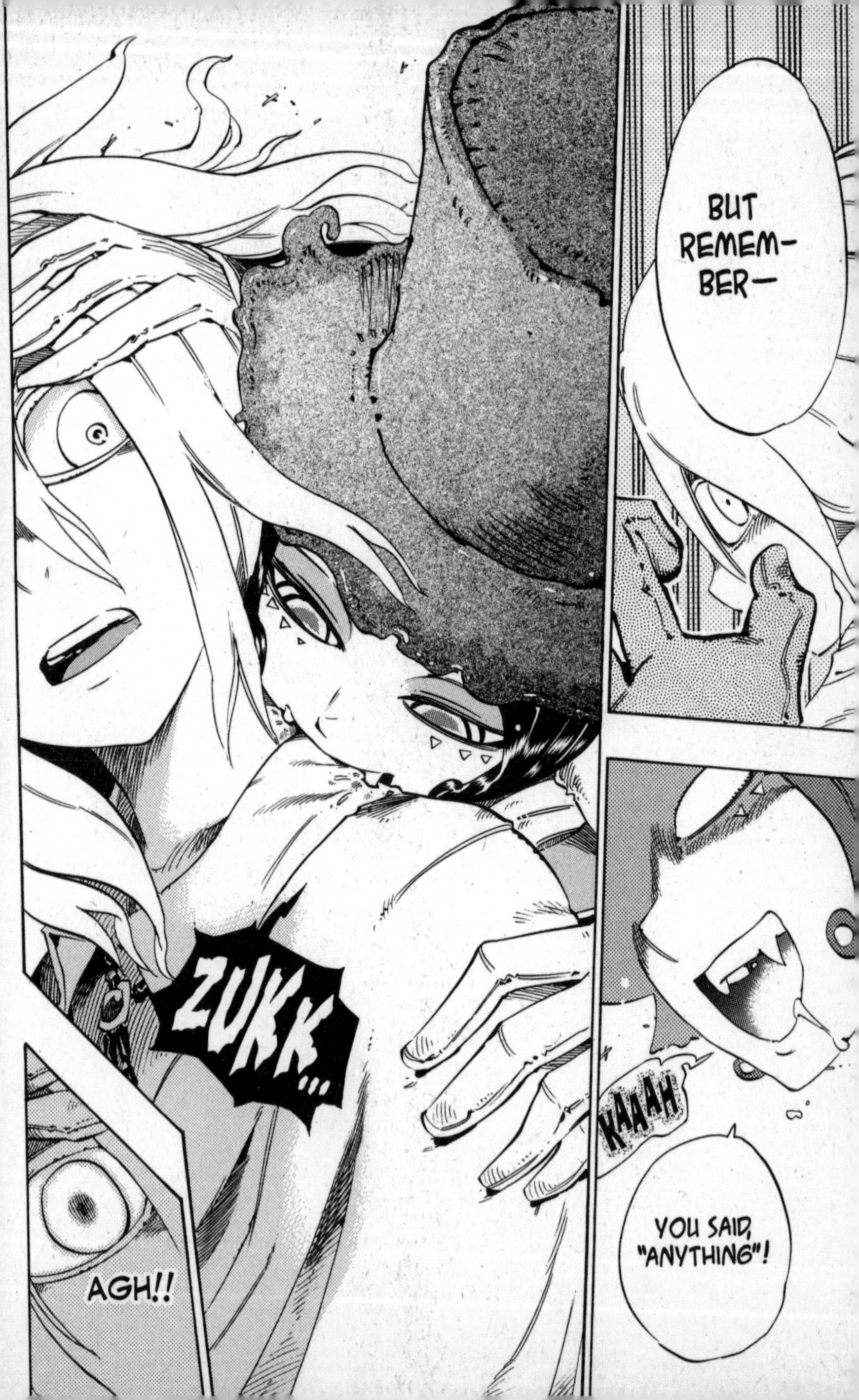
BUT REMEMBER—
KAAAH
YOU SAID, "ANYTHING"!
ZUKK...
AGH!!

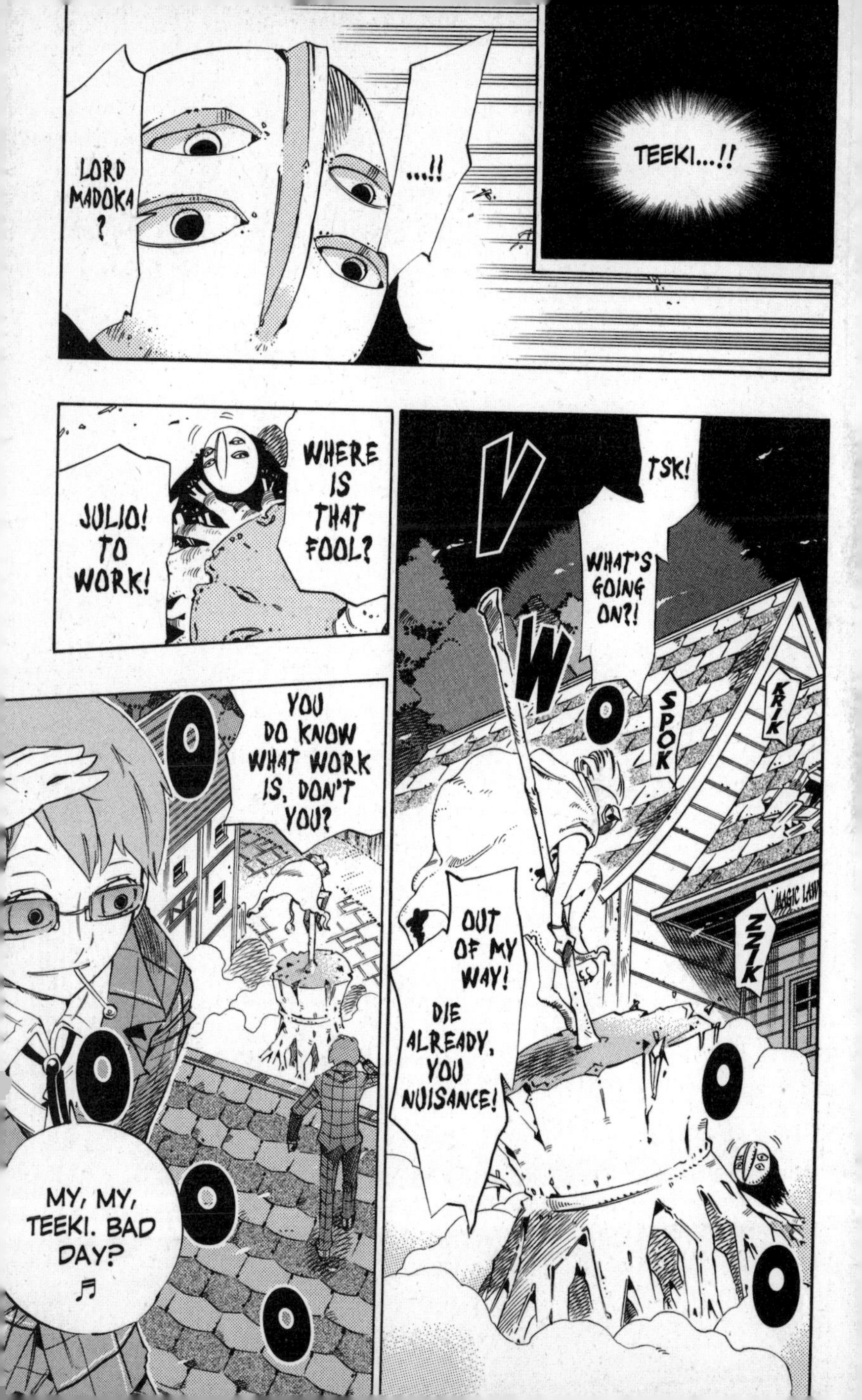
TEEKI...!!
...!!
LORD MADOKA ?
TSK!
WHAT'S GOING ON?!
V
W
KRIK
SPOK
MAGIC LAW
ZZIK
OUT OF MY WAY!
DIE ALREADY, YOU NUISANCE!
WHERE IS THAT FOOL?
JULIO! TO WORK!
YOU DO KNOW WHAT WORK IS, DON'T YOU?
MY, MY, TEEKI. BAD DAY? ♬

MR. A OF TOCHIGI PREFECTURE WRITES...

Q1: WHAT'S THAT UNDER GINJI'S LEFT EYE?
(A BAND-AID?) DID HE CUT HIMSELF?

Q2: WAS MICK'S RIGHT EYE ALWAYS LIKE THAT?

Q3: WHERE DOES ROJI COOK WHEN HE'S AT THE OFFICE?
THERE ISN'T A KITCHEN THERE, IS THERE?

Q4: IN VOLUME 11, ISABI MENDS PAGE'S WOUNDS. HOW'D THAT FEEL
FOR PAGE? JUST OKAY? OR SURPRISINGLY GOOD?

Q5: IN VOLUME 2, WE FIND YOICHI BURIED IN THE SNOW. HOW
LONG WAS HE IN THERE? AND DIDN'T ANYONE NOTICE HIM?

Q6: DO YOUR OWN GHOSTS EVER SCARE YOU?

Q7: HOW DID YOU COME UP WITH NAMES FOR EVERYONE?

A1: GINJI: "YEAH... SOMETHING LIKE THAT."
THERE YOU HAVE IT. SOUNDS LIKE HE'S HIDING SOMETHING.

NISHI: "C'MON, YOU CAN TELL US—**WHAP** ...HE HIT ME.
WHERE WERE THOSE BAND-AIDS AGAIN...?

A2: WHAT'S THAT ABOUT A SCAR? AUGH!! SO, ABOUT MICK'S SCAR... ACTUALLY, LET'S
NOT ASK HIM ABOUT THAT. I'LL JUST TELL YOU.
HE WASN'T BORN WITH IT. IT'S—*EEK!* S-SORRY.
IT'S A SECRET! HELP!!

A3: I'LL BE POSTING BLUEPRINTS FOR THE OFFICE IN VOLUME
16, SO CHECK IT OUT!

A4: APPARENTLY, HAVING MUSHROOMS GROWING OUT OF
YOUR BACK FEELS REALLY CREEPY, AND HE'D RATHER
NOT THINK ABOUT THAT.

A5: HERE'S THE TIMELINE: 1) MUHYO DECIDES TO GO TO THE
ASSOCIATION. 2) HE CALLS YOICHI. 3) YOICHI IS WAITING FOR
HIM AT THE ASSOCIATION. 4) MUHYO ARRIVES. 5) NANA RUNS
OUT OF THE PORTAL. 6) YOICHI IS TRAMPLED. 7) HE FEELS HER UP.

A6: THEY DO! ESPECIALLY THE GHOSTS IN THE ONE-SHOT
STORIES. I HAVE TO STOP WRITING AND JUST GO TO BED.
WITH THE LIGHT STILL ON. YEAH, I'M IN GRADE SCHOOL,
I KNOW.

A7: I START BY THINKING ABOUT THE CHARACTER'S PERSONALITY,
THEN I FIND SOMETHING THAT SOUNDS RIGHT. SOMETIMES IT
JUST WON'T COME TO ME, AND IT TAKES
FOREVER...

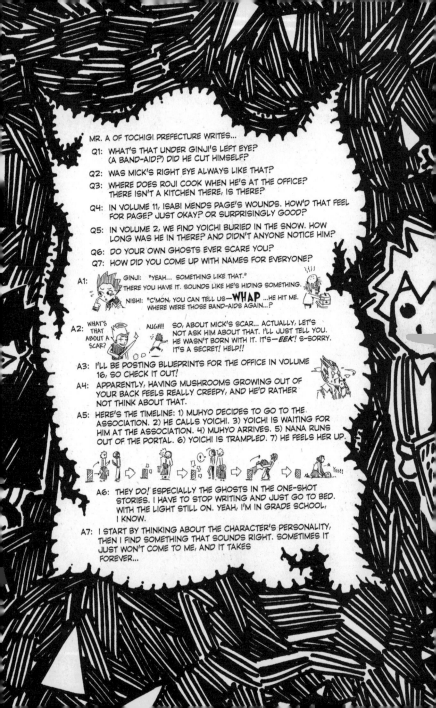

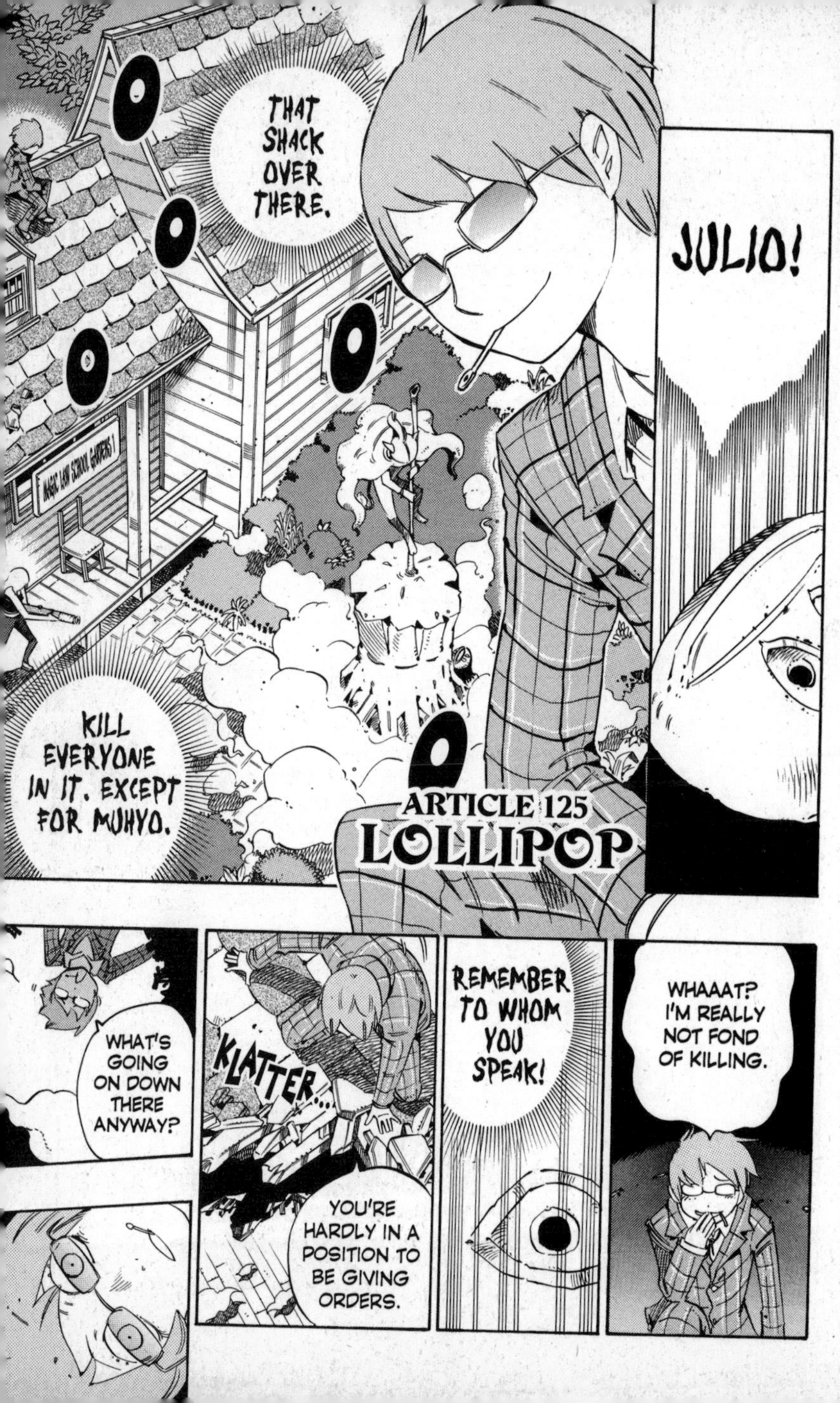
JULIO!
THAT SHACK OVER THERE.
MAGIC LAW SCHOOL GARDENS
KILL EVERYONE IN IT. EXCEPT FOR MUHYO.
ARTICLE 125
LOLLIPOP
WHAAAT? I'M REALLY NOT FOND OF KILLING.
REMEMBER TO WHOM YOU SPEAK!
KLATTER...
YOU'RE HARDLY IN A POSITION TO BE GIVING ORDERS.
WHAT'S GOING ON DOWN THERE ANYWAY?

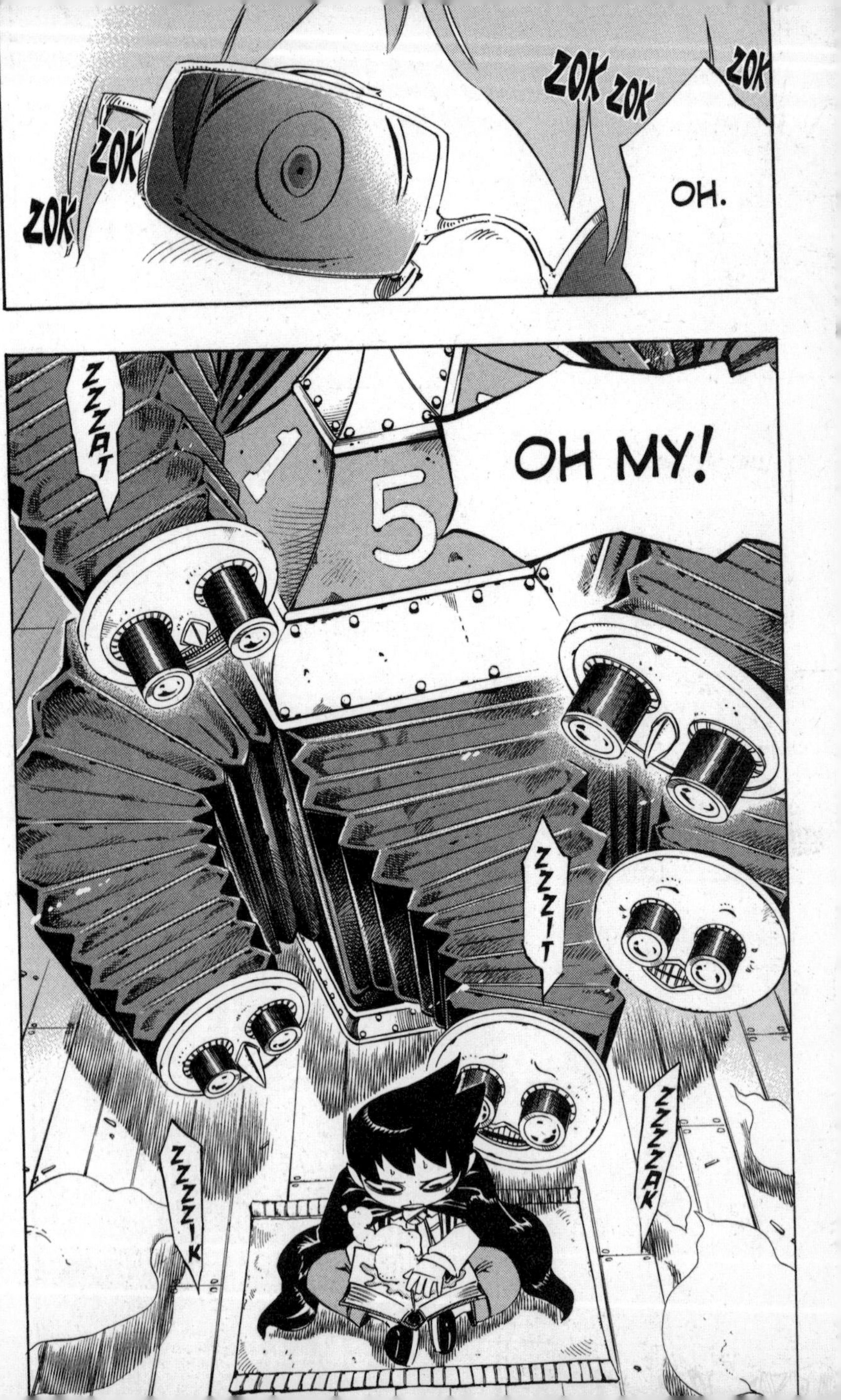
ZOK
ZOK ZOK
OH.
ZOK
ZOK
OH MY!
ZZZIT
ZZZZAK
ZZZAT
ZZZZIK

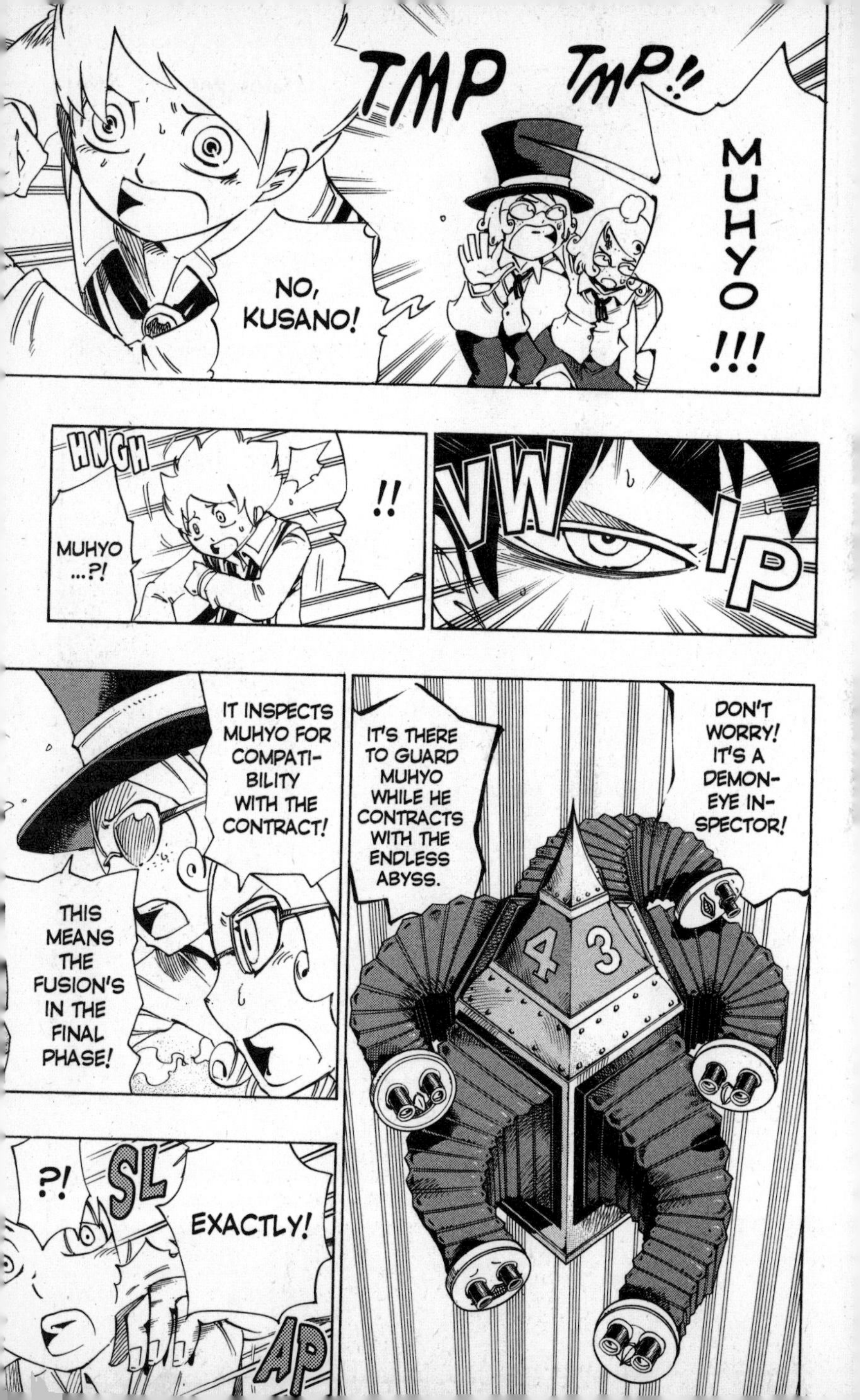
TMP TMP!!
MUHYO!!!
NO, KUSANO!
VWIP
!!
MUHYO ...?!
HNGH
DON'T WORRY! IT'S A DEMON-EYE INSPECTOR!
IT'S THERE TO GUARD MUHYO WHILE HE CONTRACTS WITH THE ENDLESS ABYSS.
IT INSPECTS MUHYO FOR COMPATIBILITY WITH THE CONTRACT!
THIS MEANS THE FUSION'S IN THE FINAL PHASE!
EXACTLY!
SLAP
?!

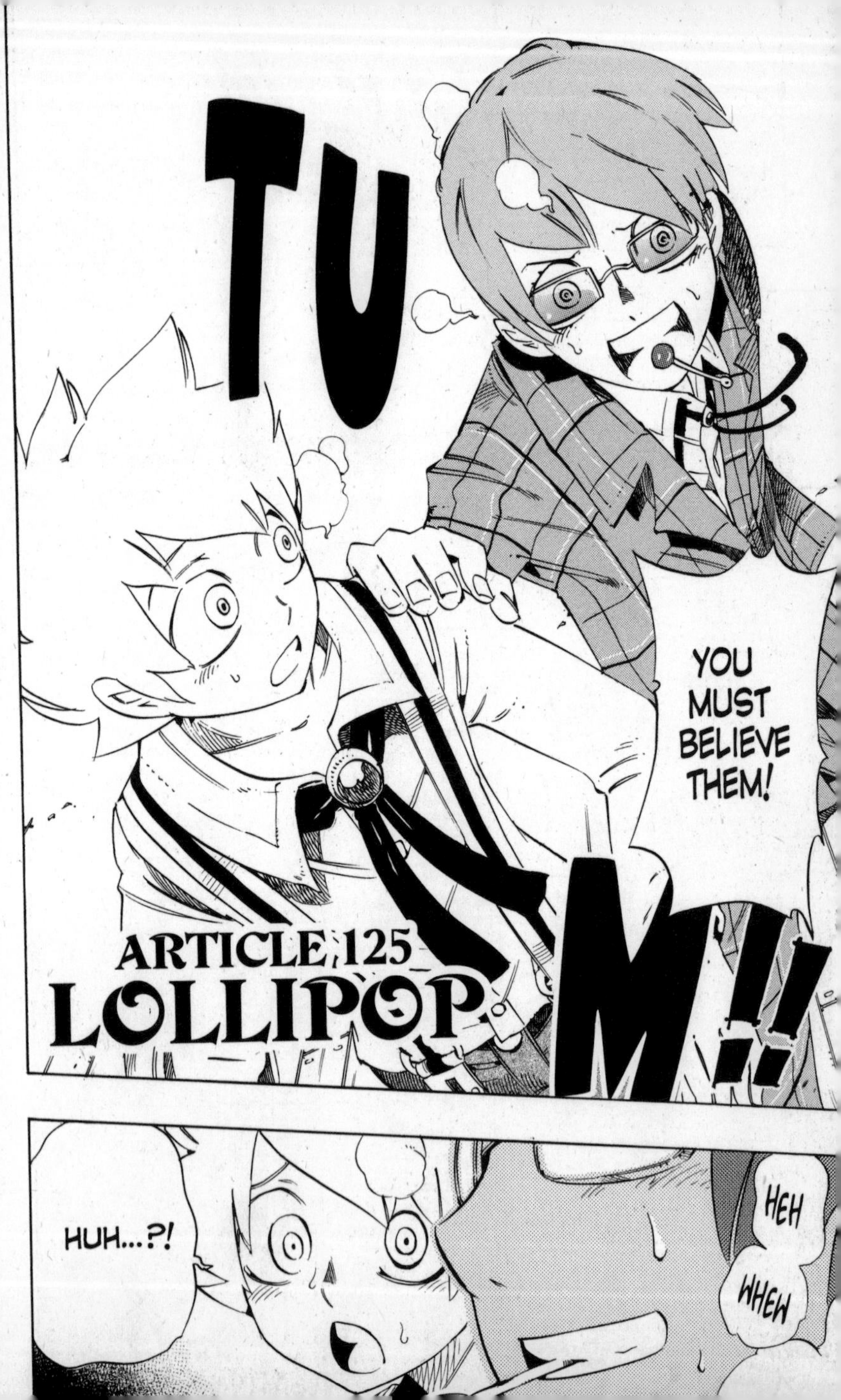
TU
M!!
YOU MUST BELIEVE THEM!
ARTICLE 125
LOLLIPOP
HEH
WHEW
HUH...?!

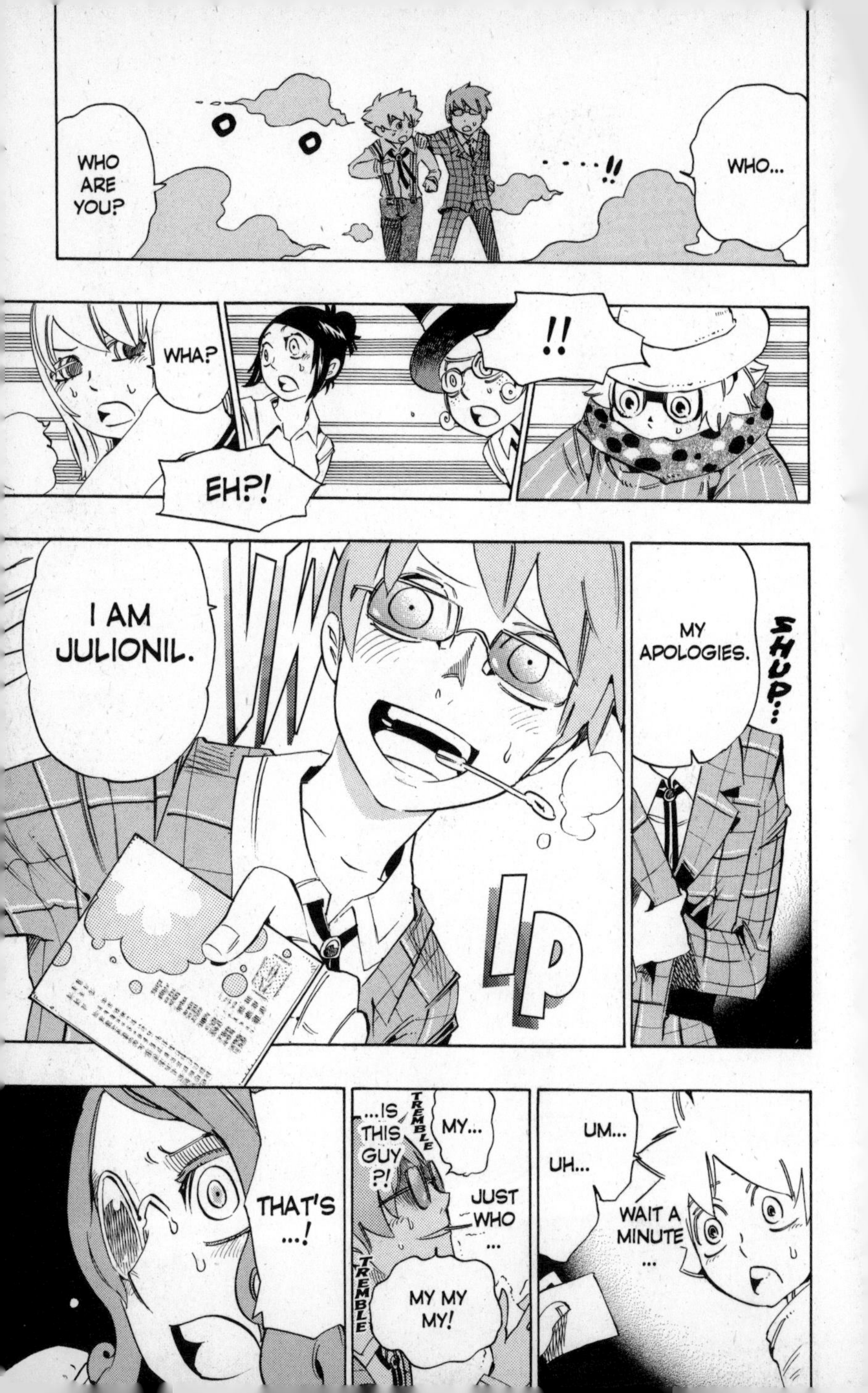
WHO...
....!!
O
O
WHO ARE YOU?
!!
EH?!
WHA?
MY APOLOGIES.
SHUP...
I AM JULIONIL.
IP
UM...
UH...
WAIT A MINUTE ...
MY...
JUST WHO ...
...IS THIS GUY ?!
TREMBLE
MY MY MY!
TREMBLE
THAT'S ...!

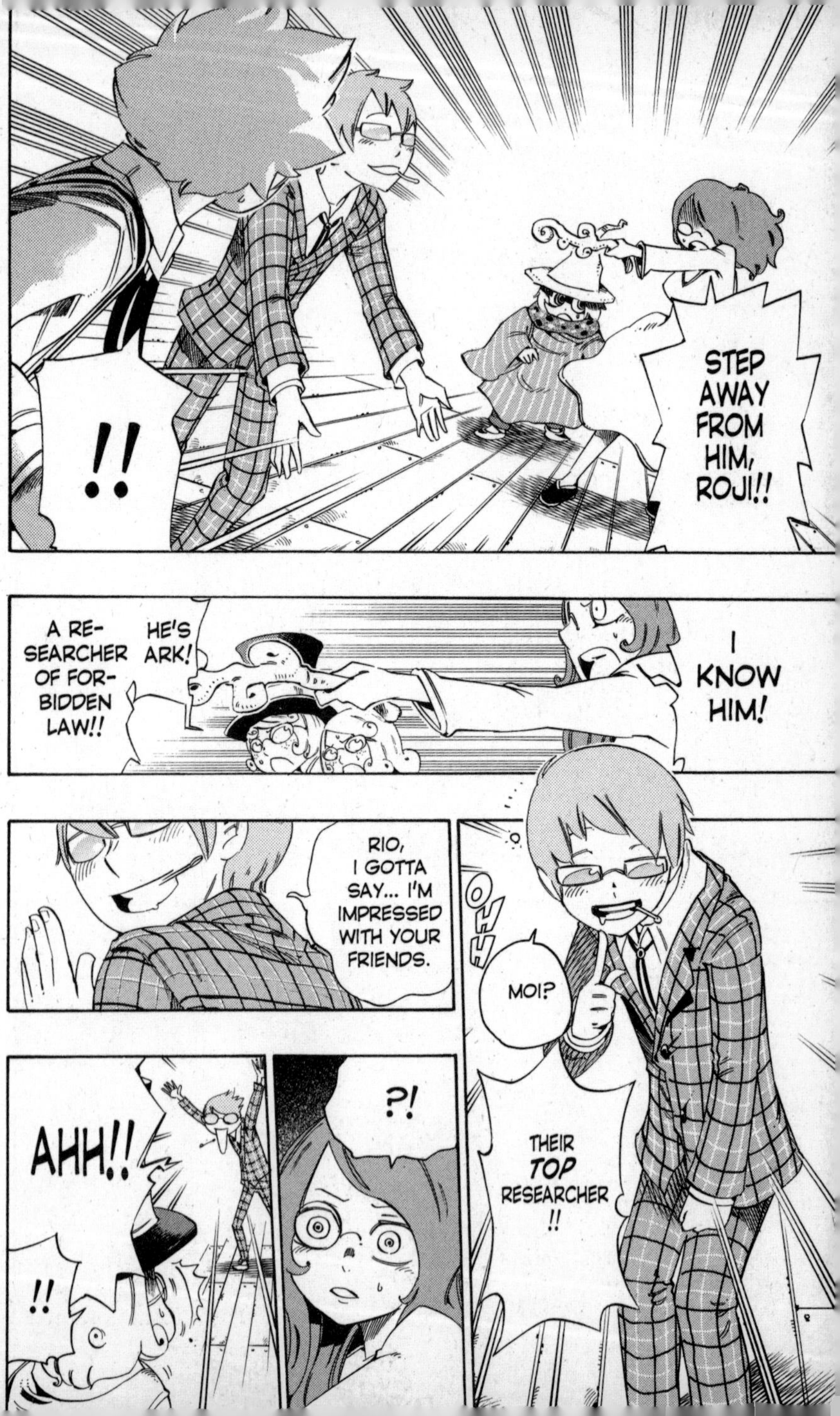
STEP AWAY FROM HIM, ROJI!!
!!
I KNOW HIM!
HE'S ARK!
A RE-SEARCHER OF FOR-BIDDEN LAW!!
MOI?
THEIR *TOP* RESEARCHER!!
RIO, I GOTTA SAY... I'M IMPRESSED WITH YOUR FRIENDS.
?!
AHH!!
!!

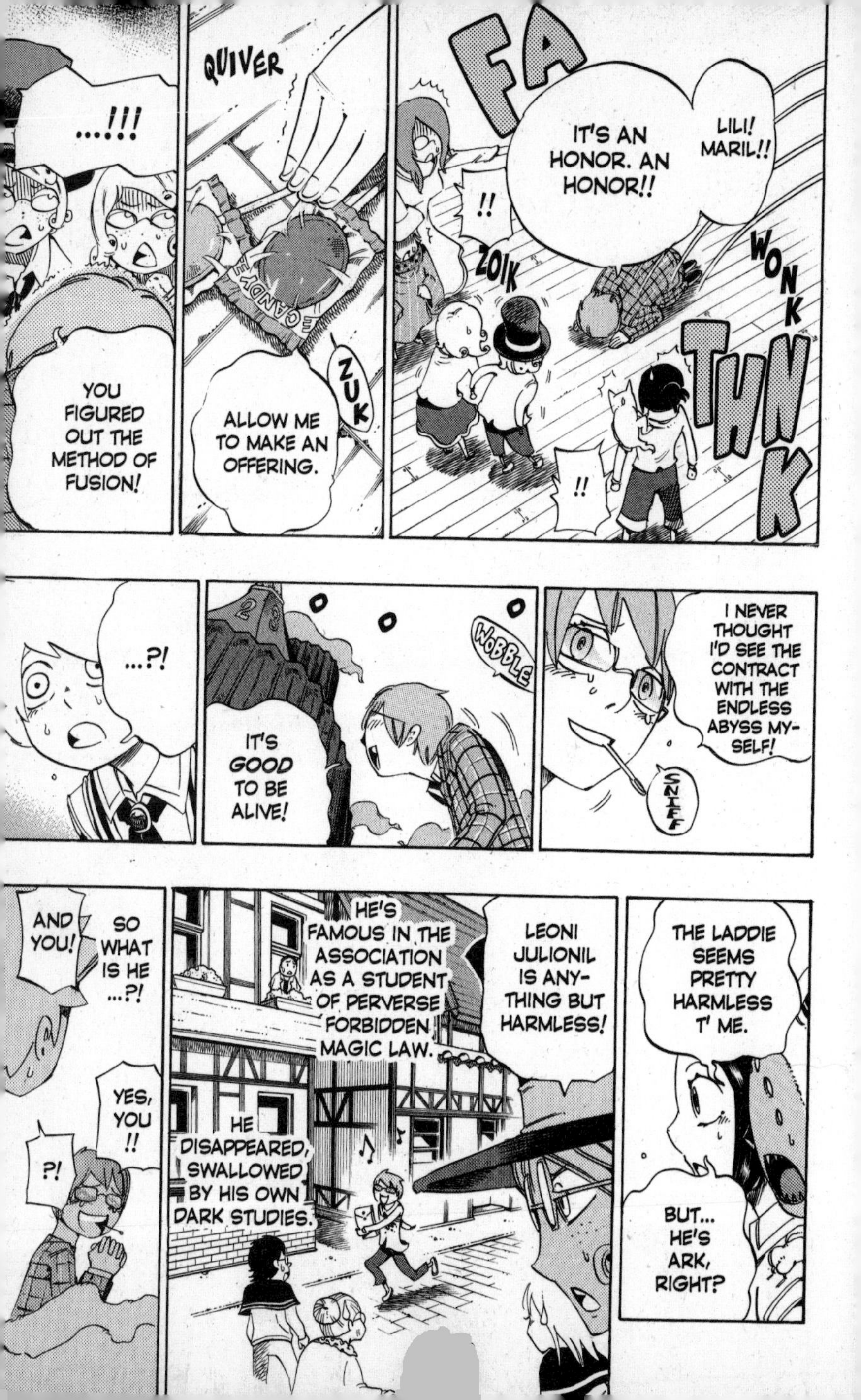
FA
LILI! MARIL!!
IT'S AN HONOR. AN HONOR!!
!!
ZOIK
WONK
THUNK
!!
QUIVER
ZUK
ALLOW ME TO MAKE AN OFFERING.
...!!!
YOU FIGURED OUT THE METHOD OF FUSION!
I NEVER THOUGHT I'D SEE THE CONTRACT WITH THE ENDLESS ABYSS MY-SELF!
SNIFF
WOBBLE
IT'S *GOOD* TO BE ALIVE!
...?!
THE LADDIE SEEMS PRETTY HARMLESS T' ME.
BUT... HE'S ARK, RIGHT?
LEONI JULIONIL IS ANY-THING BUT HARMLESS!
HE'S FAMOUS IN THE ASSOCIATION AS A STUDENT OF PERVERSE FORBIDDEN MAGIC LAW.
HE DISAPPEARED, SWALLOWED BY HIS OWN DARK STUDIES.
SO WHAT IS HE ...?!
AND YOU!
YES, YOU!!
?!

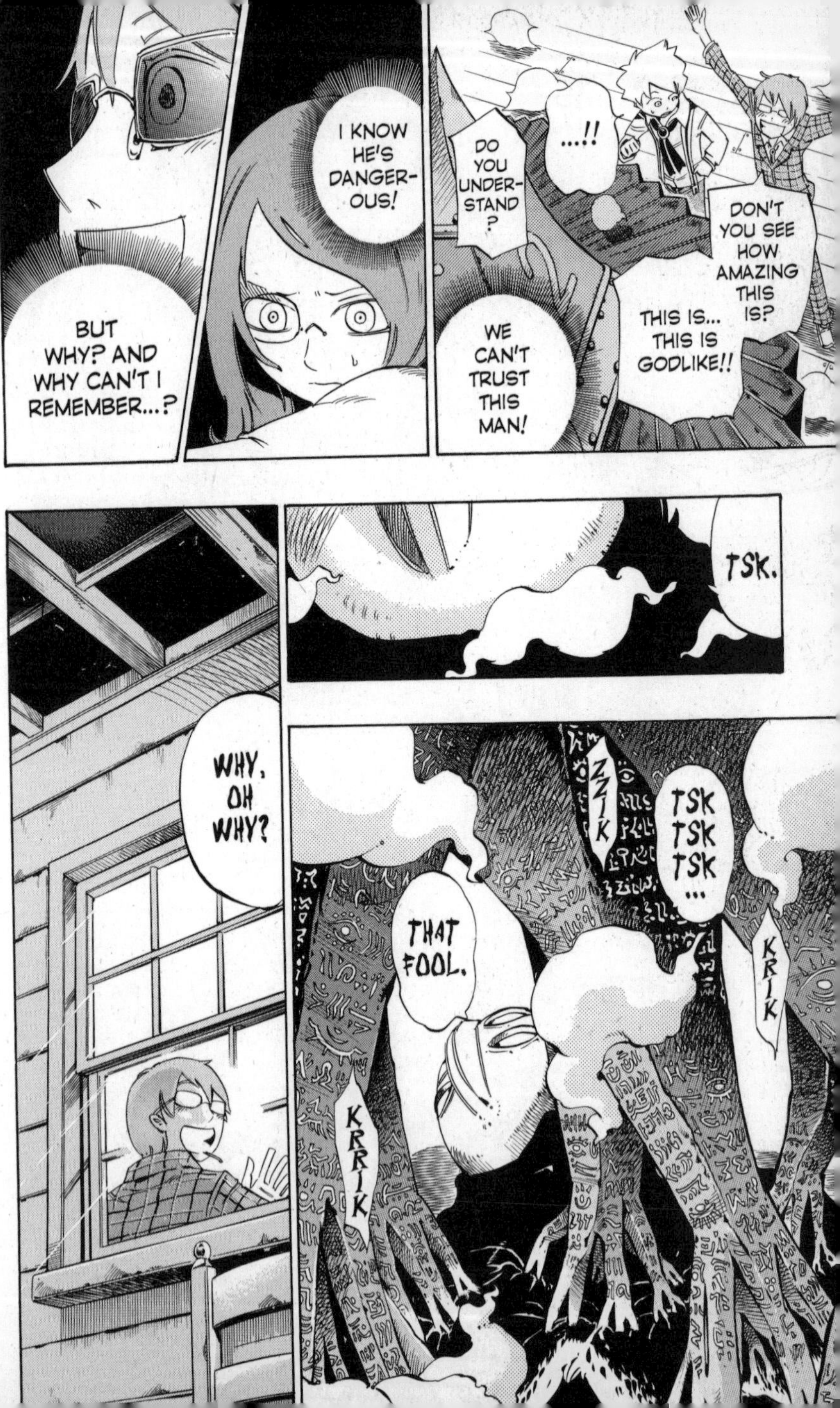
...!!
DO YOU UNDERSTAND?
DON'T YOU SEE HOW AMAZING THIS IS?
THIS IS... THIS IS GODLIKE!!
WE CAN'T TRUST THIS MAN!
I KNOW HE'S DANGEROUS!
BUT WHY? AND WHY CAN'T I REMEMBER...?
TSK.
KRIK
TSK TSK TSK...
ZZIK
THAT FOOL.
KRRIK
WHY, OH WHY?

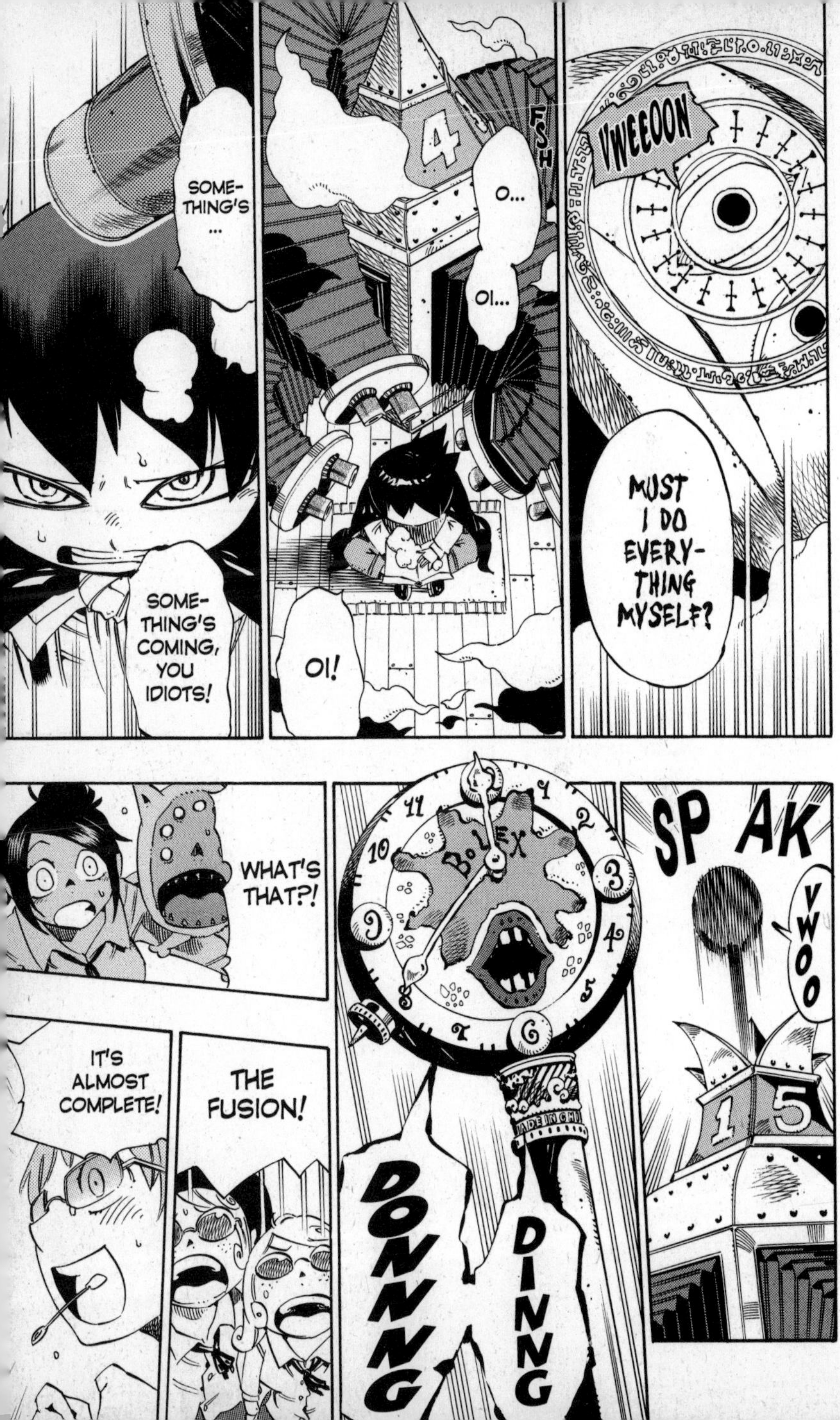
VWEEOON
MUST I DO EVERY-THING MYSELF?
FSH
O...
OI...
OI!
SOME-THING'S ...
SOME-THING'S COMING, YOU IDIOTS!
SP AK
VWOO
DINNG
DONNG
WHAT'S THAT?!
THE FUSION!
IT'S ALMOST COMPLETE!

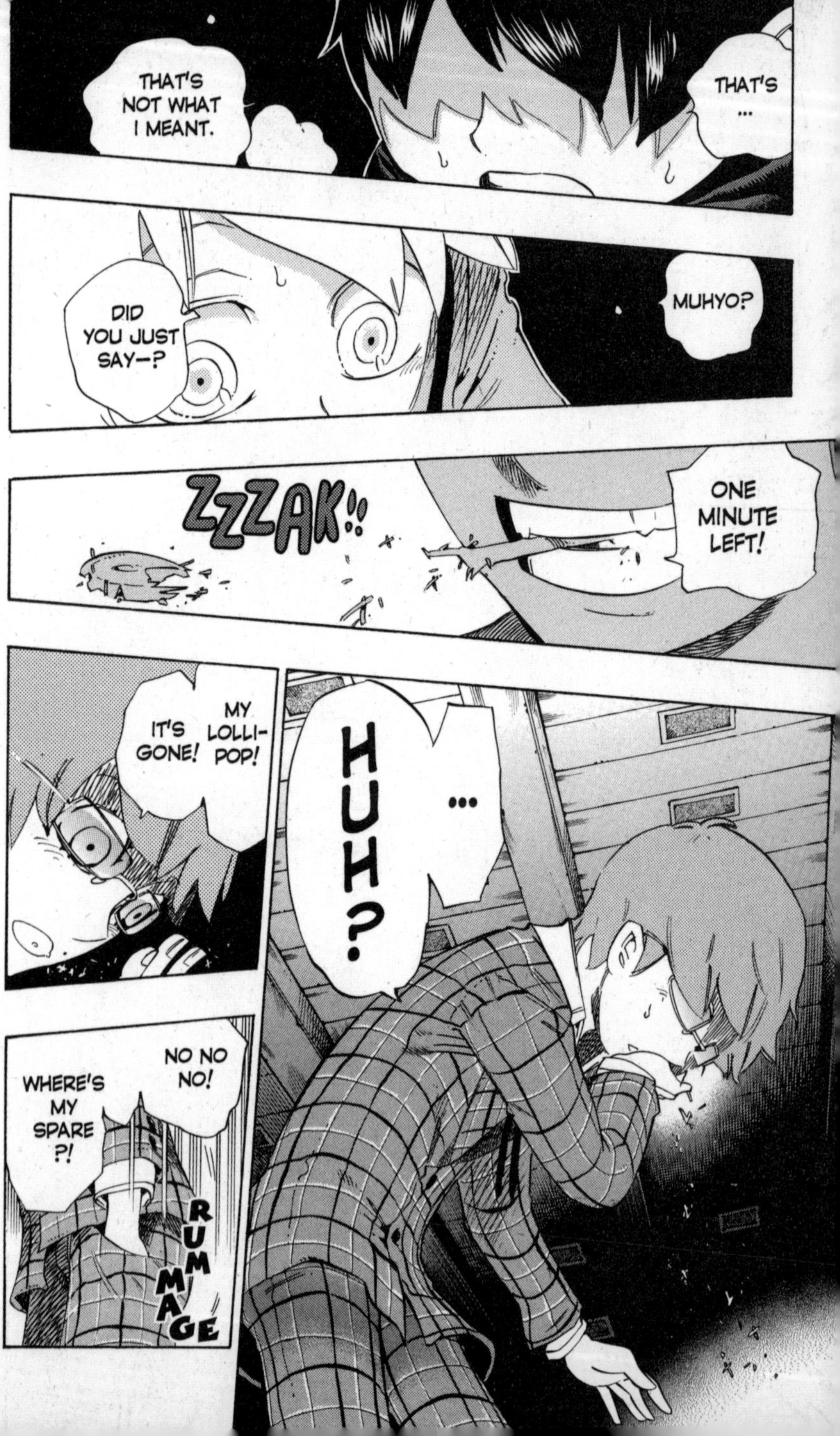
THAT'S ...
THAT'S NOT WHAT I MEANT.
MUHYO?
DID YOU JUST SAY—?
ONE MINUTE LEFT!
ZZZAK!!
HUH?
...
MY LOLLI-POP!
IT'S GONE!
NO NO NO!
WHERE'S MY SPARE?!
RUMMAGE

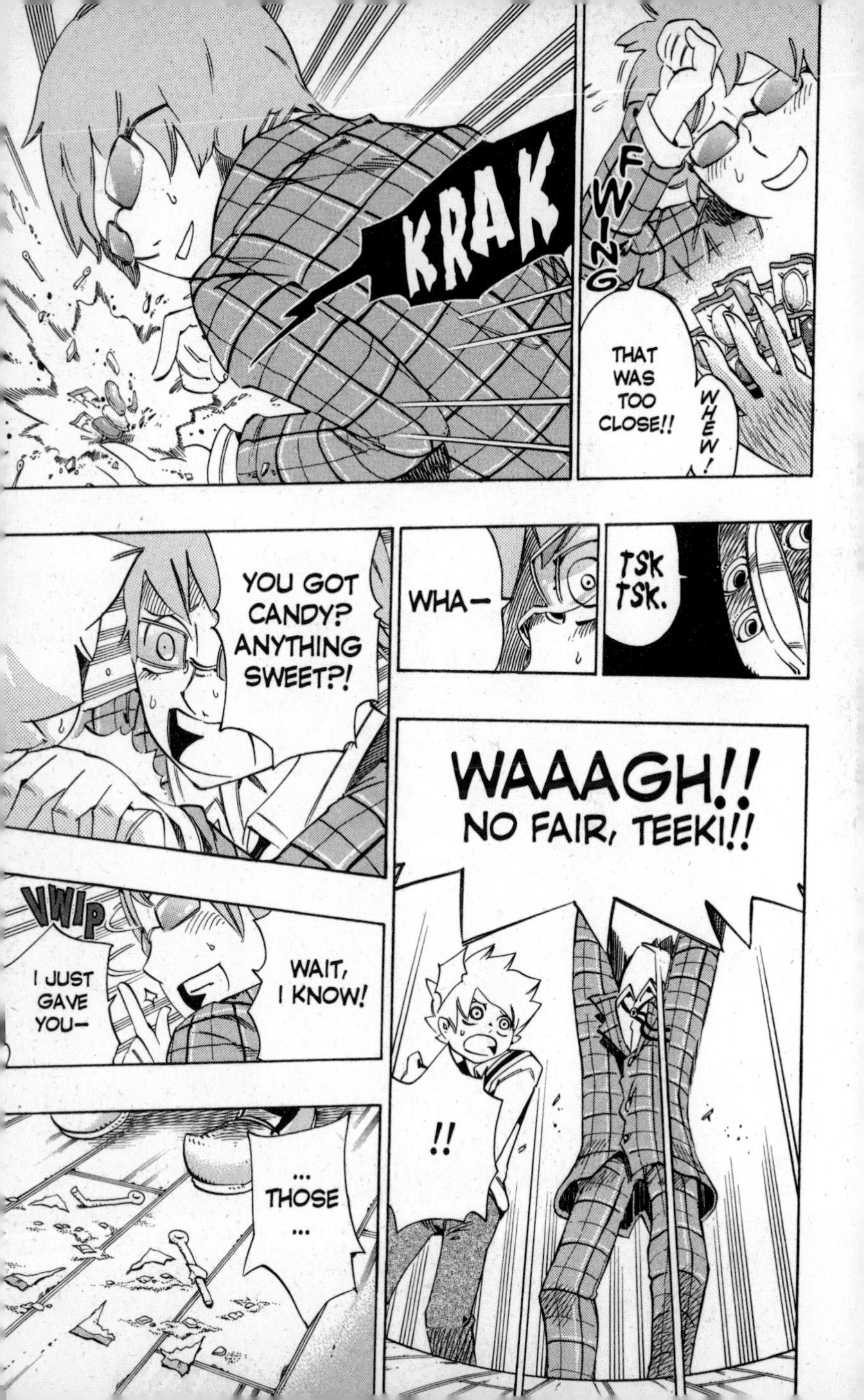
FWING
THAT WAS TOO CLOSE!!
WHEW!
KRAK
TSK TSK.
WHA—
YOU GOT CANDY? ANYTHING SWEET?!
VWIP
WAIT, I KNOW!
I JUST GAVE YOU—
... THOSE ...
WAAAGH!! NO FAIR, TEEKI!!
!!

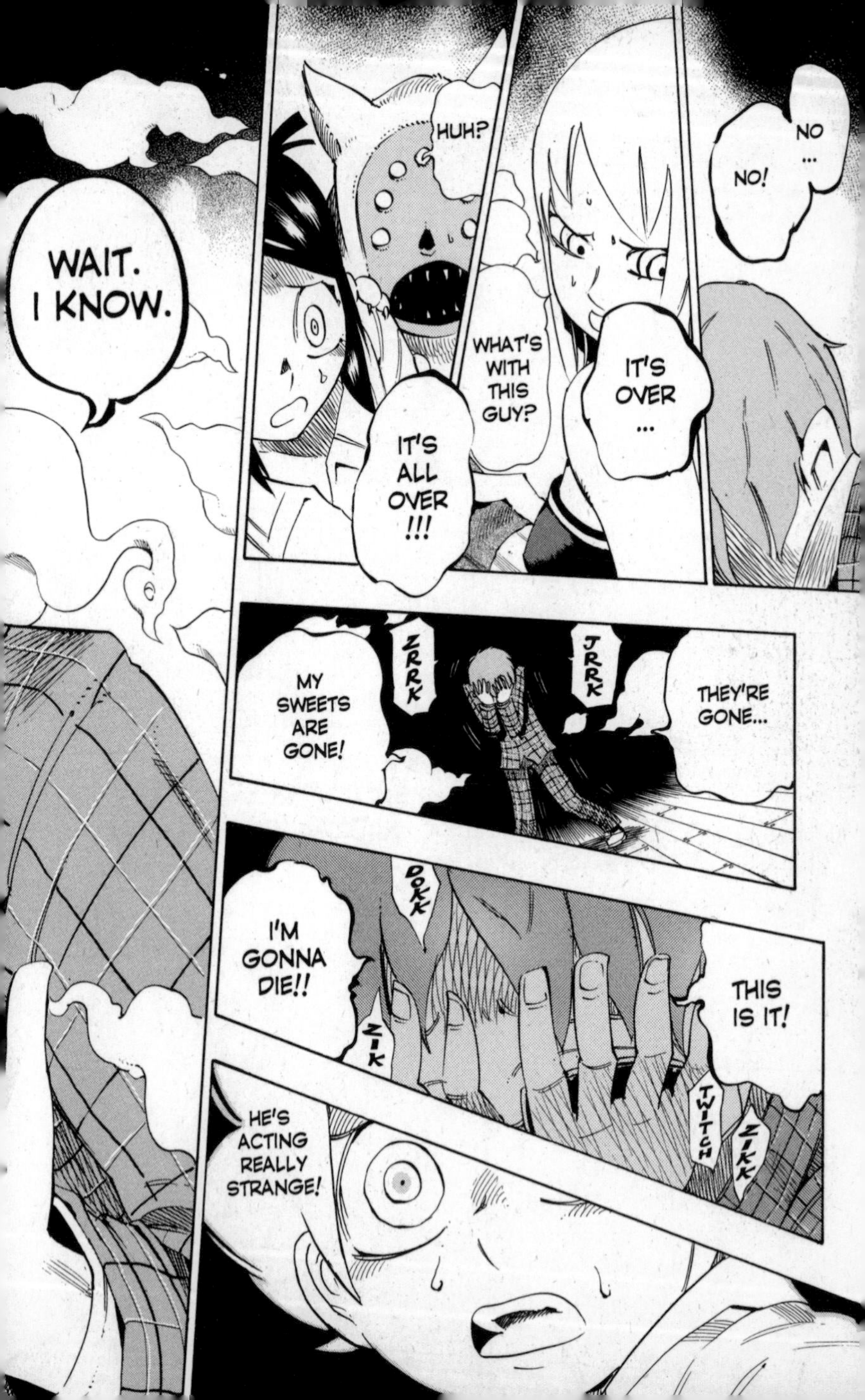
NO ... NO!
IT'S OVER ...
WHAT'S WITH THIS GUY?
HUH?
IT'S ALL OVER!!!
THEY'RE GONE...
JRRK
ZRRK
MY SWEETS ARE GONE!
THIS IS IT!
DOKK
I'M GONNA DIE!!
ZIK
ZIKK
TWITCH
HE'S ACTING REALLY STRANGE!
WAIT. I KNOW.

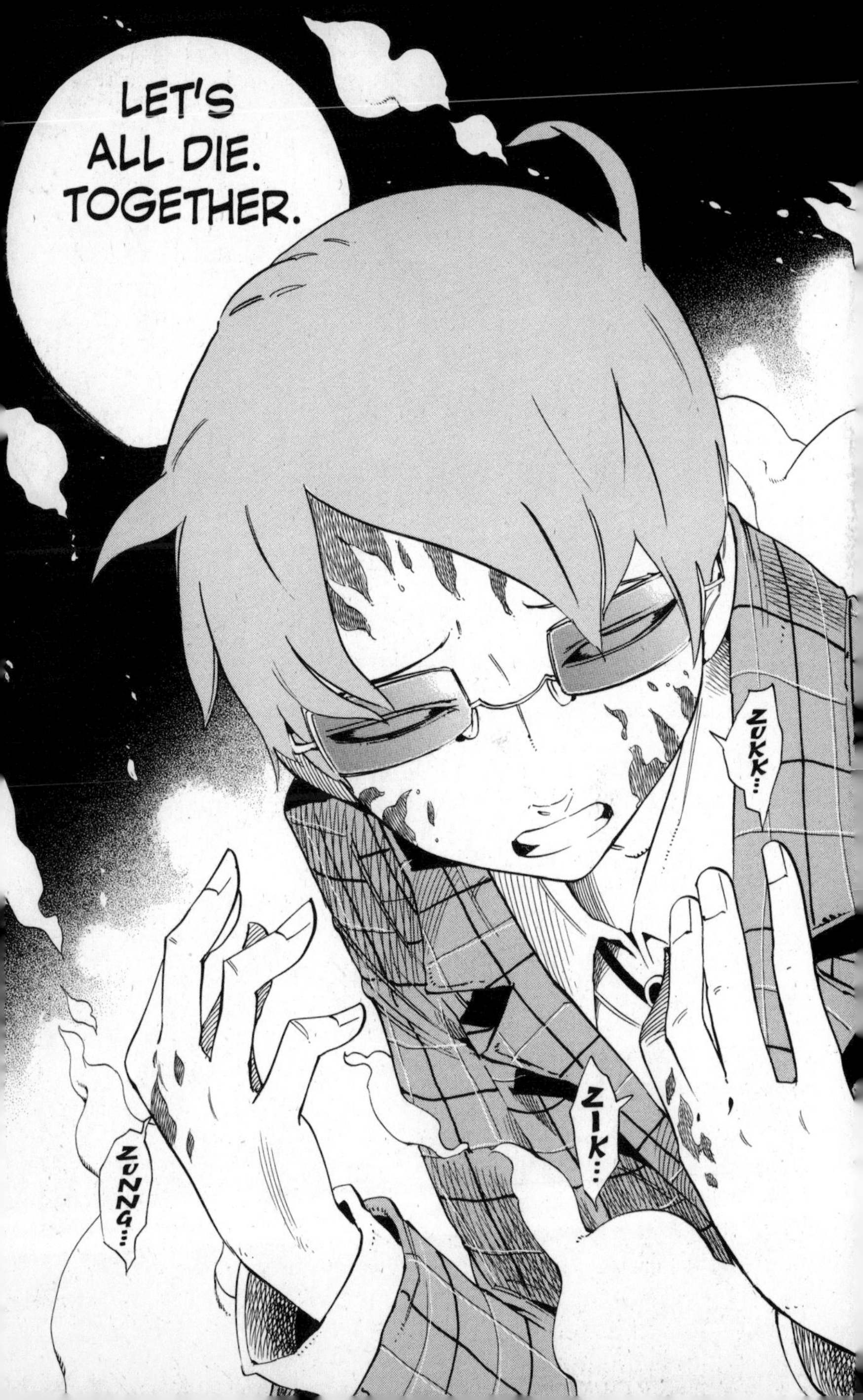
LET'S ALL DIE. TOGETHER.
ZUKK...
ZIK...
ZUNNG...

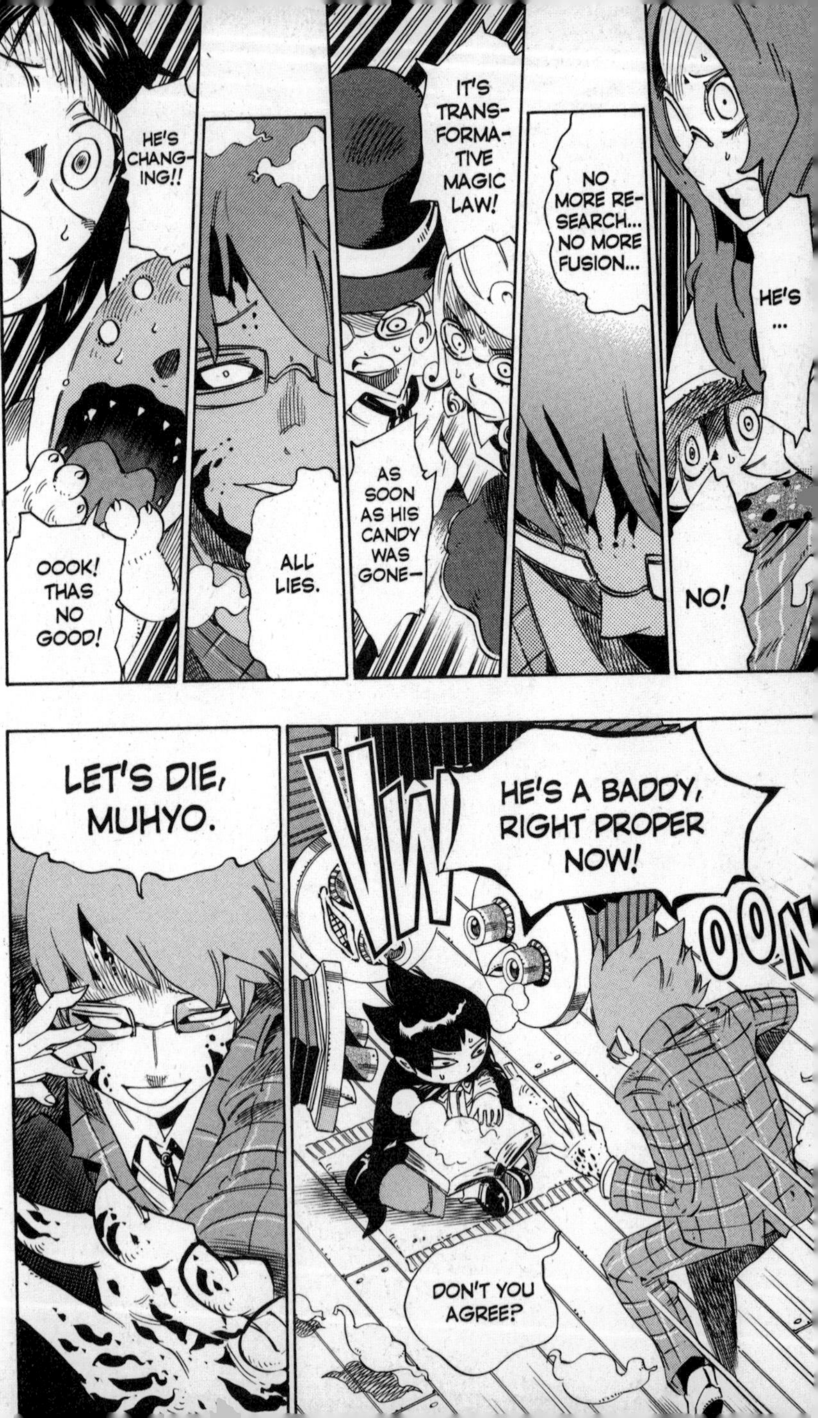
HE'S ...
NO!
NO MORE RESEARCH... NO MORE FUSION...
IT'S TRANSFORMATIVE MAGIC LAW!
AS SOON AS HIS CANDY WAS GONE—
ALL LIES.
HE'S CHANGING!!
OOOK! THAS NO GOOD!
HE'S A BADDY, RIGHT PROPER NOW!
VWOON
DON'T YOU AGREE?
LET'S DIE, MUHYO.

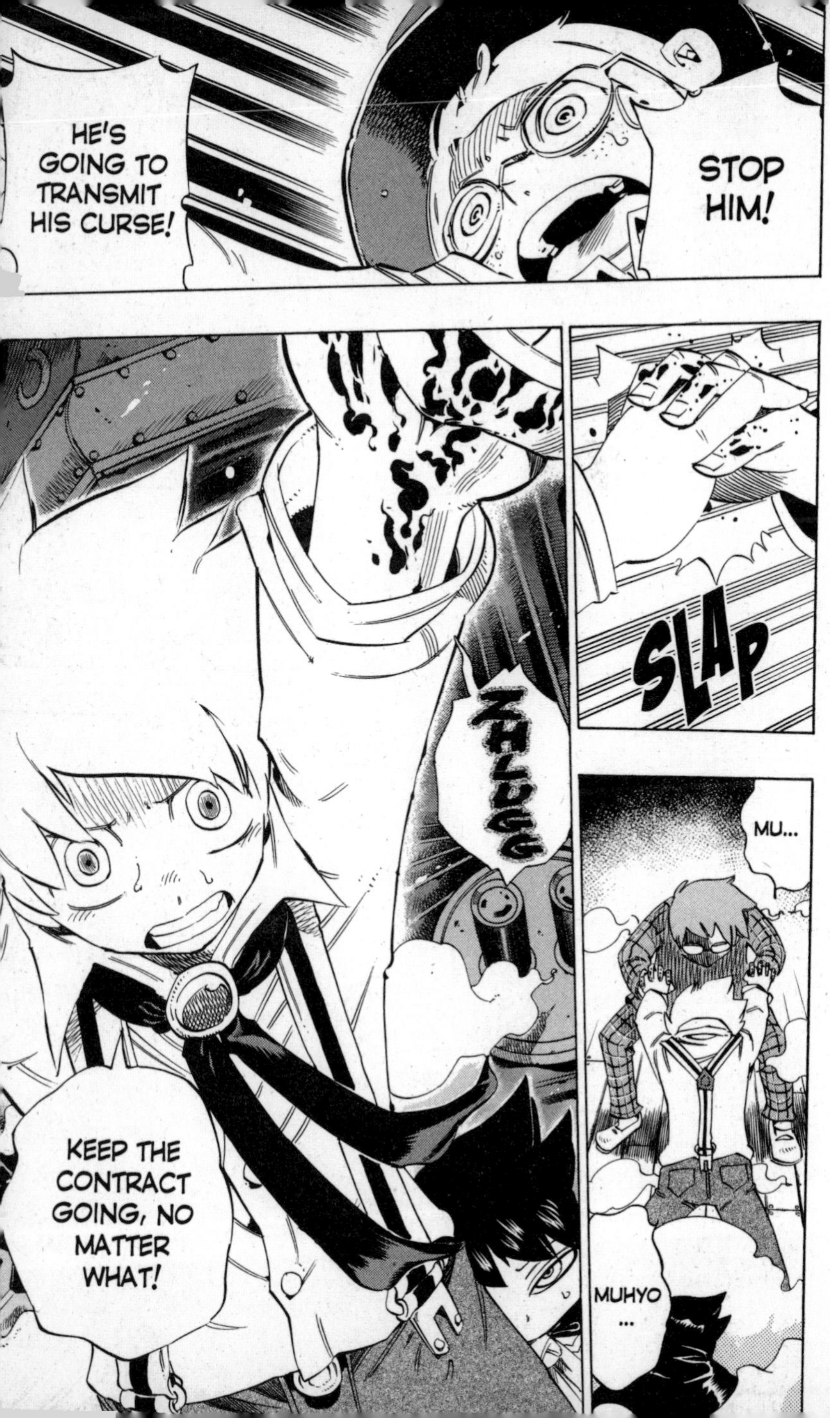
STOP HIM!
HE'S GOING TO TRANSMIT HIS CURSE!
SLAP
MU...
MUHYO ...
ZHLUGG
KEEP THE CONTRACT GOING, NO MATTER WHAT!

I'LL HOLD HIM AS LONG AS I CAN!

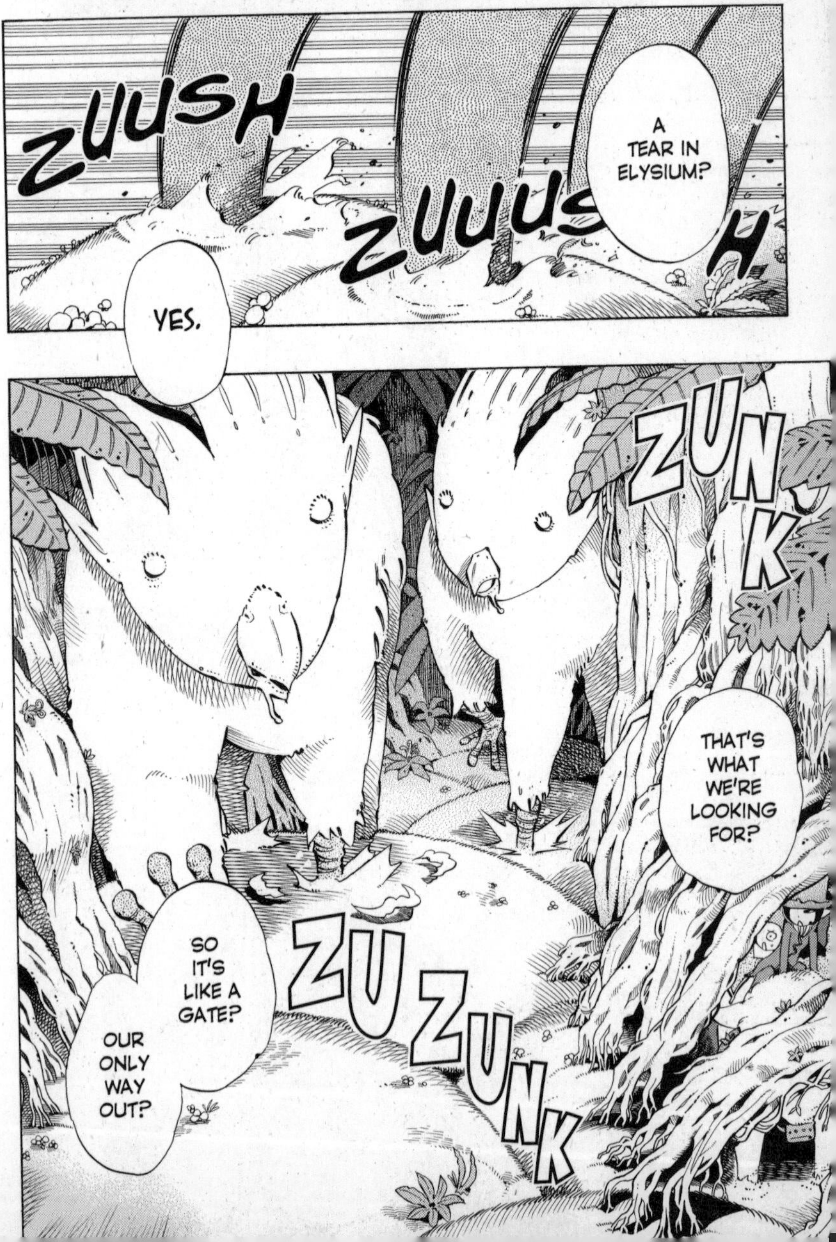
A TEAR IN ELYSIUM?
ZUUUSH
ZUUSH
YES.
ZUNK
THAT'S WHAT WE'RE LOOKING FOR?
ZUZUNK
SO IT'S LIKE A GATE?
OUR ONLY WAY OUT?

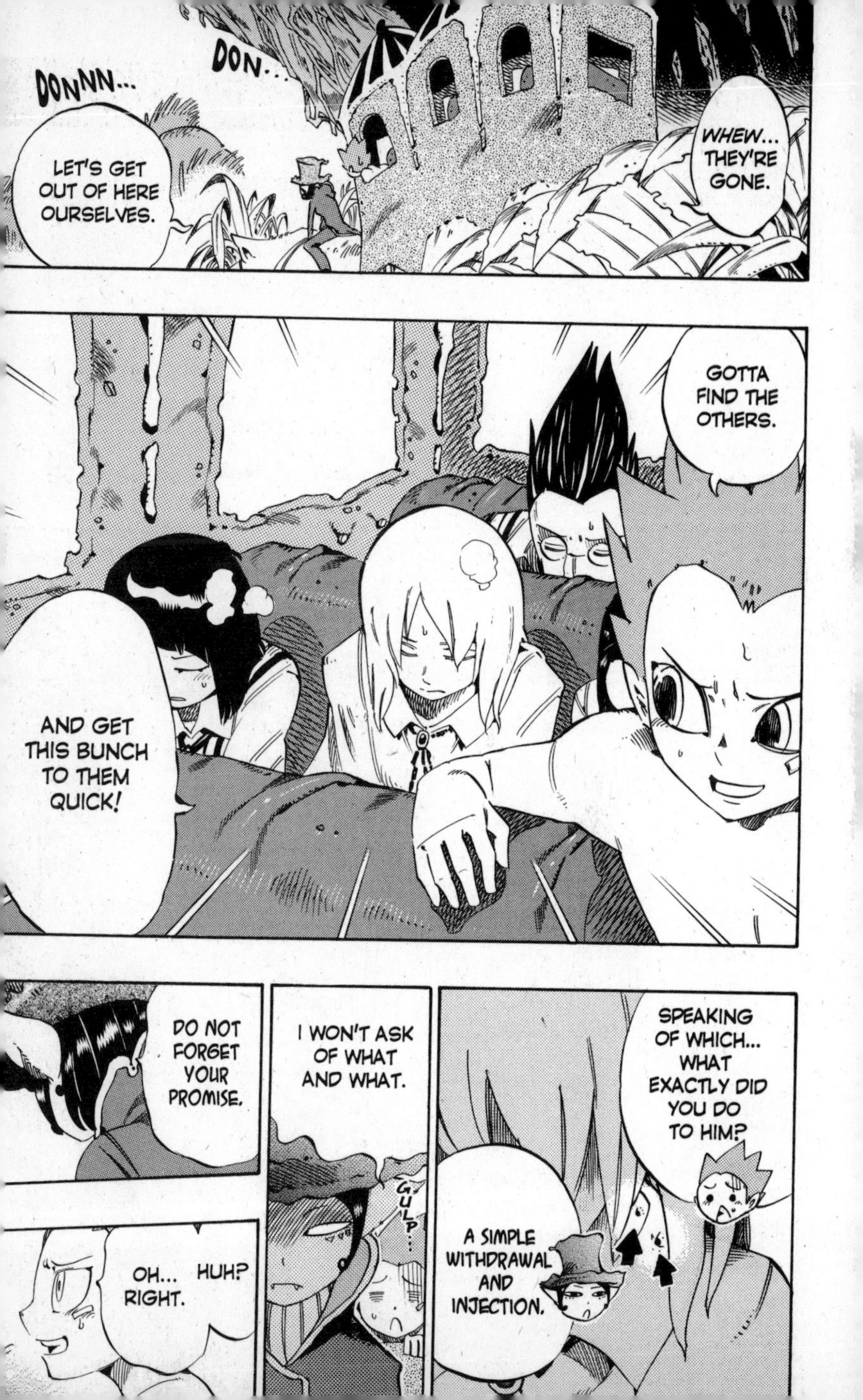
WHEW... THEY'RE GONE.
DON...
DONNN...
LET'S GET OUT OF HERE OURSELVES.
GOTTA FIND THE OTHERS.
AND GET THIS BUNCH TO THEM QUICK!
SPEAKING OF WHICH... WHAT EXACTLY DID YOU DO TO HIM?
A SIMPLE WITHDRAWAL AND INJECTION.
I WON'T ASK OF WHAT AND WHAT.
GULP...
DO NOT FORGET YOUR PROMISE.
HUH?
OH... RIGHT.

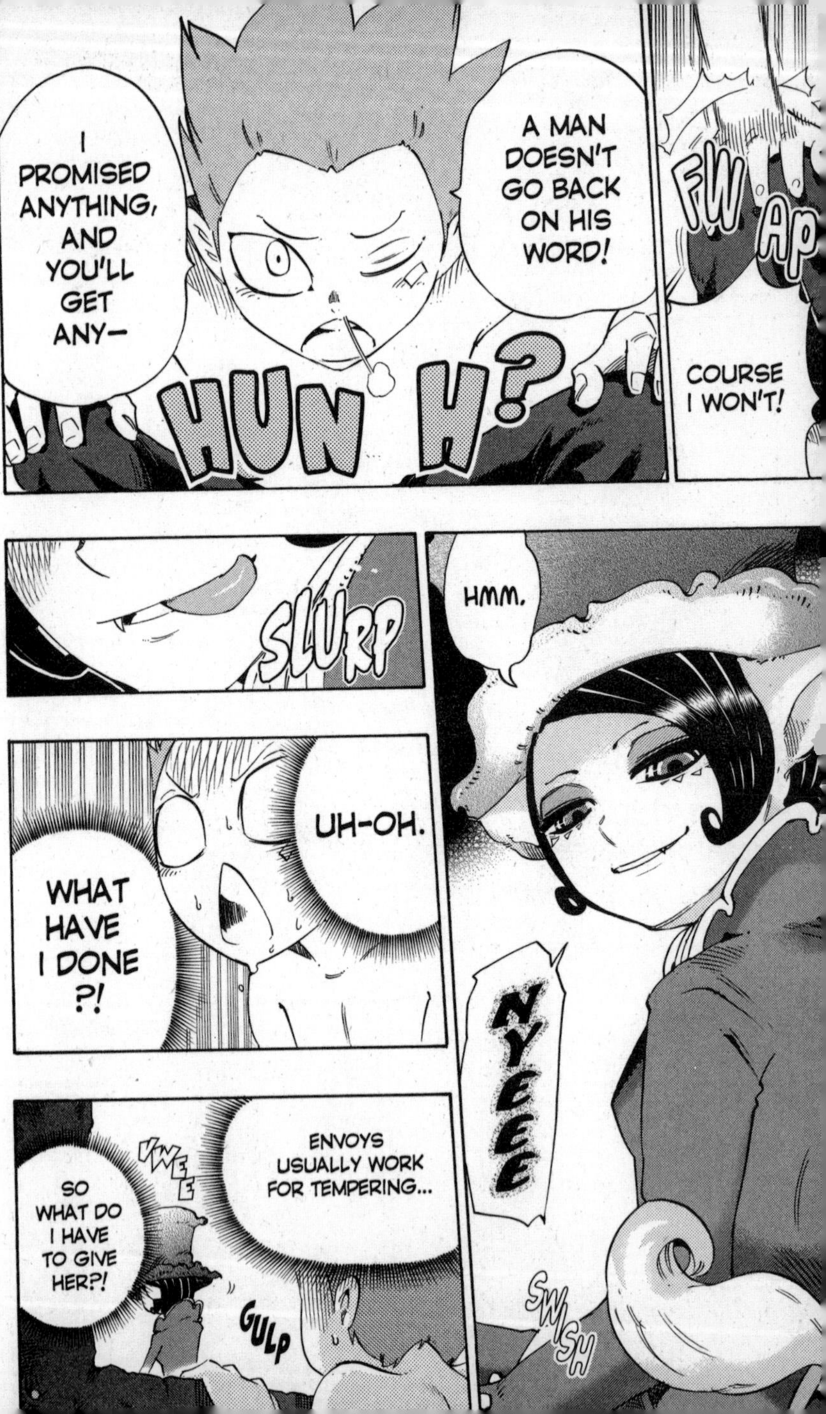
FWAP
COURSE I WON'T!
A MAN DOESN'T GO BACK ON HIS WORD!
I PROMISED ANYTHING, AND YOU'LL GET ANY—
HUNH?
HMM.
NYEEEE
SWISH
SLURP
UH-OH.
WHAT HAVE I DONE?!
ENVOYS USUALLY WORK FOR TEMPERING...
VWEE
SO WHAT DO I HAVE TO GIVE HER?!
GULP

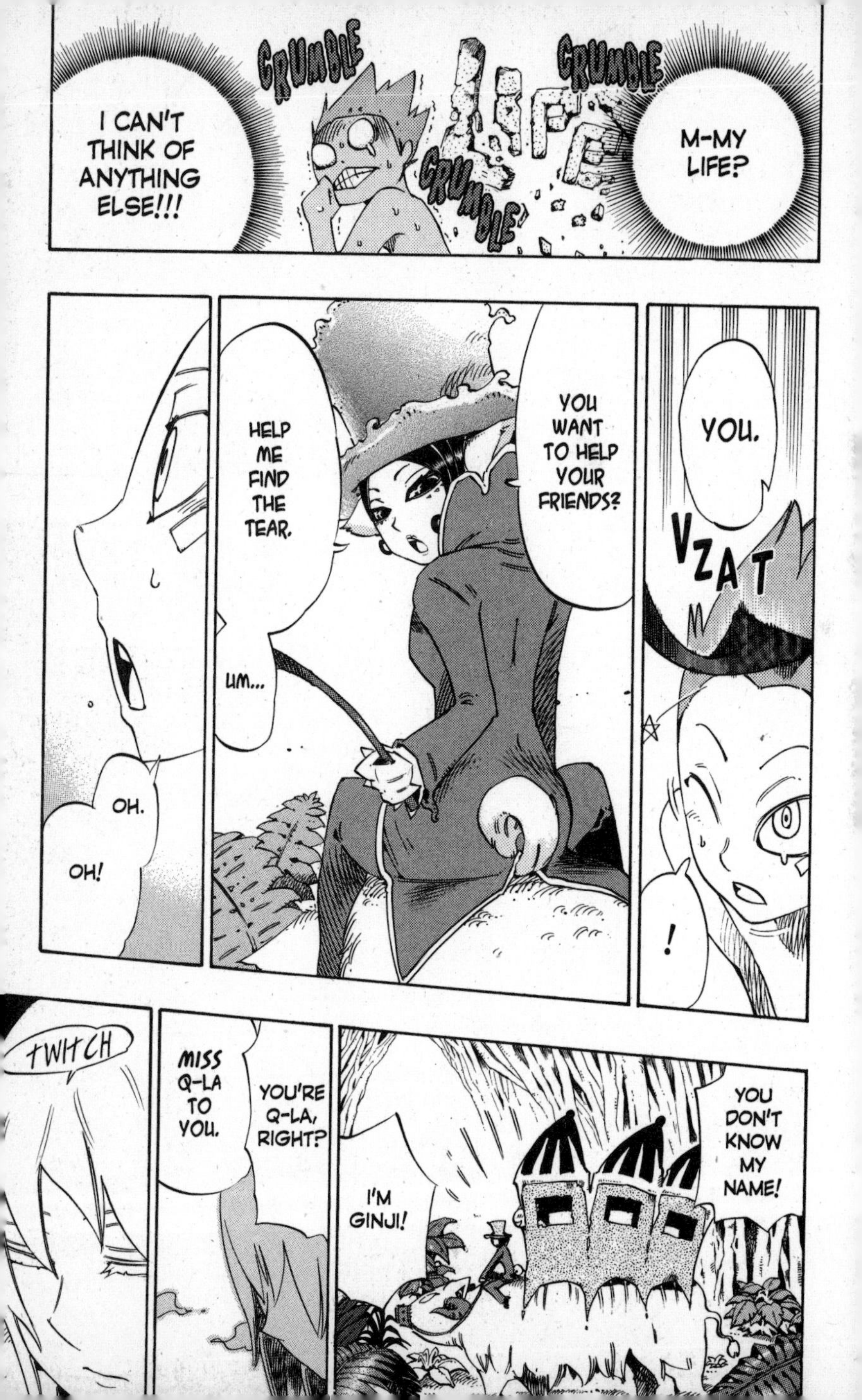
M-MY LIFE?
CRUMBLE
CRUMBLE
CRUMBLE
I CAN'T THINK OF ANYTHING ELSE!!!
YOU.
VZAT
!
YOU WANT TO HELP YOUR FRIENDS?
HELP ME FIND THE TEAR.
UM...
OH.
OH!
YOU DON'T KNOW MY NAME!
I'M GINJI!
YOU'RE Q-LA, RIGHT?
MISS Q-LA TO YOU.
TWITCH

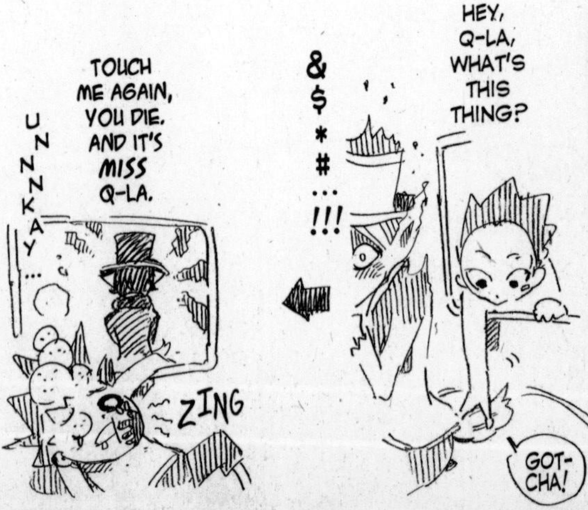

HEY, Q-LA, WHAT'S THIS THING?
&$*#...!!!
GOT-CHA!
TOUCH ME AGAIN, YOU DIE. AND IT'S MISS Q-LA.
UNNNKAY...
ZING

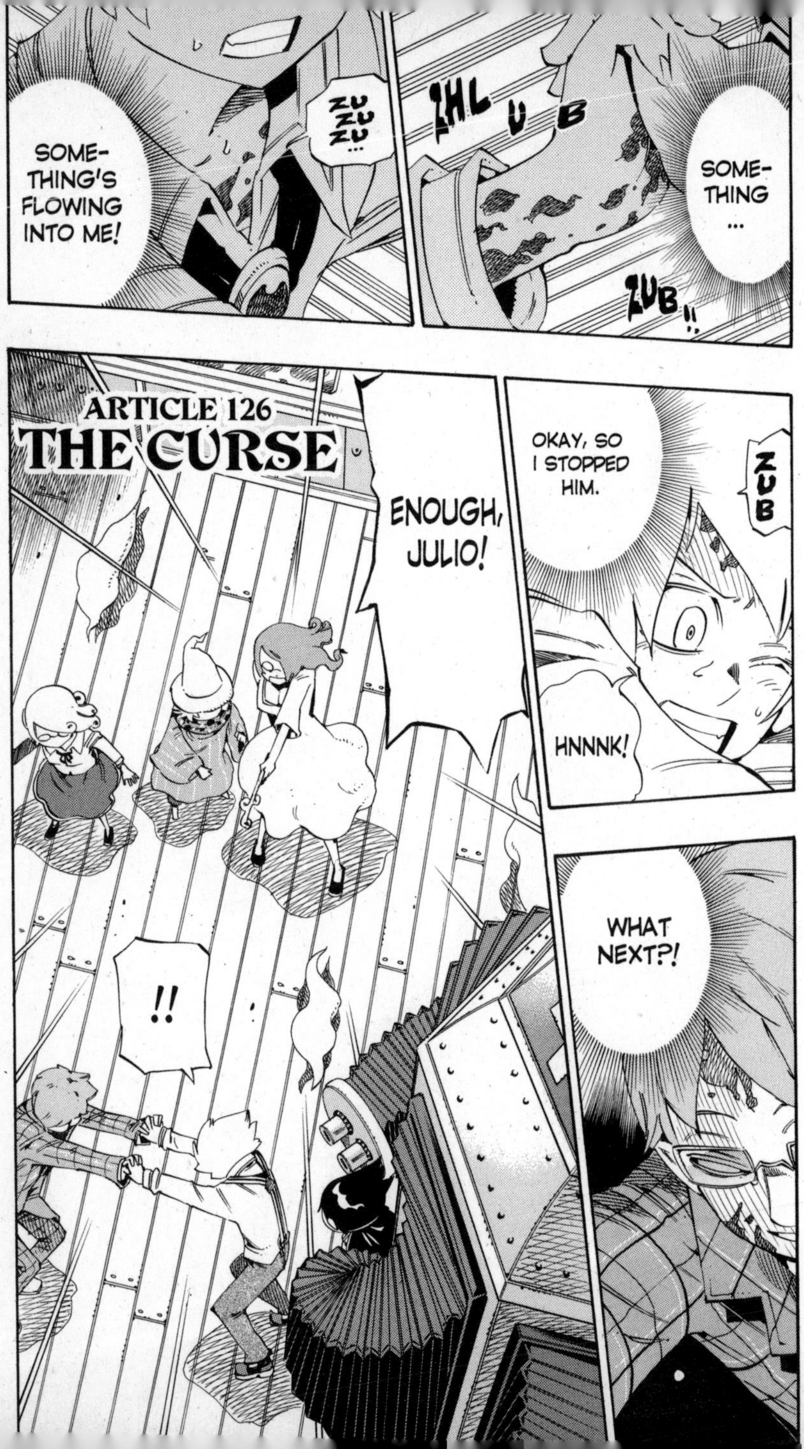
SOME-THING ...
ZHL U B
ZUB!!
ZUZUZU...
SOME-THING'S FLOWING INTO ME!
OKAY, SO I STOPPED HIM.
ZUB
HNNNK!
WHAT NEXT?!
ARTICLE 126
THE CURSE
ENOUGH, JULIO!
!!

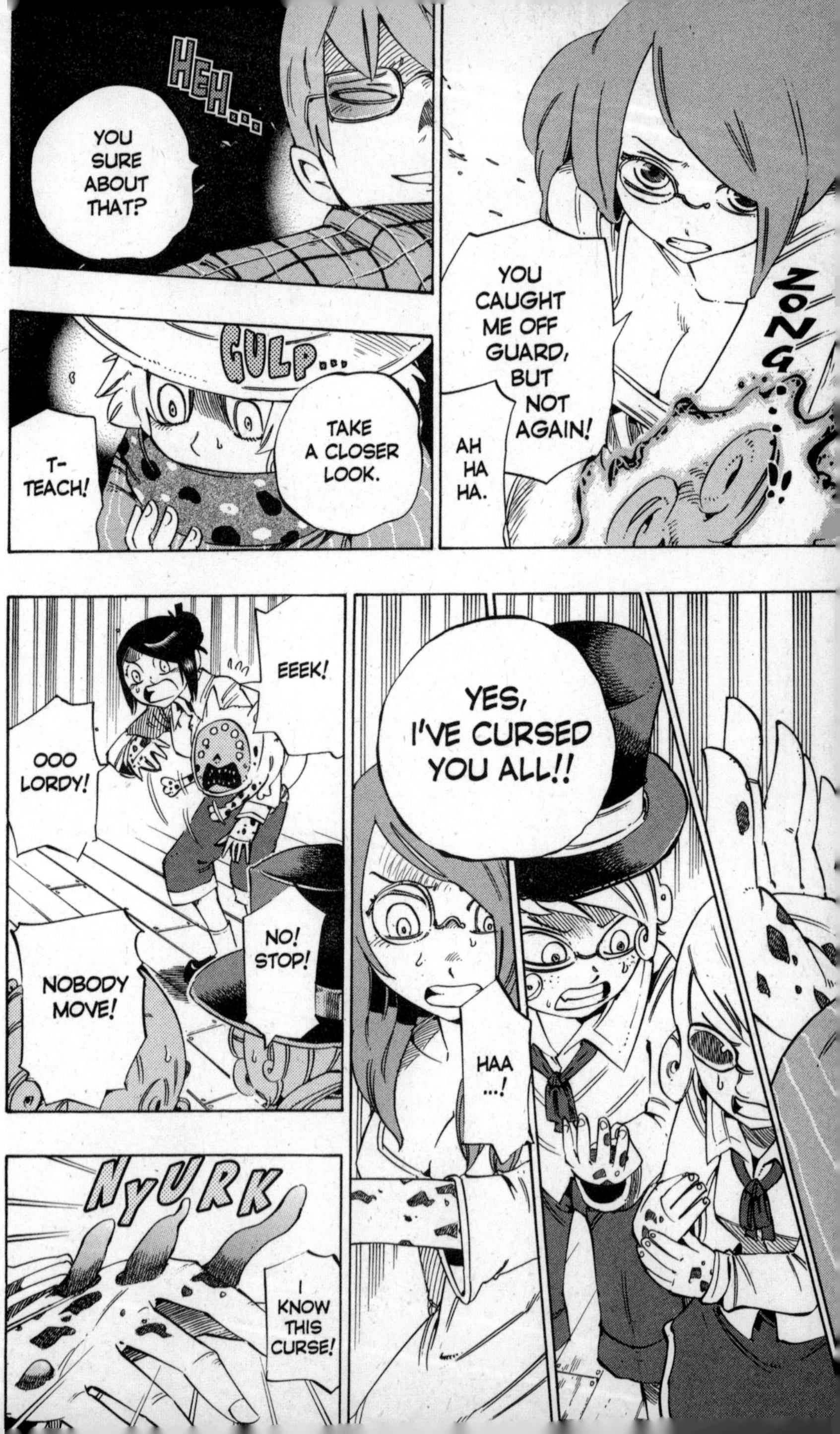
YOU CAUGHT ME OFF GUARD, BUT NOT AGAIN!
ZONG...!!
AH HA HA.
HEH...
YOU SURE ABOUT THAT?
GULP...
TAKE A CLOSER LOOK.
T-TEACH!
YES, I'VE CURSED YOU ALL!!
HAA...!
EEEK!
OOO LORDY!
NO! STOP!
NOBODY MOVE!
NyURK
I KNOW THIS CURSE!

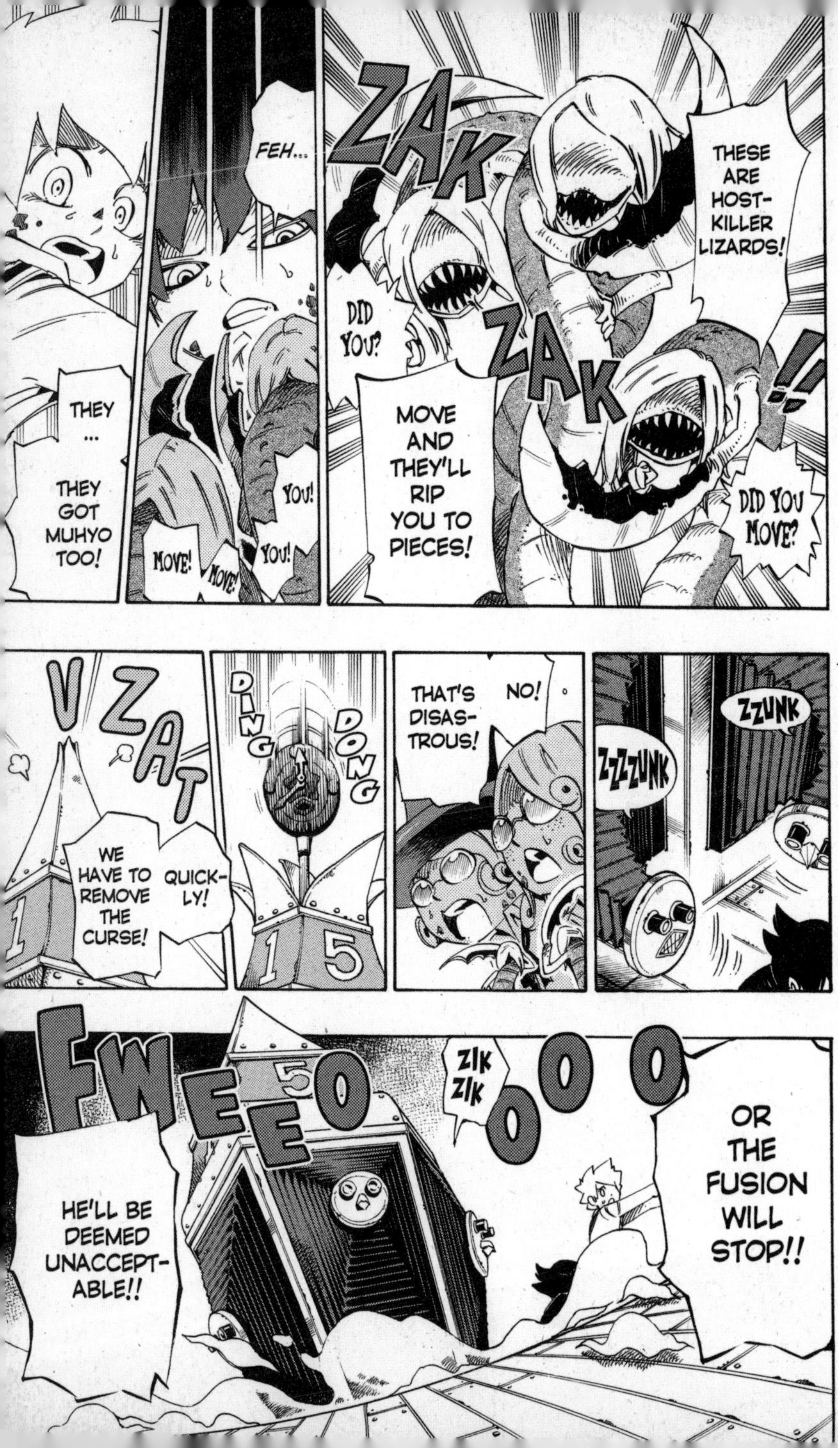
THESE ARE HOST-KILLER LIZARDS!
ZAK
ZAK!!
DID YOU MOVE?
DID YOU?
MOVE AND THEY'LL RIP YOU TO PIECES!
FEH...
YOU!
YOU!
MOVE!
MOVE!
THEY ...
THEY GOT MUHYO TOO!
ZZUNK
ZZZZUNK
NO!
THAT'S DISASTROUS!
DING
DONG
VZAT
QUICKLY!
WE HAVE TO REMOVE THE CURSE!
OR THE FUSION WILL STOP!!
ZIK ZIK
FWEEOOOO
HE'LL BE DEEMED UNACCEPTABLE!!

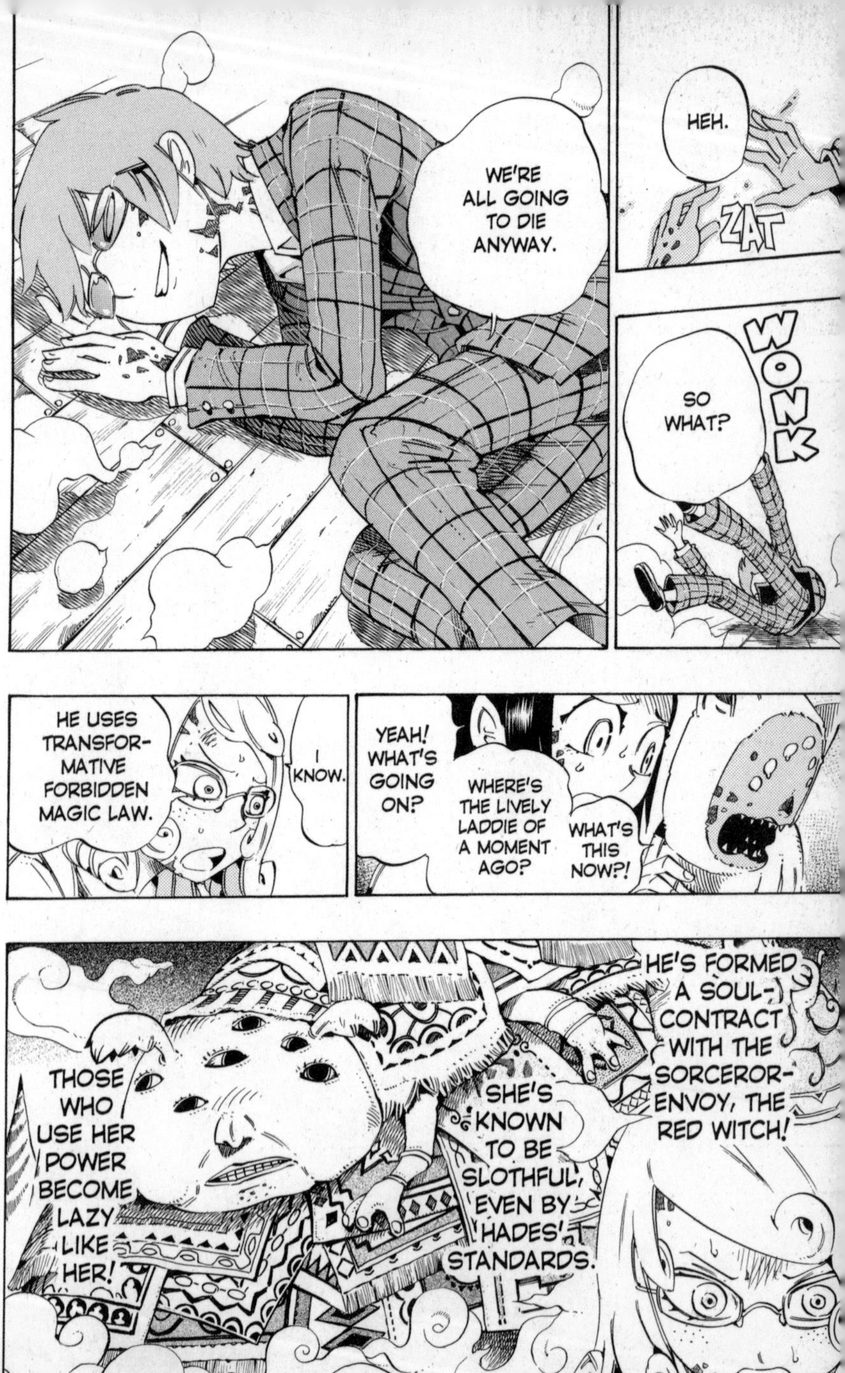
HEH.
ZAT
SO WHAT?
WONK
WE'RE ALL GOING TO DIE ANYWAY.
WHAT'S THIS NOW?!
WHERE'S THE LIVELY LADDIE OF A MOMENT AGO?
YEAH! WHAT'S GOING ON?
I KNOW.
HE USES TRANSFORMATIVE FORBIDDEN MAGIC LAW.
HE'S FORMED A SOUL-CONTRACT WITH THE SORCEROR-ENVOY, THE RED WITCH!
SHE'S KNOWN TO BE SLOTHFUL, EVEN BY HADES' STANDARDS.
THOSE WHO USE HER POWER BECOME LAZY LIKE HER!

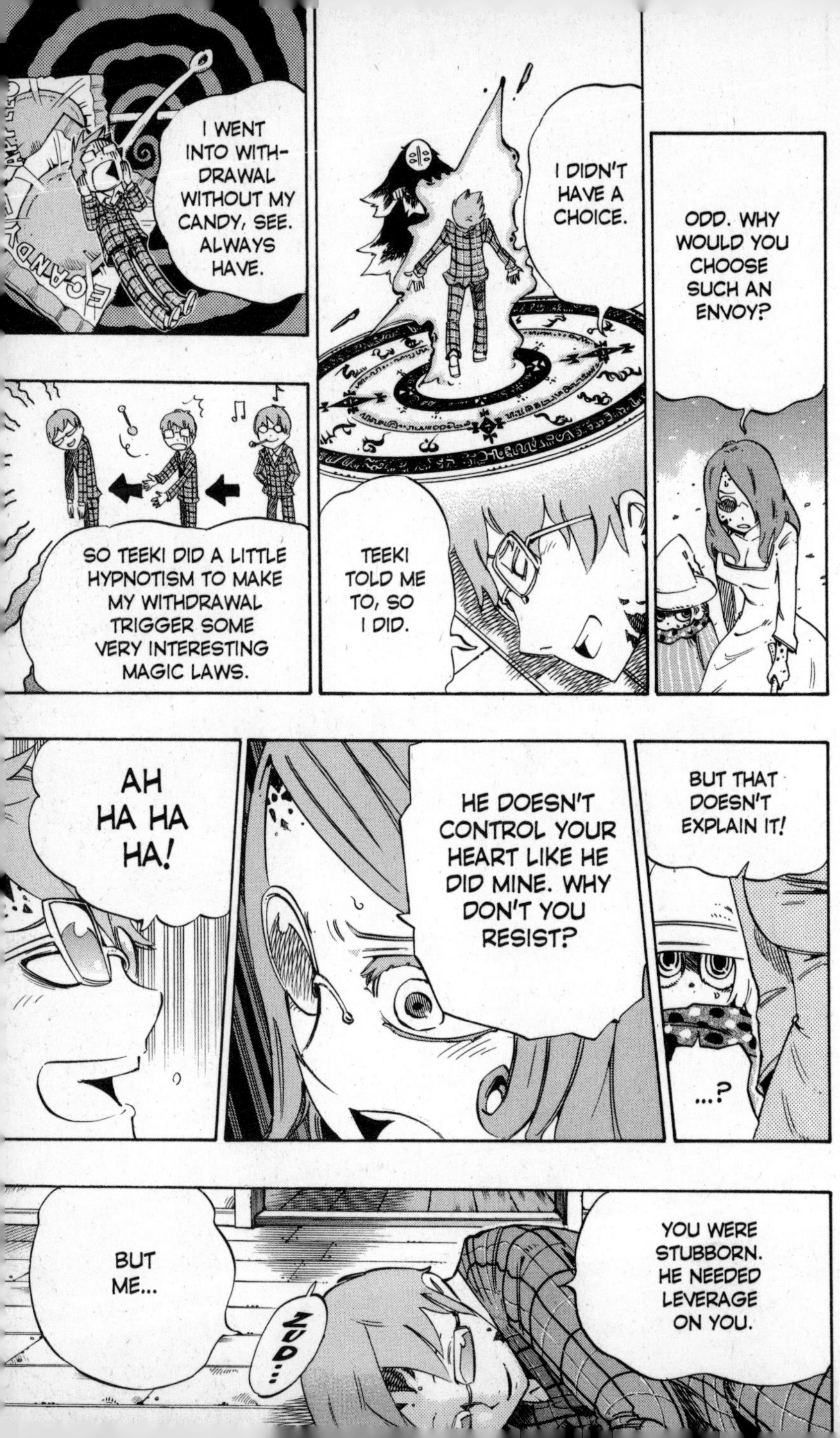
ODD. WHY WOULD YOU CHOOSE SUCH AN ENVOY?
I DIDN'T HAVE A CHOICE.
TEEKI TOLD ME TO, SO I DID.
I WENT INTO WITH-DRAWAL WITHOUT MY CANDY, SEE. ALWAYS HAVE.
SO TEEKI DID A LITTLE HYPNOTISM TO MAKE MY WITHDRAWAL TRIGGER SOME VERY INTERESTING MAGIC LAWS.
BUT THAT DOESN'T EXPLAIN IT!
...?
HE DOESN'T CONTROL YOUR HEART LIKE HE DID MINE. WHY DON'T YOU RESIST?
AH HA HA HA!
YOU WERE STUBBORN. HE NEEDED LEVERAGE ON YOU.
ZUD...
BUT ME...

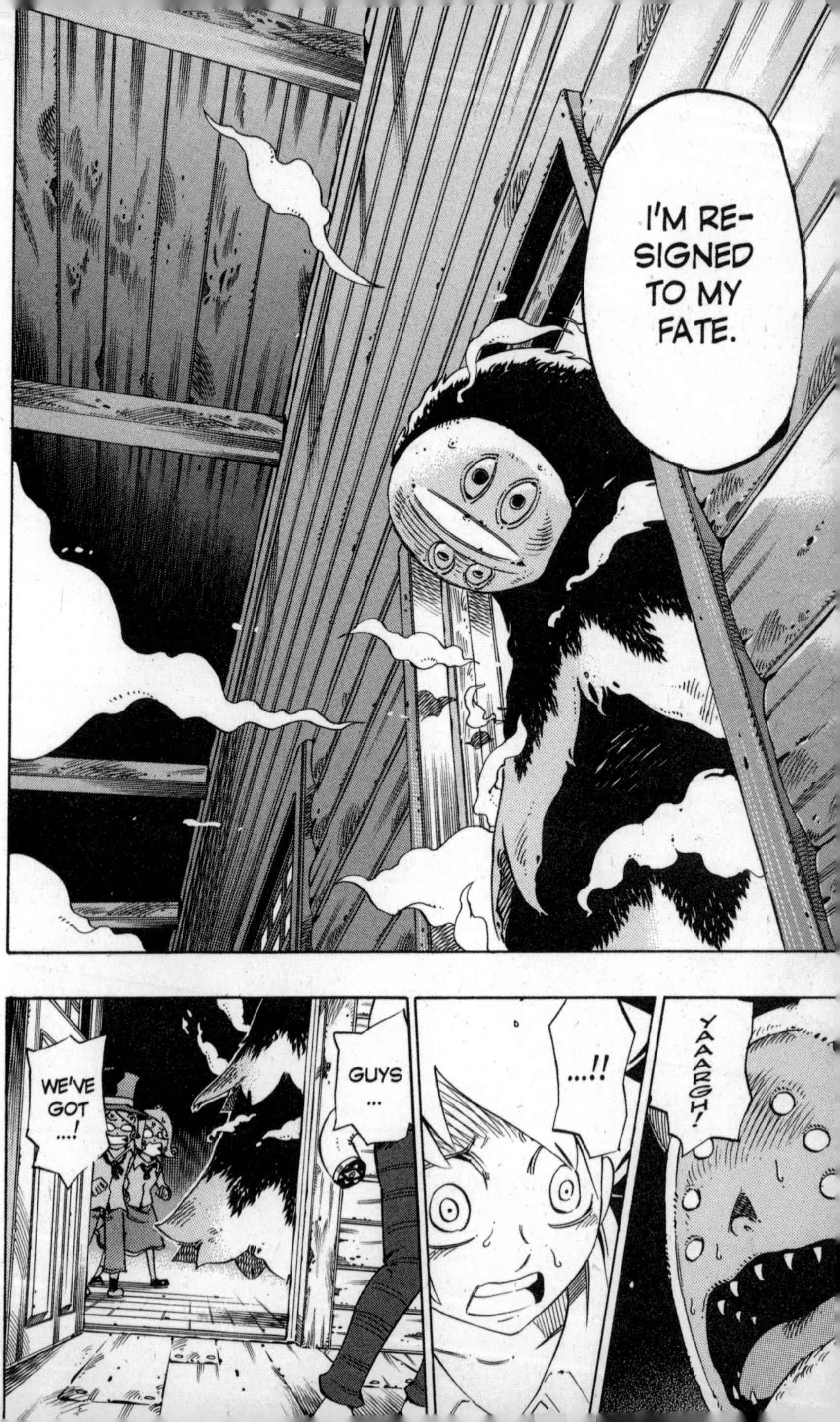
I'M RE-SIGNED TO MY FATE.
YAAARGH!
...!!
GUYS ...
WE'VE GOT ...!

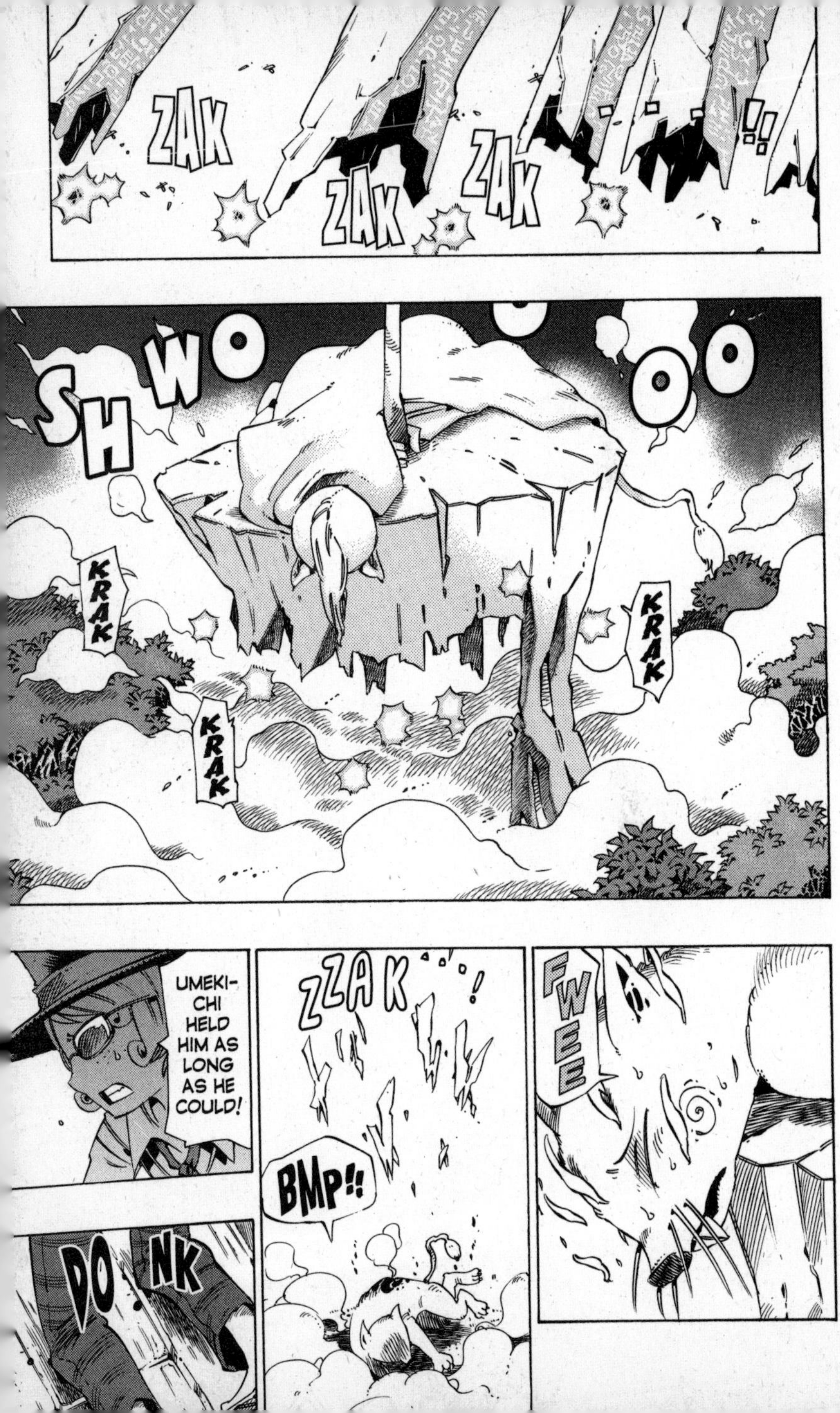
!!
ZAK
ZAK
ZAK
SHWOOOO
KRAK
KRAK
KRAK
FWEE
ZZAK
BMP!!
UMEKICHI HELD HIM AS LONG AS HE COULD!
DONK

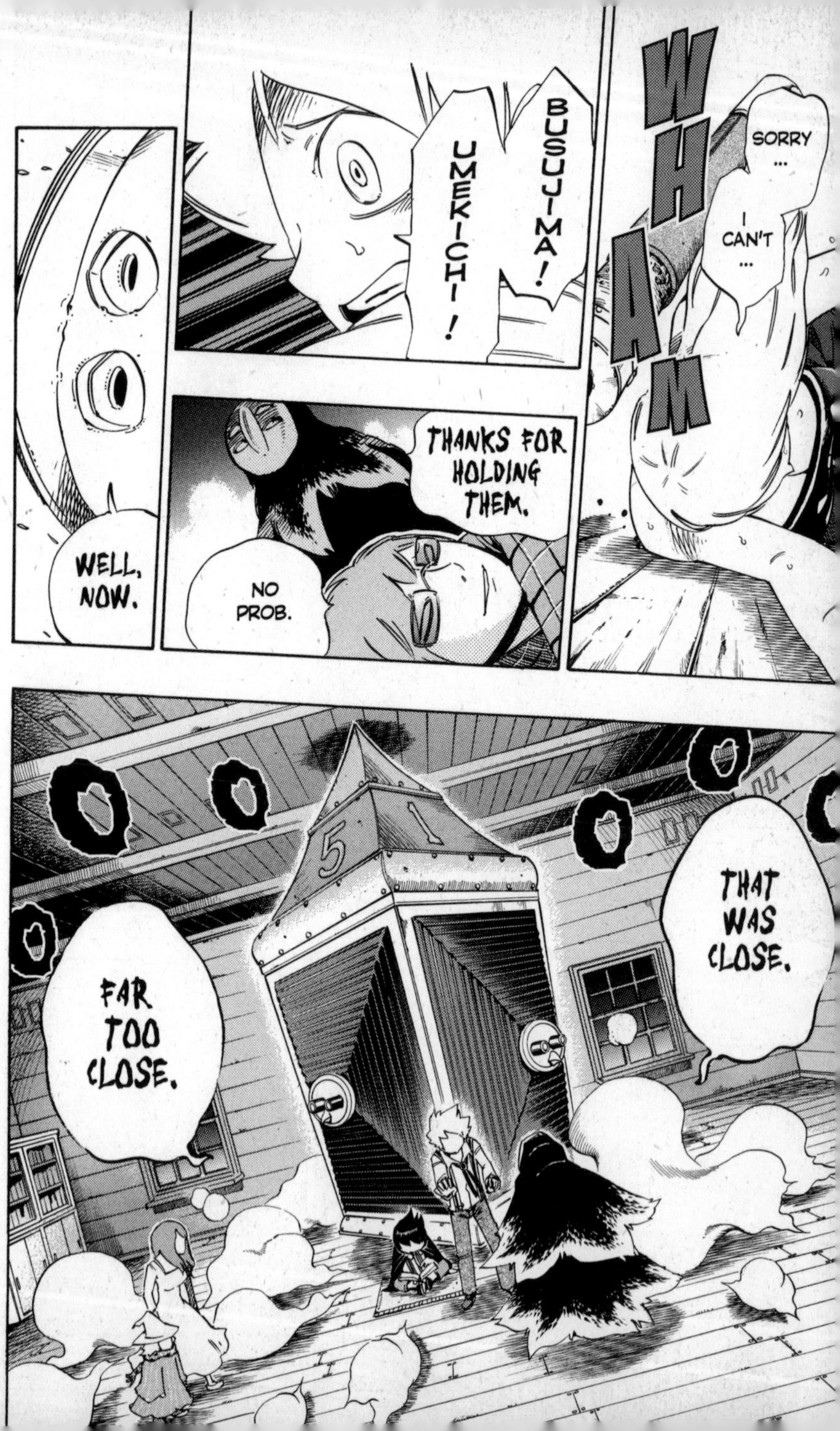
WHAM
SORRY ...
I CAN'T ...
BUSUJIMA!
UMEKICHI!
THANKS FOR HOLDING THEM.
NO PROB.
WELL, NOW.
THAT WAS CLOSE.
FAR TOO CLOSE.

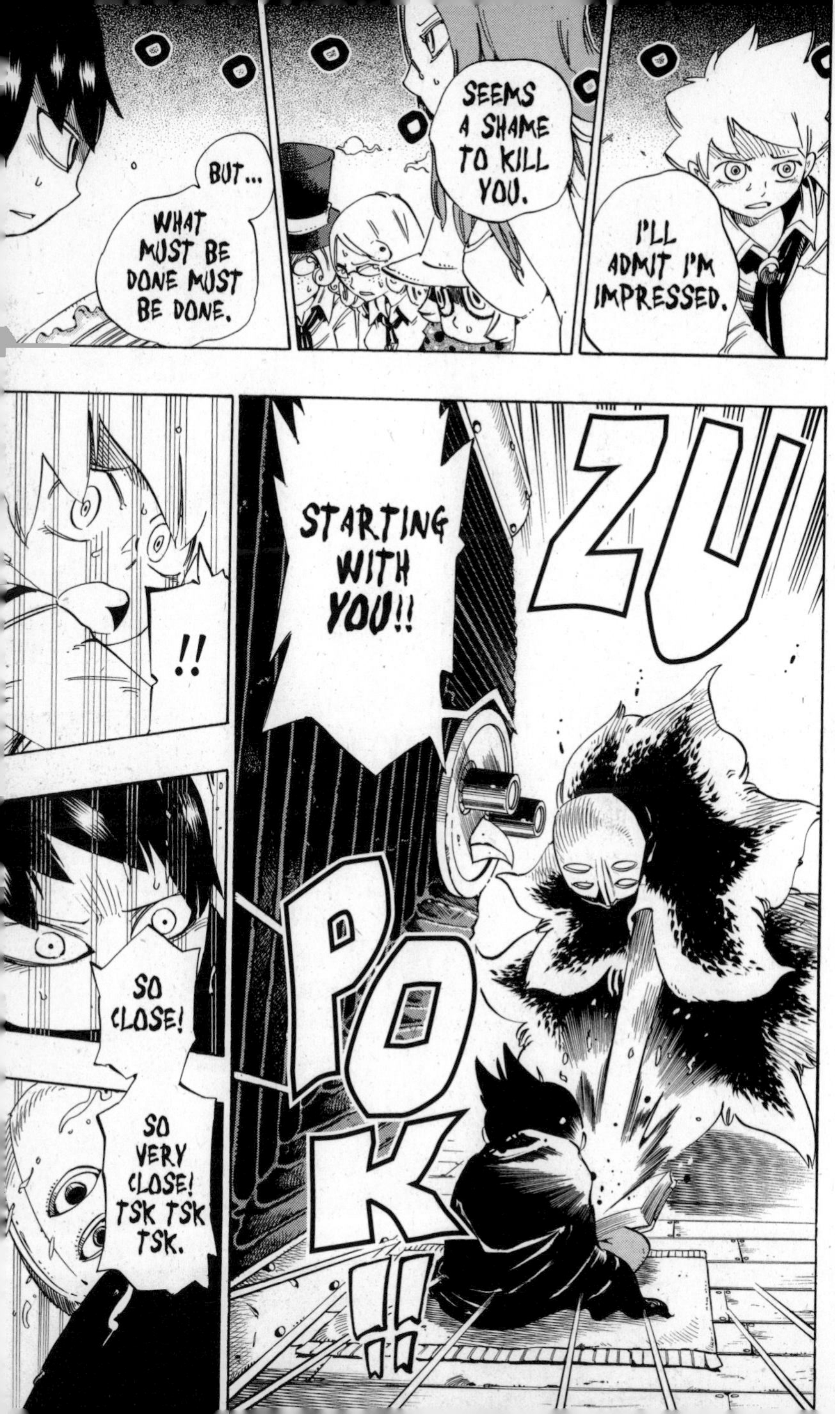
I'LL ADMIT I'M IMPRESSED.
SEEMS A SHAME TO KILL YOU.
BUT...
WHAT MUST BE DONE MUST BE DONE.
ZU
STARTING WITH YOU!!
POK!!
!!
SO CLOSE!
SO VERY CLOSE! TSK TSK TSK.

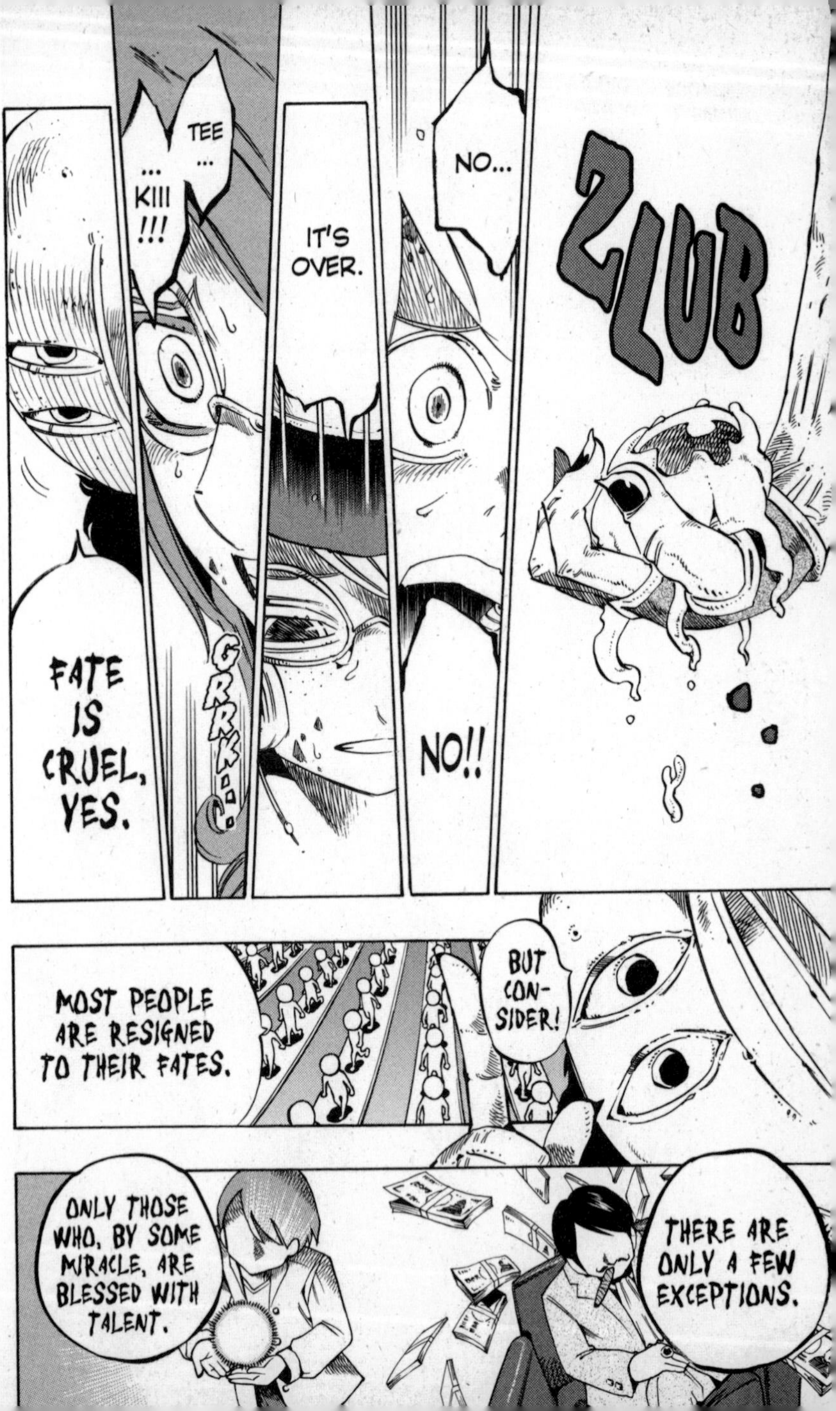
ZLUB
NO...
NO!!
IT'S OVER.
TEE ...
... KIII !!!
GRRK...
FATE IS CRUEL, YES.
BUT CON-SIDER!
MOST PEOPLE ARE RESIGNED TO THEIR FATES.
THERE ARE ONLY A FEW EXCEPTIONS.
ONLY THOSE WHO, BY SOME MIRACLE, ARE BLESSED WITH TALENT.

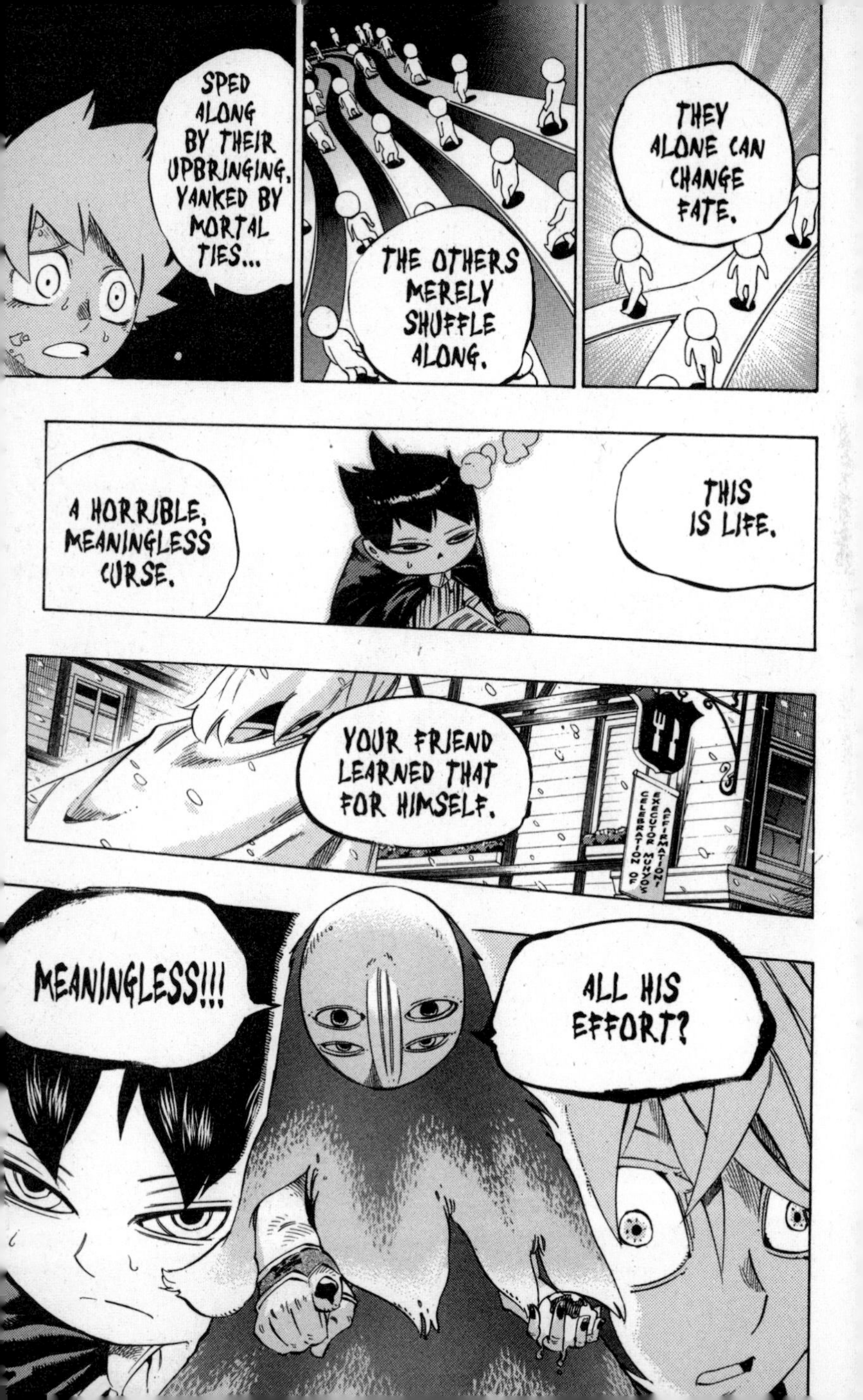
THEY ALONE CAN CHANGE FATE.
THE OTHERS MERELY SHUFFLE ALONG.
SPED ALONG BY THEIR UPBRINGING, YANKED BY MORTAL TIES...
THIS IS LIFE.
A HORRIBLE, MEANINGLESS CURSE.
YOUR FRIEND LEARNED THAT FOR HIMSELF.
CELEBRATION OF EXECUTOR MUHYO'S AFFIRMATION!
ALL HIS EFFORT?
MEANINGLESS!!!

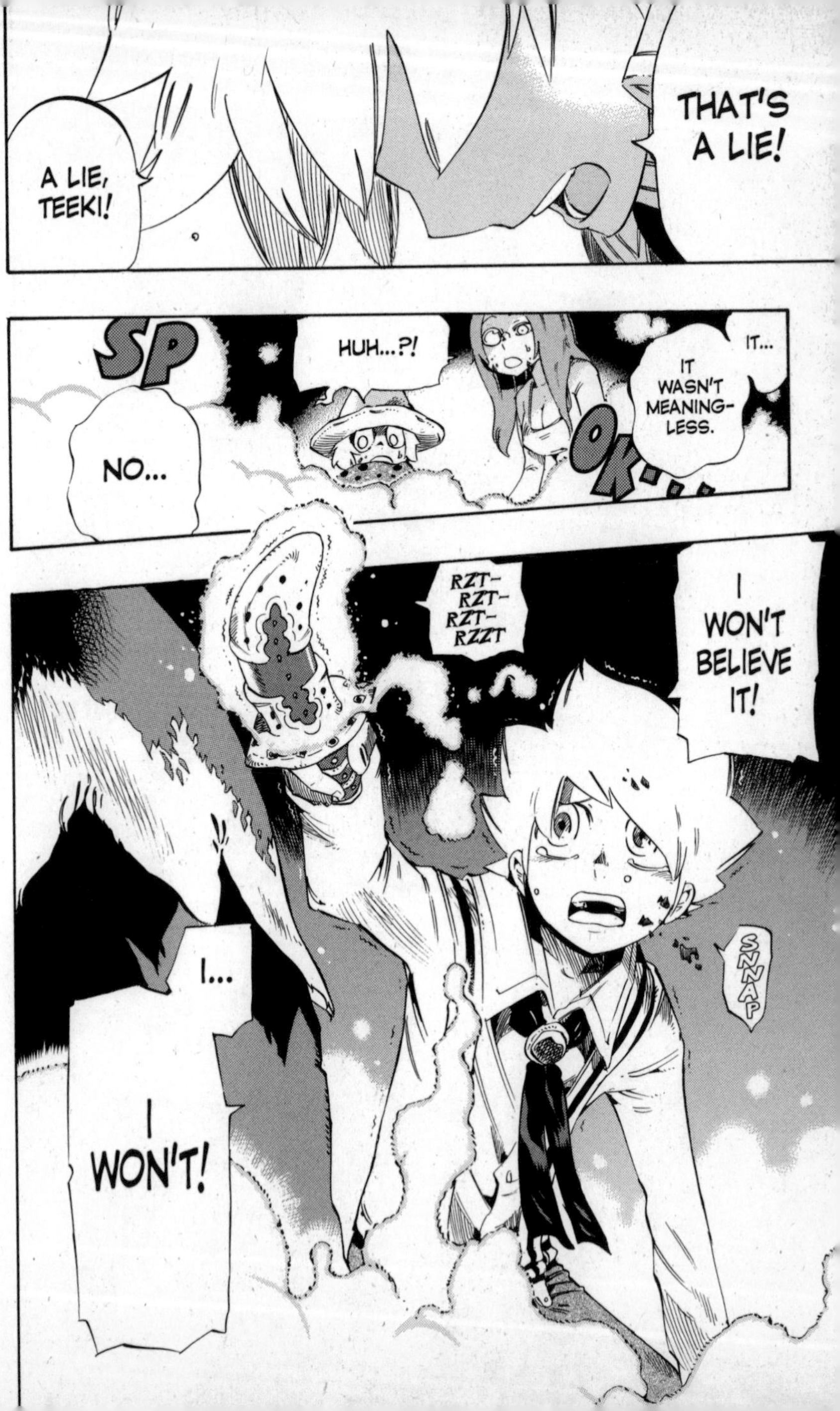
THAT'S A LIE!
A LIE, TEEKI!
IT...
IT WASN'T MEANING-LESS.
OK...
HUH...?!
SP
NO...
I WON'T BELIEVE IT!
RZT- RZT- RZT- RZZT
SNNAP
I...
I WON'T!

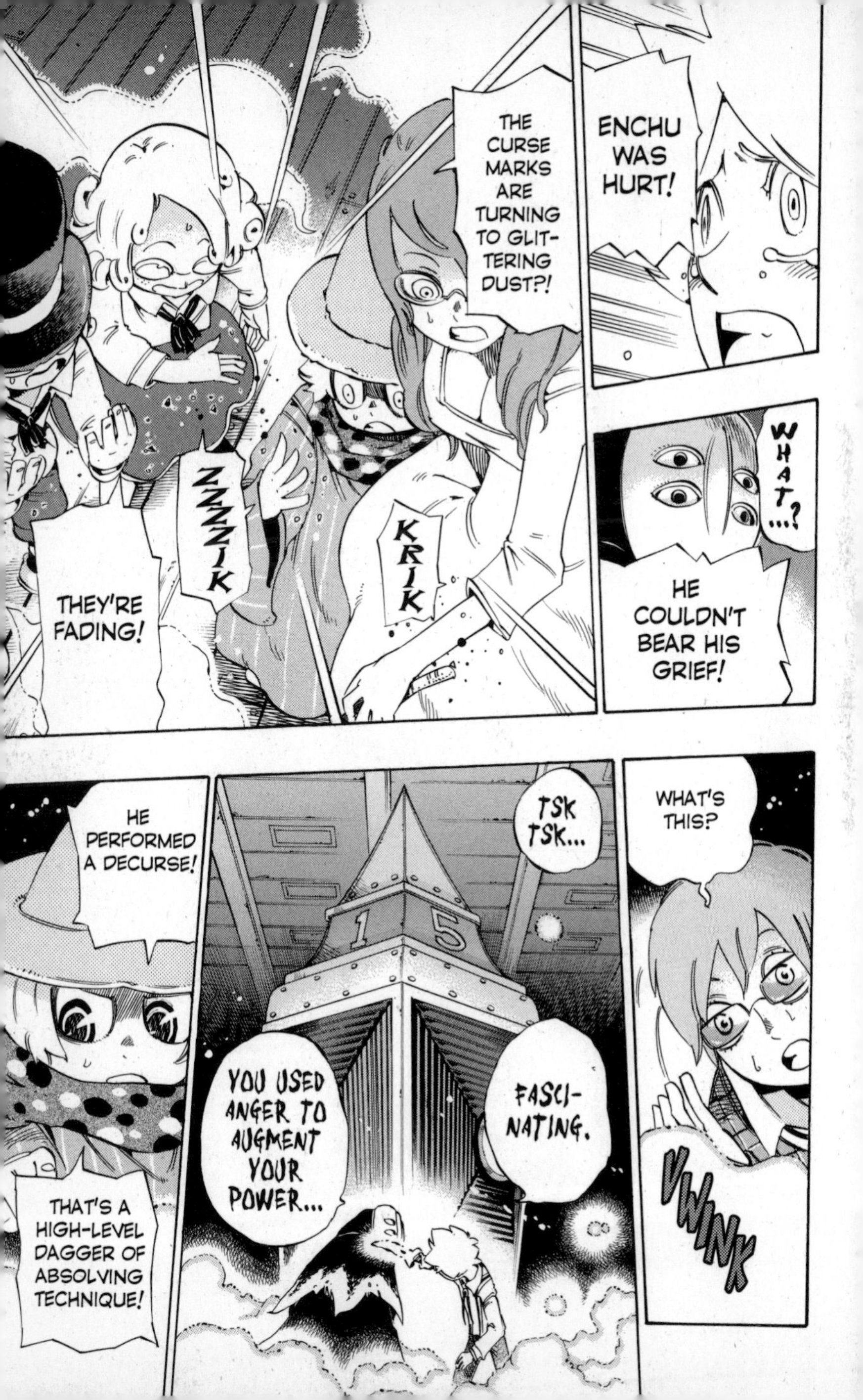
ENCHU WAS HURT!
WHAT...?
HE COULDN'T BEAR HIS GRIEF!
THE CURSE MARKS ARE TURNING TO GLITTERING DUST?!
KRIK
ZZZZIK
THEY'RE FADING!
WHAT'S THIS?
VWINK
TSK TSK...
FASCI-NATING.
YOU USED ANGER TO AUGMENT YOUR POWER...
HE PERFORMED A DECURSE!
THAT'S A HIGH-LEVEL DAGGER OF ABSOLVING TECHNIQUE!

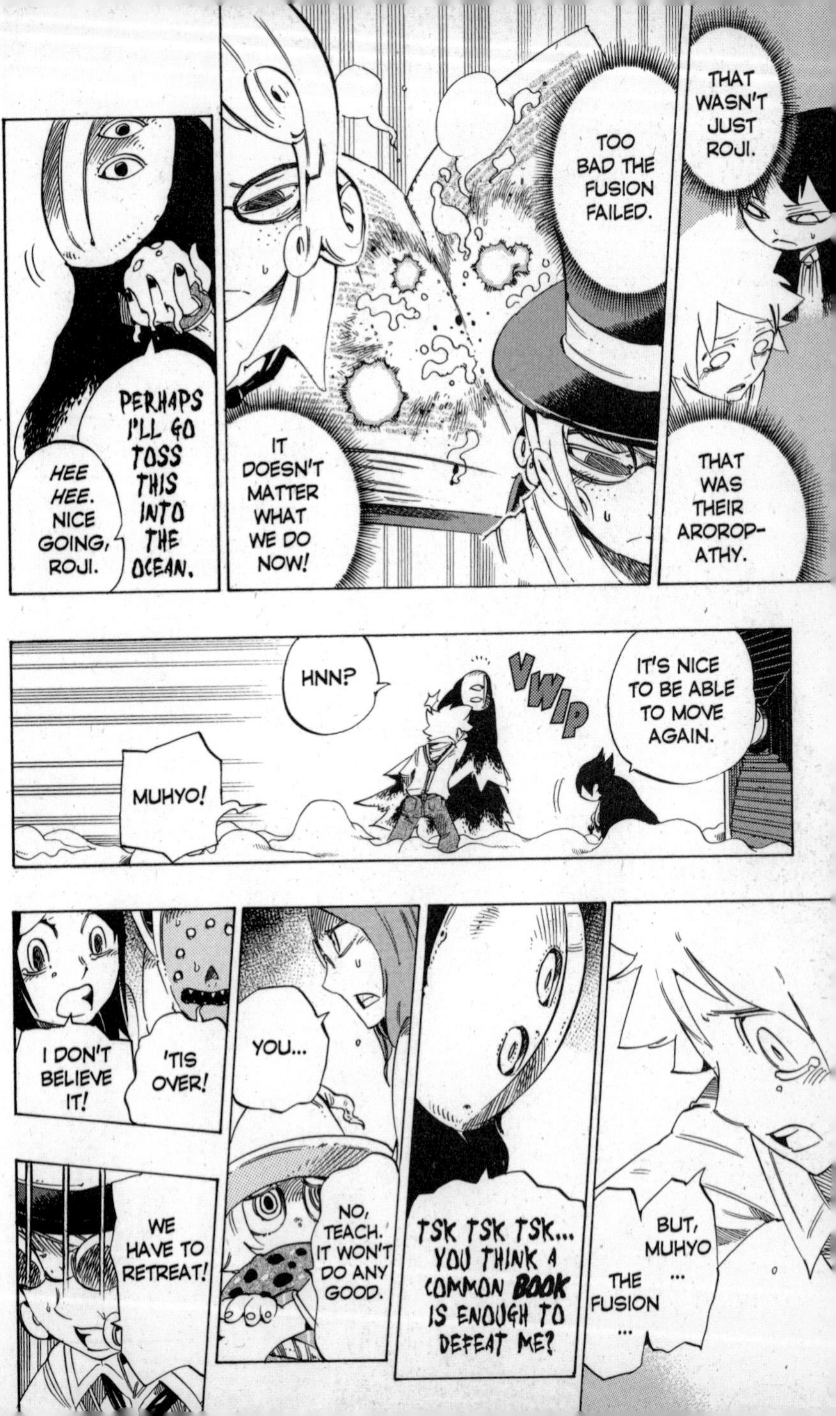
THAT WASN'T JUST ROJI.
THAT WAS THEIR ARAROPATHY.
TOO BAD THE FUSION FAILED.
IT DOESN'T MATTER WHAT WE DO NOW!
PERHAPS I'LL GO TOSS THIS INTO THE OCEAN.
HEE HEE. NICE GOING, ROJI.
IT'S NICE TO BE ABLE TO MOVE AGAIN.
VWIP
HNN?
MUHYO!
BUT, MUHYO...
THE FUSION...
TSK TSK TSK... YOU THINK A COMMON **BOOK** IS ENOUGH TO DEFEAT ME?
YOU...
'TIS OVER!
I DON'T BELIEVE IT!
NO, TEACH. IT WON'T DO ANY GOOD.
WE HAVE TO RETREAT!

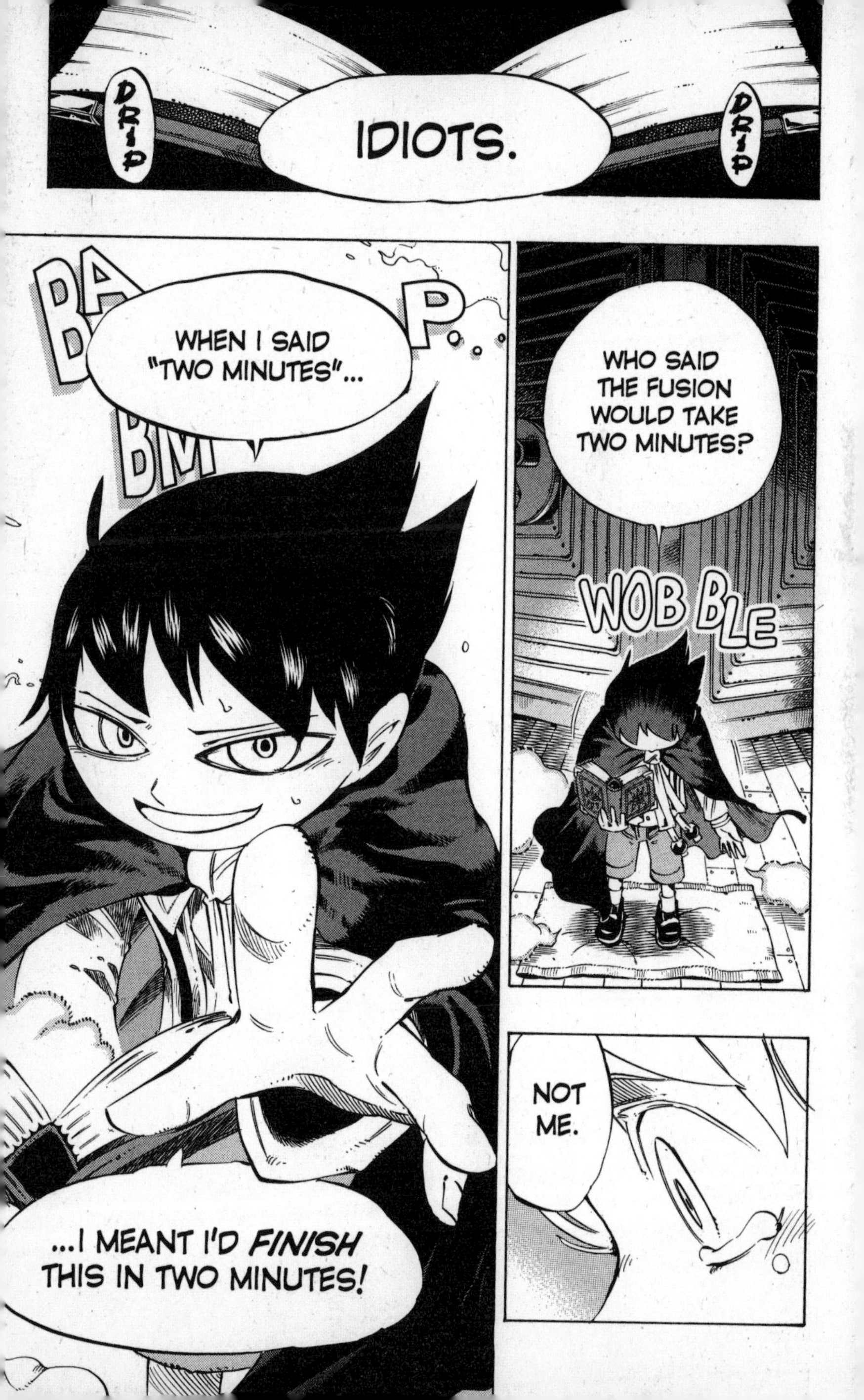
DRIP
IDIOTS.
DRIP
WHO SAID THE FUSION WOULD TAKE TWO MINUTES?
WOBBLE
NOT ME.
BA P
BM
WHEN I SAID "TWO MINUTES"...
...I MEANT I'D *FINISH* THIS IN TWO MINUTES!

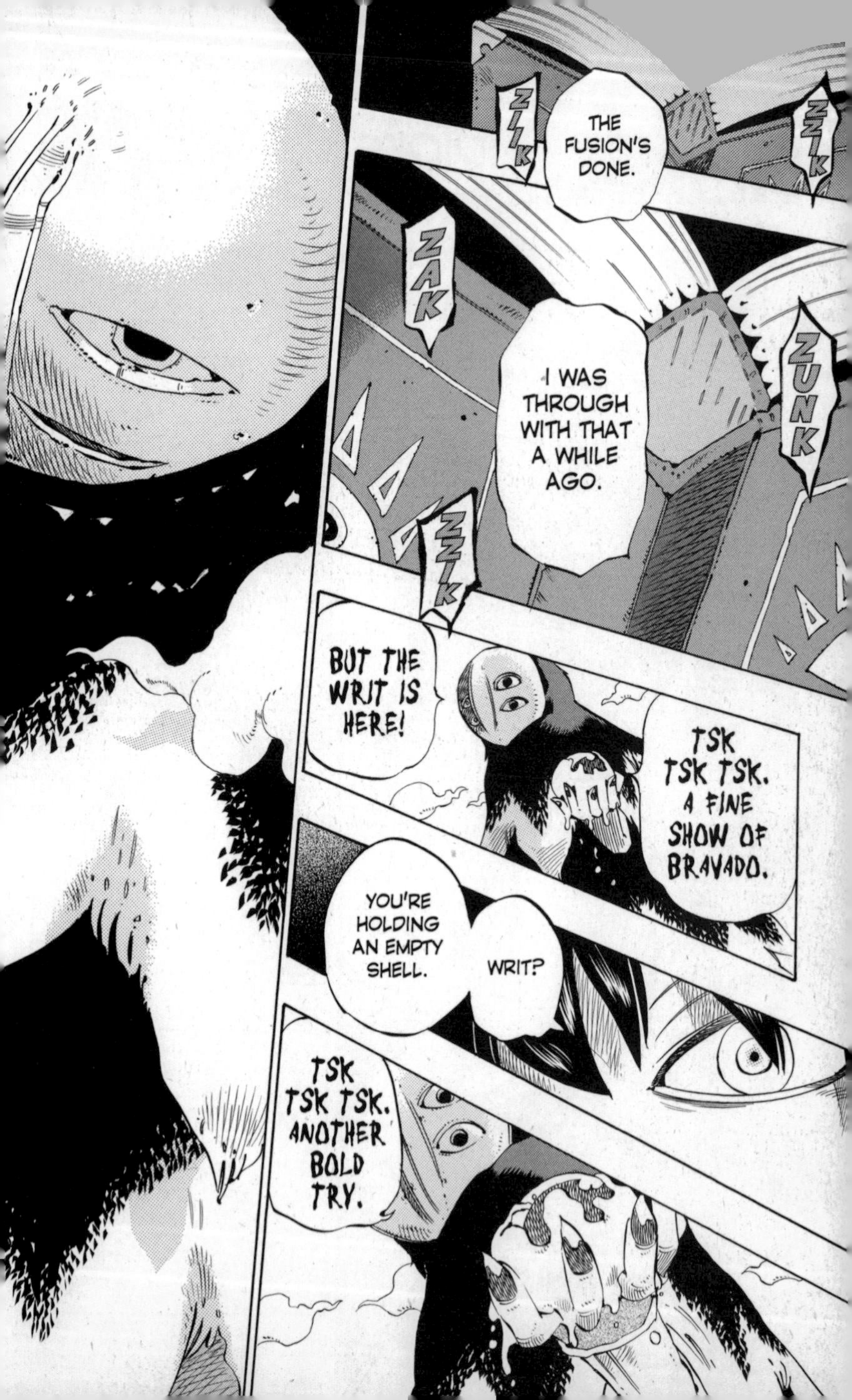
ZZIK
THE FUSION'S DONE.
ZIIK
ZUNK
ZAK
I WAS THROUGH WITH THAT A WHILE AGO.
ZZIK
BUT THE WRIT IS HERE!
TSK TSK TSK. A FINE SHOW OF BRAVADO.
WRIT?
YOU'RE HOLDING AN EMPTY SHELL.
TSK TSK TSK. ANOTHER BOLD TRY.

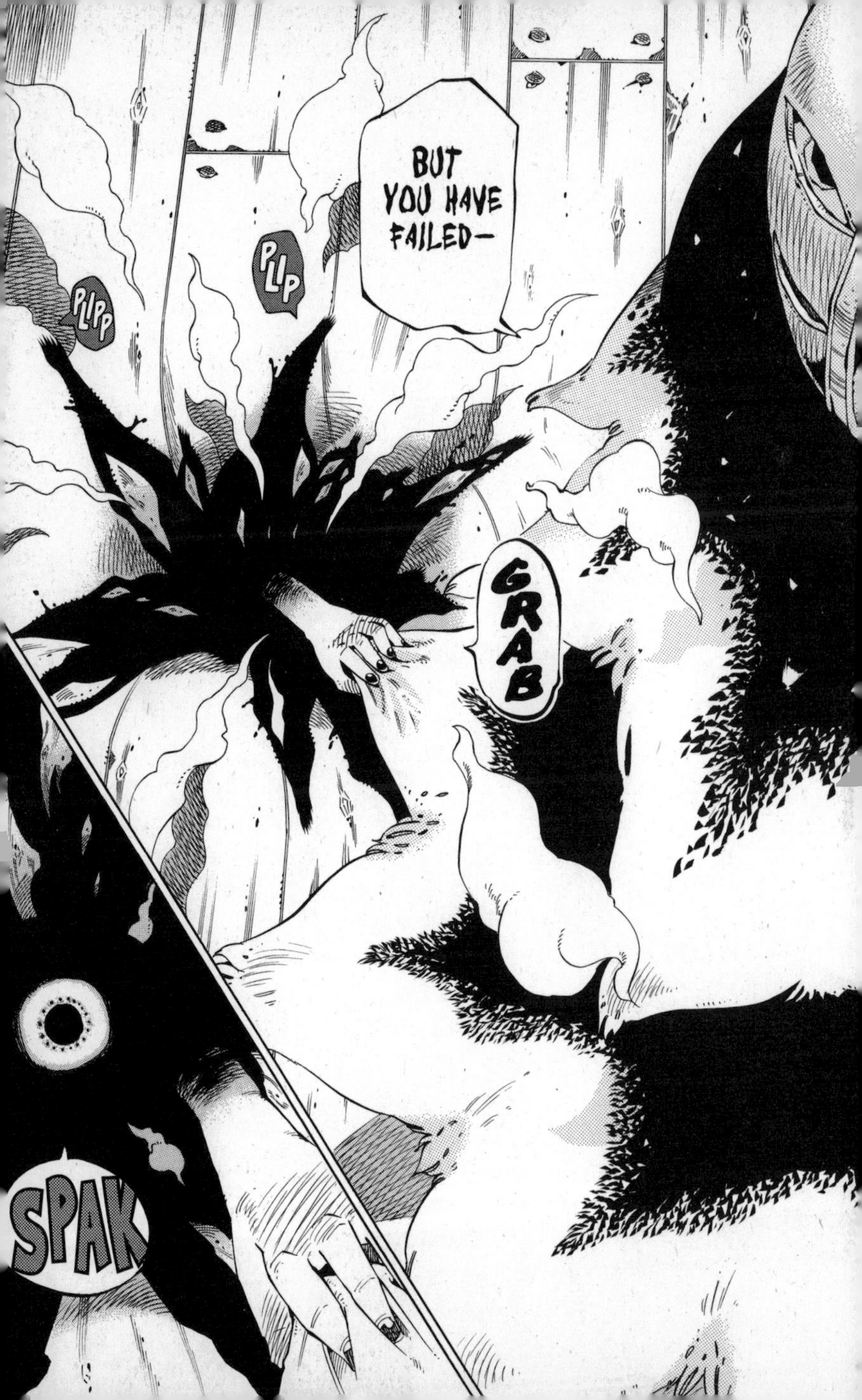
BUT YOU HAVE FAILED—
PLIP
PLIPP
GRAB
SPAK

Muhyo & Roji's
Bureau of Supernatural Investigation
BSI

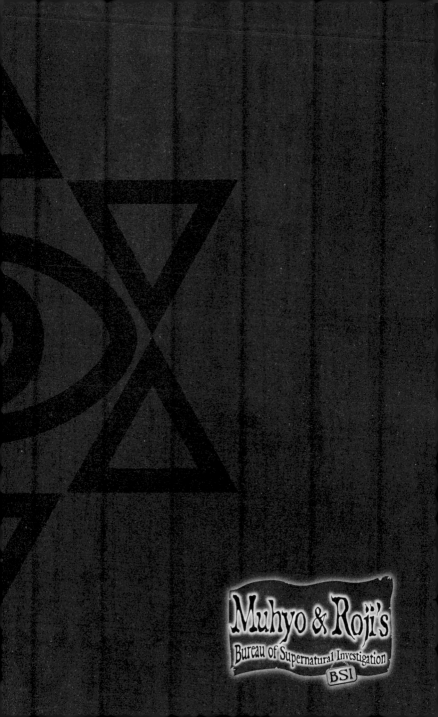

ARTICLE 127
HADES

BY THE LAWS
OF MAGIC,
ARTICLE 13...

...

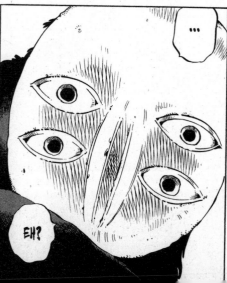

I GET IT
NOW!

...

EH?

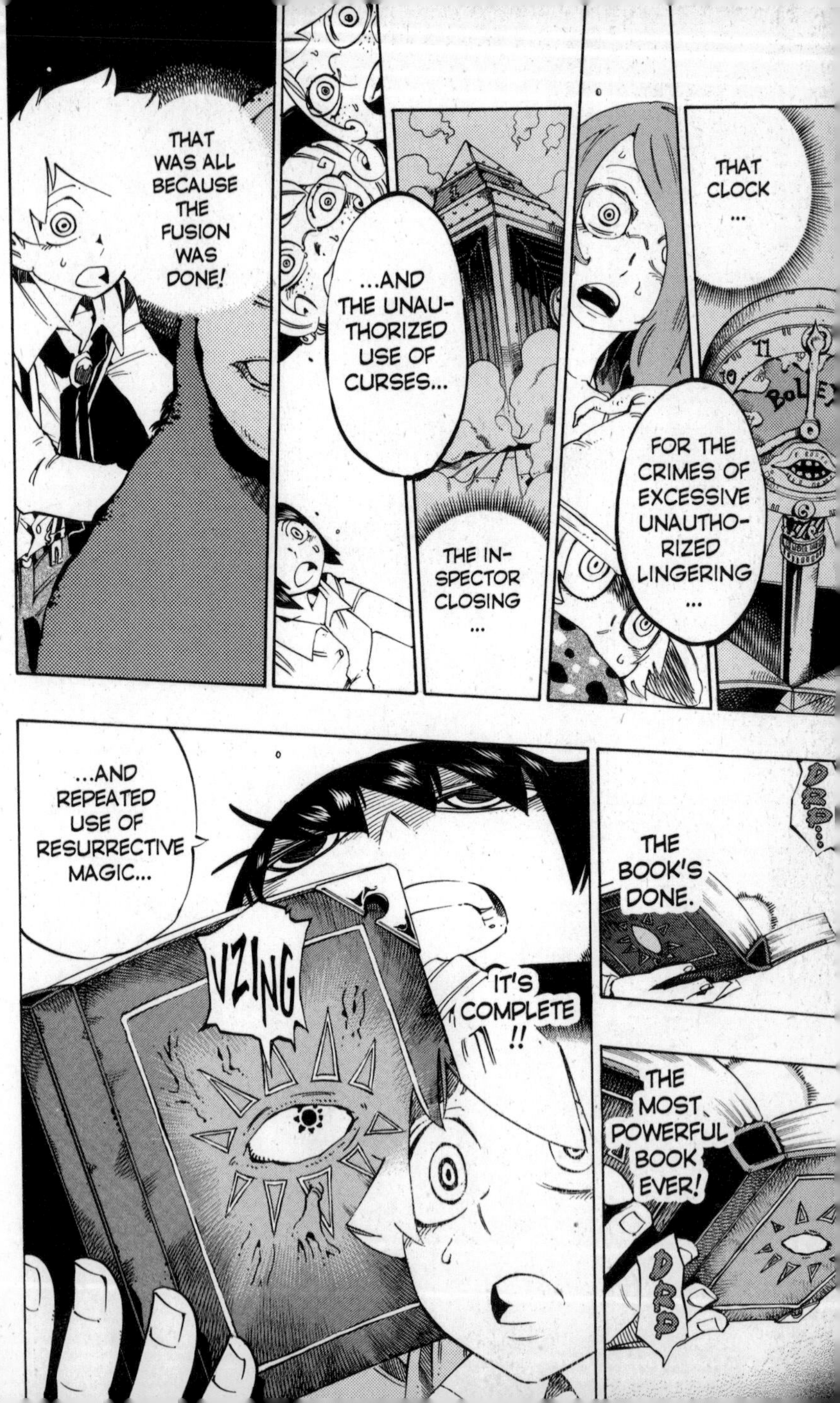
THAT CLOCK ...
FOR THE CRIMES OF EXCESSIVE UNAUTHORIZED LINGERING ...
THE INSPECTOR CLOSING ...
...AND THE UNAUTHORIZED USE OF CURSES...
THAT WAS ALL BECAUSE THE FUSION WAS DONE!
DRP...
THE BOOK'S DONE.
THE MOST POWERFUL BOOK EVER!
DRP
...AND REPEATED USE OF RESURRECTIVE MAGIC...
VZING
IT'S COMPLETE !!

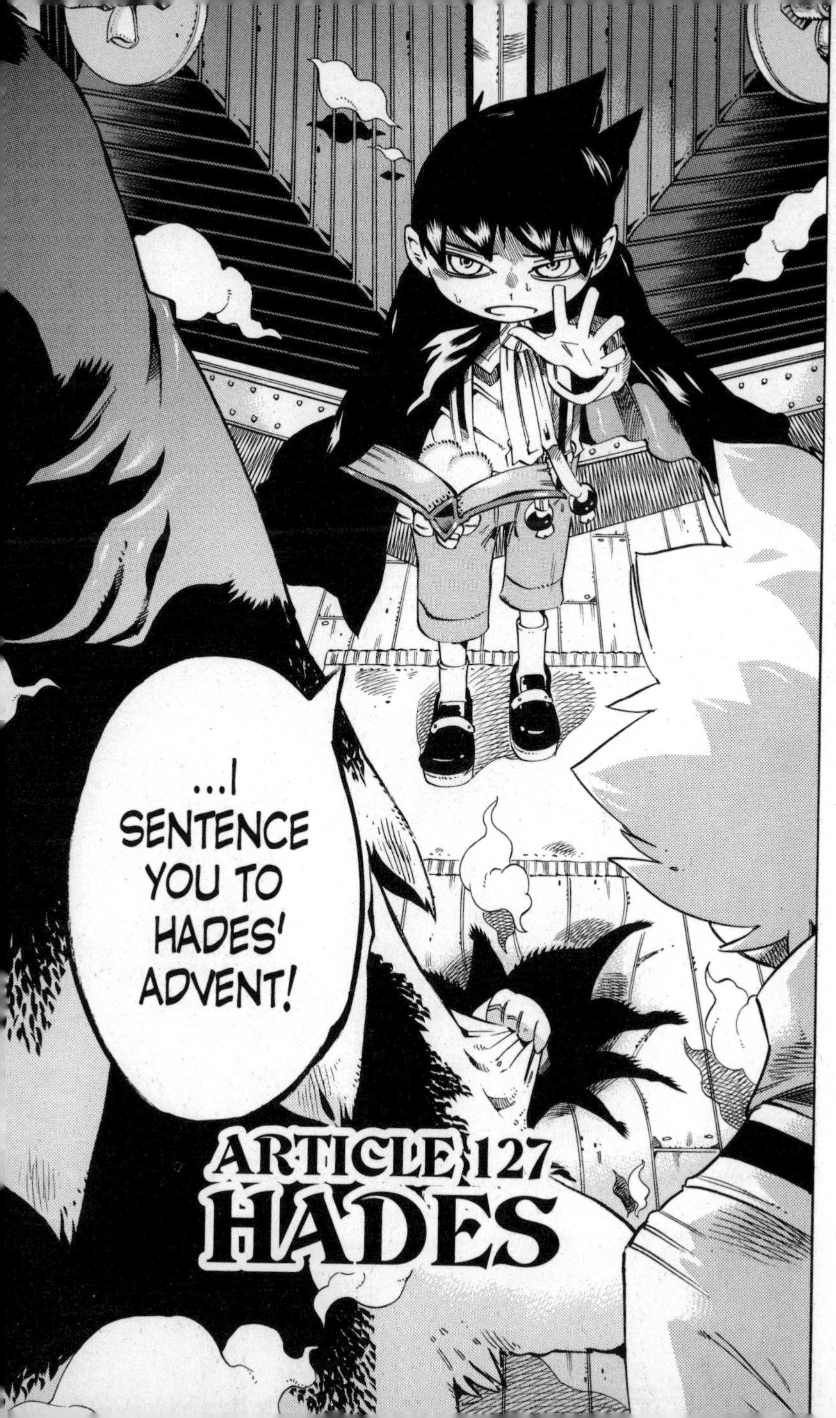
...I SENTENCE YOU TO HADES' ADVENT!
ARTICLE 127
HADES

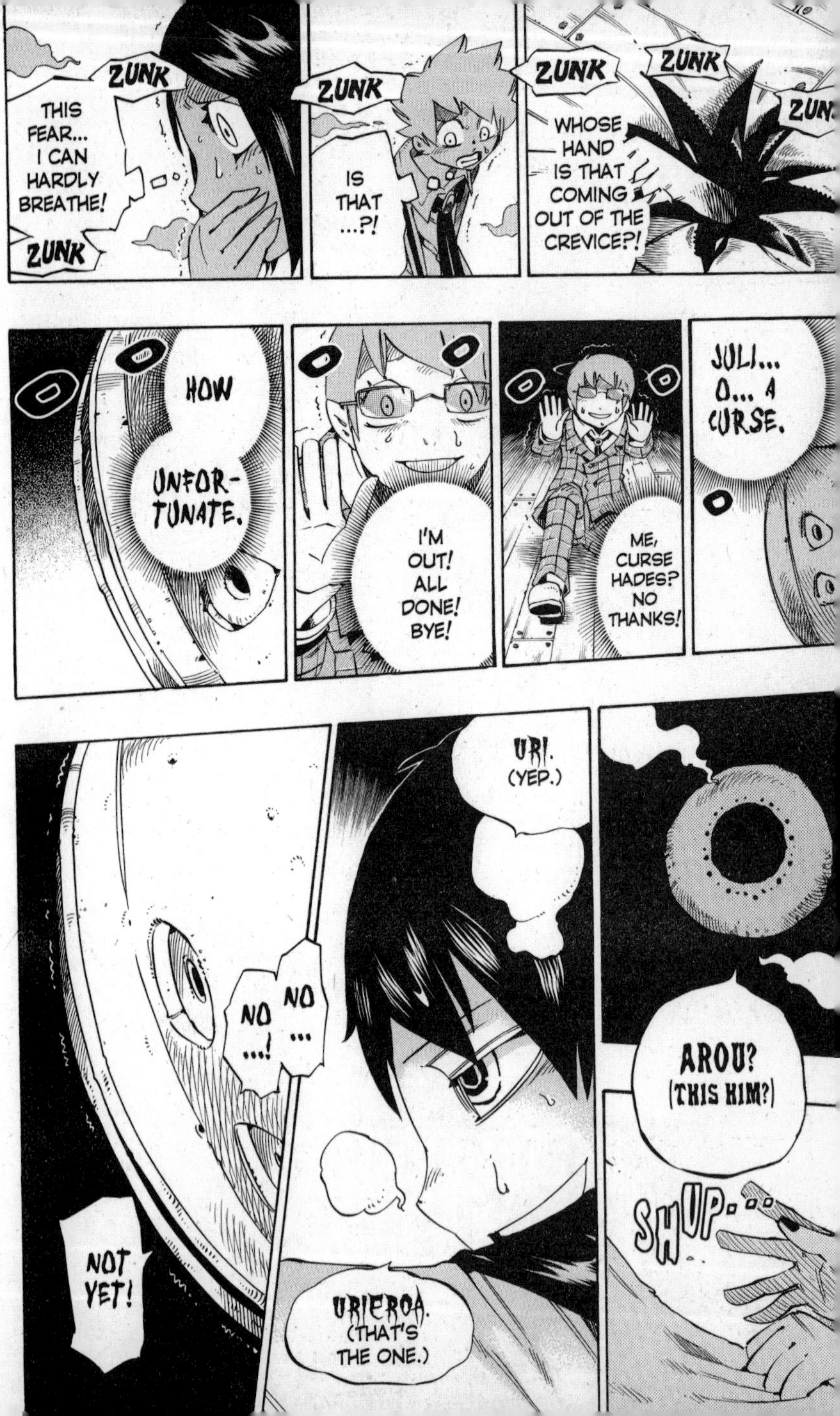
ZUNK
ZUNK
ZUN
WHOSE HAND IS THAT COMING OUT OF THE CREVICE?!
ZUNK
IS THAT ...?!
ZUNK
THIS FEAR... I CAN HARDLY BREATHE!
ZUNK
JULI... O... A CURSE.
ME, CURSE HADES? NO THANKS!
I'M OUT! ALL DONE! BYE!
HOW UNFORTUNATE.
AROU? (THIS HIM?)
SHUP...
URI. (YEP.)
URIEROA. (THAT'S THE ONE.)
NO ...
NO ...!
NOT YET!

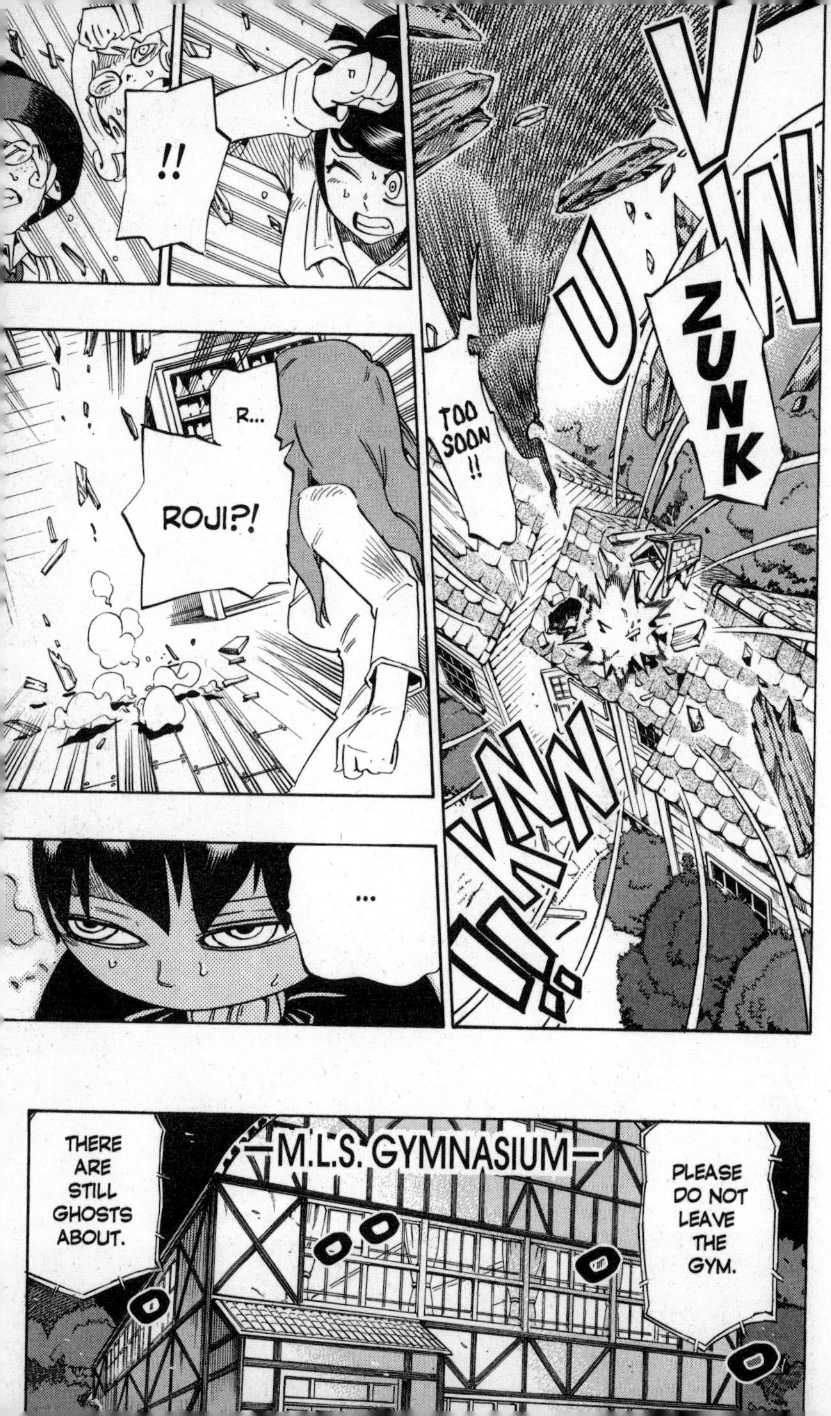
ZUNK
TOO SOON!!
!!
R...
ROJI?!
...
—M.L.S. GYMNASIUM—
PLEASE DO NOT LEAVE THE GYM.
THERE ARE STILL GHOSTS ABOUT.

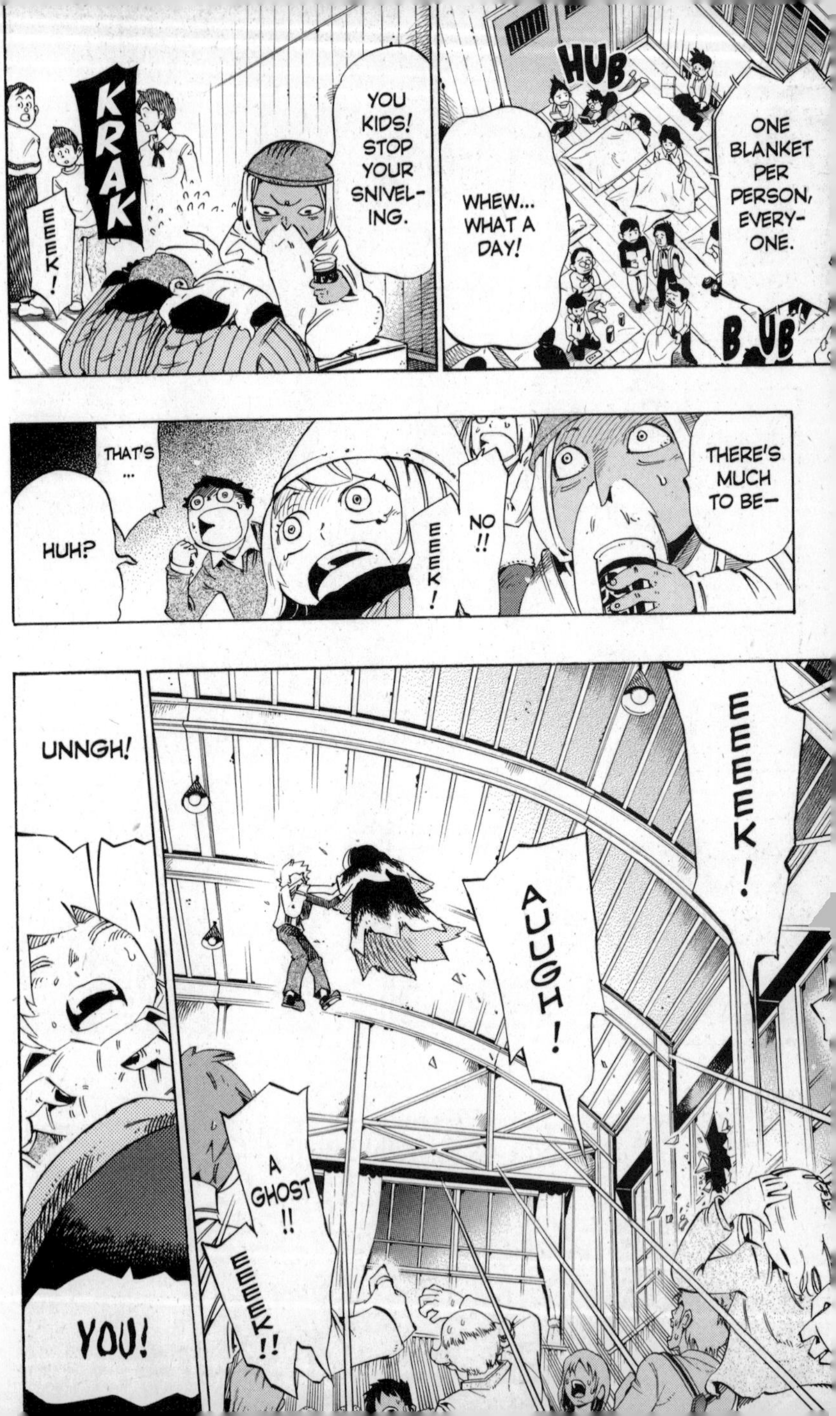
ONE BLANKET PER PERSON, EVERY-ONE.
HUB
B UB
WHEW... WHAT A DAY!
YOU KIDS! STOP YOUR SNIVEL-ING.
KRAK
EEEK!
THERE'S MUCH TO BE—
NO!!
EEEK!
THAT'S ...
HUH?
EEEEK!
AUUGH!
A GHOST!!
EEEEK!!
UNNGH!
YOU!

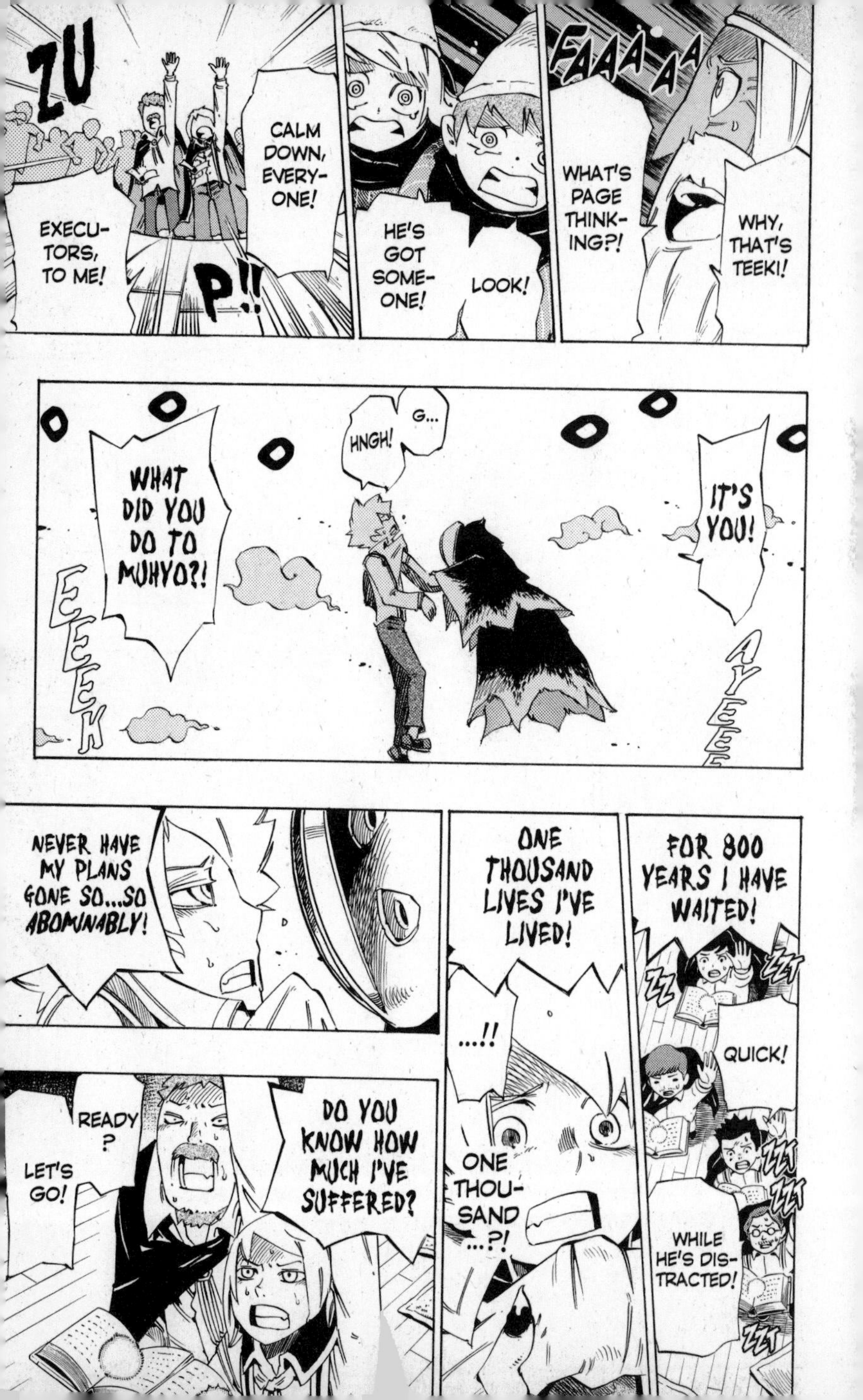
FAAAAA
WHY, THAT'S TEEKI!
WHAT'S PAGE THINKING?!
LOOK!
HE'S GOT SOMEONE!
CALM DOWN, EVERYONE!
ZU
EXECUTORS, TO ME!
P!!
IT'S YOU!
AYEEE
G... HNGH!
WHAT DID YOU DO TO MUHYO?!
EEEEK
FOR 800 YEARS I HAVE WAITED!
QUICK!
WHILE HE'S DISTRACTED!
ONE THOUSAND LIVES I'VE LIVED!
...!!
ONE THOUSAND...?!
NEVER HAVE MY PLANS GONE SO...SO ABOMINABLY!
DO YOU KNOW HOW MUCH I'VE SUFFERED?
READY?
LET'S GO!

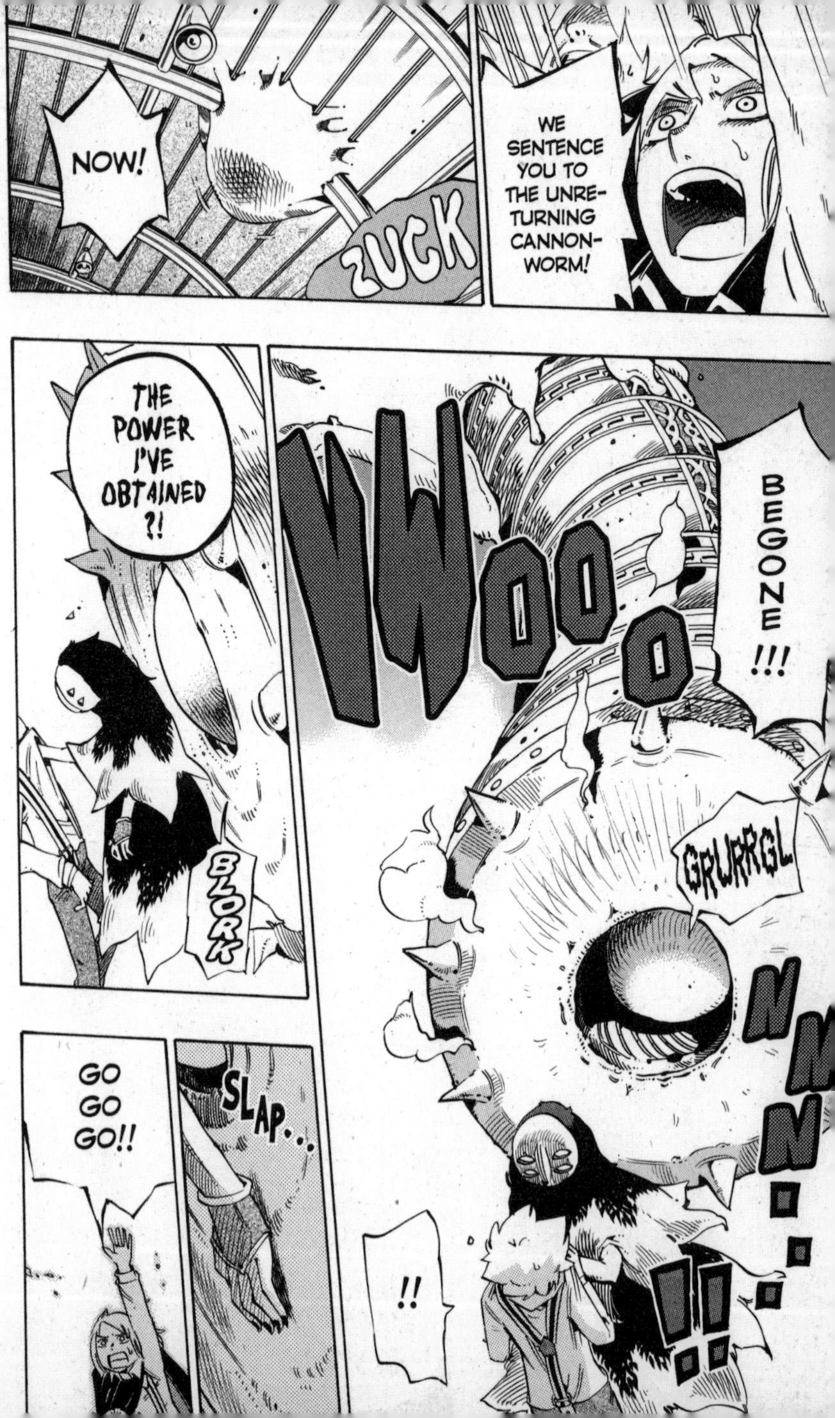
WE SENTENCE YOU TO THE UNRE-TURNING CANNON-WORM!
ZUCK
NOW!
BEGONE!!!
VWOOOO
GRURRGL
NNN...
!!!
!!
THE POWER I'VE OBTAINED?!
BLORK
SLAP...
GO GO GO!!

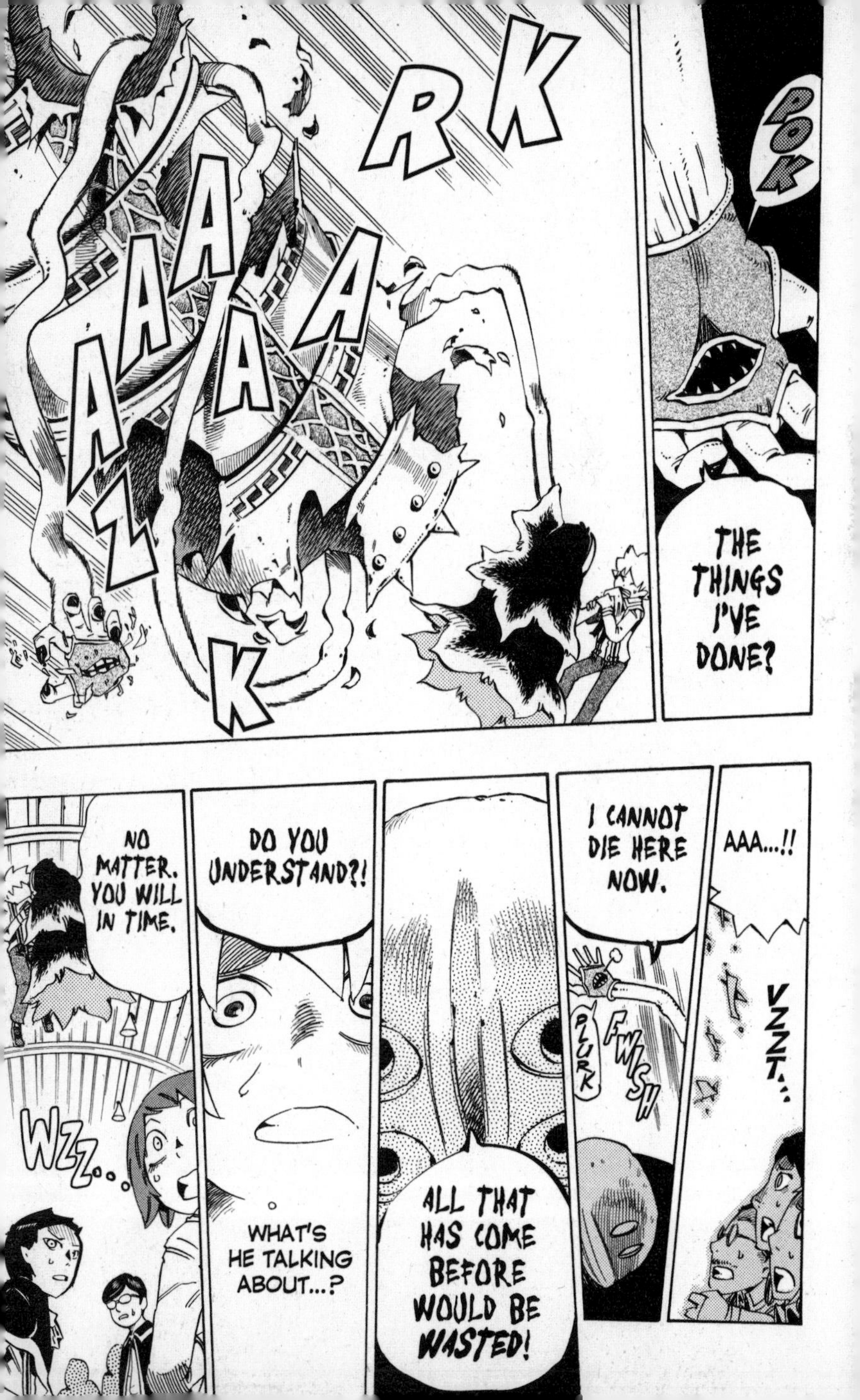
POK
THE THINGS I'VE DONE?
ZAAAAARK
K
AAA...!!
VZZT...
I CANNOT DIE HERE NOW.
PLURK
FWISH
ALL THAT HAS COME BEFORE WOULD BE WASTED!
DO YOU UNDERSTAND?!
WHAT'S HE TALKING ABOUT...?
NO MATTER. YOU WILL IN TIME.
WZZ...

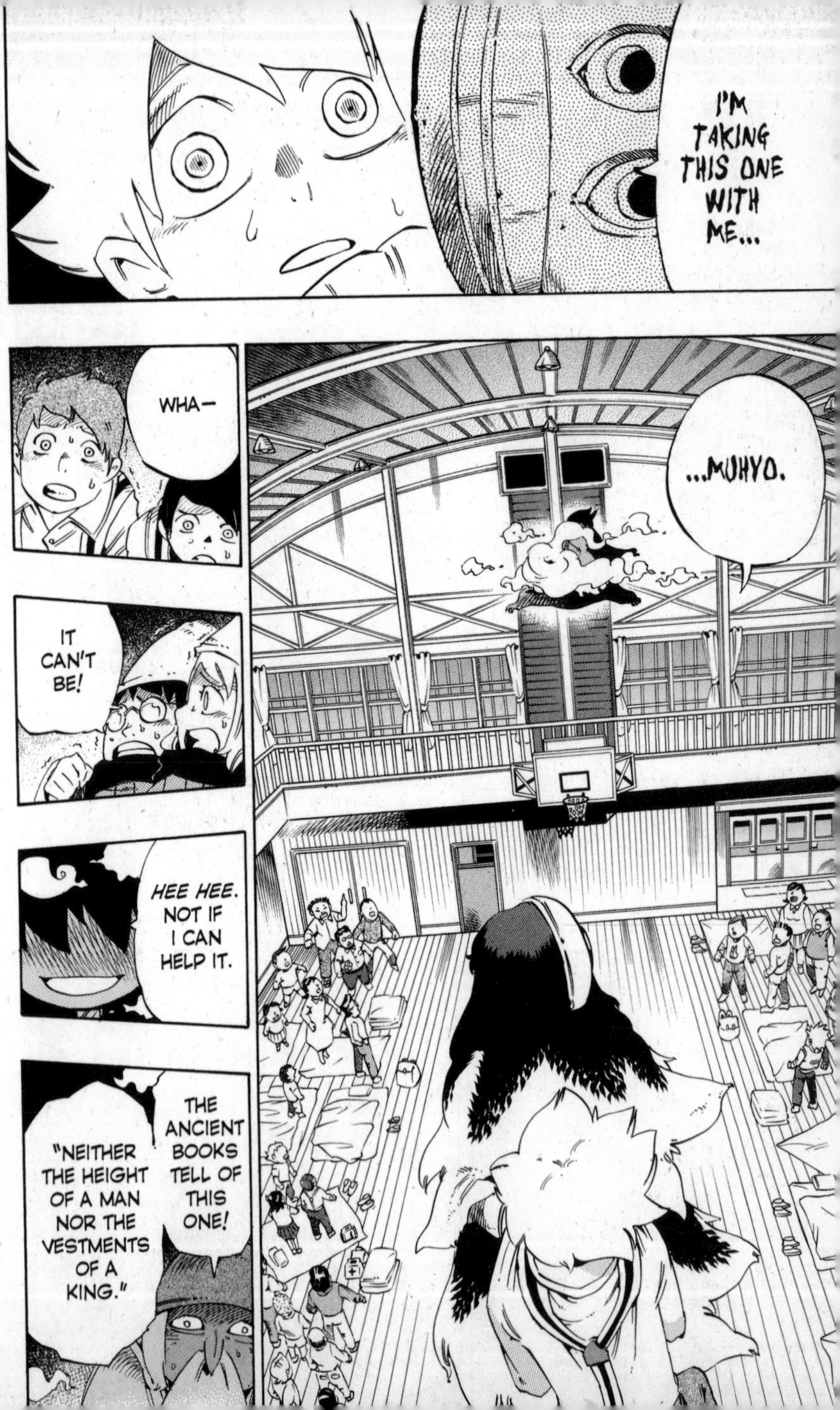
I'M TAKING THIS ONE WITH ME...
...MUHYO.
WHA—
IT CAN'T BE!
HEE HEE. NOT IF I CAN HELP IT.
THE ANCIENT BOOKS TELL OF THIS ONE!
"NEITHER THE HEIGHT OF A MAN NOR THE VESTMENTS OF A KING."

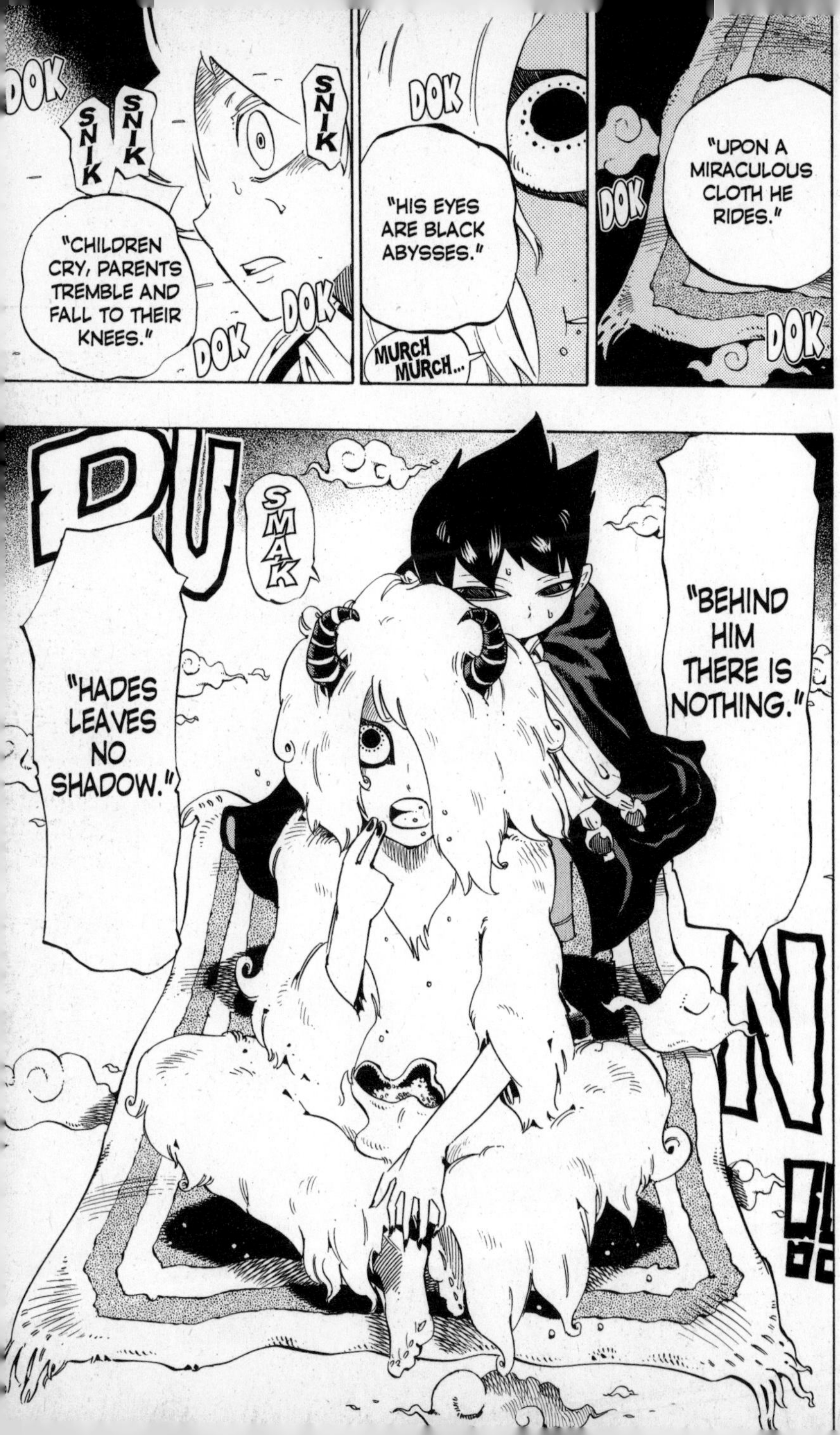
"UPON A MIRACULOUS CLOTH HE RIDES."
DOK
DOK
DOK
"HIS EYES ARE BLACK ABYSSES."
MURCH MURCH...
SNIK
DOK
SNIK
SNIK
"CHILDREN CRY, PARENTS TREMBLE AND FALL TO THEIR KNEES."
DOK
DOK
"BEHIND HIM THERE IS NOTHING."
N
DU
SMAK
"HADES LEAVES NO SHADOW."

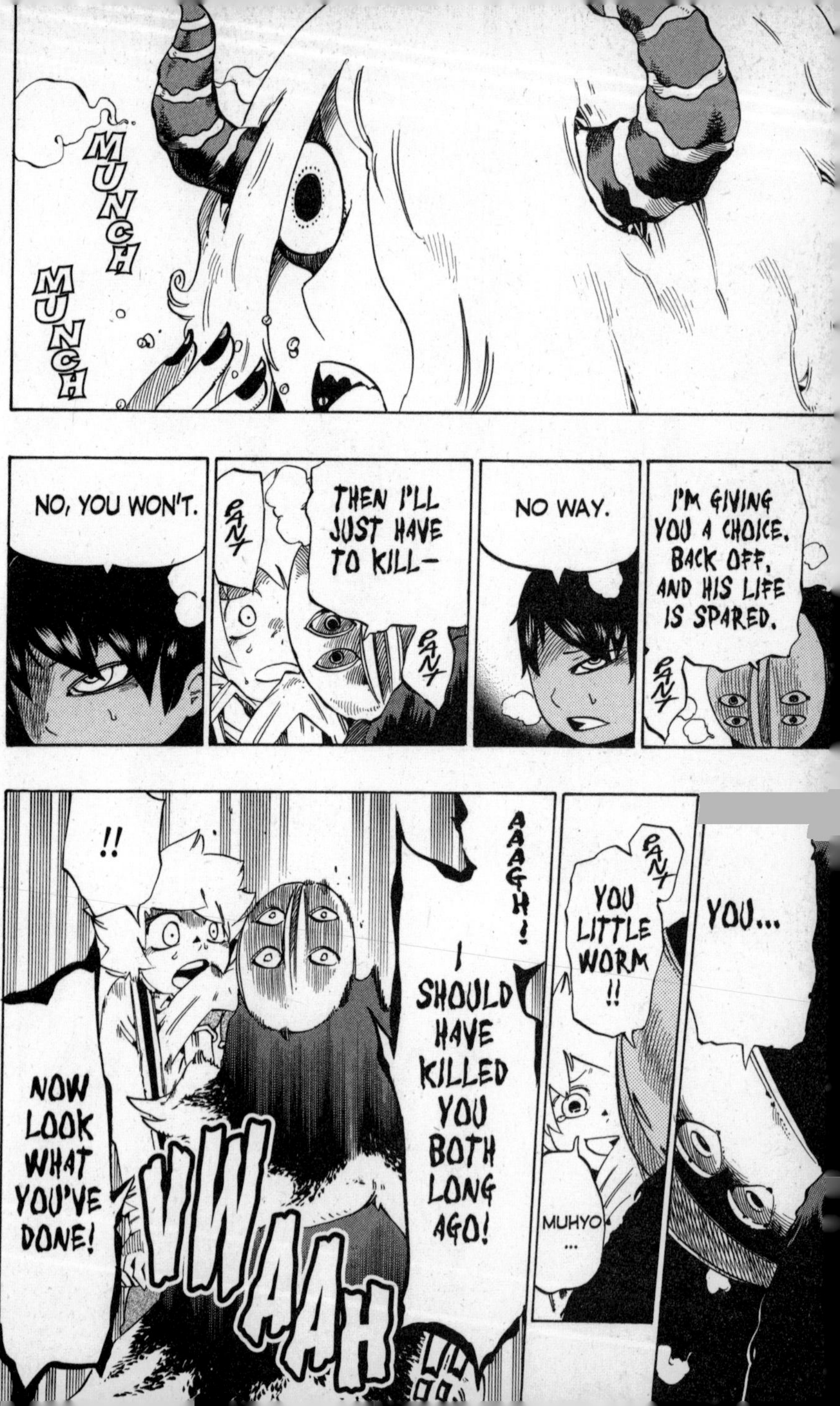
MUNCH
MUNCH
PANT
I'M GIVING YOU A CHOICE. BACK OFF, AND HIS LIFE IS SPARED.
NO WAY.
PANT
THEN I'LL JUST HAVE TO KILL—
PANT
NO, YOU WON'T.
YOU...
PANT
YOU LITTLE WORM!!
MUHYO...
AAAGH!
I SHOULD HAVE KILLED YOU BOTH LONG AGO!
!!
NOW LOOK WHAT YOU'VE DONE!
VWAAH

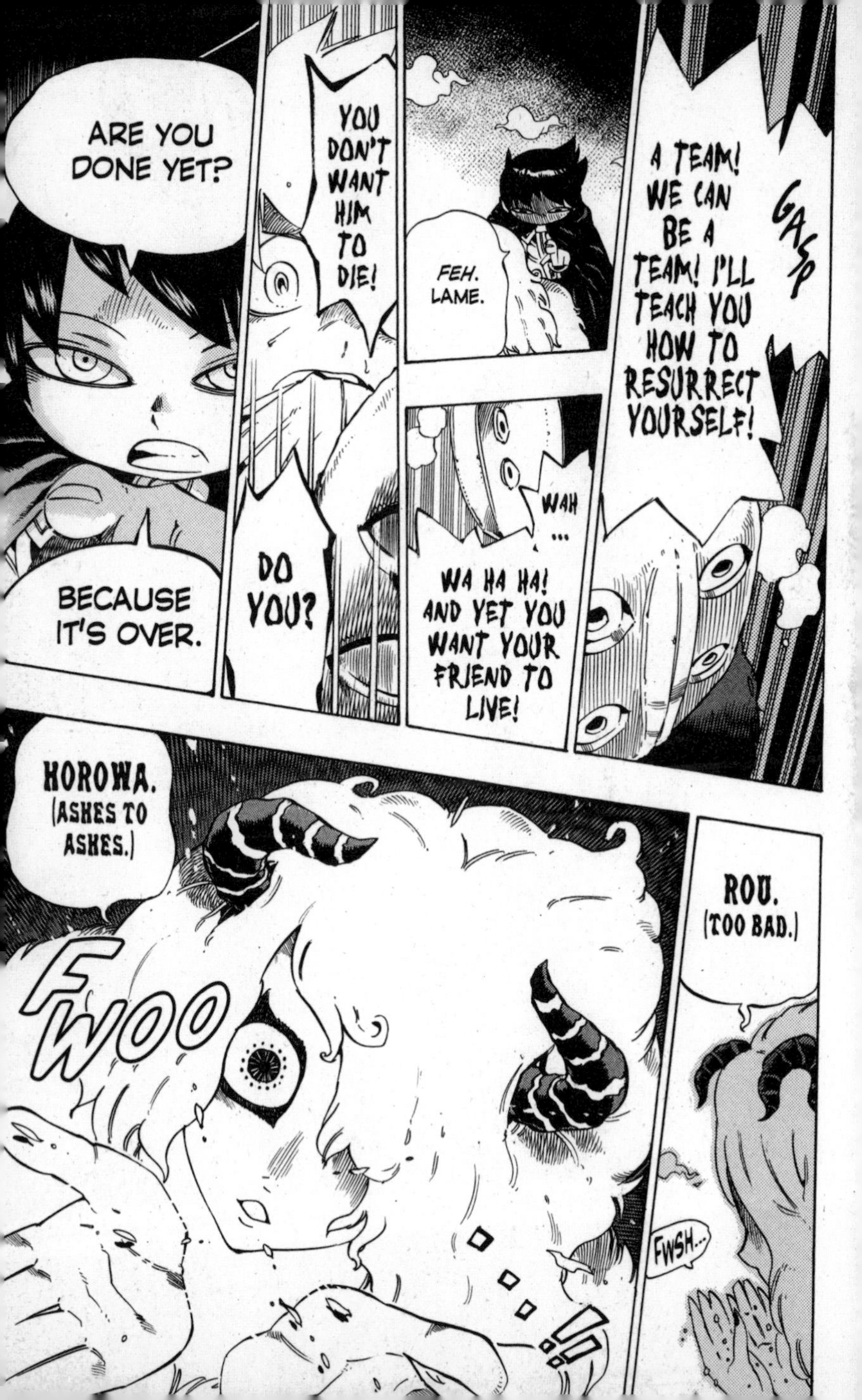
A TEAM! WE CAN BE A TEAM! I'LL TEACH YOU HOW TO RESURRECT YOURSELF!
GASP
FEH. LAME.
WAH...
WA HA HA! AND YET YOU WANT YOUR FRIEND TO LIVE!
YOU DON'T WANT HIM TO DIE!
DO YOU?
ARE YOU DONE YET?
BECAUSE IT'S OVER.
ROU. (TOO BAD.)
FWSH...
HOROWA. (ASHES TO ASHES.)
FWOO

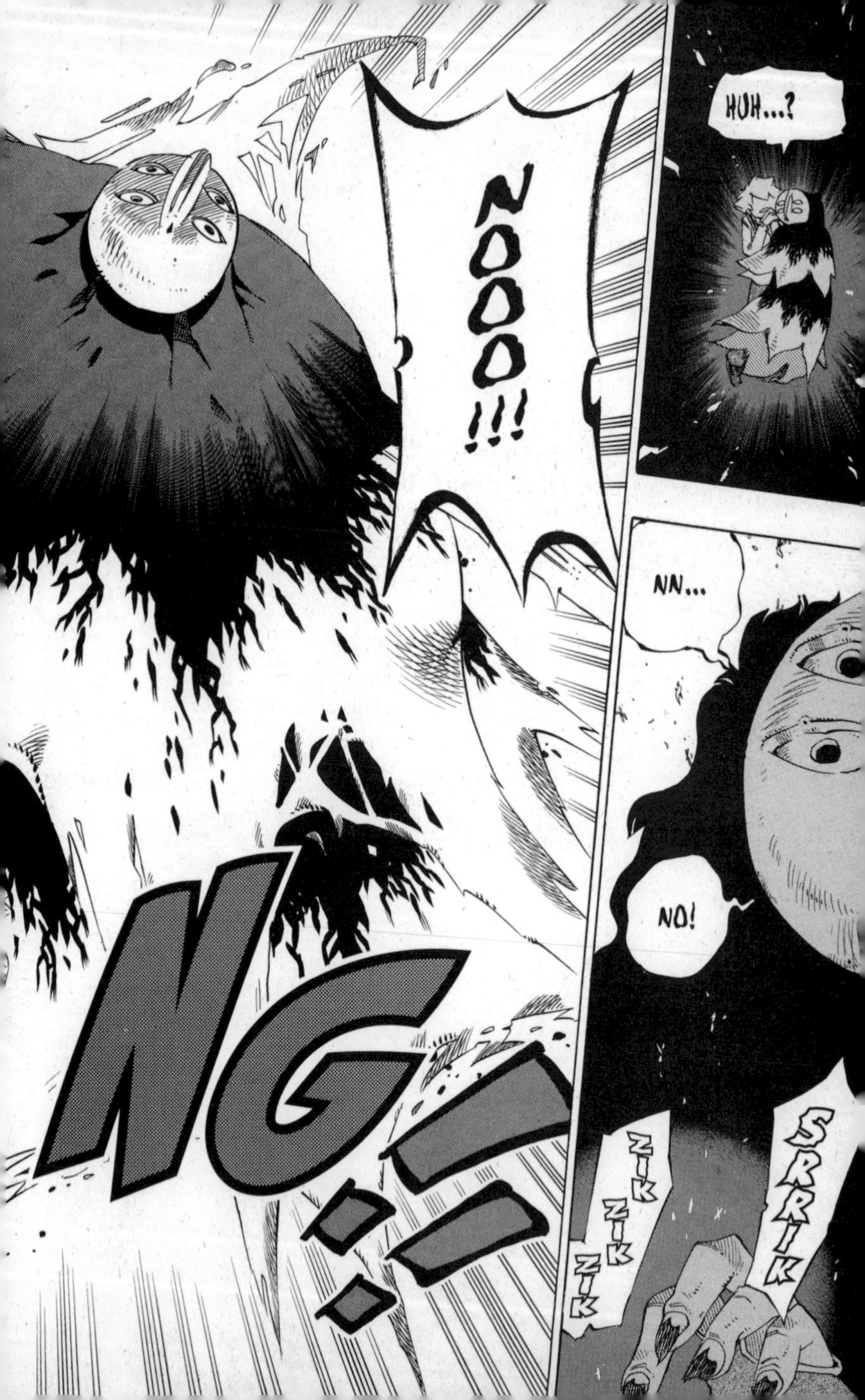
HUH...?
NN...
NO!
SRRIK
ZIK ZIK ZIK
NOOO!!!
NG!!

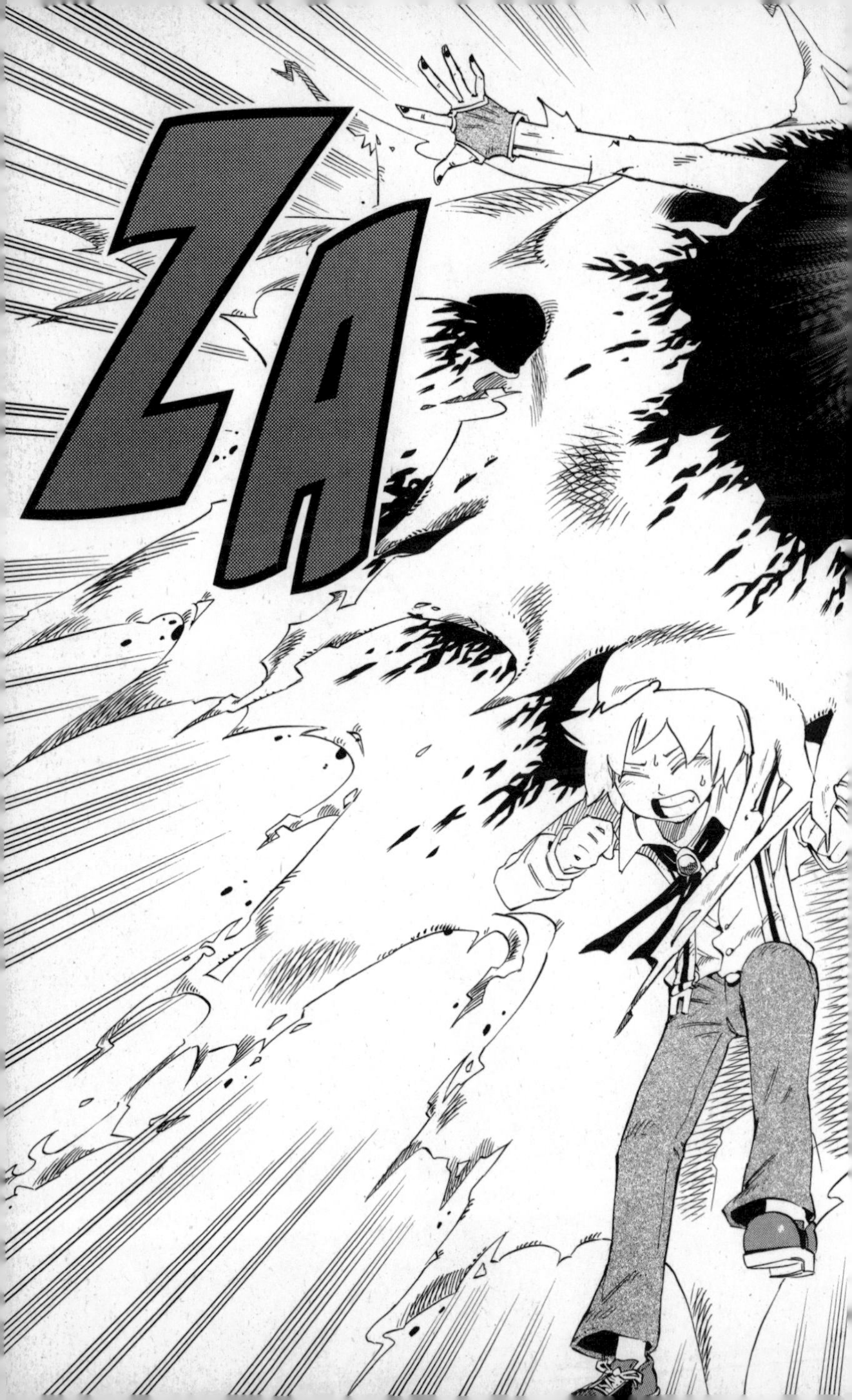
ZA

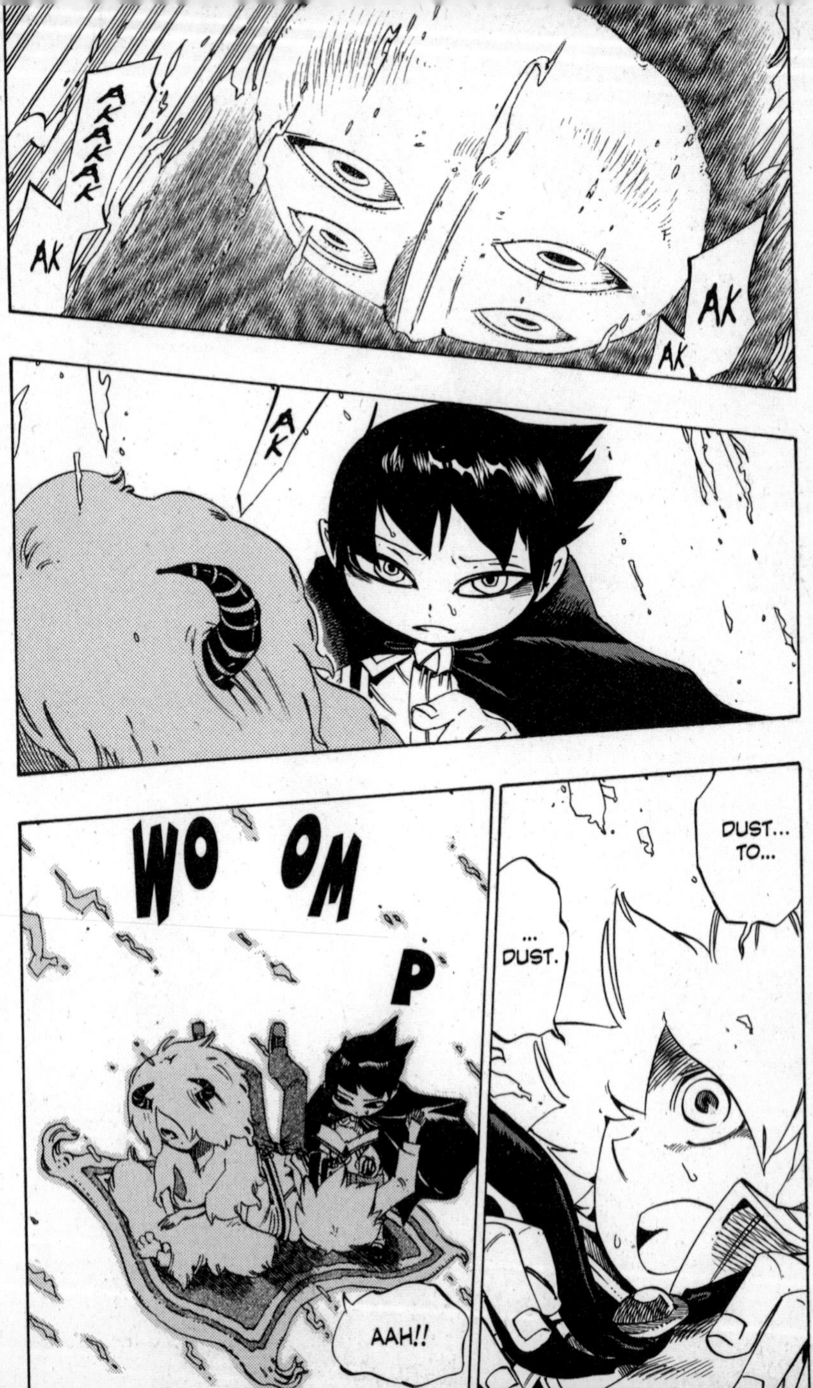
AKAKAK
AK
AK
AK
AK
DUST... TO...
... DUST.
WOOMP
AAH!!

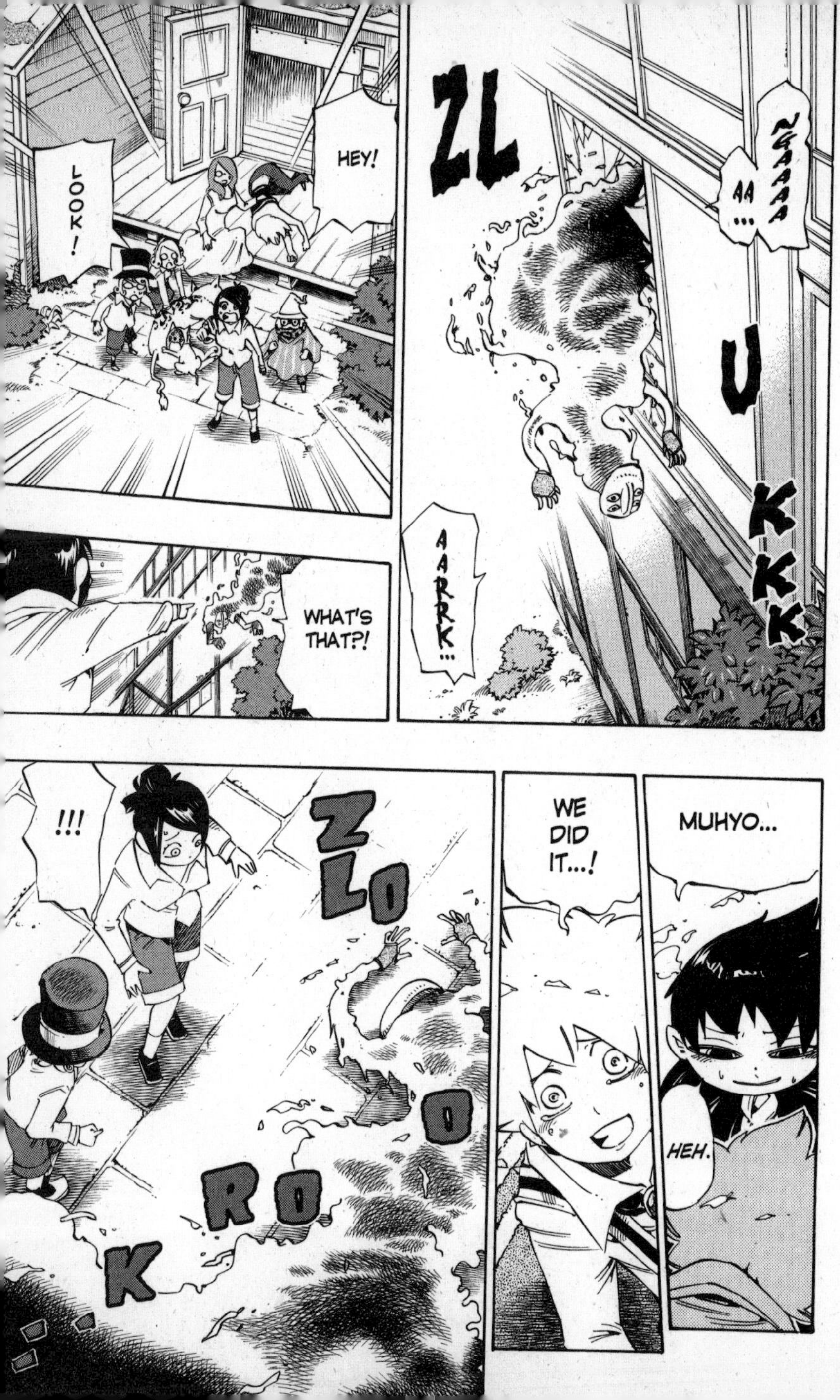
NGAAAAA AA...
ZLUKKKK
AARRRK...
HEY!
LOOK!
WHAT'S THAT?!
MUHYO...
HEH.
WE DID IT...!
ZLOOROROK
!!!

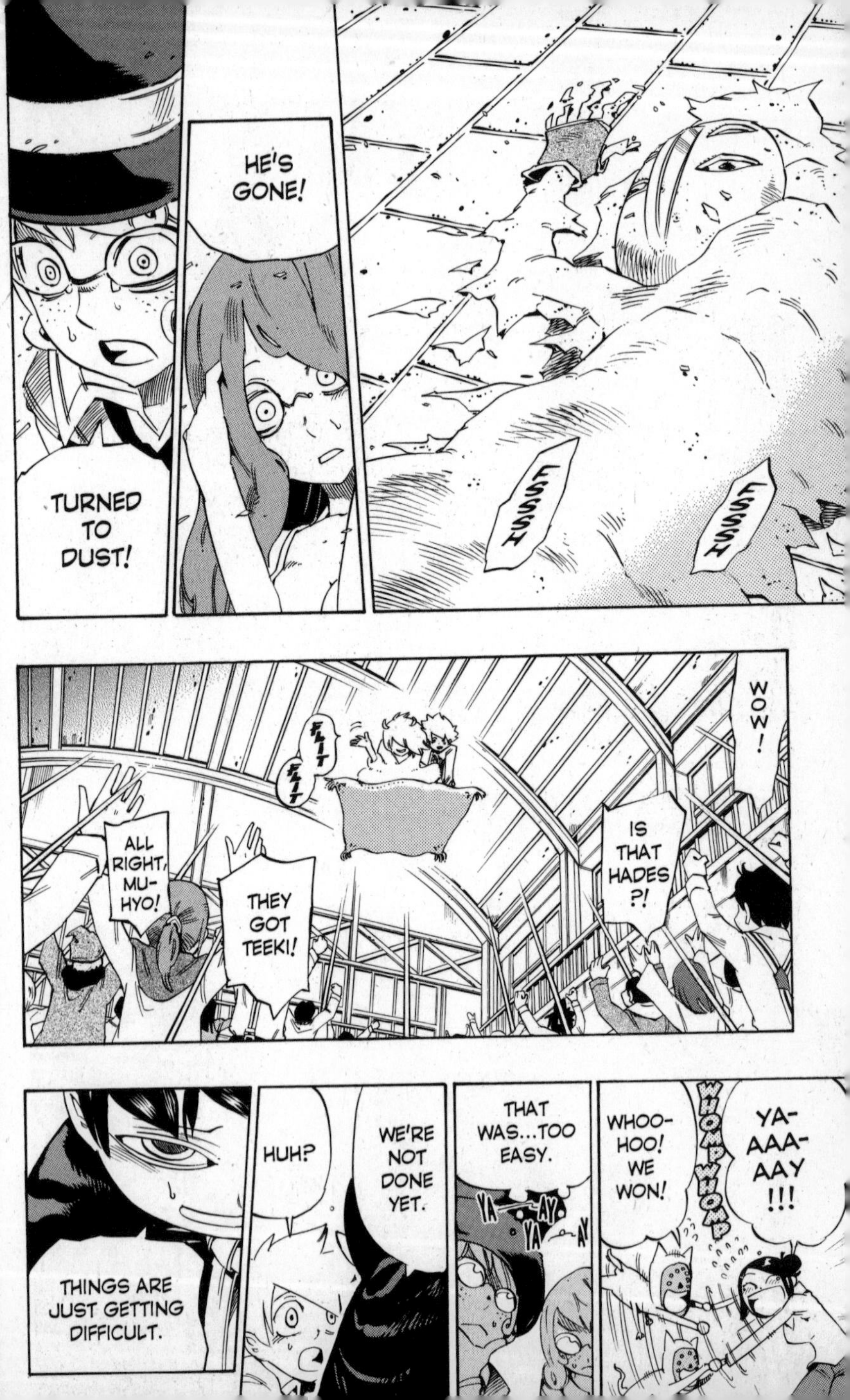
FSSSH
FSSSH
HE'S GONE!
TURNED TO DUST!
WOW!
IS THAT HADES?!
FLIT
FLIT
THEY GOT TEEKI!
ALL RIGHT, MU-HYO!
YA-AAA-AAY!!!
WHOMP WHOMP
WHOO-HOO! WE WON!
THAT WAS...TOO EASY.
YA-AY
YA-AY
WE'RE NOT DONE YET.
HUH?
THINGS ARE JUST GETTING DIFFICULT.

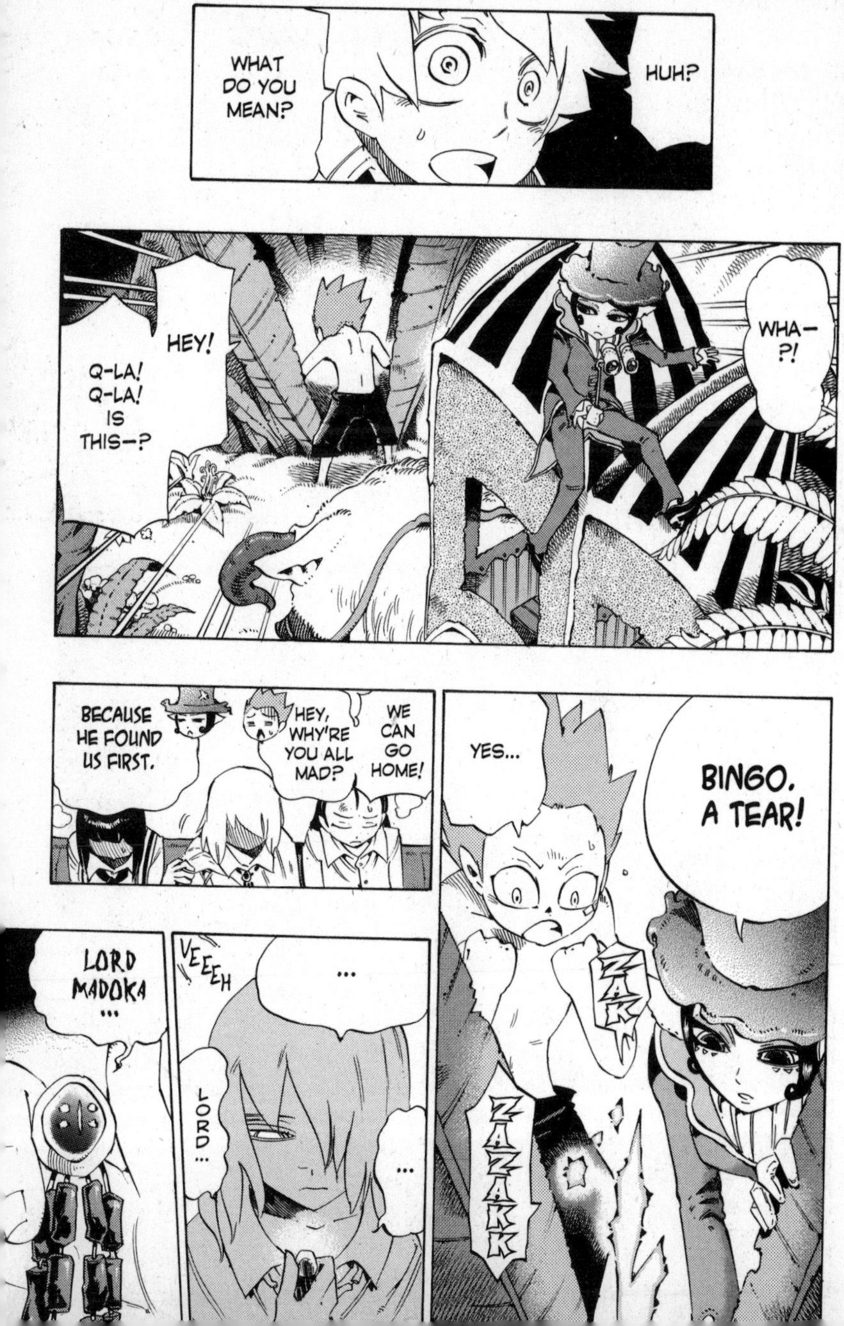
HUH?
WHAT DO YOU MEAN?
WHA--?!
HEY!
Q-LA! Q-LA! IS THIS--?
BINGO. A TEAR!
YES...
ZAK
ZAZAKK
WE CAN GO HOME!
HEY, WHY'RE YOU ALL MAD?
BECAUSE HE FOUND US FIRST.
...
VEEEH
LORD...
...
LORD MADOKA...

Muhyo & Roji's
Bureau of Supernatural Investigation
BSI

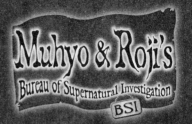

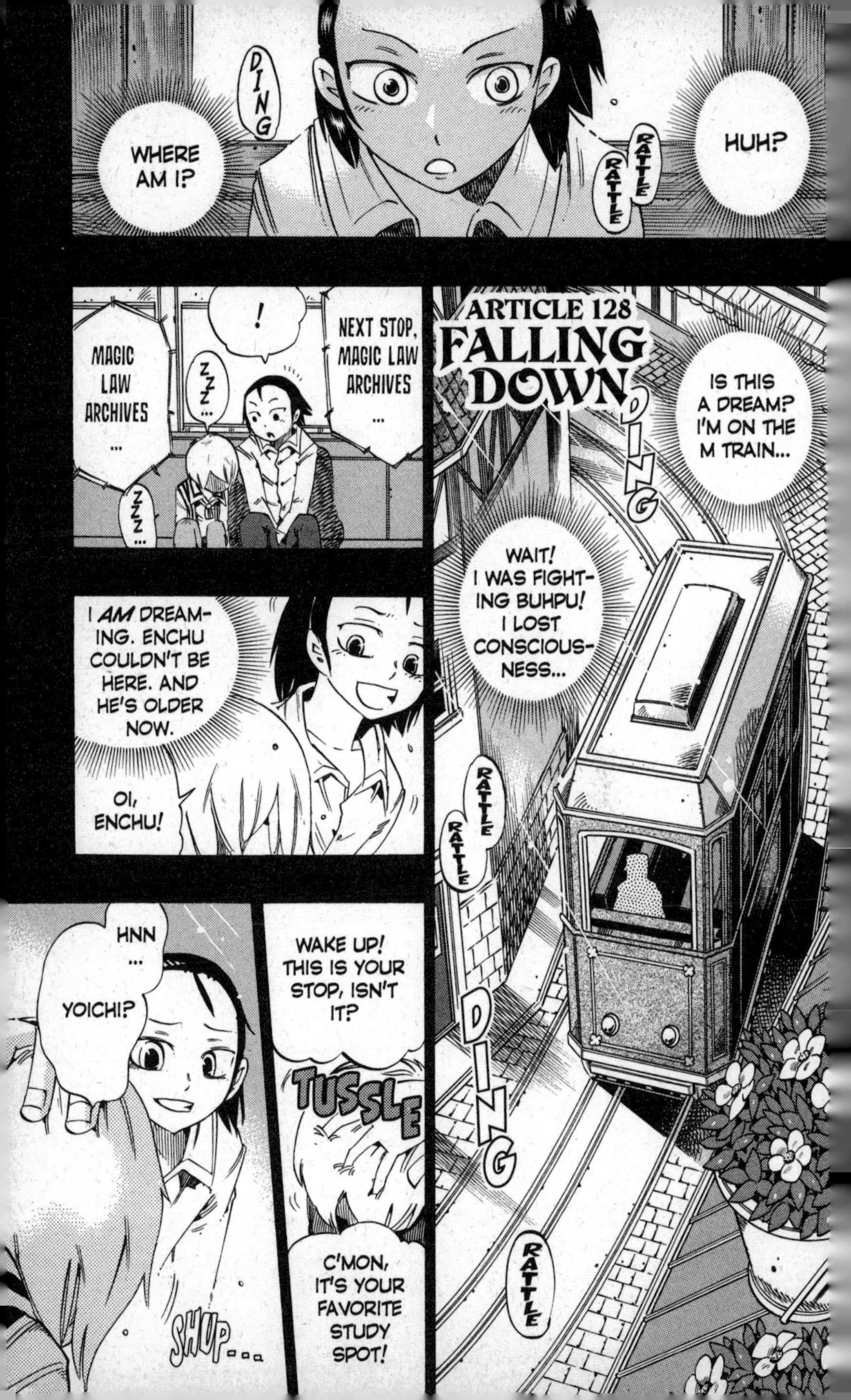
HUH?
RATTLE
RATTLE
DING
WHERE AM I?
ARTICLE 128
FALLING DOWN
IS THIS A DREAM? I'M ON THE M TRAIN...
DING
WAIT! I WAS FIGHT-ING BUHPU! I LOST CONSCIOUS-NESS...
RATTLE
RATTLE
DING
RATTLE
NEXT STOP, MAGIC LAW ARCHIVES ...
!
ZZZ ...
MAGIC LAW ARCHIVES ...
ZZZ ...
I AM DREAM-ING. ENCHU COULDN'T BE HERE. AND HE'S OLDER NOW.
OI, ENCHU!
WAKE UP! THIS IS YOUR STOP, ISN'T IT?
TUSSLE
C'MON, IT'S YOUR FAVORITE STUDY SPOT!
HNN ...
YOICHI?
SHUP...

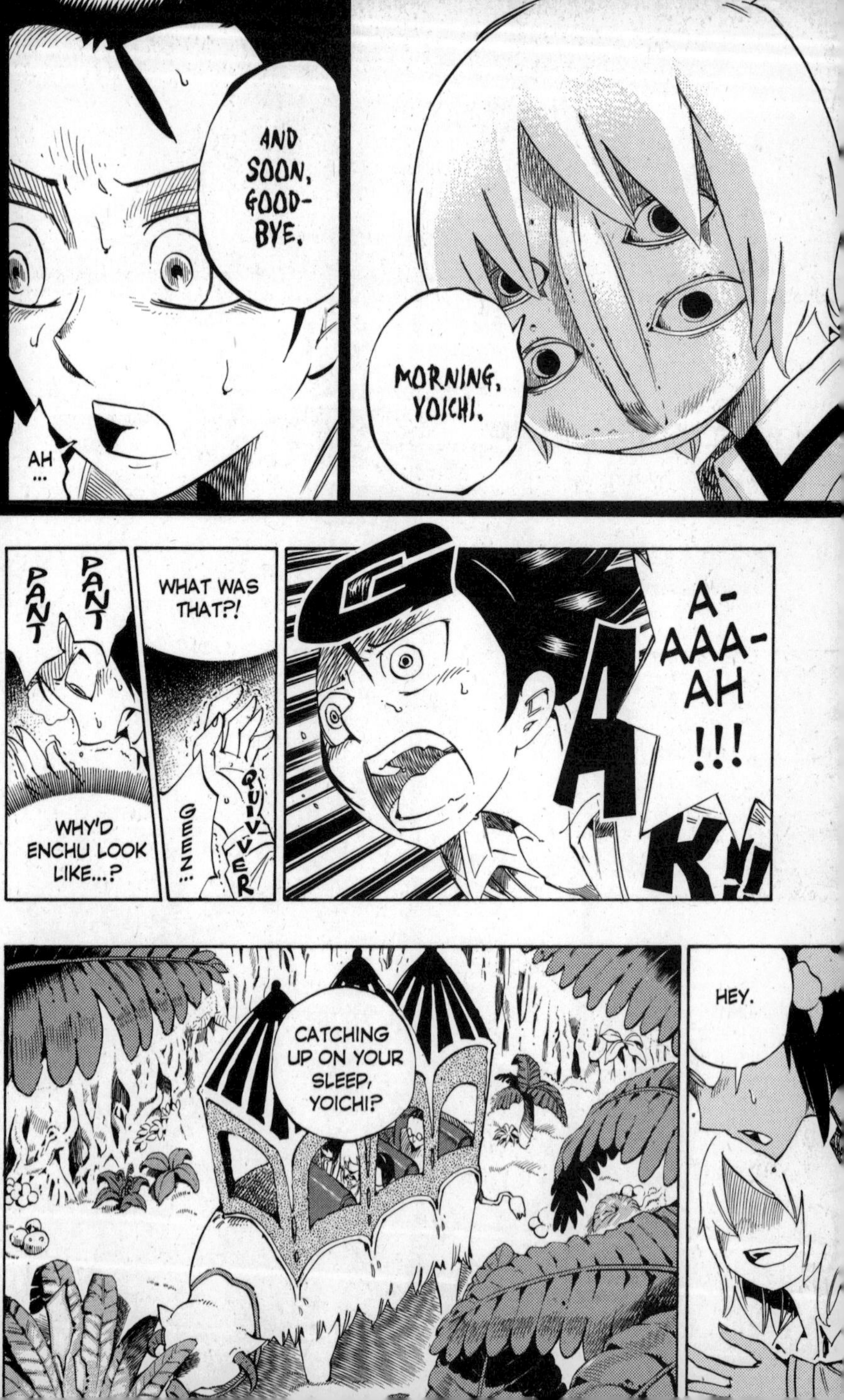
MORNING, YOICHI.
AND SOON, GOOD-BYE.
AH ...
A-AAAA-AH!!!
GAK!!
WHAT WAS THAT?!
QUIVVER
GEEZ...
PANT
PANT
WHY'D ENCHU LOOK LIKE...?
HEY.
CATCHING UP ON YOUR SLEEP, YOICHI?

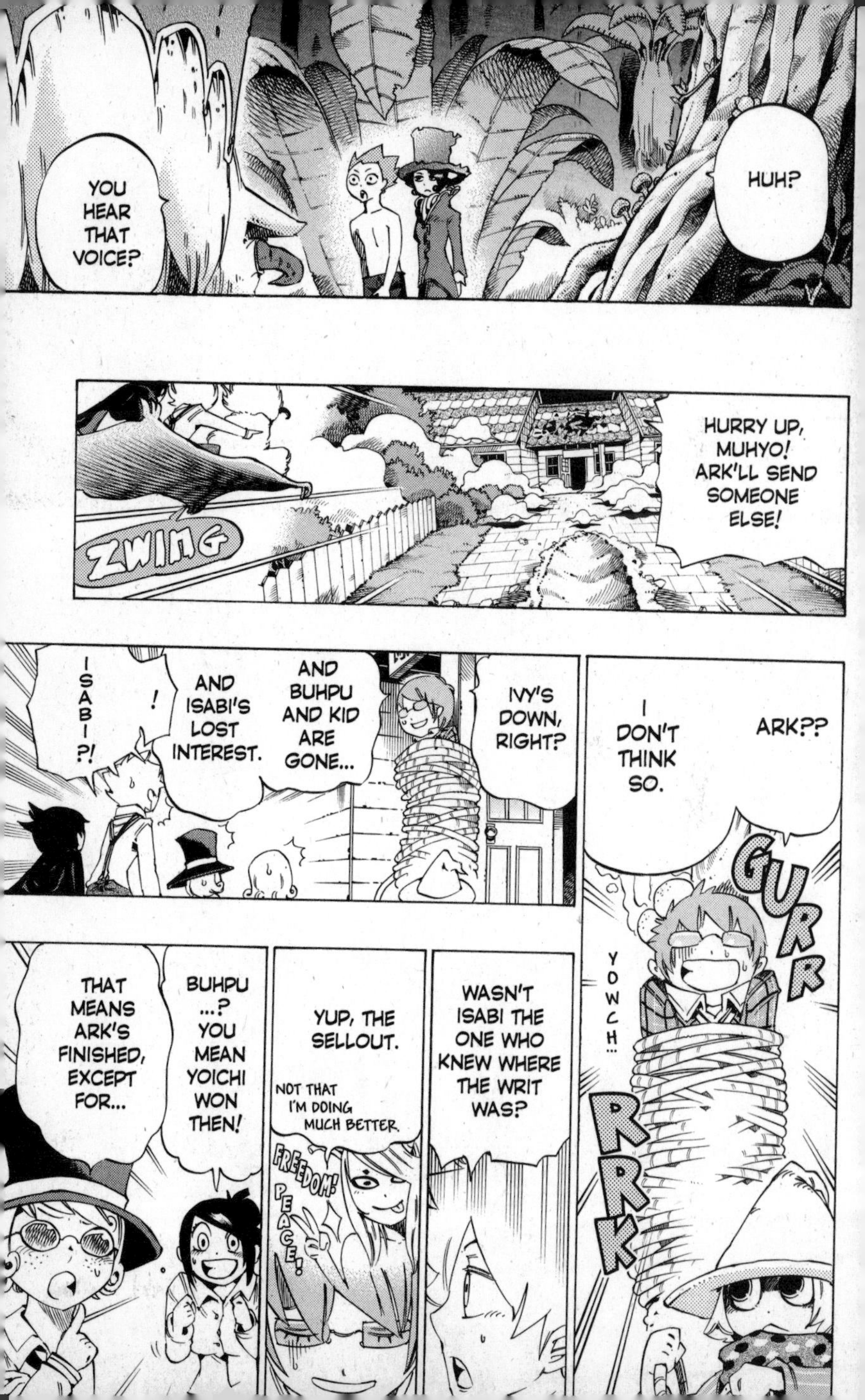
HUH?
YOU HEAR THAT VOICE?
HURRY UP, MUHYO! ARK'LL SEND SOMEONE ELSE!
ZWING
ARK??
I DON'T THINK SO.
GURR
RRK
YOWCH!!
IVY'S DOWN, RIGHT?
AND BUHPU AND KID ARE GONE...
AND ISABI'S LOST INTEREST.
!
ISABI?!
WASN'T ISABI THE ONE WHO KNEW WHERE THE WRIT WAS?
YUP, THE SELLOUT.
NOT THAT I'M DOING MUCH BETTER.
FREEDOM!
PEACE!
BUHPU...? YOU MEAN YOICHI WON THEN!
THAT MEANS ARK'S FINISHED, EXCEPT FOR...

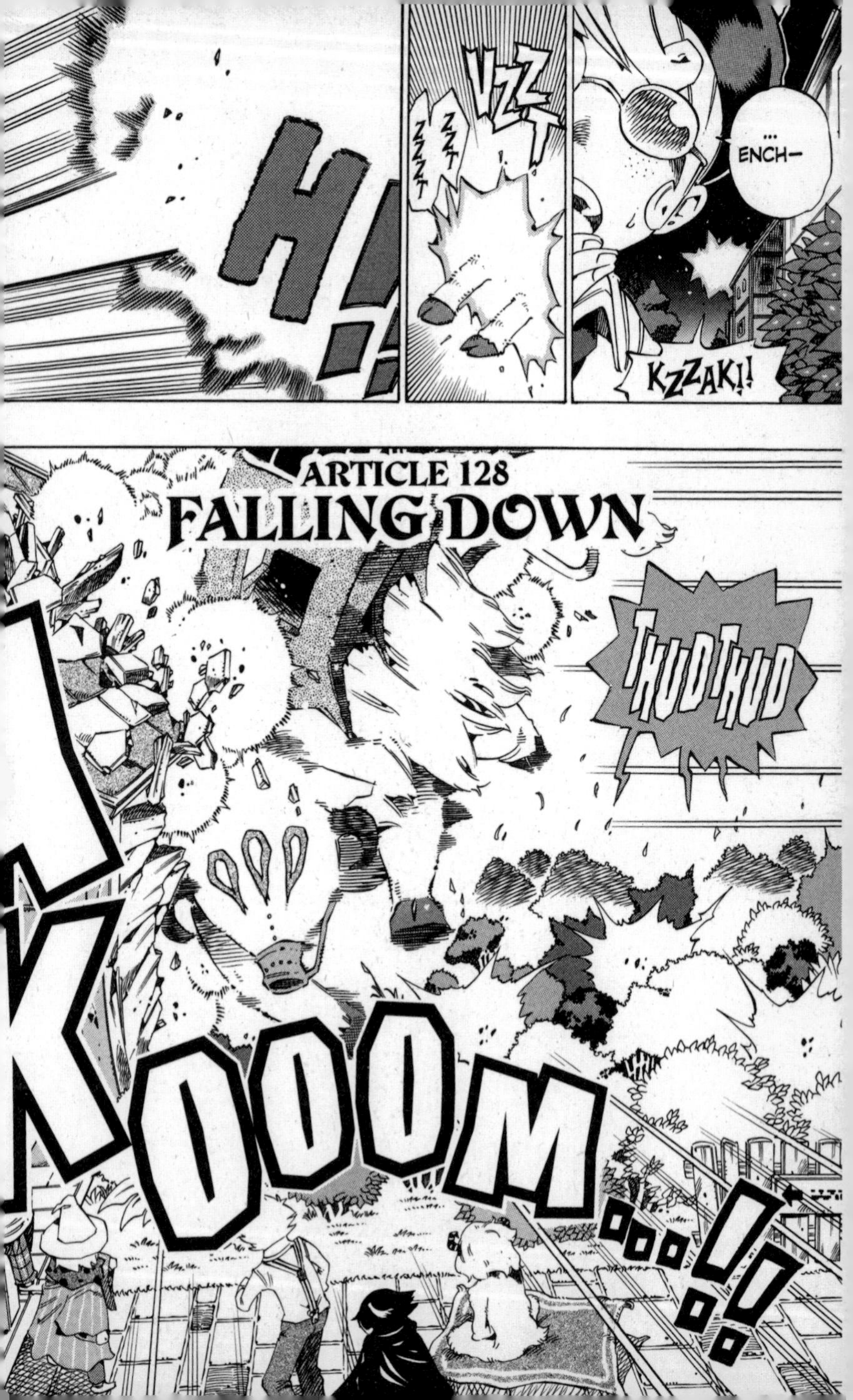
... ENCH—
KZZAKI!
VZZZT
ZZZT
ZZZZT
H!!
ARTICLE 128
FALLING DOWN
THUD THUD
KOOOM...!!

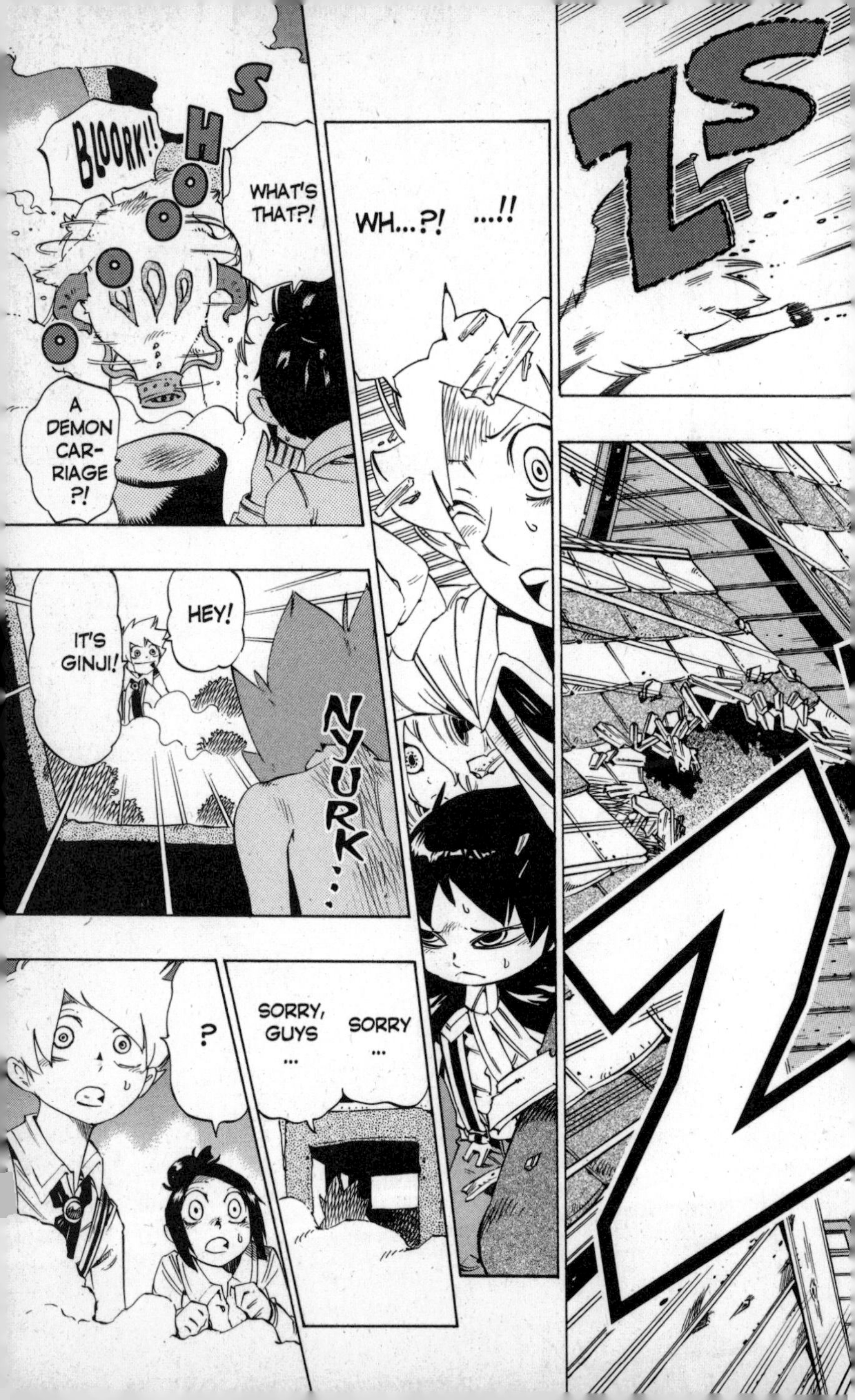
ZS
Z
...!!
WH...?!
SHOOOO
WHAT'S THAT?!
BLOORK!!
A DEMON CAR-RIAGE?!
NYURK...
HEY!
IT'S GINJI!
SORRY...
SORRY, GUYS...
?

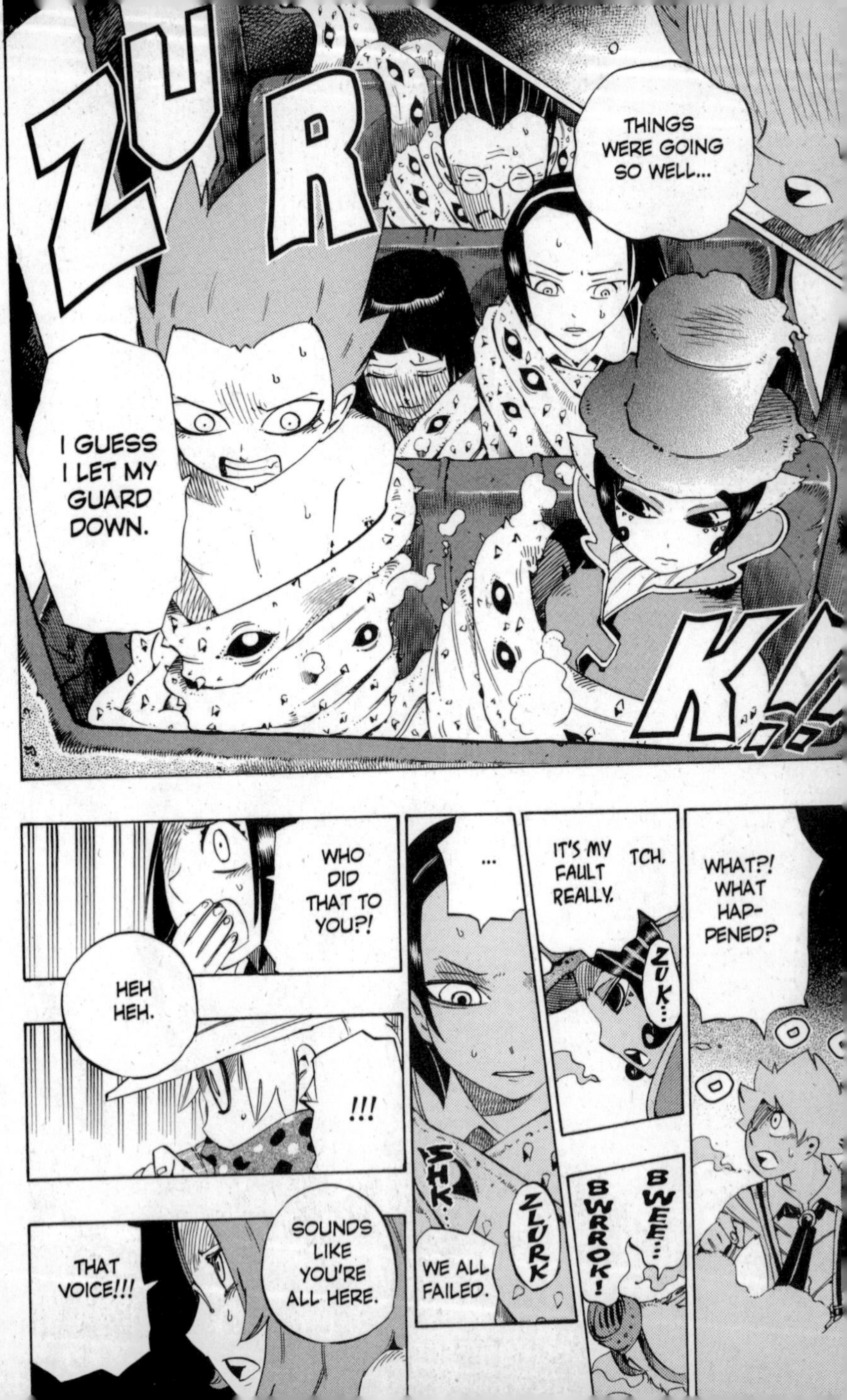
ZUR
THINGS WERE GOING SO WELL...
I GUESS I LET MY GUARD DOWN.
WHAT?! WHAT HAP-PENED?
BWEE...
BWRROK!
TCH.
IT'S MY FAULT REALLY.
ZUK...
...
WE ALL FAILED.
ZLURK
SHK...
WHO DID THAT TO YOU?!
HEH HEH.
!!!
SOUNDS LIKE YOU'RE ALL HERE.
THAT VOICE!!!

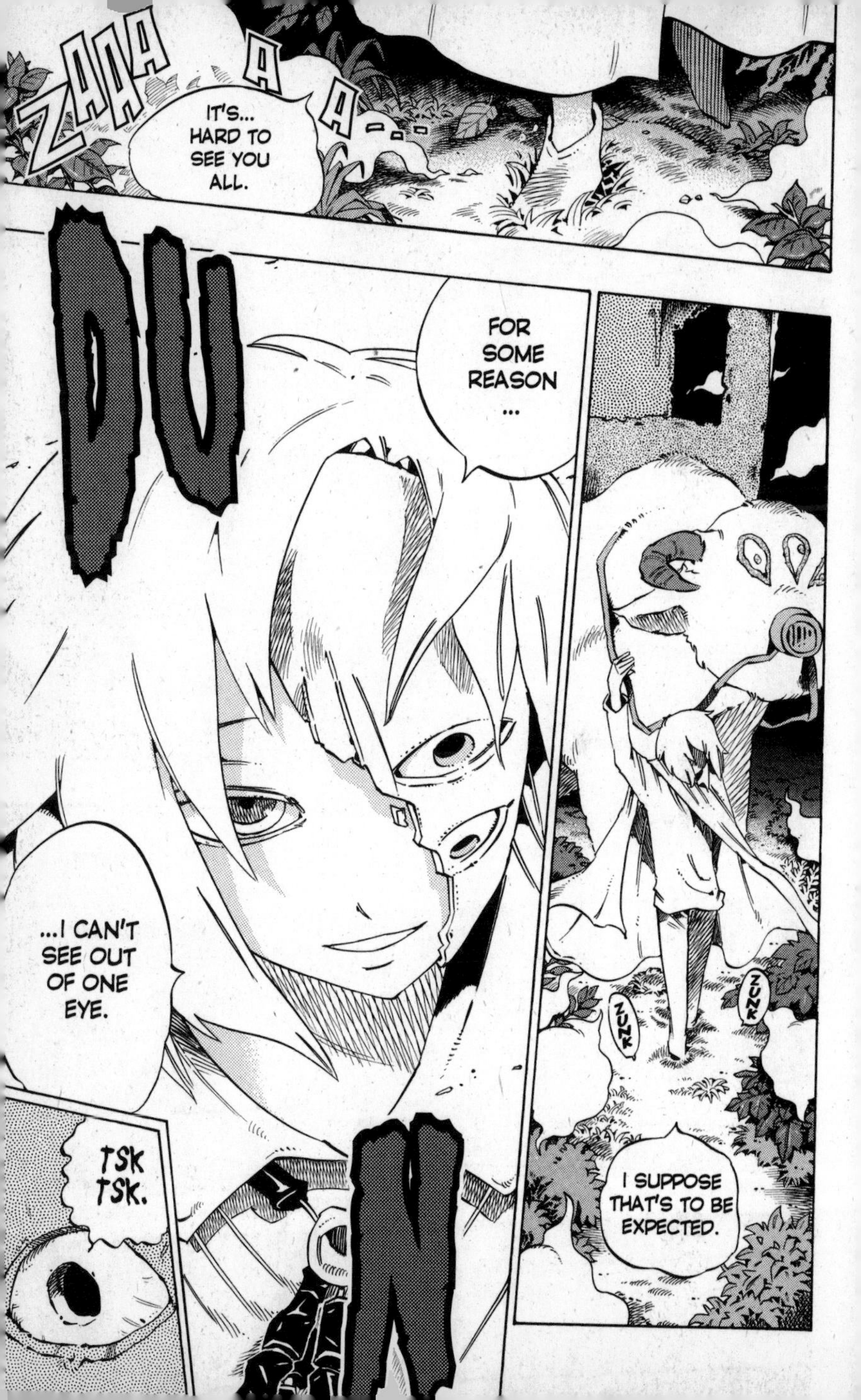
ZAAAA A A
IT'S... HARD TO SEE YOU ALL.
ZUNK
ZUNK
I SUPPOSE THAT'S TO BE EXPECTED.
DU
FOR SOME REASON ...
...I CAN'T SEE OUT OF ONE EYE.
N
TSK TSK.

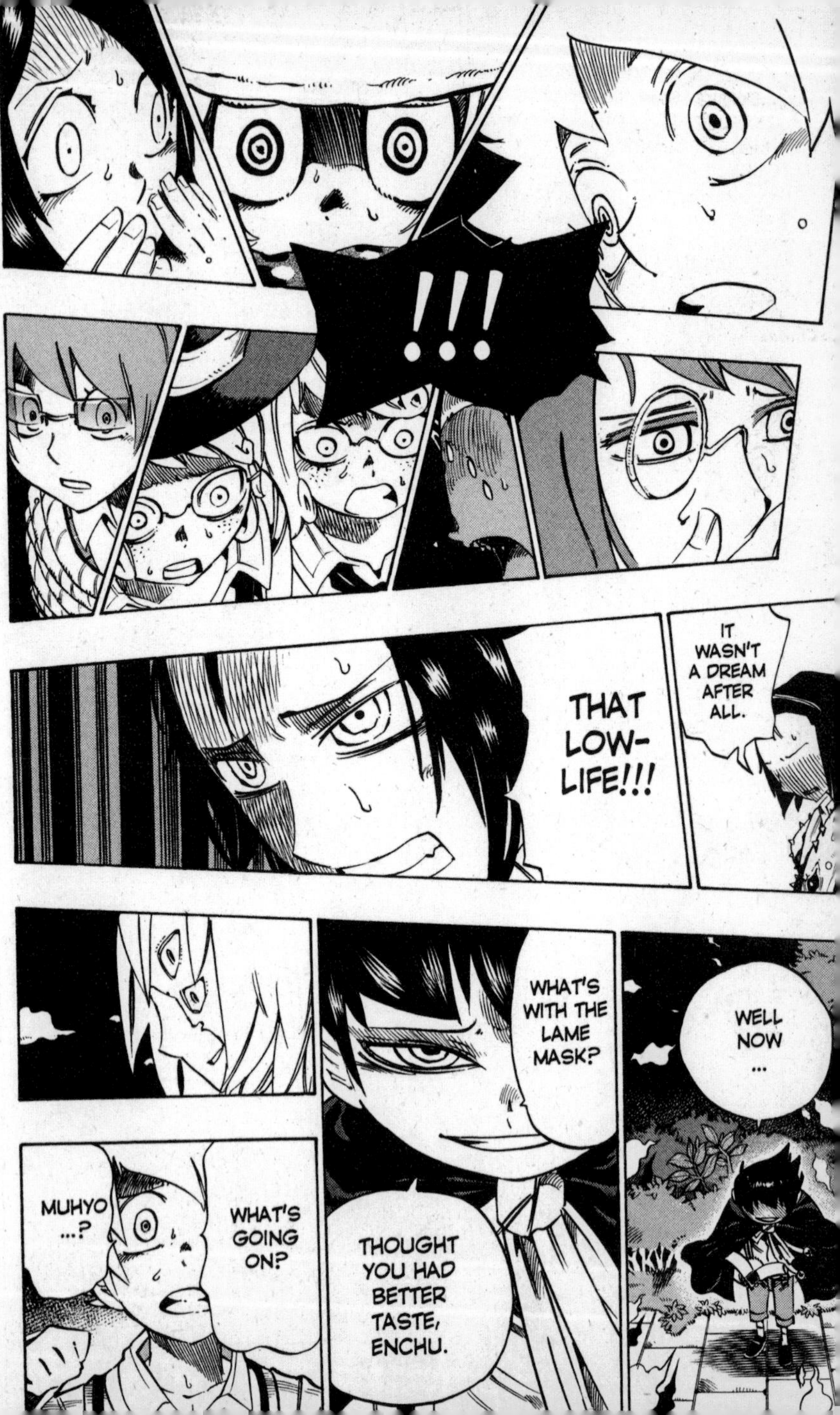
!!!
IT WASN'T A DREAM AFTER ALL.
THAT LOW-LIFE!!!
WELL NOW ...
WHAT'S WITH THE LAME MASK?
THOUGHT YOU HAD BETTER TASTE, ENCHU.
WHAT'S GOING ON?
MUHYO ...?

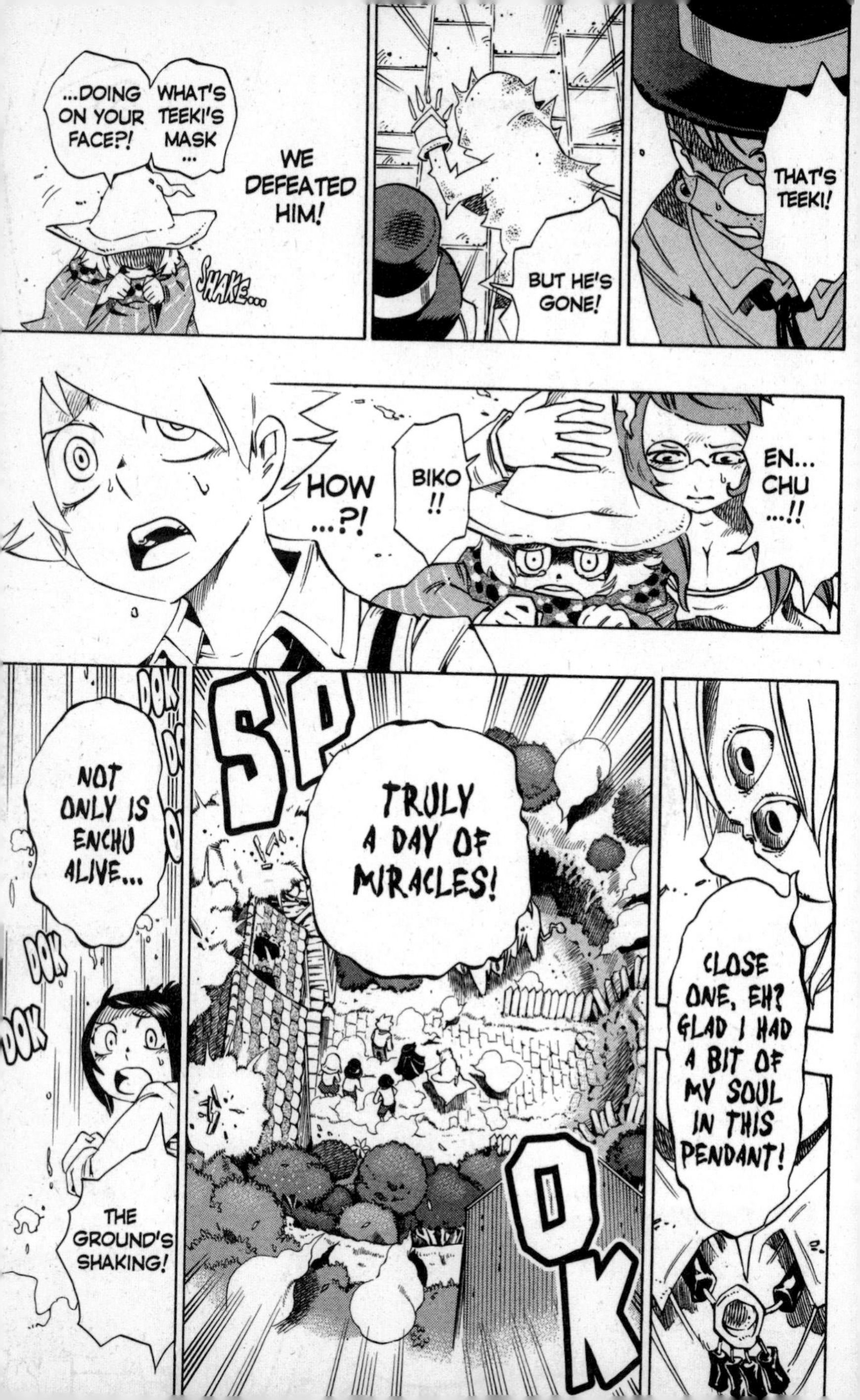
THAT'S TEEKI!
WE DEFEATED HIM!
BUT HE'S GONE!
WHAT'S TEEKI'S MASK ...
...DOING ON YOUR FACE?!
SHAKE...
EN... CHU ...!!
BIKO !!
HOW ...?!
CLOSE ONE, EH? GLAD I HAD A BIT OF MY SOUL IN THIS PENDANT!
SP
TRULY A DAY OF MIRACLES!
OK
DOK
NOT ONLY IS ENCHU ALIVE...
DOK
DOK
THE GROUND'S SHAKING!

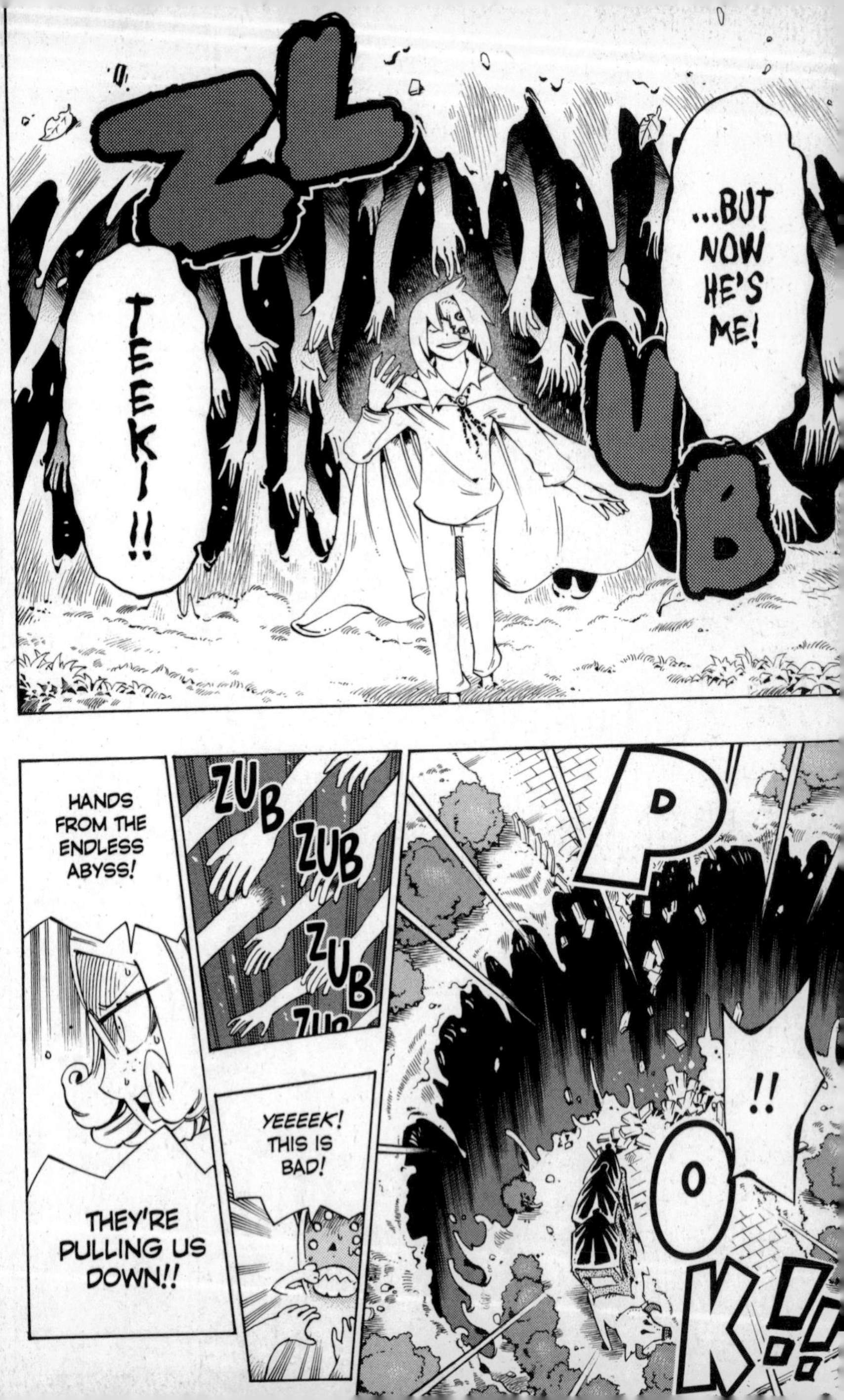
...BUT NOW HE'S ME!
ZUB
TEEKI!!
POK!!
!!
ZUB
ZUB
ZUB
YEEEEK! THIS IS BAD!
HANDS FROM THE ENDLESS ABYSS!
THEY'RE PULLING US DOWN!!

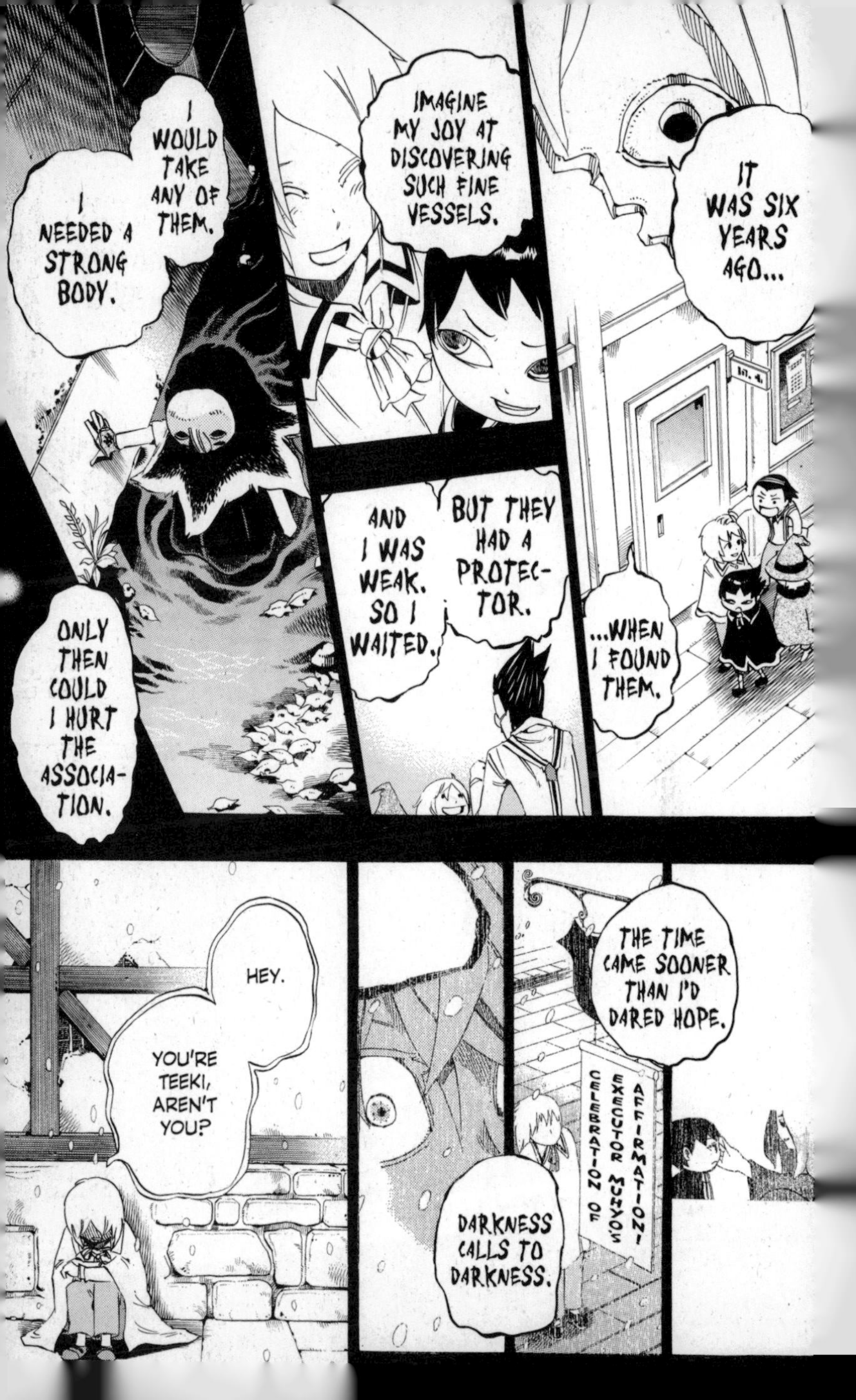
IT WAS SIX YEARS AGO...
...WHEN I FOUND THEM.
IMAGINE MY JOY AT DISCOVERING SUCH FINE VESSELS.
BUT THEY HAD A PROTECTOR.
AND I WAS WEAK. SO I WAITED.
I WOULD TAKE ANY OF THEM.
I NEEDED A STRONG BODY.
ONLY THEN COULD I HURT THE ASSOCIATION.
THE TIME CAME SOONER THAN I'D DARED HOPE.
CELEBRATION OF EXECUTOR MUHYO'S AFFIRMATION!
DARKNESS CALLS TO DARKNESS.
HEY.
YOU'RE TEEKI, AREN'T YOU?

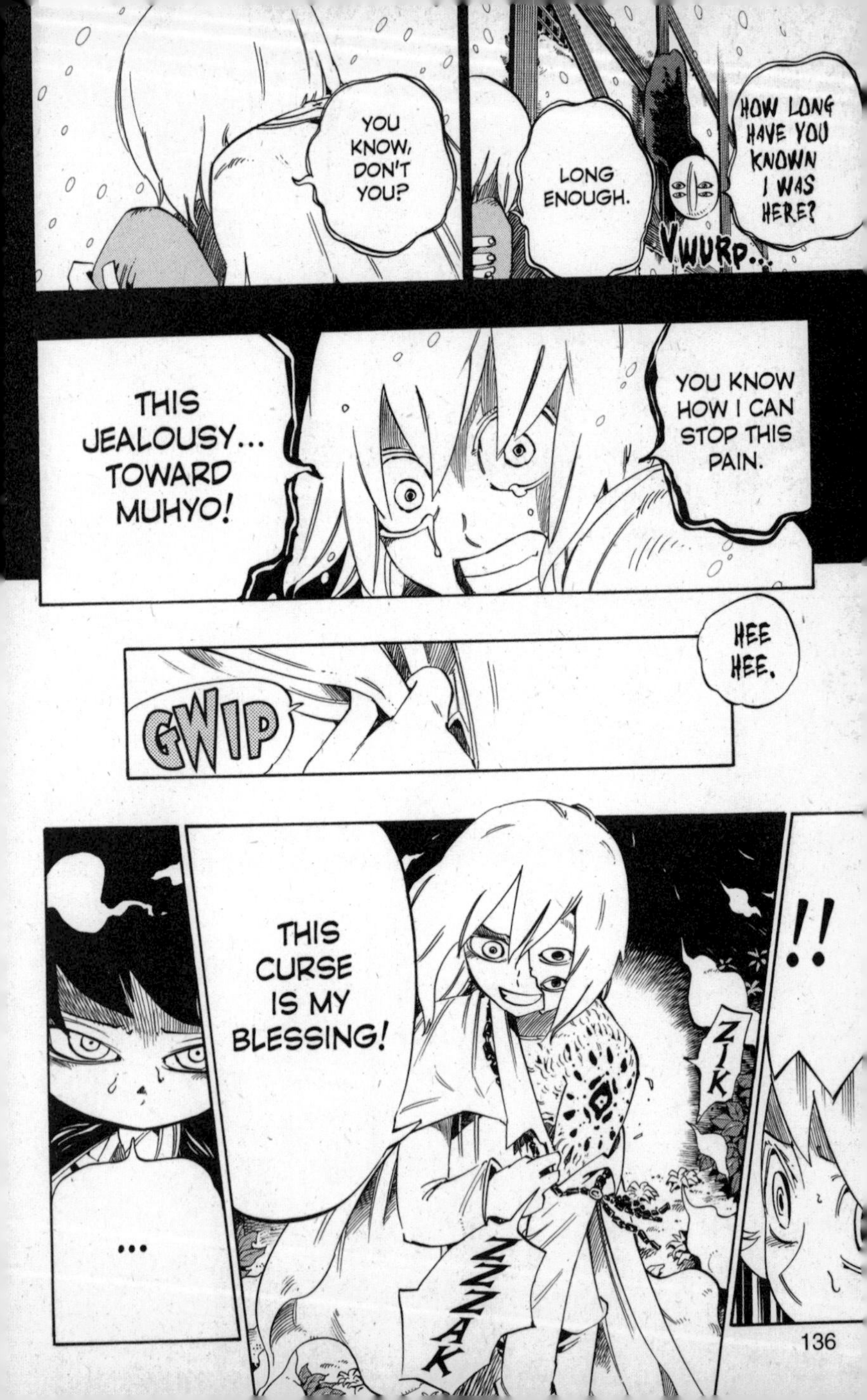

HOW LONG HAVE YOU KNOWN I WAS HERE?
LONG ENOUGH.
VWURP...
YOU KNOW, DON'T YOU?
YOU KNOW HOW I CAN STOP THIS PAIN.
THIS JEALOUSY... TOWARD MUHYO!
HEE HEE.
GWIP
!!
THIS CURSE IS MY BLESSING!
ZIK
ZZZAK
...

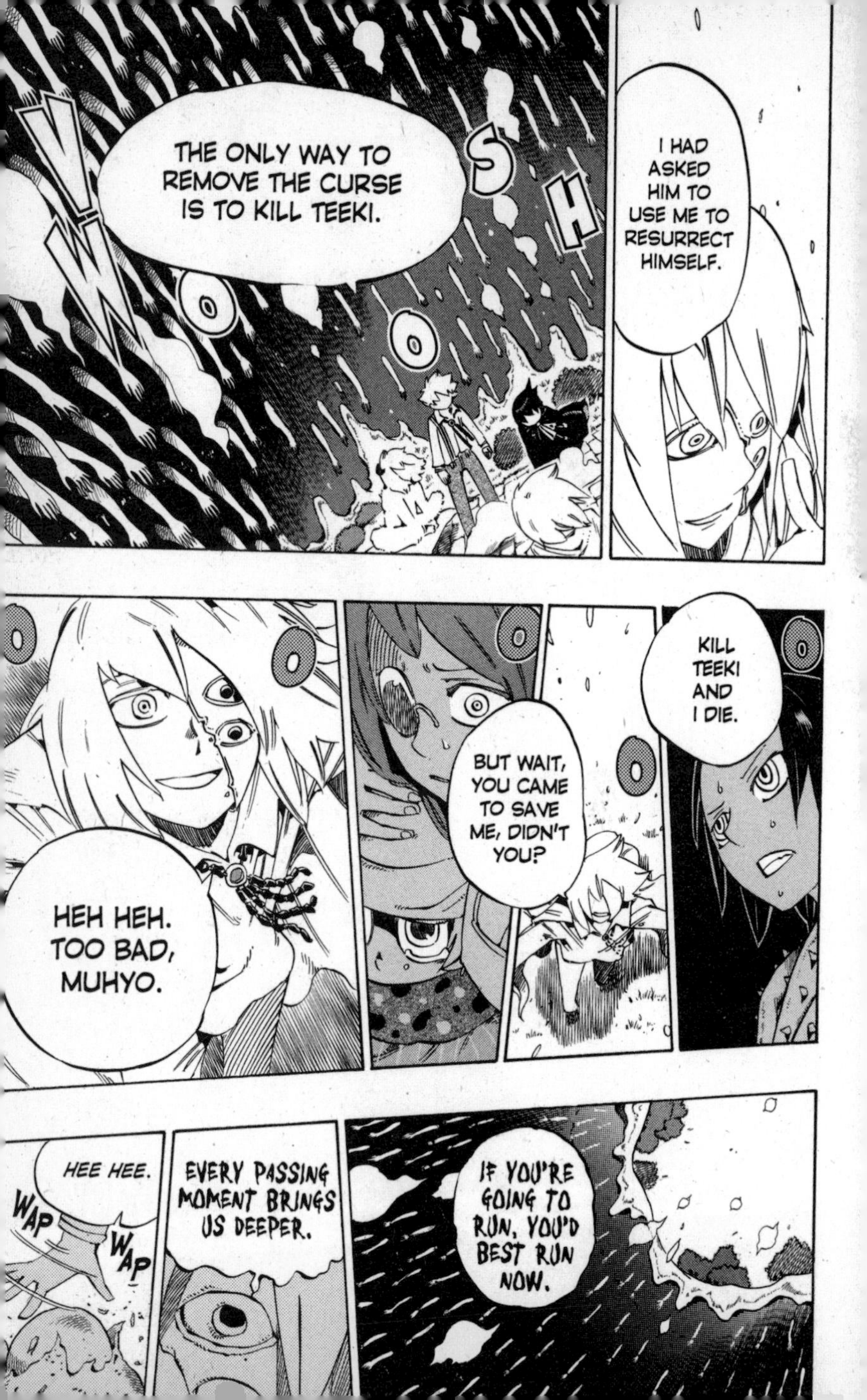
I HAD ASKED HIM TO USE ME TO RESURRECT HIMSELF.
THE ONLY WAY TO REMOVE THE CURSE IS TO KILL TEEKI.
KILL TEEKI AND I DIE.
BUT WAIT, YOU CAME TO SAVE ME, DIDN'T YOU?
HEH HEH. TOO BAD, MUHYO.
IF YOU'RE GOING TO RUN, YOU'D BEST RUN NOW.
EVERY PASSING MOMENT BRINGS US DEEPER.
HEE HEE.
WAP
WAP

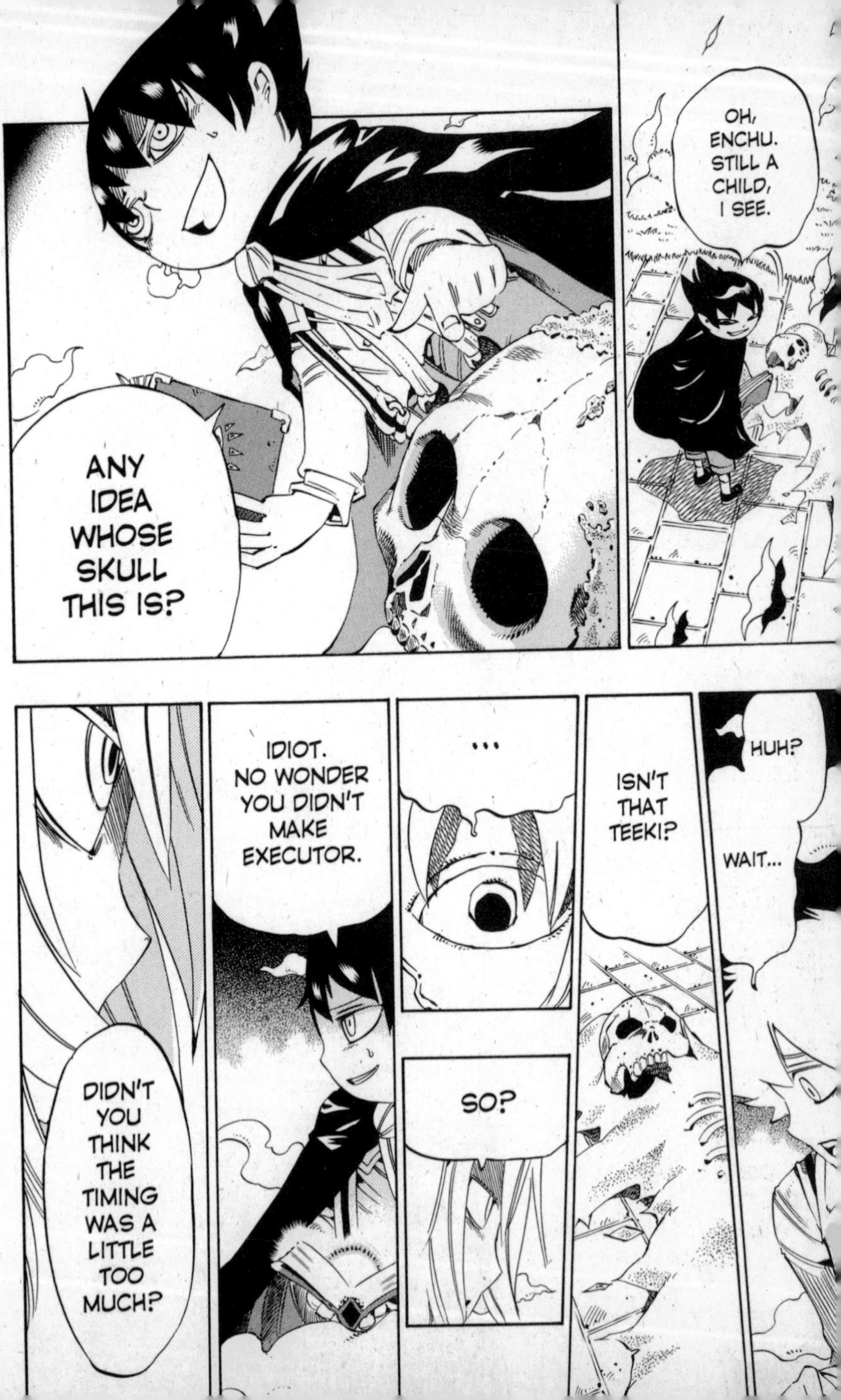

OH, ENCHU. STILL A CHILD, I SEE.
ANY IDEA WHOSE SKULL THIS IS?
HUH?
WAIT...
ISN'T THAT TEEKI?
...
SO?
IDIOT. NO WONDER YOU DIDN'T MAKE EXECUTOR.
DIDN'T YOU THINK THE TIMING WAS A LITTLE TOO MUCH?

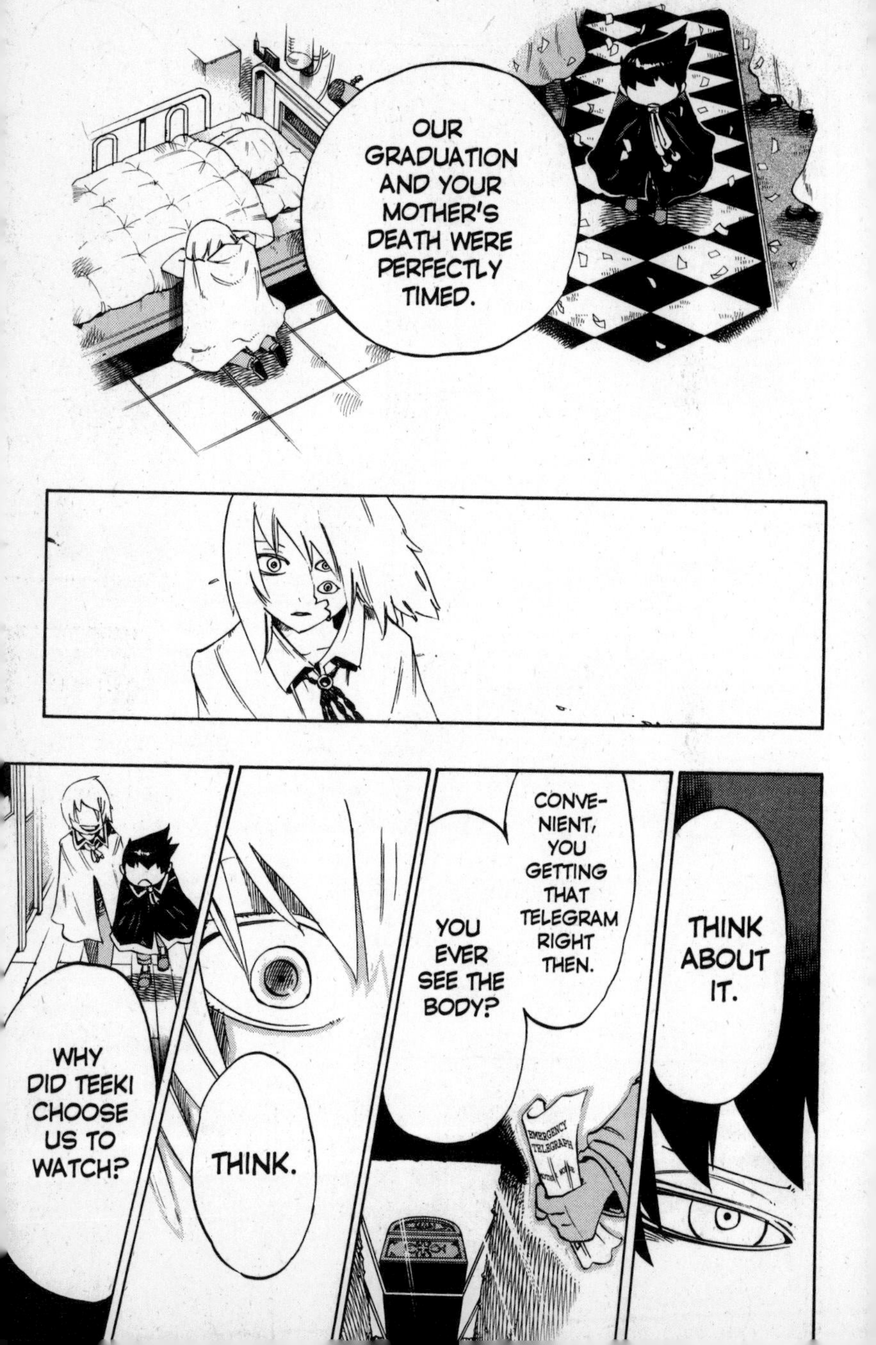
OUR GRADUATION AND YOUR MOTHER'S DEATH WERE PERFECTLY TIMED.
THINK ABOUT IT.
EMERGENCY TELEGRAPH
CONVENIENT, YOU GETTING THAT TELEGRAM RIGHT THEN.
YOU EVER SEE THE BODY?
THINK.
WHY DID TEEKI CHOOSE US TO WATCH?

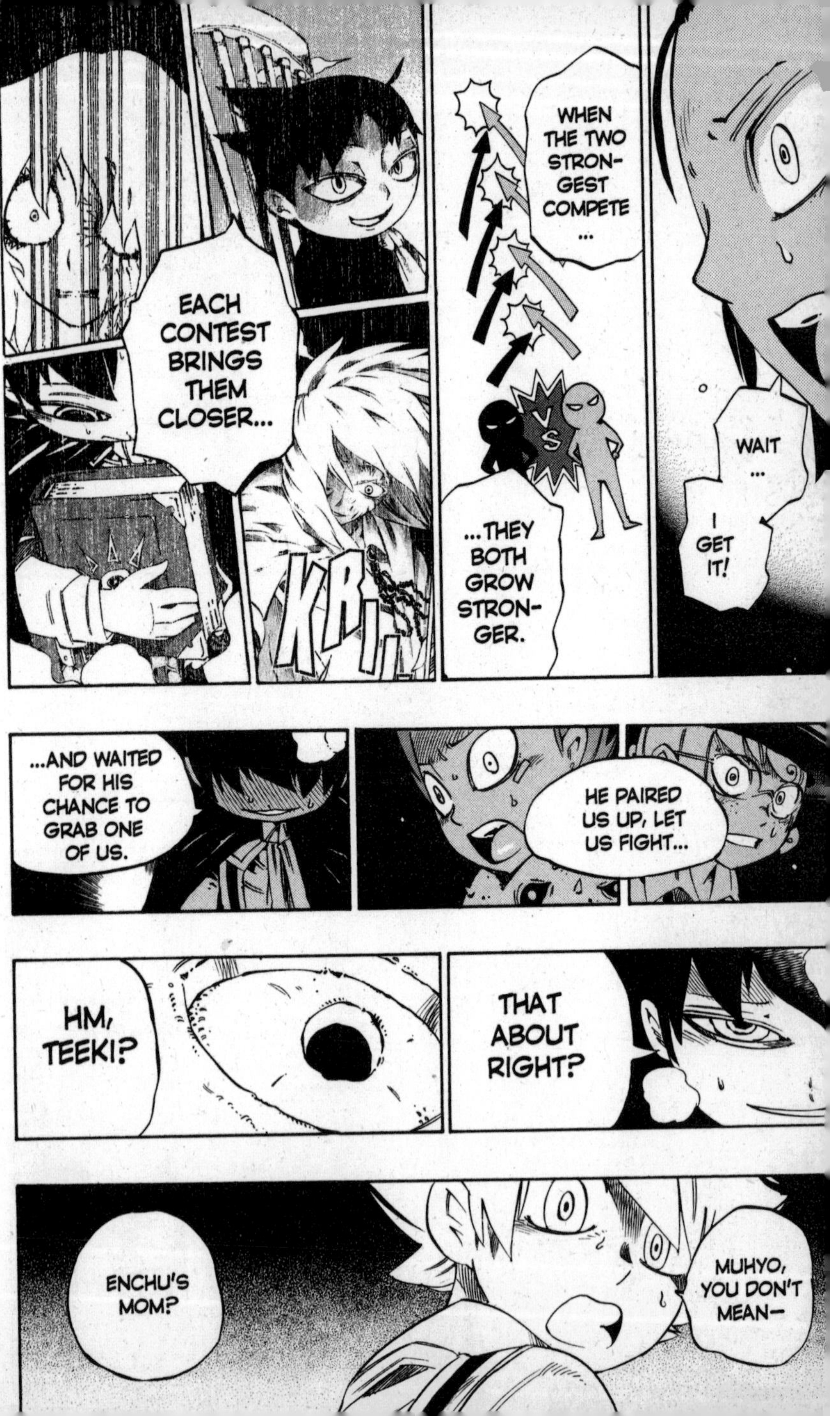
WAIT... I GET IT!
WHEN THE TWO STRONGEST COMPETE...
...THEY BOTH GROW STRONGER.
VS
EACH CONTEST BRINGS THEM CLOSER...
KRII
HE PAIRED US UP, LET US FIGHT...
...AND WAITED FOR HIS CHANCE TO GRAB ONE OF US.
THAT ABOUT RIGHT?
HM, TEEKI?
MUHYO, YOU DON'T MEAN—
ENCHU'S MOM?

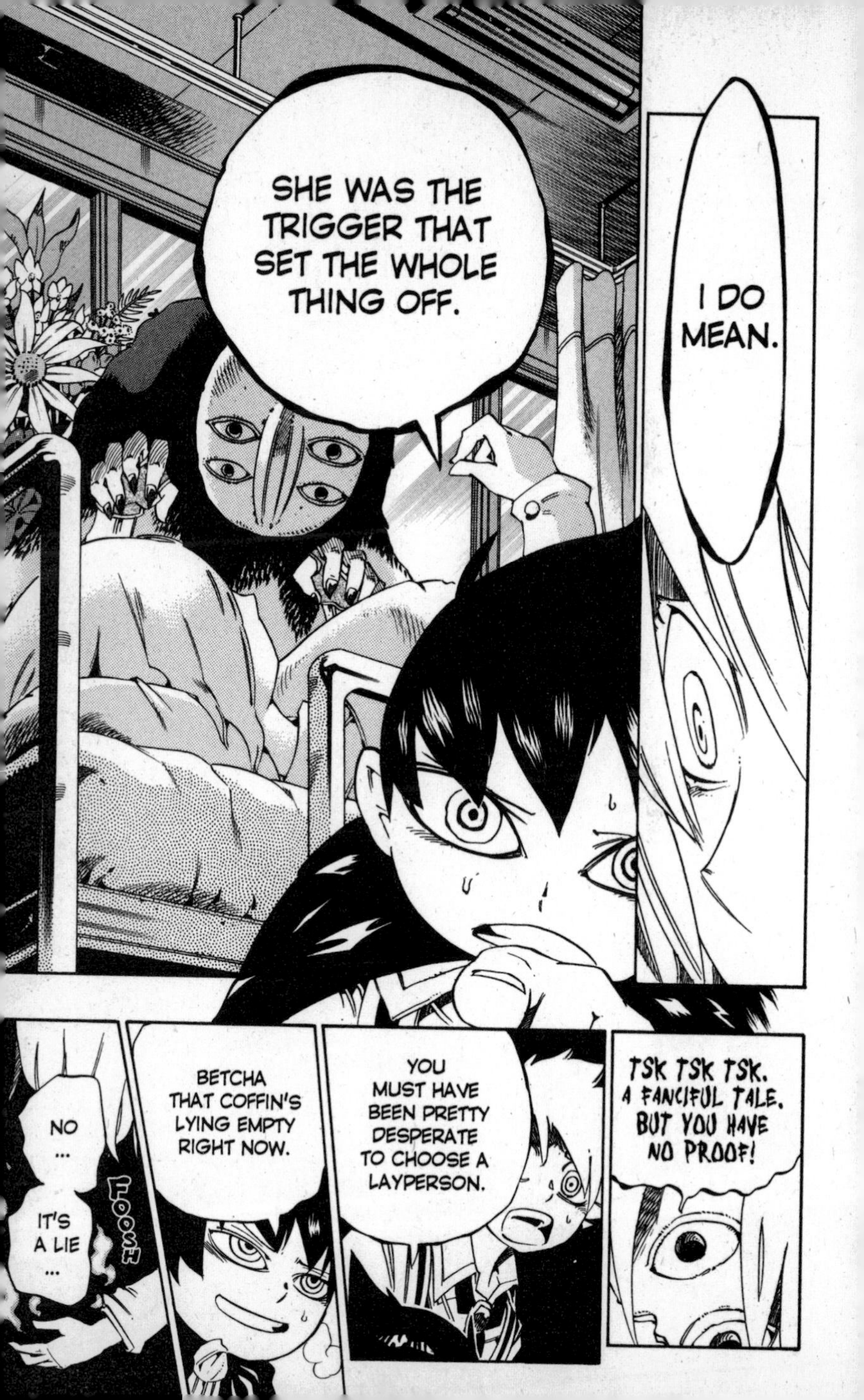
I DO MEAN.
SHE WAS THE TRIGGER THAT SET THE WHOLE THING OFF.
TSK TSK TSK. A FANCIFUL TALE. BUT YOU HAVE NO PROOF!
YOU MUST HAVE BEEN PRETTY DESPERATE TO CHOOSE A LAYPERSON.
BETCHA THAT COFFIN'S LYING EMPTY RIGHT NOW.
FOOSH
NO ... IT'S A LIE ...

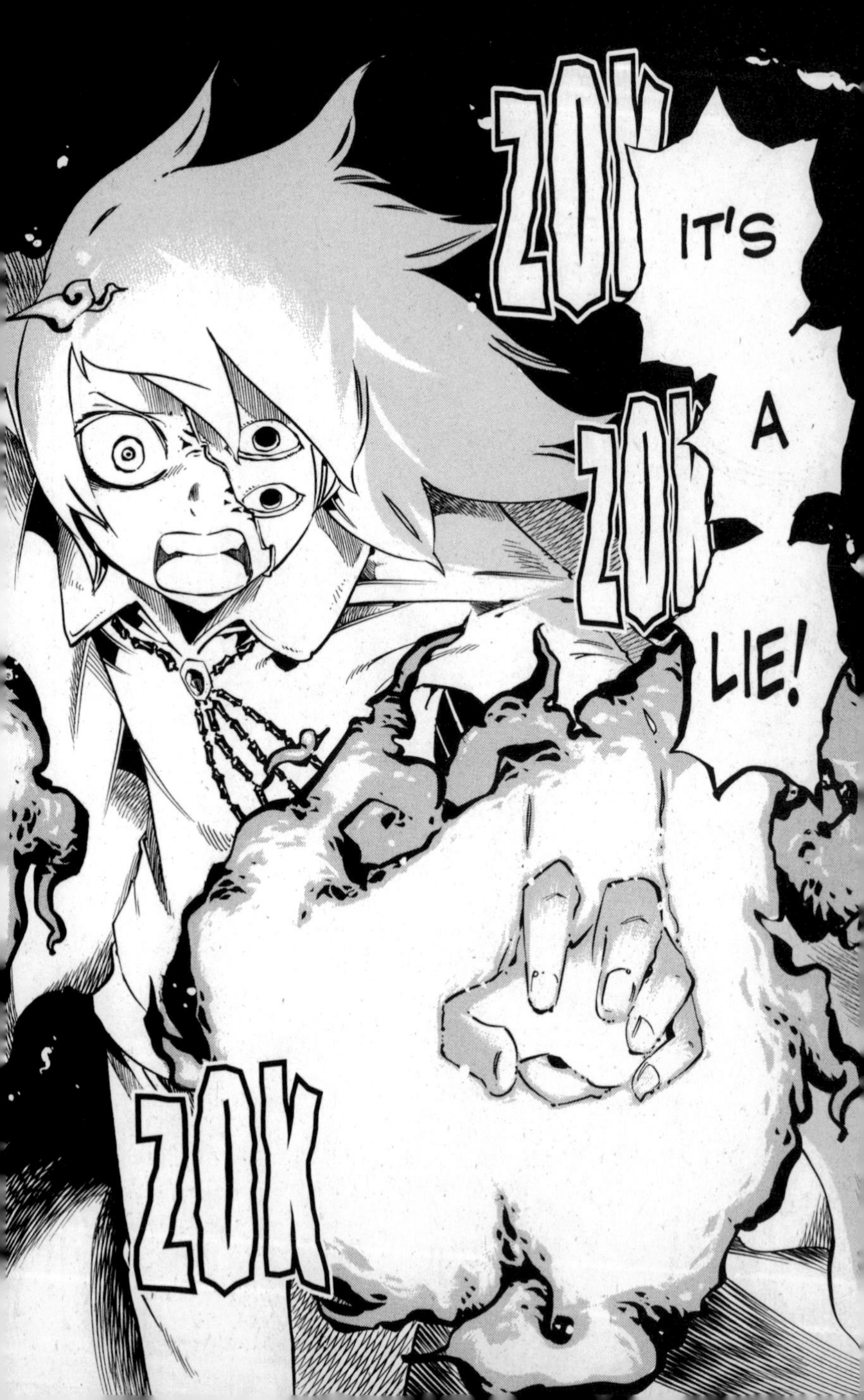
IT'S A LIE!
ZOK
ZOK
ZOK

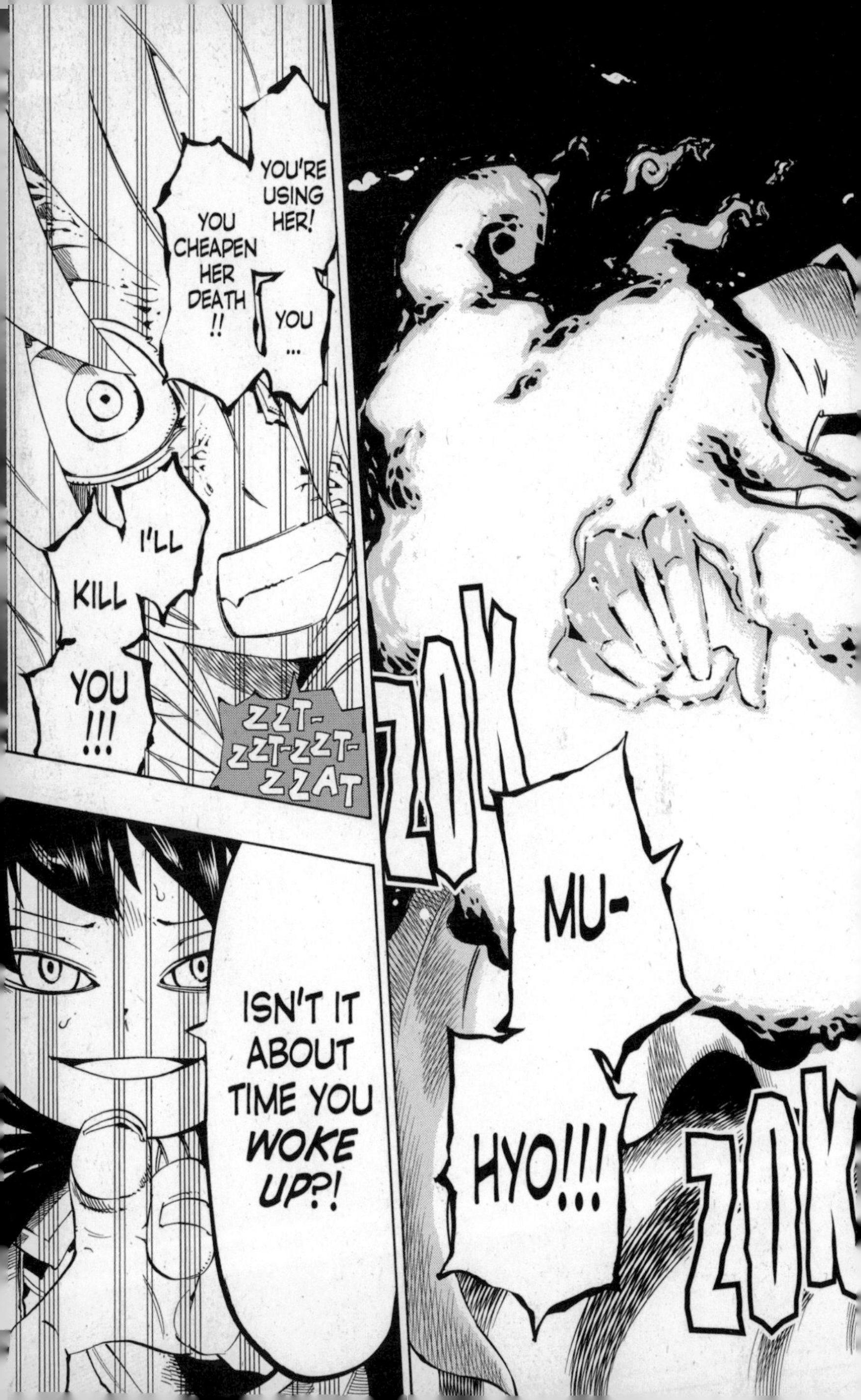
ZOK
MU-HYO!!!
ZOK
YOU'RE USING HER!
YOU CHEAPEN HER DEATH!!
YOU...
I'LL KILL YOU!!!
ZZT-ZZT-ZZT-ZZAT
ISN'T IT ABOUT TIME YOU *WOKE UP*?!

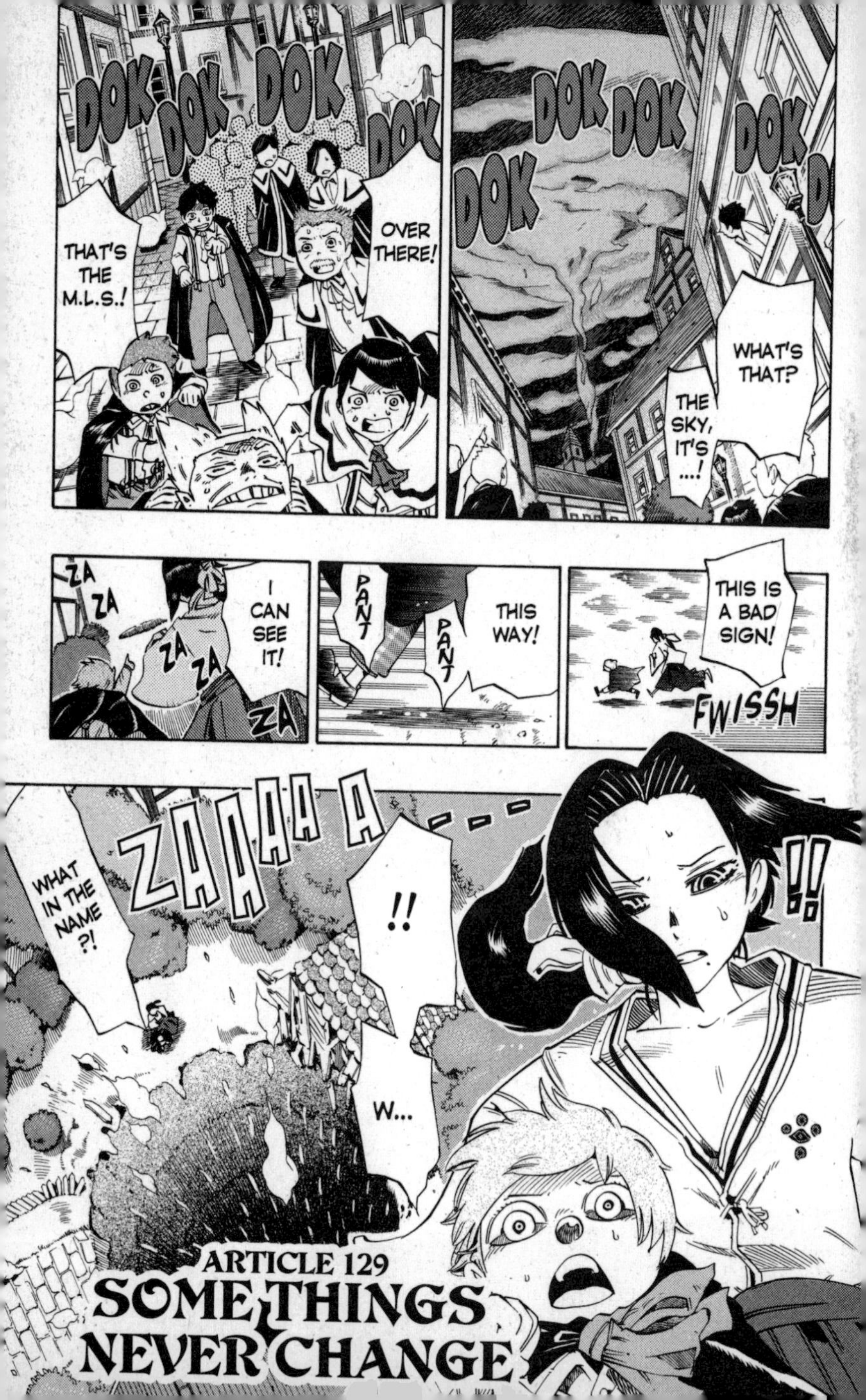
DOK DOK DOK DOK
WHAT'S THAT?
THE SKY, IT'S ...!
DOK DOK DOK DOK DOK
OVER THERE!
THAT'S THE M.L.S.!
THIS IS A BAD SIGN!
FWISSH
THIS WAY!
PANT PANT
I CAN SEE IT!
ZA ZA ZA ZA ZA
!!
ZAAAA A
!!
W...
WHAT IN THE NAME ?!
ARTICLE 129
SOME THINGS NEVER CHANGE

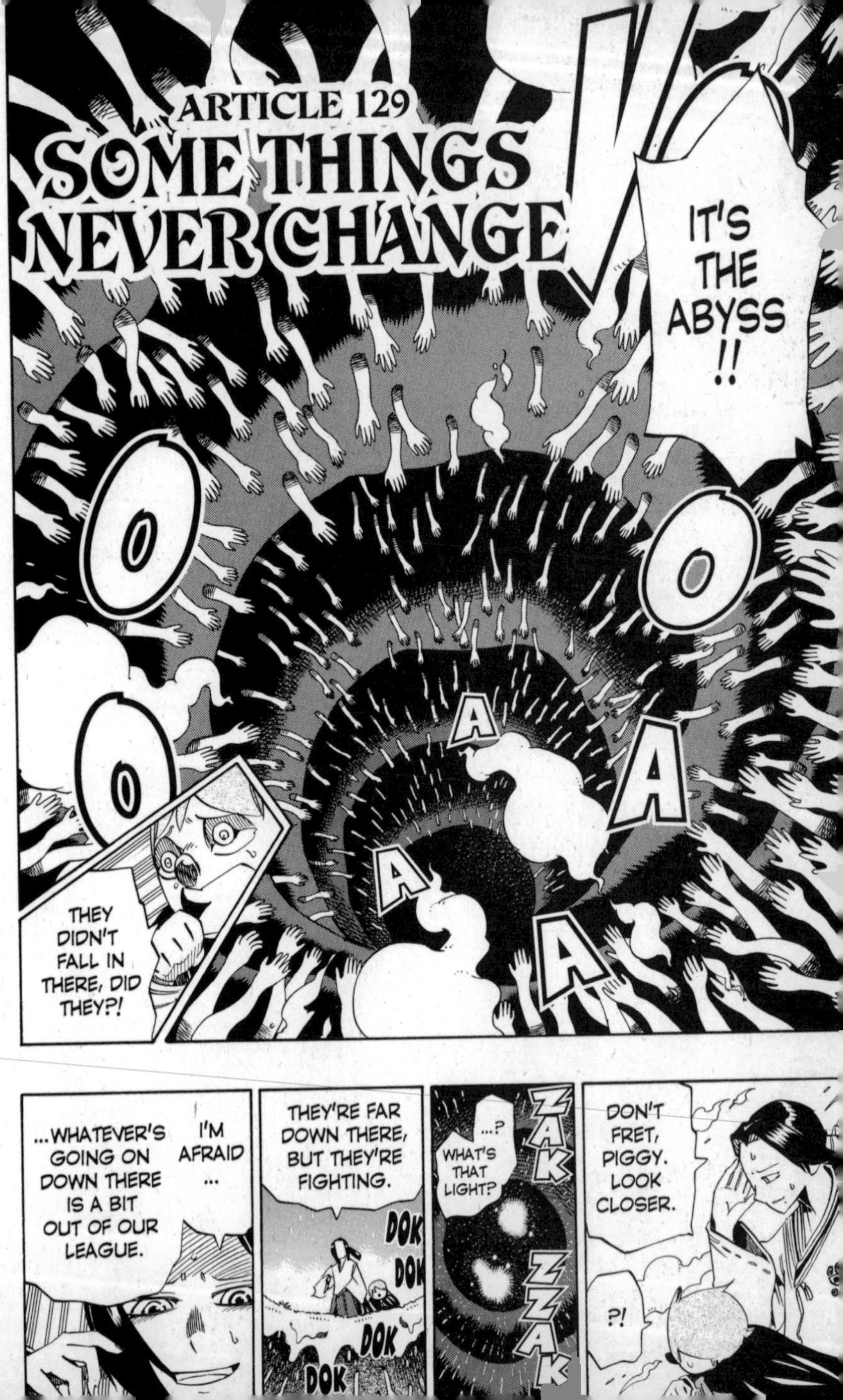
ARTICLE 129
SOME THINGS NEVER CHANGE
IT'S THE ABYSS !!
O
O
A
A
A
A
THEY DIDN'T FALL IN THERE, DID THEY?!
DON'T FRET, PIGGY. LOOK CLOSER.
?!
ZAK
...? WHAT'S THAT LIGHT?
ZZZAK
THEY'RE FAR DOWN THERE, BUT THEY'RE FIGHTING.
DOK
DOK
DOK
DOK
I'M AFRAID ...
...WHATEVER'S GOING ON DOWN THERE IS A BIT OUT OF OUR LEAGUE.

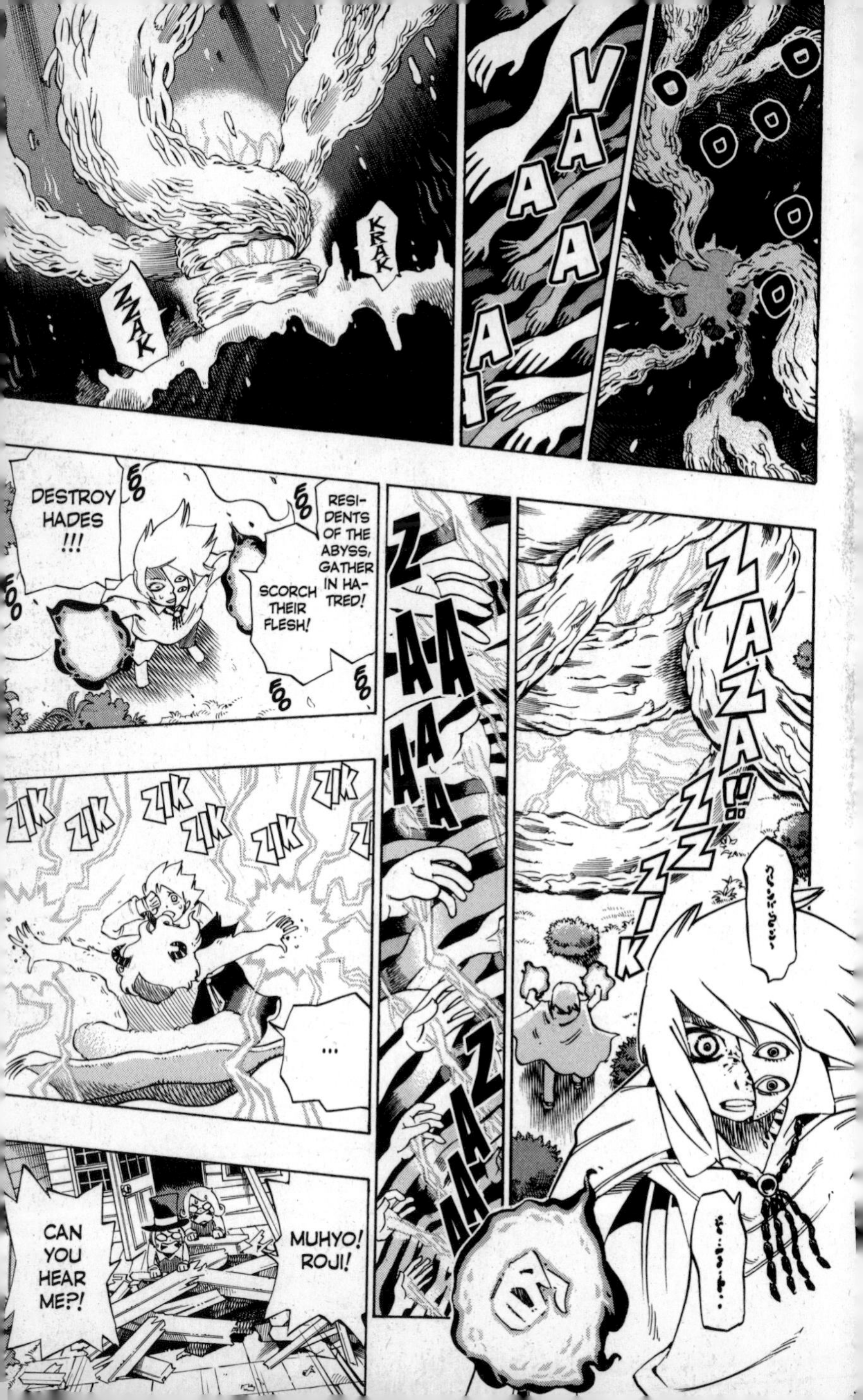
VAAAAAA
KRAK
ZZAK
ZAZAA!!
ZZZZIK
ZAAAAAA
ZAAAA
RESIDENTS OF THE ABYSS, GATHER IN HATRED!
SCORCH THEIR FLESH!
EOO
DESTROY HADES!!!
ZIK
ZIK
ZIK
ZIK
ZIK
ZIK
ZIK
...
MUHYO! ROJI!
CAN YOU HEAR ME?!

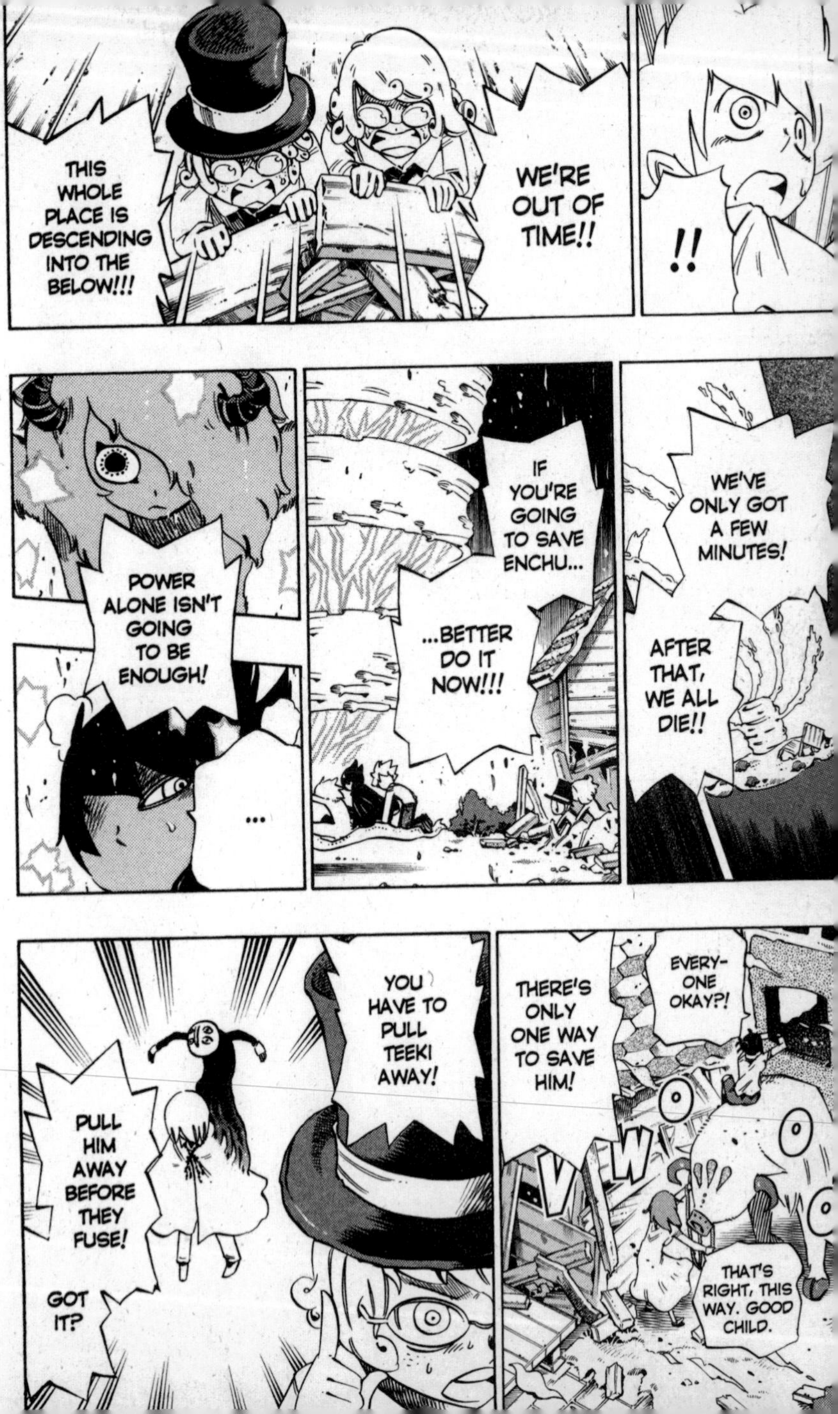
!!
WE'RE OUT OF TIME!!
THIS WHOLE PLACE IS DESCENDING INTO THE BELOW!!!
WE'VE ONLY GOT A FEW MINUTES!
AFTER THAT, WE ALL DIE!!
IF YOU'RE GOING TO SAVE ENCHU...
...BETTER DO IT NOW!!!
POWER ALONE ISN'T GOING TO BE ENOUGH!
...
EVERY-ONE OKAY?!
THERE'S ONLY ONE WAY TO SAVE HIM!
VEW
THAT'S RIGHT, THIS WAY. GOOD CHILD.
YOU HAVE TO PULL TEEKI AWAY!
PULL HIM AWAY BEFORE THEY FUSE!
GOT IT?

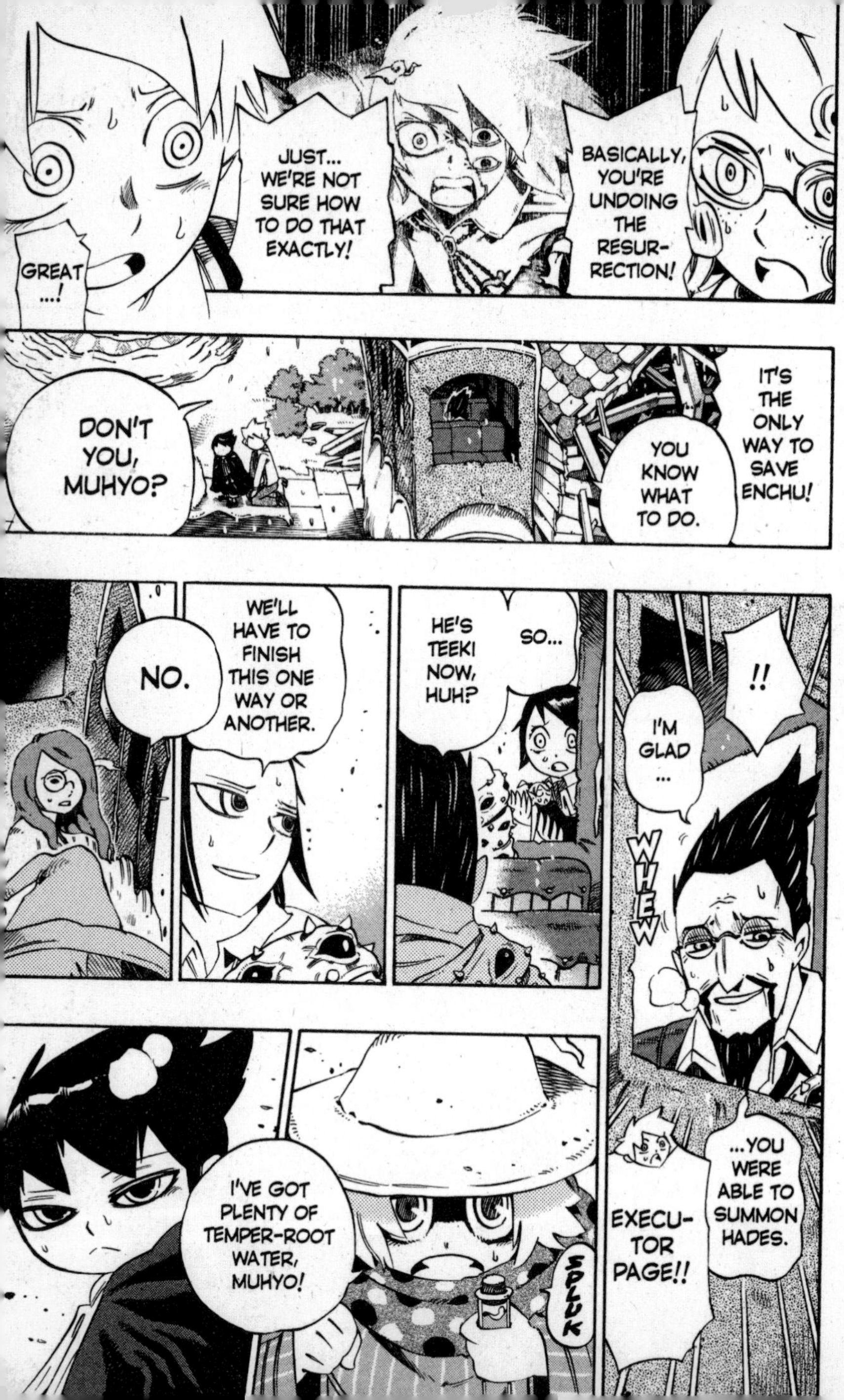
BASICALLY, YOU'RE UNDOING THE RESURRECTION!
JUST... WE'RE NOT SURE HOW TO DO THAT EXACTLY!
GREAT ....!
IT'S THE ONLY WAY TO SAVE ENCHU!
YOU KNOW WHAT TO DO.
DON'T YOU, MUHYO?
!!
I'M GLAD ...
WHEW
...YOU WERE ABLE TO SUMMON HADES.
EXECUTOR PAGE!!
SO...
HE'S TEEKI NOW, HUH?
WE'LL HAVE TO FINISH THIS ONE WAY OR ANOTHER.
NO.
SPLUK
I'VE GOT PLENTY OF TEMPER-ROOT WATER, MUHYO!

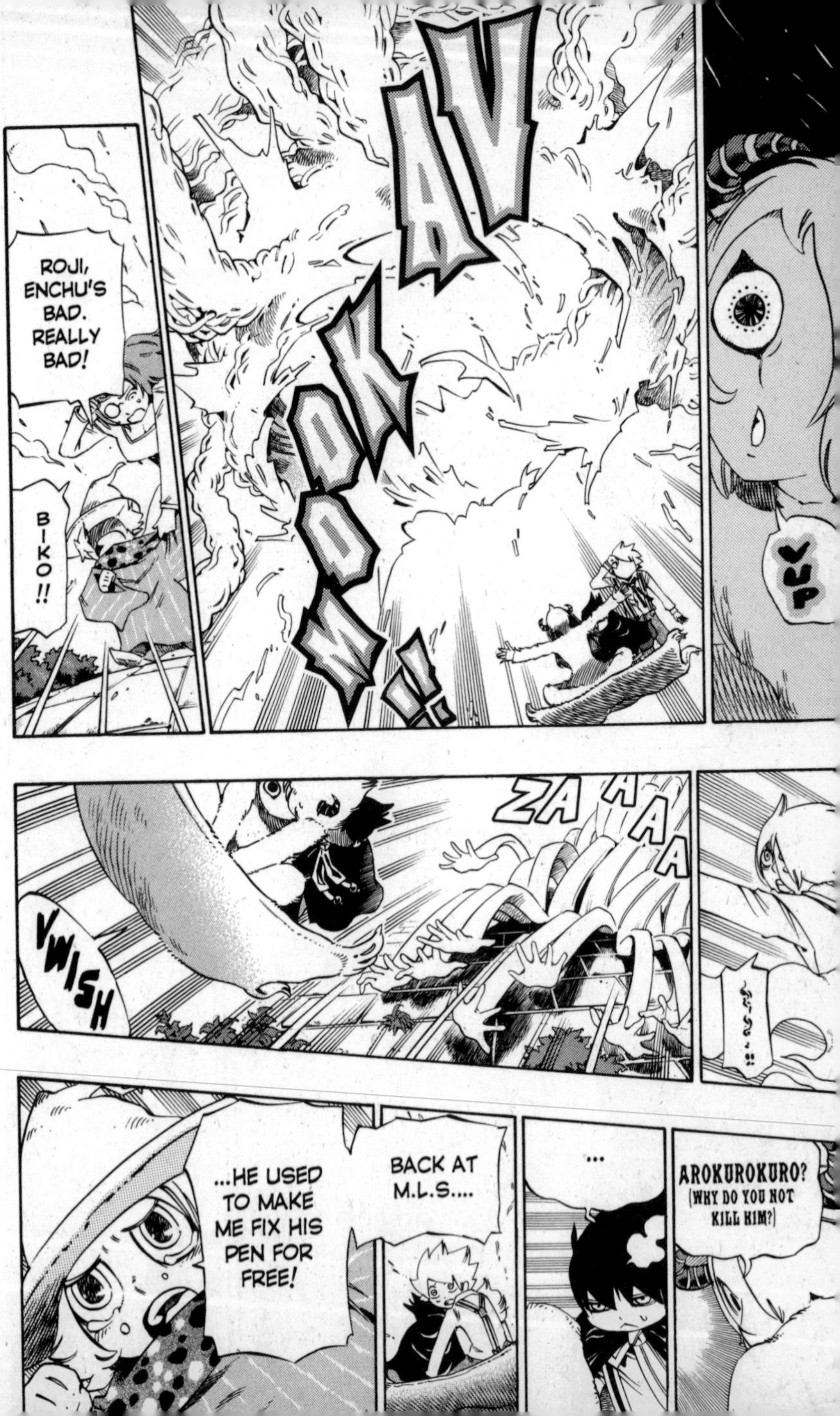
VUP
ROJI, ENCHU'S BAD. REALLY BAD!
BIKO!!
ZAAAA
VWISH
ARO KURO KURO? (WHY DO YOU NOT KILL HIM?)
...
BACK AT M.L.S....
...HE USED TO MAKE ME FIX HIS PEN FOR FREE!

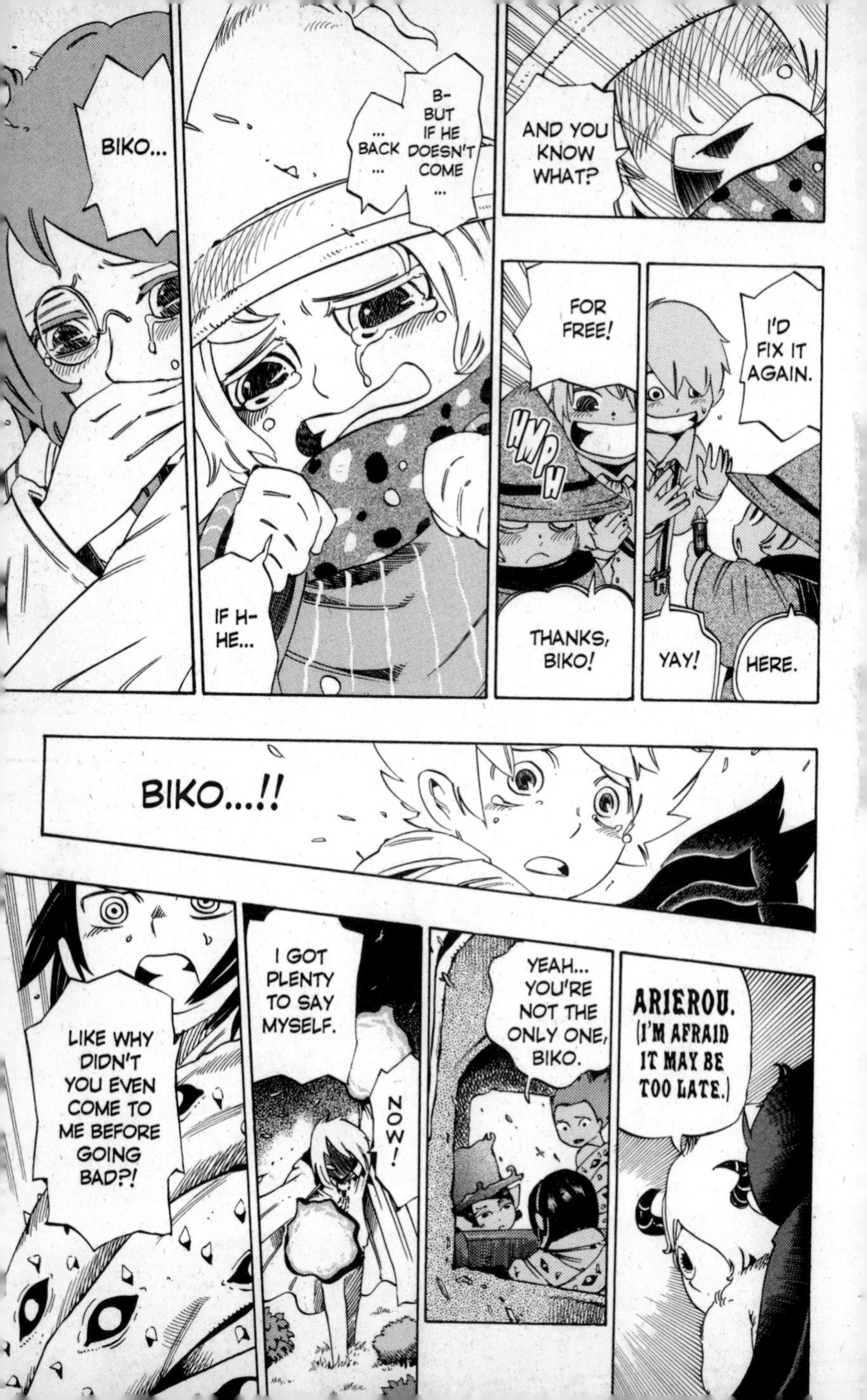
AND YOU KNOW WHAT?
I'D FIX IT AGAIN.
HERE.
YAY!
FOR FREE!
HMPH
THANKS, BIKO!
B-BUT IF HE DOESN'T COME ...
... BACK ...
IF H-HE...
BIKO...
BIKO...!!
ARIEROU.
(I'M AFRAID IT MAY BE TOO LATE.)
YEAH... YOU'RE NOT THE ONLY ONE, BIKO.
I GOT PLENTY TO SAY MYSELF.
NOW!
LIKE WHY DIDN'T YOU EVEN COME TO ME BEFORE GOING BAD?!

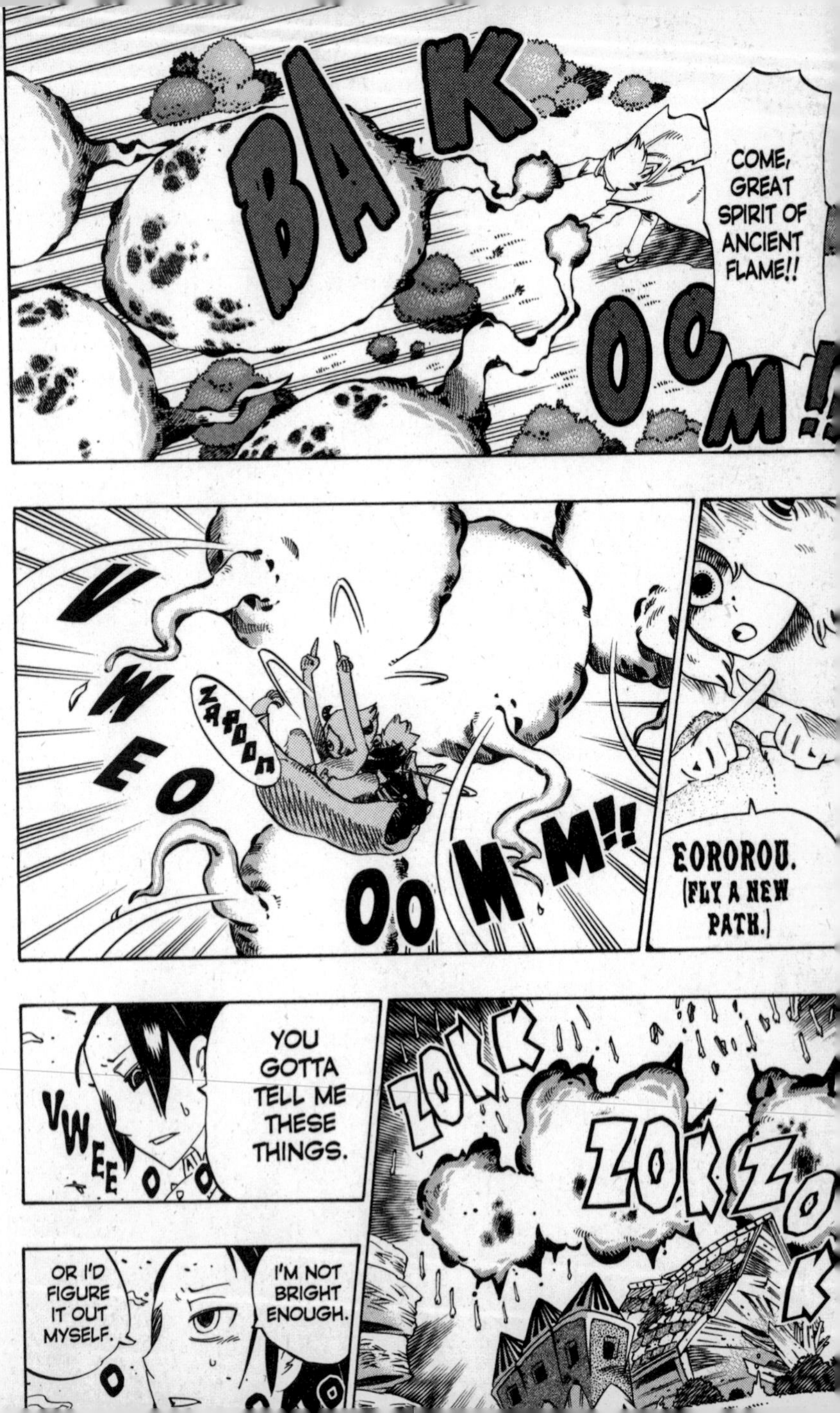
COME, GREAT SPIRIT OF ANCIENT FLAME!!
BAK
BOOOM!!
EORORU. (FLY A NEW PATH.)
VWEOOOMMM!!
ZAPOOM
ZOK
ZOK ZOK ZOK
YOU GOTTA TELL ME THESE THINGS.
VWEEOO
I'M NOT BRIGHT ENOUGH.
OR I'D FIGURE IT OUT MYSELF.

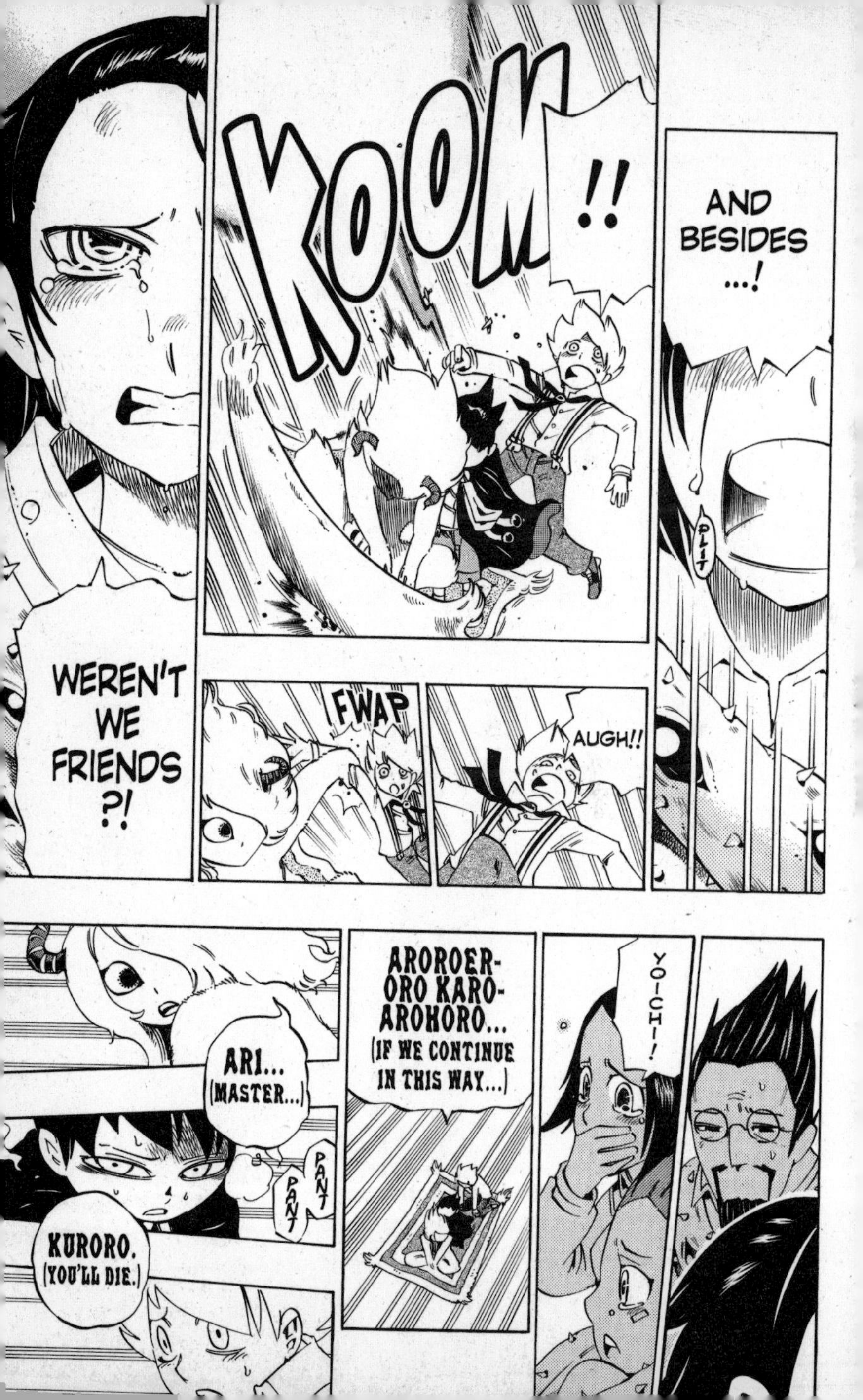
AND BESIDES ...!
PLIT
KOOM!!
AUGH!!
FWAP
WEREN'T WE FRIENDS ?!
YOICHI!
AROROER-ORO KARO-AROHORO... (IF WE CONTINUE IN THIS WAY...)
ARI... (MASTER...)
PANT PANT
KURORO. (YOU'LL DIE.)

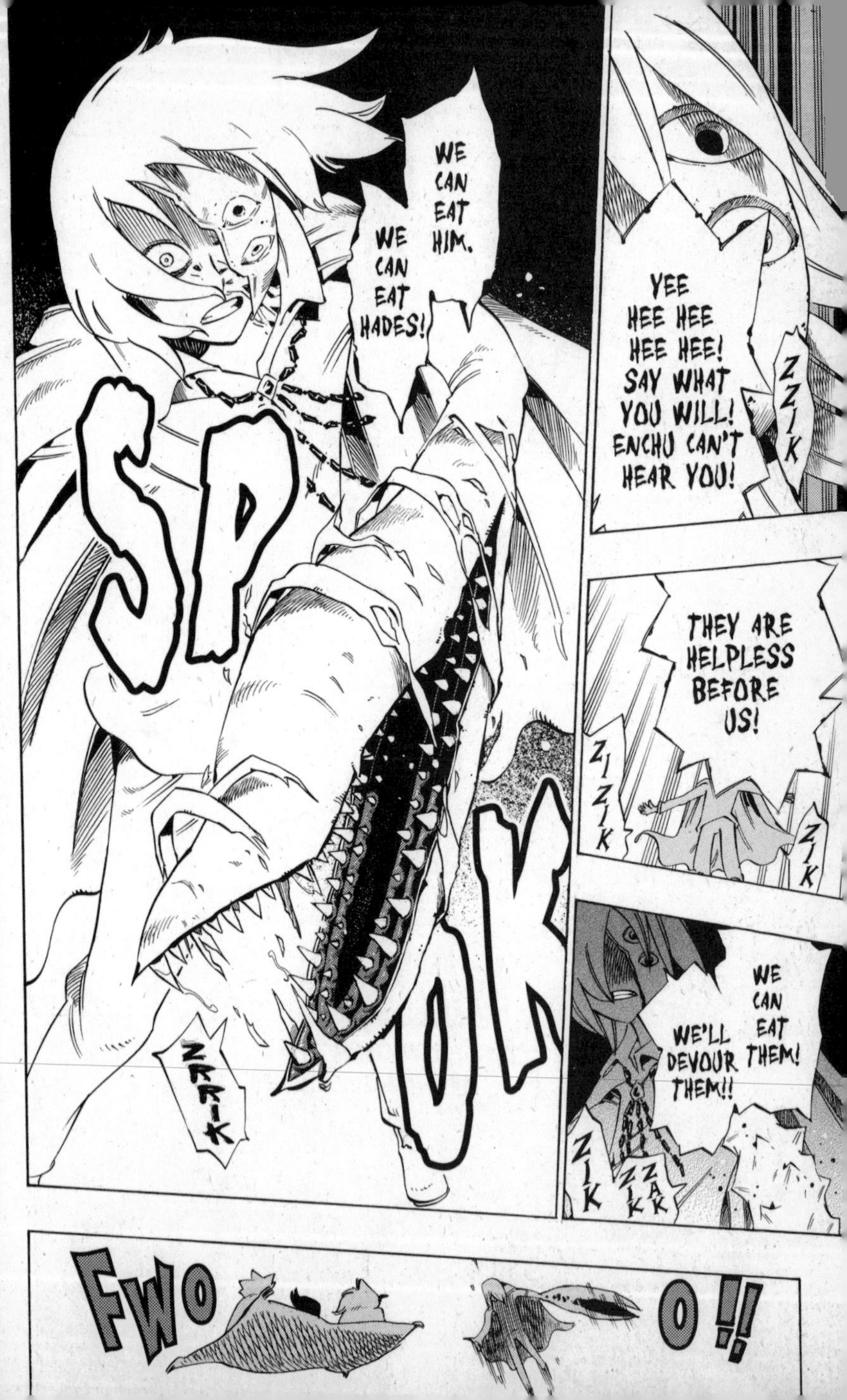

YEE HEE HEE HEE HEE! SAY WHAT YOU WILL! ENCHU CAN'T HEAR YOU!
ZZIK
THEY ARE HELPLESS BEFORE US!
ZIZIK
ZIK
WE CAN EAT THEM!
WE'LL DEVOUR THEM!!
ZIK
ZIK
ZAK
ZIK
WE CAN EAT HIM.
WE CAN EAT HADES!
SPOK
ZRRIK
FWO O!!

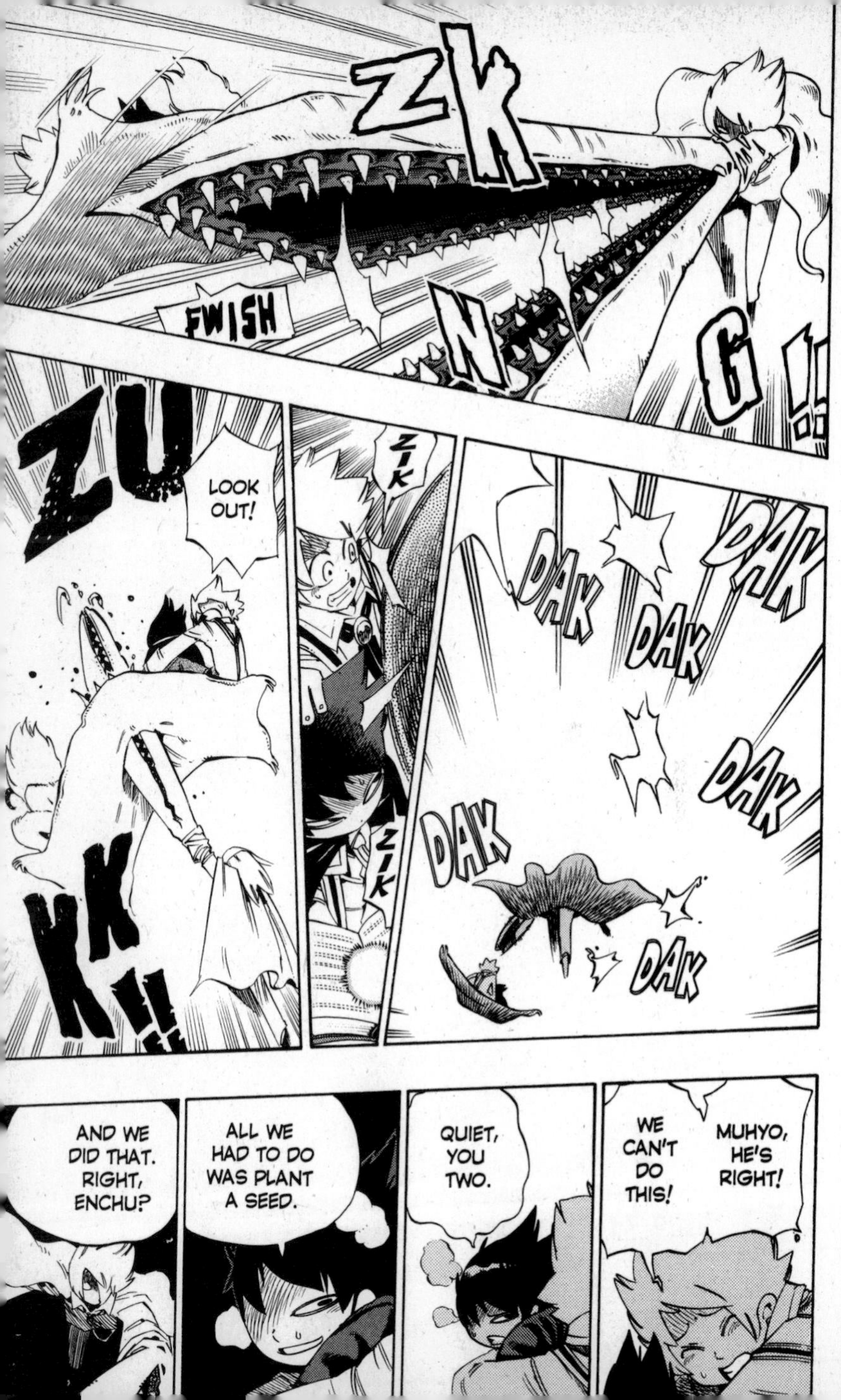
ZK
N
G!!
FWISH
DAK
DAK
DAK
DAK
DAK
DAK
ZIK
ZIK
ZU
LOOK OUT!
KK!!
MUHYO, HE'S RIGHT!
WE CAN'T DO THIS!
QUIET, YOU TWO.
ALL WE HAD TO DO WAS PLANT A SEED.
AND WE DID THAT. RIGHT, ENCHU?

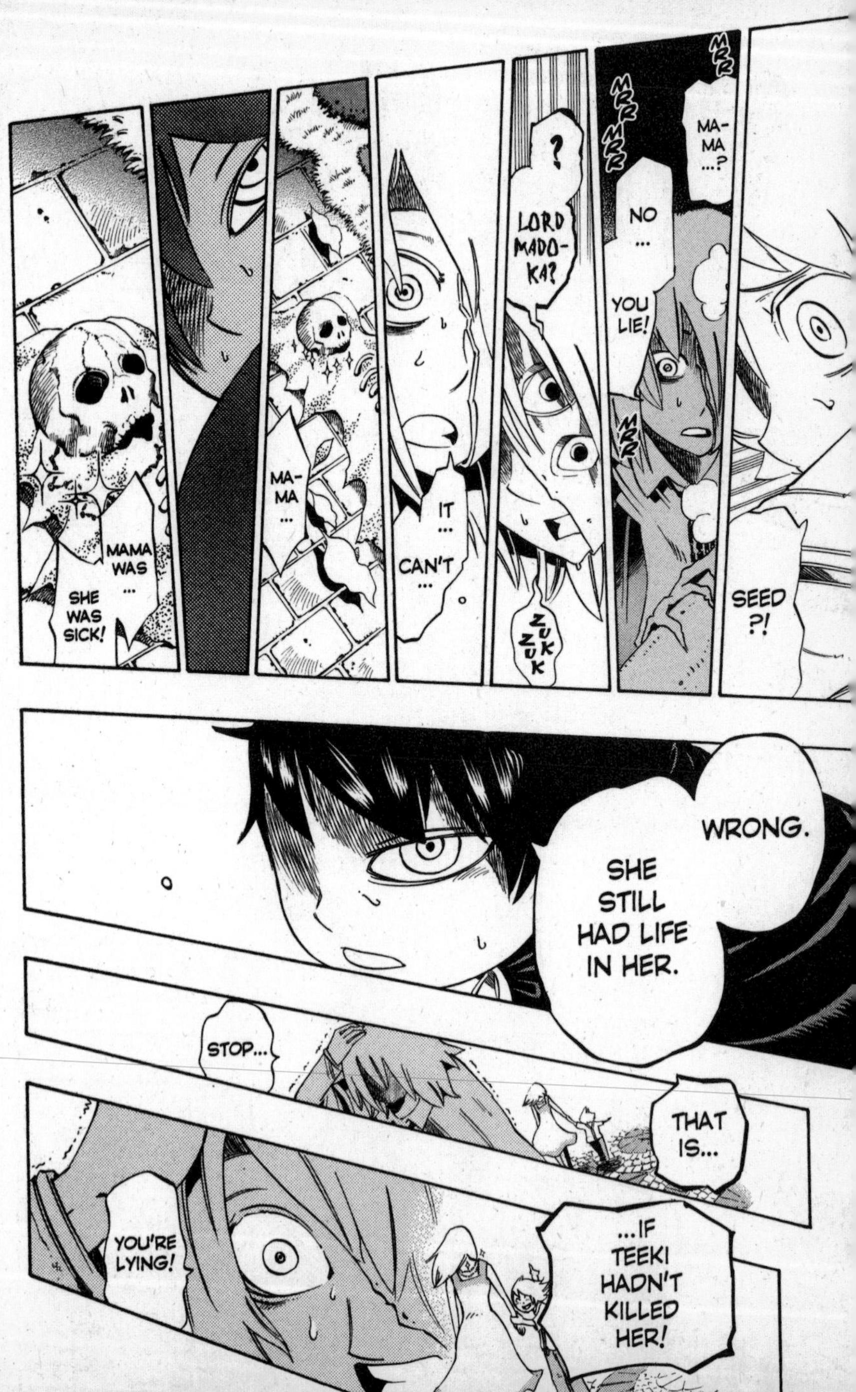
SEED ?!
MRR
MAMA ...?
MRR MRR
NO ...
YOU LIE!
MRR
?
LORD MADO-KA?
ZUK ZUK
IT ... CAN'T ...
MA-MA ...
MAMA WAS ...
SHE WAS SICK!
WRONG.
SHE STILL HAD LIFE IN HER.
STOP...
THAT IS...
...IF TEEKI HADN'T KILLED HER!
YOU'RE LYING!

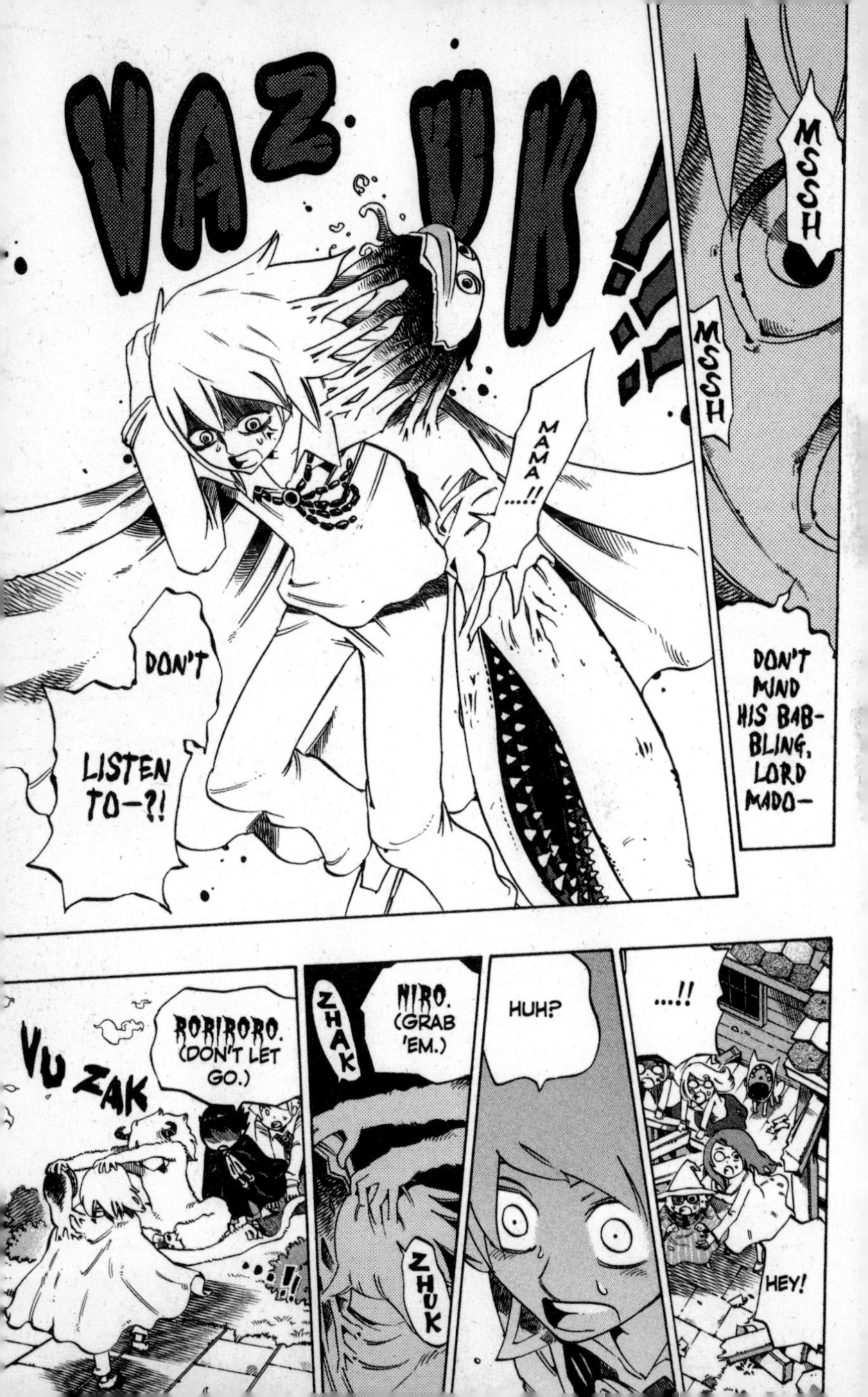
MSSH
MSSH
DON'T MIND HIS BAB-BLING, LORD MADO-
VAZUK!!
MAMA ....!!
DON'T LISTEN TO-?!
...!!
HEY!
HUH?
ZHAK
NIRO. (GRAB 'EM.)
ZHUK
RORIRORO. (DON'T LET GO.)
VU ZAK
..!!

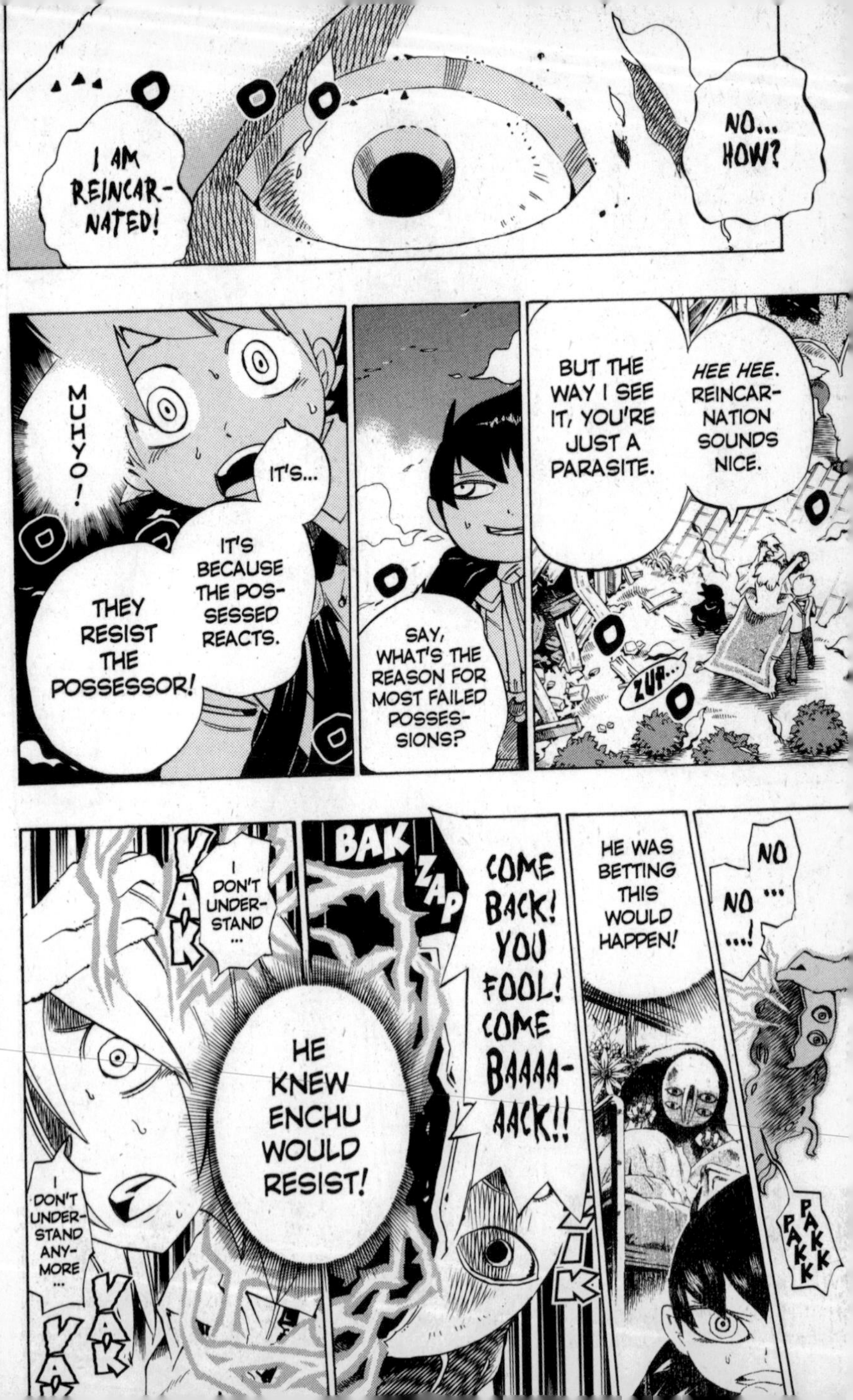
NO... HOW?
I AM REINCARNATED!
HEE HEE. REINCARNATION SOUNDS NICE.
BUT THE WAY I SEE IT, YOU'RE JUST A PARASITE.
ZUP...
SAY, WHAT'S THE REASON FOR MOST FAILED POSSESSIONS?
MUHYO!
IT'S...
IT'S BECAUSE THE POSSESSED REACTS.
THEY RESIST THE POSSESSOR!
NO
NO ... ...!
PAKK PAKK
HE WAS BETTING THIS WOULD HAPPEN!
COME BACK! YOU FOOL! COME BAAAAAACK!!
BAK
ZAP
HE KNEW ENCHU WOULD RESIST!
VAK
I DON'T UNDERSTAND ...
I DON'T UNDERSTAND ANYMORE ...
VAK
VAK

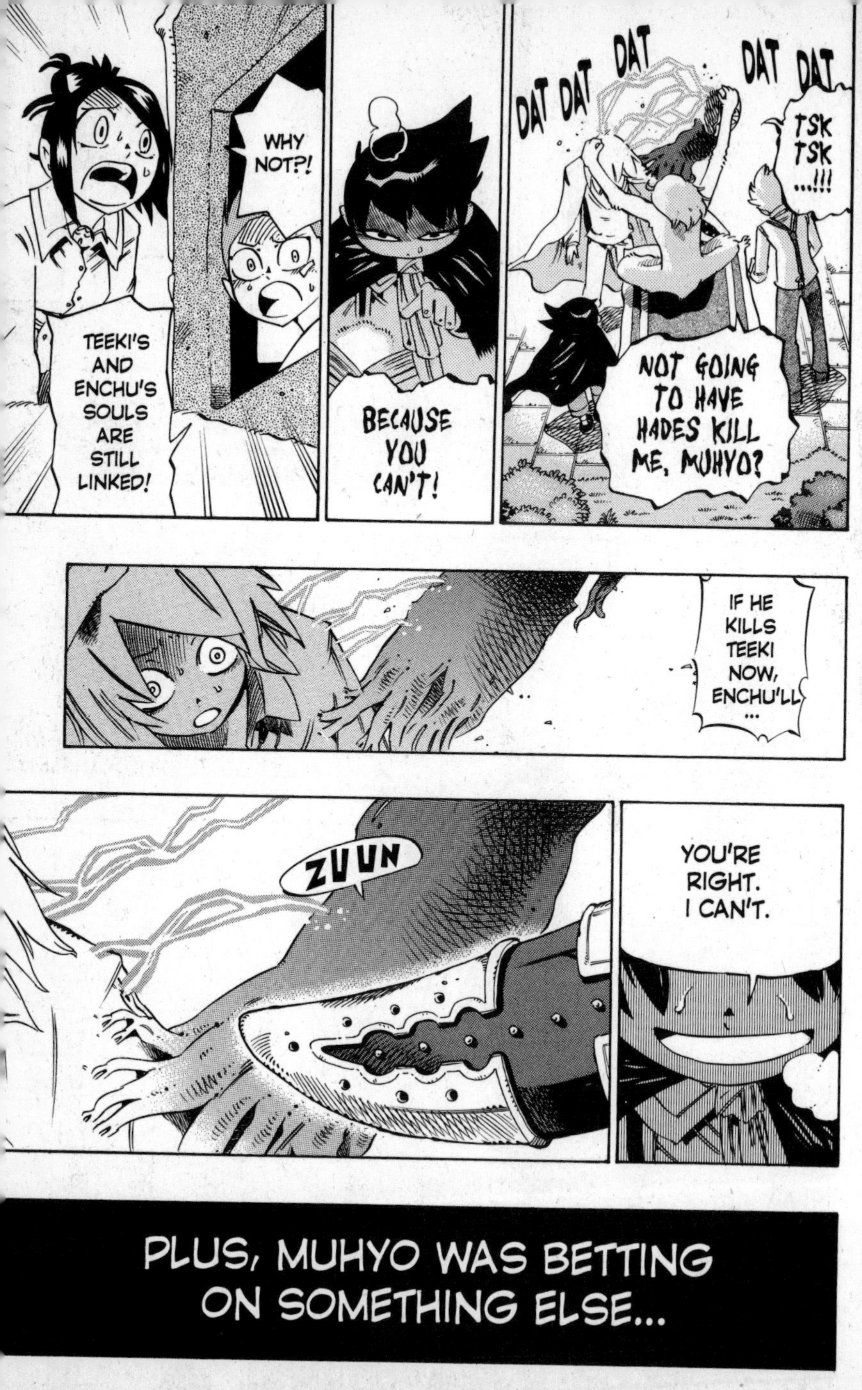
DAT DAT DAT
DAT DAT
TSK TSK ...!!!
NOT GOING TO HAVE HADES KILL ME, MUHYO?
BECAUSE YOU CAN'T!
WHY NOT?!
TEEKI'S AND ENCHU'S SOULS ARE STILL LINKED!
IF HE KILLS TEEKI NOW, ENCHU'LL ...
YOU'RE RIGHT. I CAN'T.
ZUUN
PLUS, MUHYO WAS BETTING ON SOMETHING ELSE...

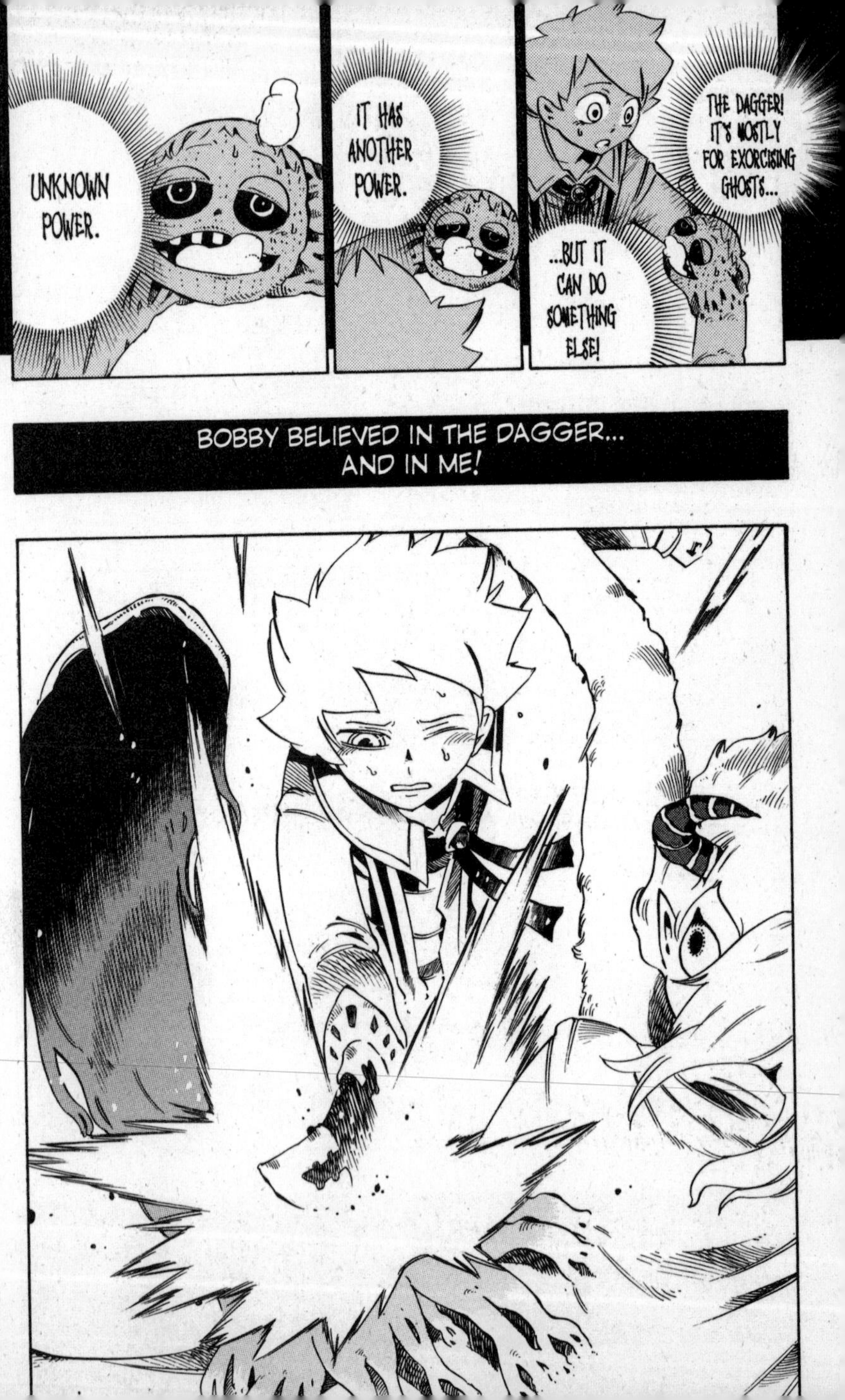
THE DAGGER! IT'S MOSTLY FOR EXORCISING GHOSTS...
...BUT IT CAN DO SOMETHING ELSE!
IT HAS ANOTHER POWER.
UNKNOWN POWER.
BOBBY BELIEVED IN THE DAGGER... AND IN ME!

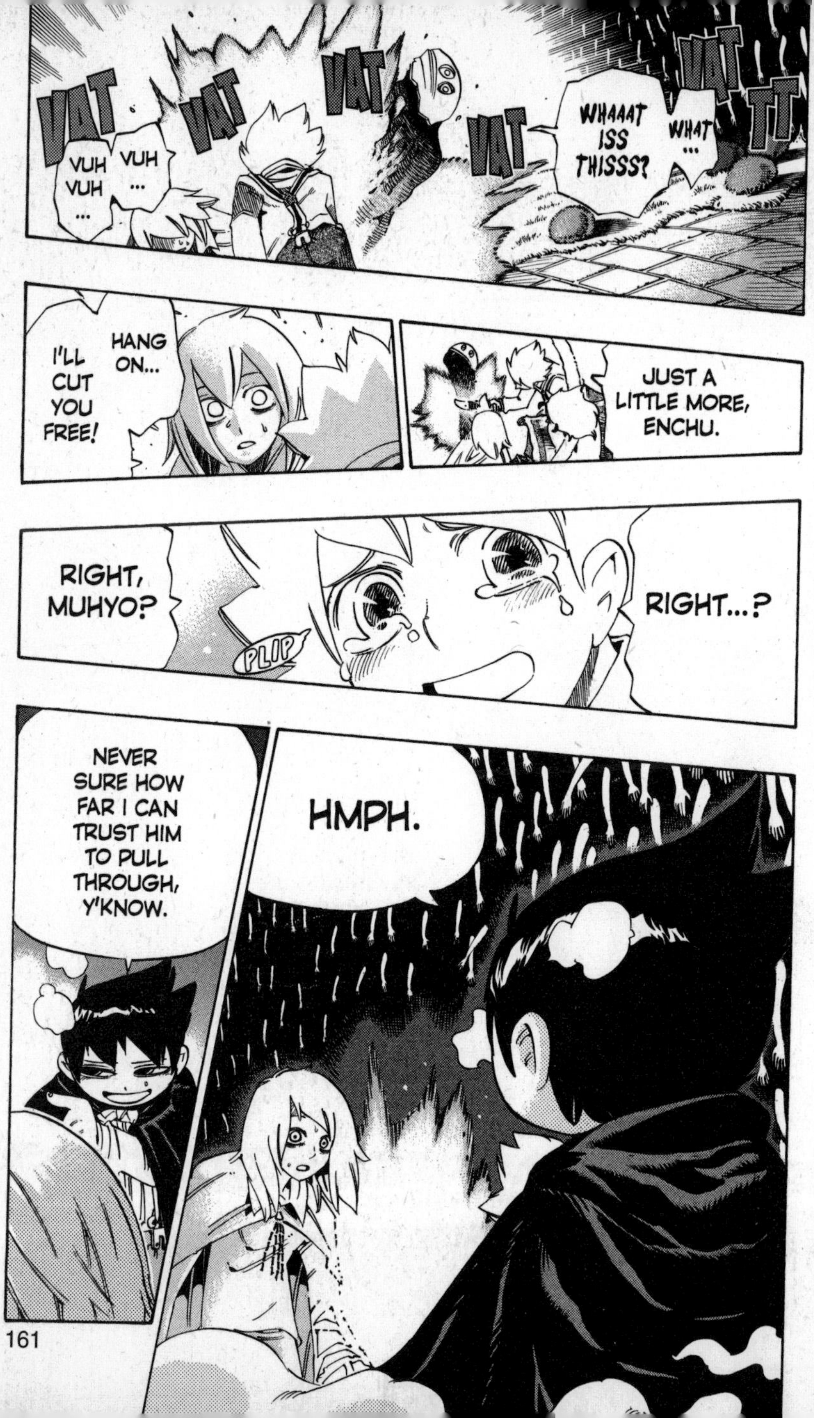

VAT TT
WHAT ...
WHAAAT ISS THISSS?
VAT
VAT
VAT
VUH ...
VAT
VUH VUH ...
JUST A LITTLE MORE, ENCHU.
HANG ON...
I'LL CUT YOU FREE!
RIGHT...?
PLIP
RIGHT, MUHYO?
HMPH.
NEVER SURE HOW FAR I CAN TRUST HIM TO PULL THROUGH, Y'KNOW.

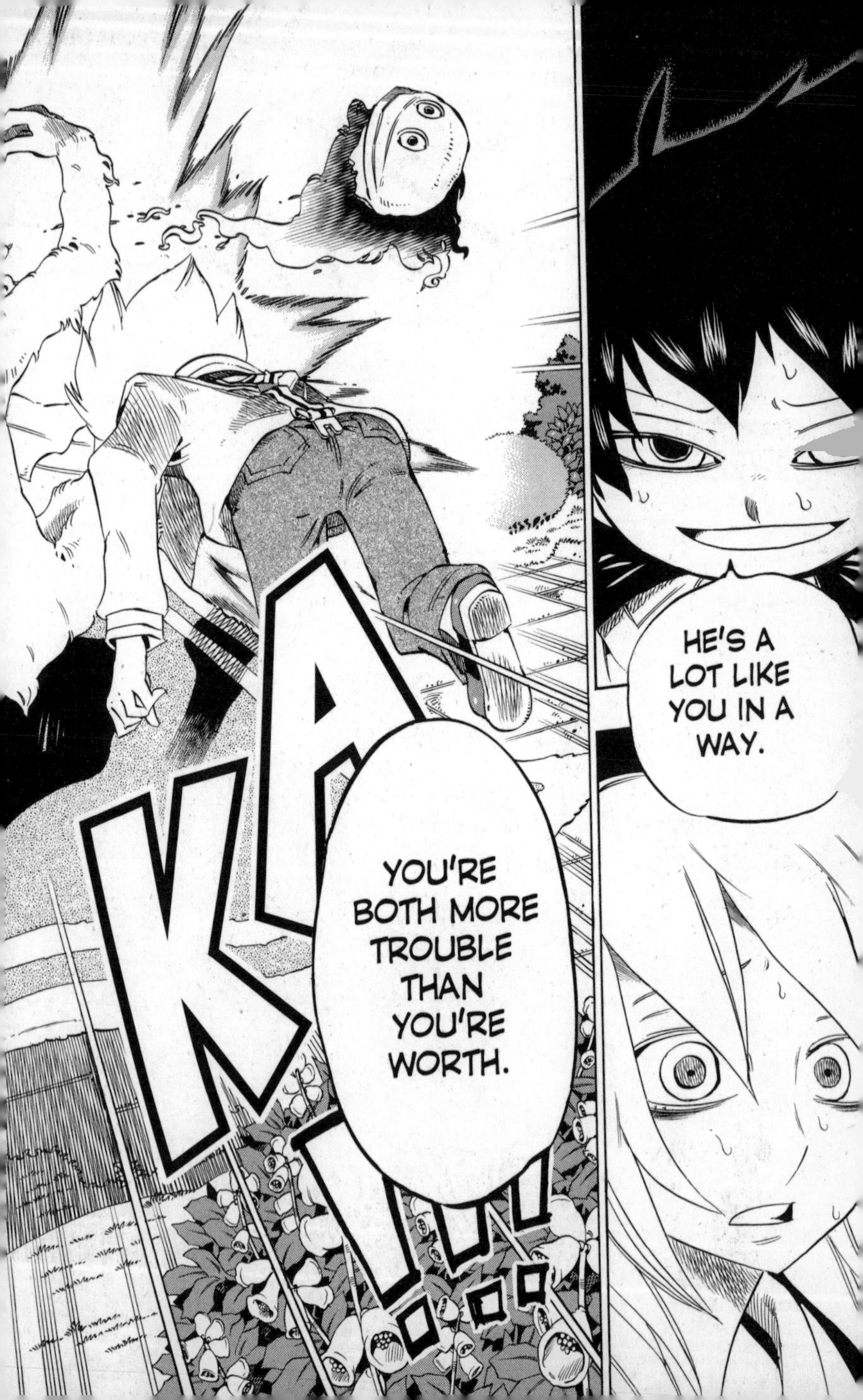
HE'S A LOT LIKE YOU IN A WAY.
YOU'RE BOTH MORE TROUBLE THAN YOU'RE WORTH.
KA...

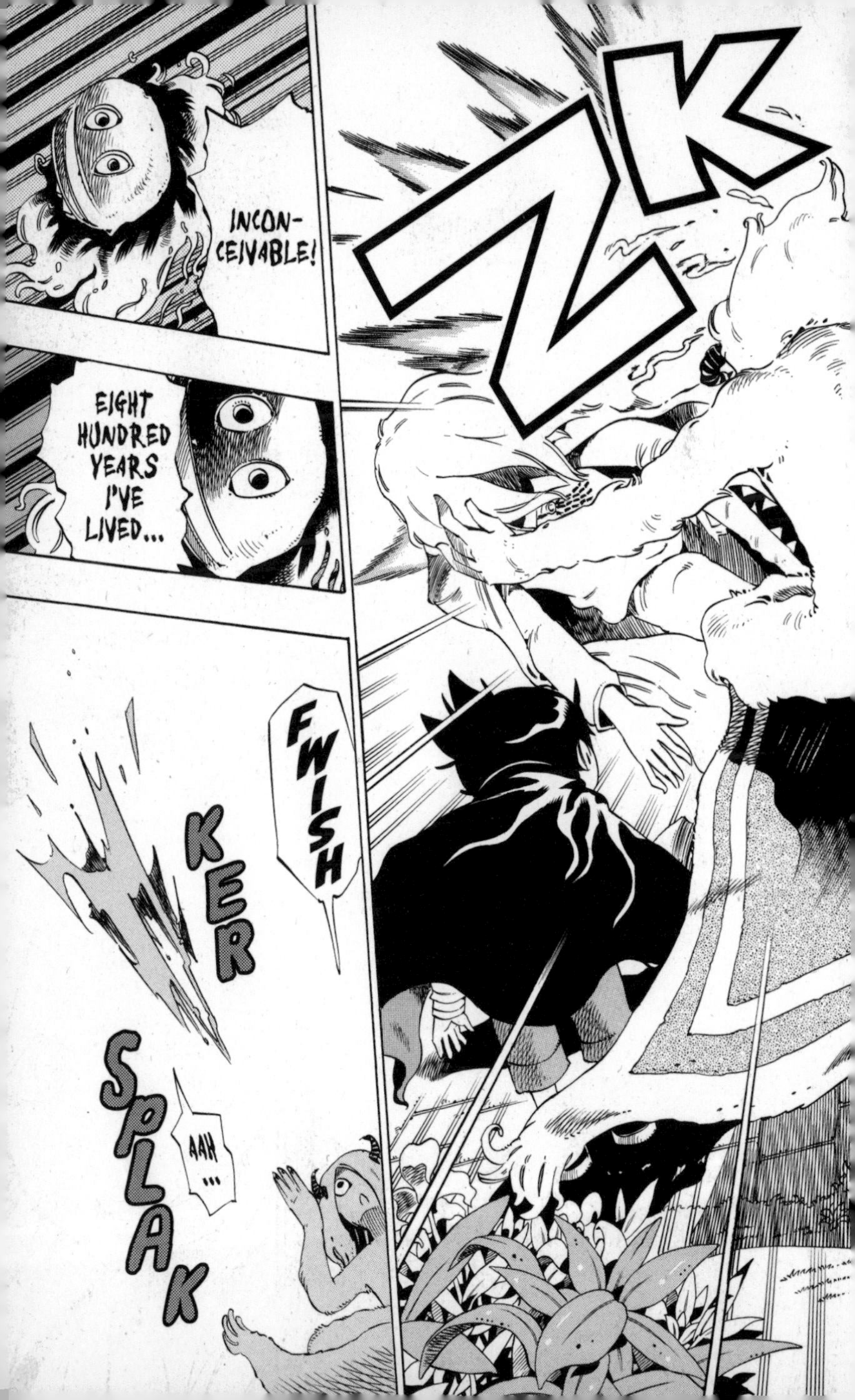
ZK
INCON-CEIVABLE!
EIGHT HUNDRED YEARS I'VE LIVED...
FWISH
KER
SPLAK
AAH...

ARTICLE 130
THE LONG NIGHTMARE

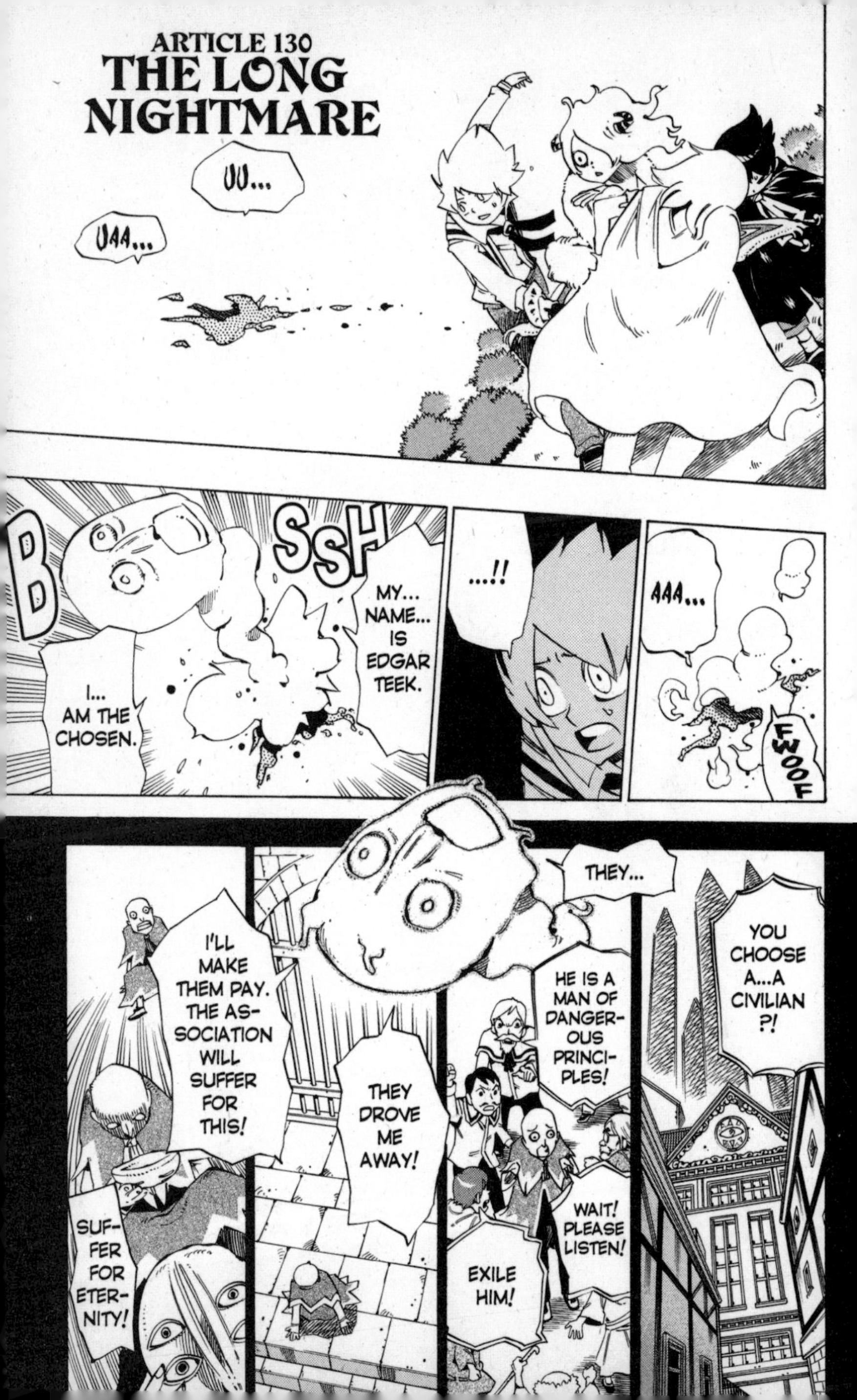
UU...
UAA...
AAA...
FWOOF
...!!
BSSH
MY... NAME... IS EDGAR TEEK.
I... AM THE CHOSEN.
YOU CHOOSE A...A CIVILIAN?!
THEY...
HE IS A MAN OF DANGEROUS PRINCIPLES!
WAIT! PLEASE LISTEN!
EXILE HIM!
THEY DROVE ME AWAY!
I'LL MAKE THEM PAY. THE ASSOCIATION WILL SUFFER FOR THIS!
SUFFER FOR ETERNITY!

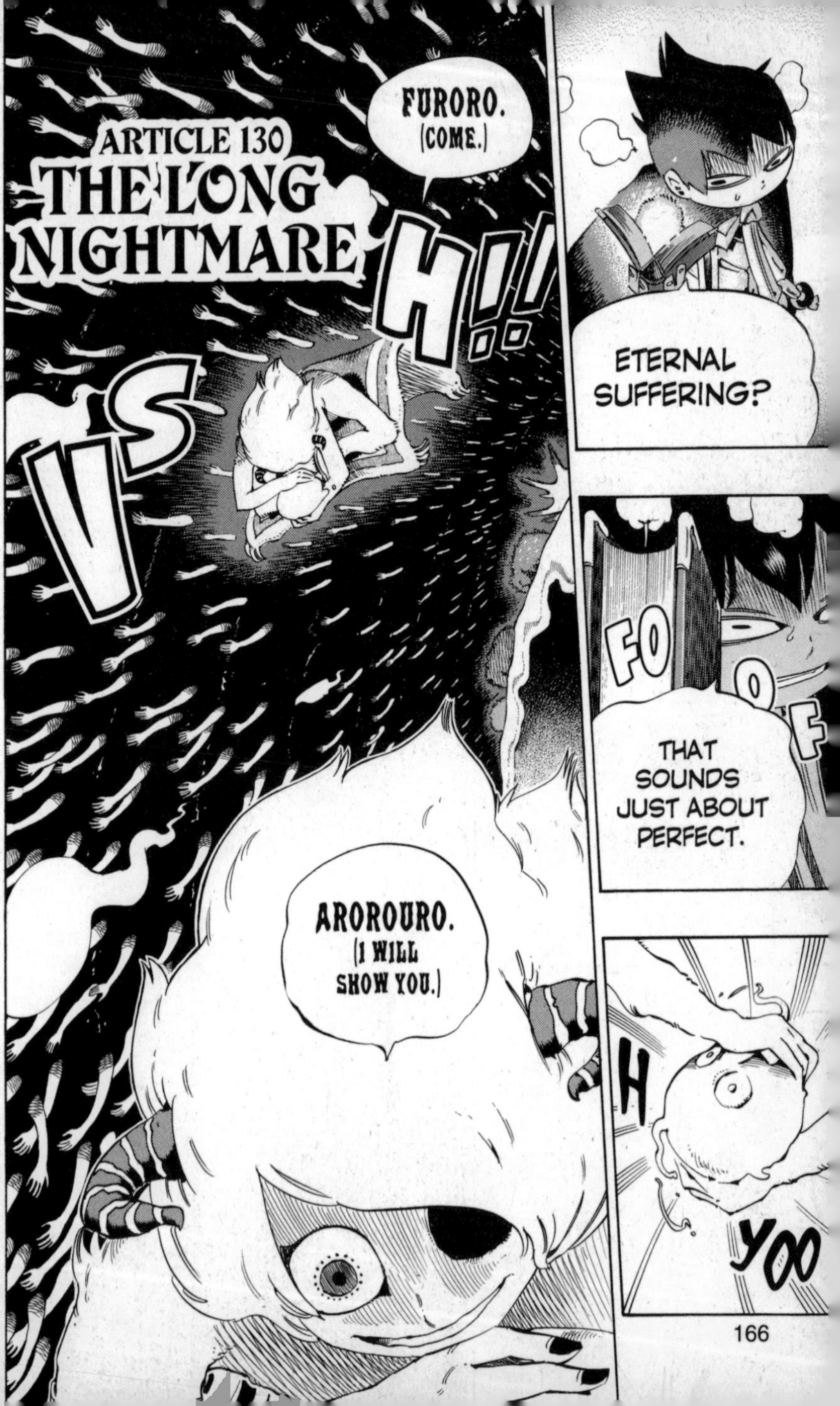
ETERNAL SUFFERING?
FOOF
THAT SOUNDS JUST ABOUT PERFECT.
H
YOO
ARTICLE 130
THE LONG NIGHTMARE
FURORO. (COME.)
H!!!
VS
ARORORURO. (I WILL SHOW YOU.)

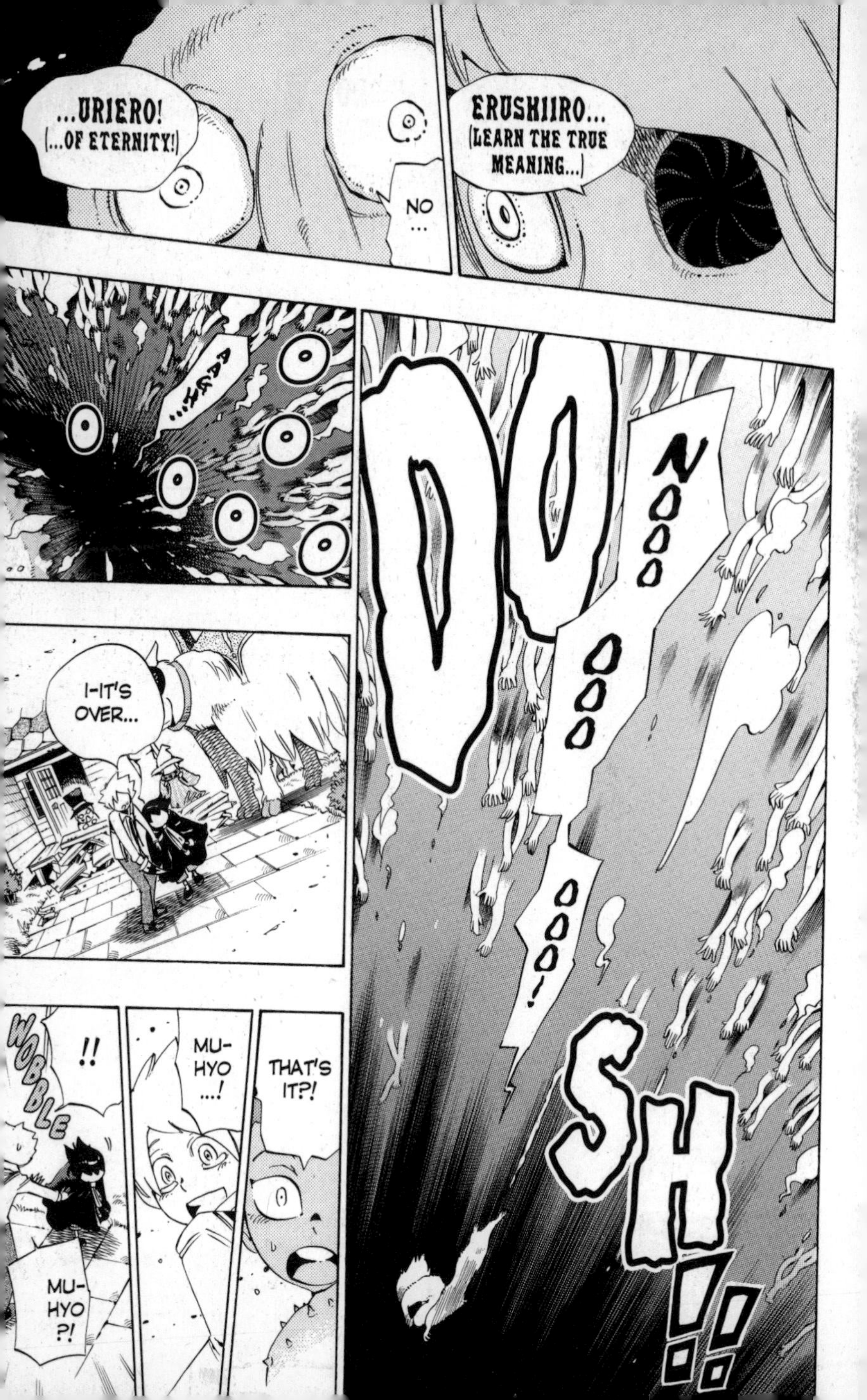
ERUSHIIRO... (LEARN THE TRUE MEANING...)
NO ...
...URIERO! (...OF ETERNITY!)
DO
NOOOOOOOOOO!
SH!!!
AAGH...
I-IT'S OVER...
THAT'S IT?!
MU-HYO ...!
!!
WOBBLE
MU-HYO ?!

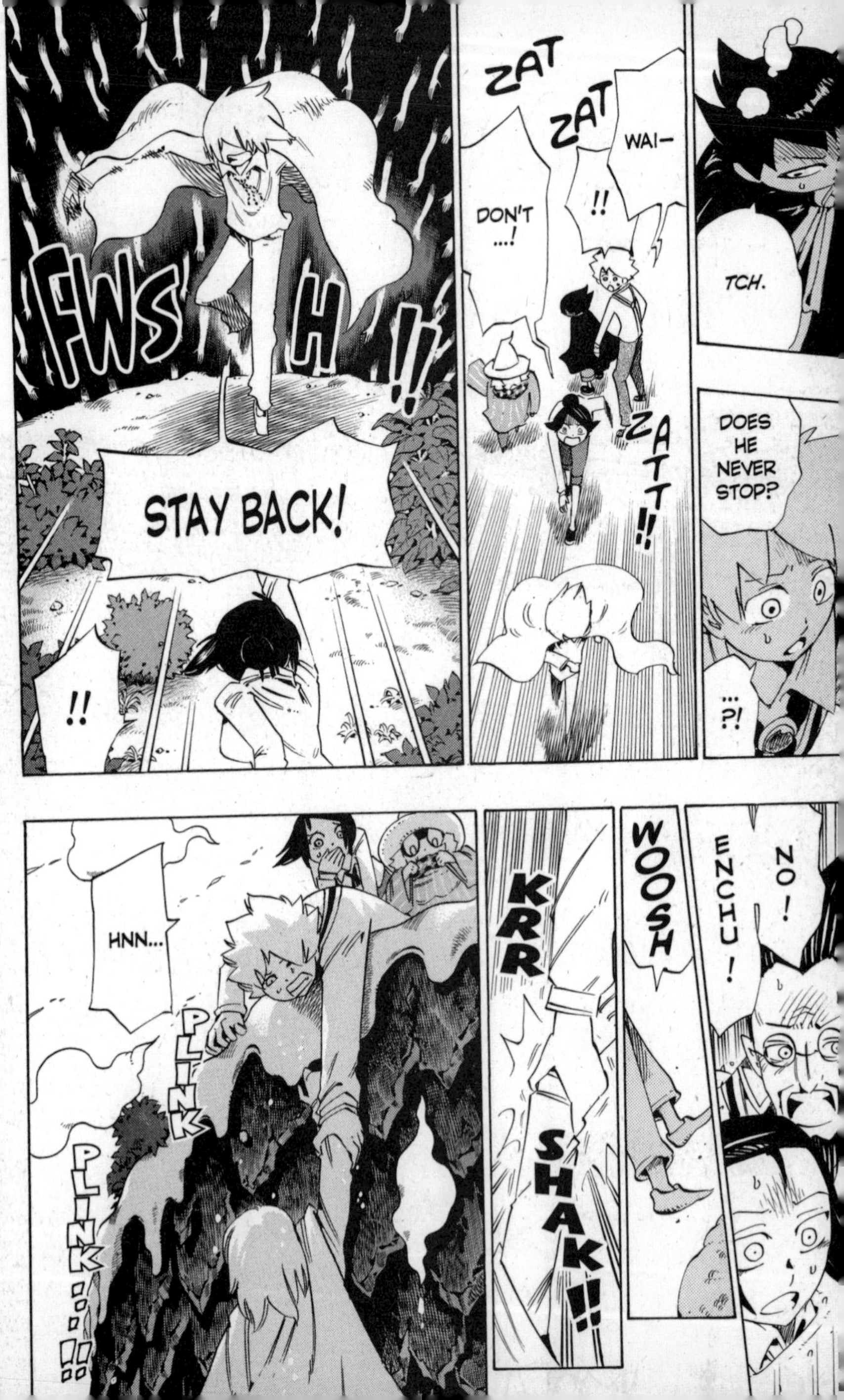
TCH.
DOES HE NEVER STOP?
...?!
WAI—
ZAT
ZAT
!!
DON'T ...!
ZATT!!
FWSH!!
STAY BACK!
!!
NO!
ENCHU!
WOOSH
KRR
SHAK!!
HNN...
PLINK
PLINK...!!

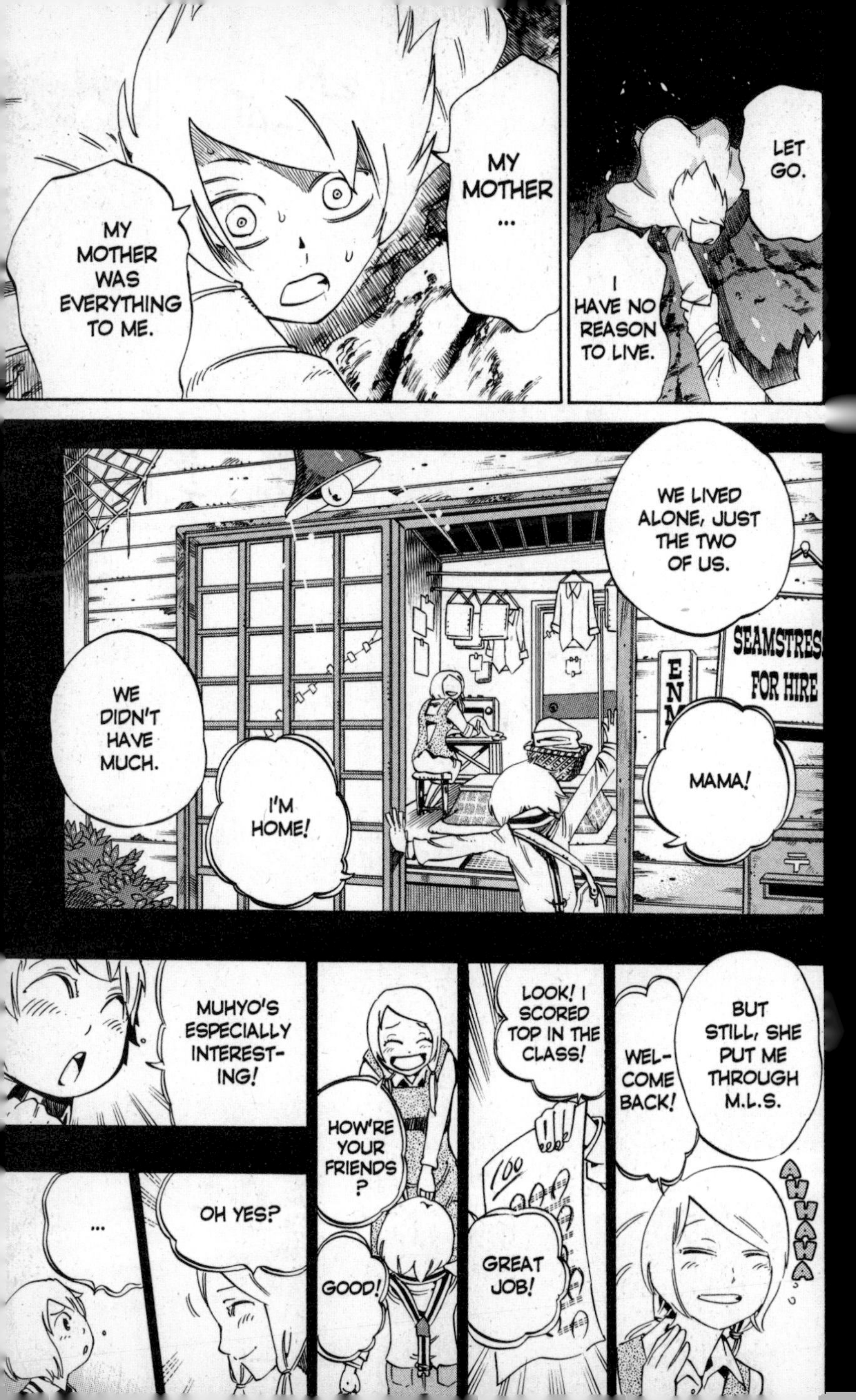
LET GO.
I HAVE NO REASON TO LIVE.
MY MOTHER ...
MY MOTHER WAS EVERYTHING TO ME.
WE LIVED ALONE, JUST THE TWO OF US.
SEAMSTRES
FOR HIRE
MAMA!
I'M HOME!
WE DIDN'T HAVE MUCH.
BUT STILL, SHE PUT ME THROUGH M.L.S.
AHAHAHA
WEL-COME BACK!
LOOK! I SCORED TOP IN THE CLASS!
100
GREAT JOB!
HOW'RE YOUR FRIENDS?
GOOD!
MUHYO'S ESPECIALLY INTEREST-ING!
OH YES?
...

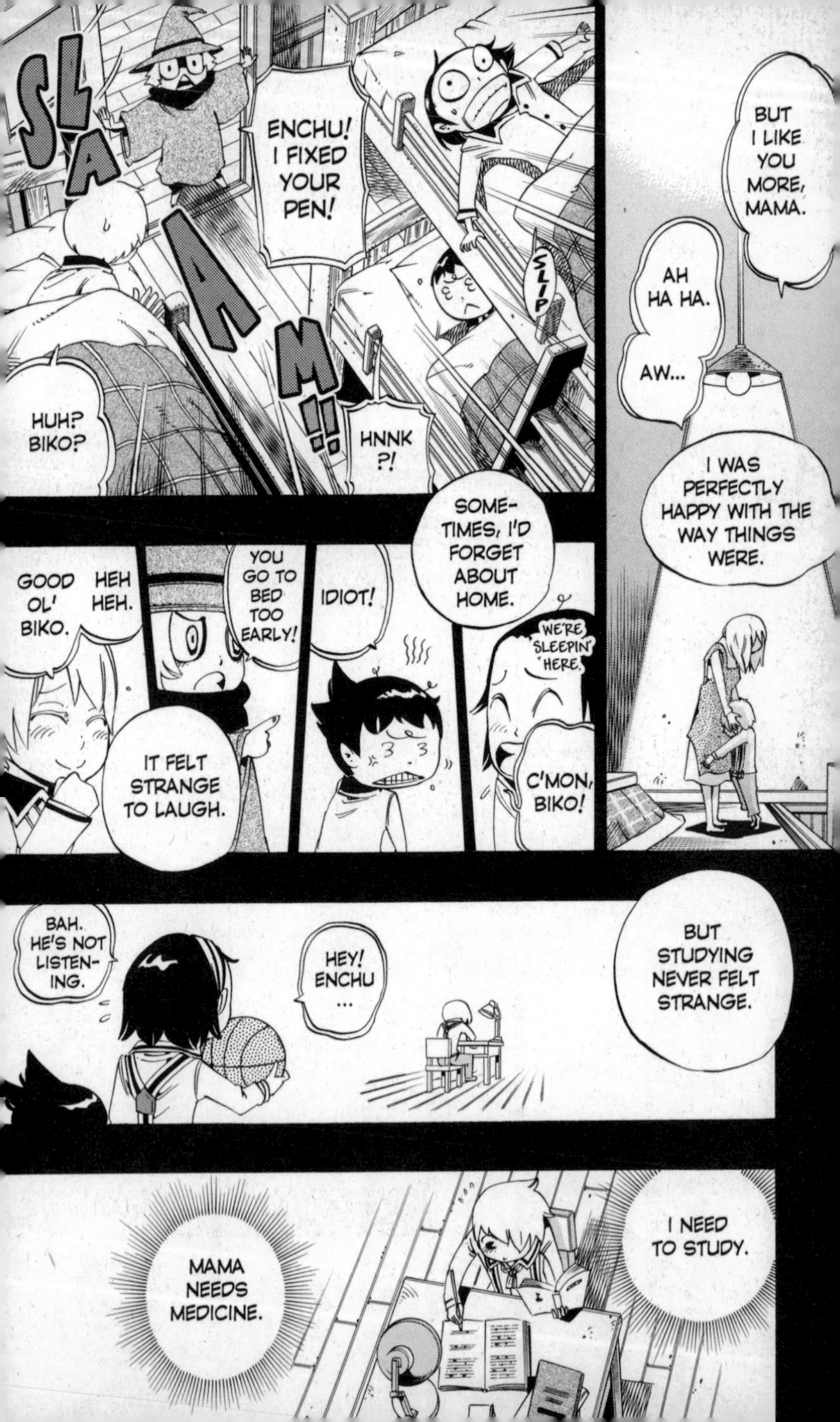
BUT I LIKE YOU MORE, MAMA.
AH HA HA.
AW...
I WAS PERFECTLY HAPPY WITH THE WAY THINGS WERE.
ENCHU! I FIXED YOUR PEN!
SLAM!!
SLIP
HNNK ?!
HUH? BIKO?
SOME-TIMES, I'D FORGET ABOUT HOME.
WE'RE SLEEPIN' HERE.
C'MON, BIKO!
IDIOT!
YOU GO TO BED TOO EARLY!
HEH HEH.
GOOD OL' BIKO.
IT FELT STRANGE TO LAUGH.
BUT STUDYING NEVER FELT STRANGE.
HEY! ENCHU ...
BAH. HE'S NOT LISTEN-ING.
I NEED TO STUDY.
MAMA NEEDS MEDICINE.

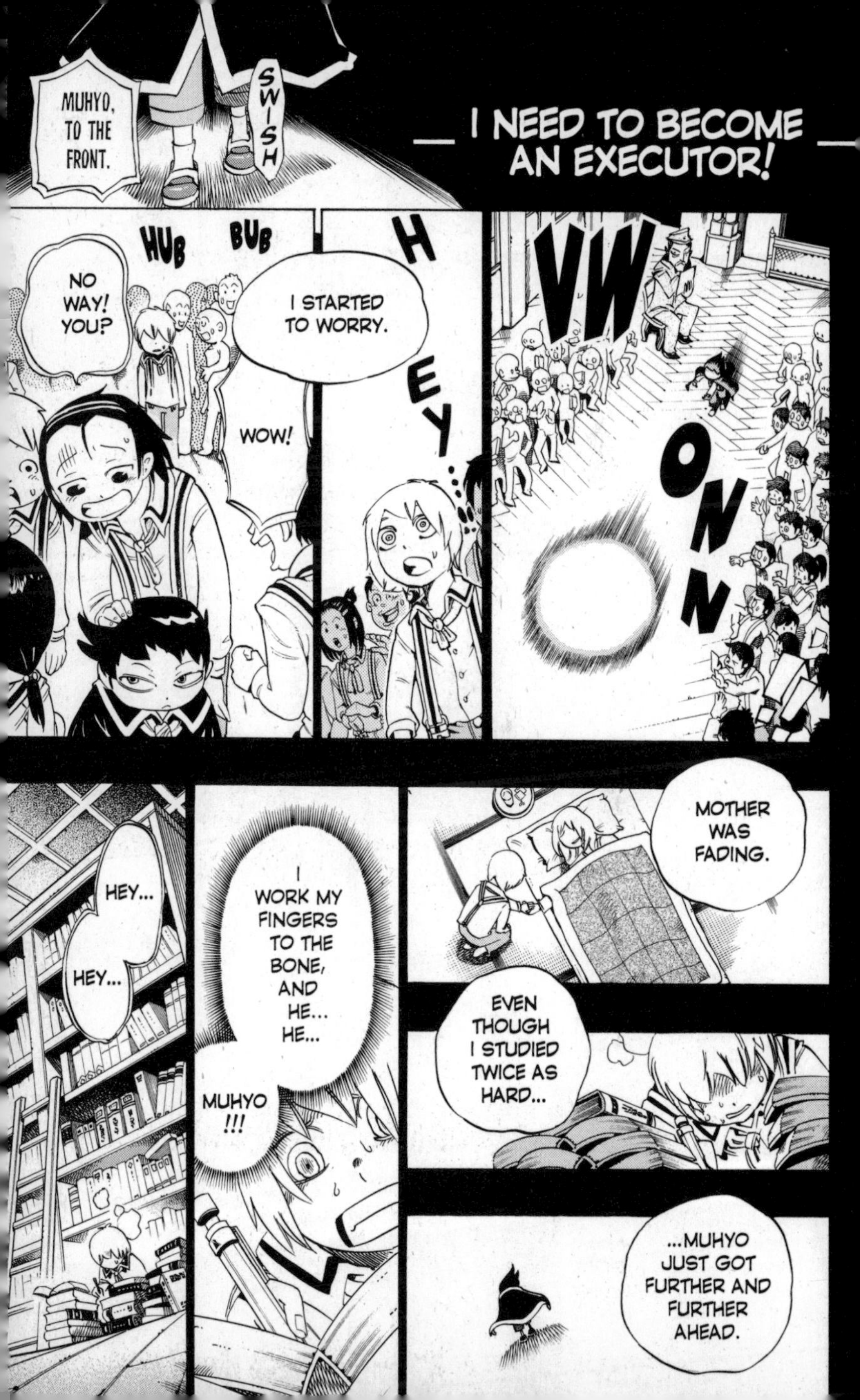
I NEED TO BECOME AN EXECUTOR!
SWISH
MUHYO, TO THE FRONT.
VWONN
HEY
I STARTED TO WORRY.
HUB BUB
NO WAY! YOU?
WOW!
MOTHER WAS FADING.
EVEN THOUGH I STUDIED TWICE AS HARD...
...MUHYO JUST GOT FURTHER AND FURTHER AHEAD.
I WORK MY FINGERS TO THE BONE, AND HE... HE...
MUHYO!!!
HEY...
HEY...

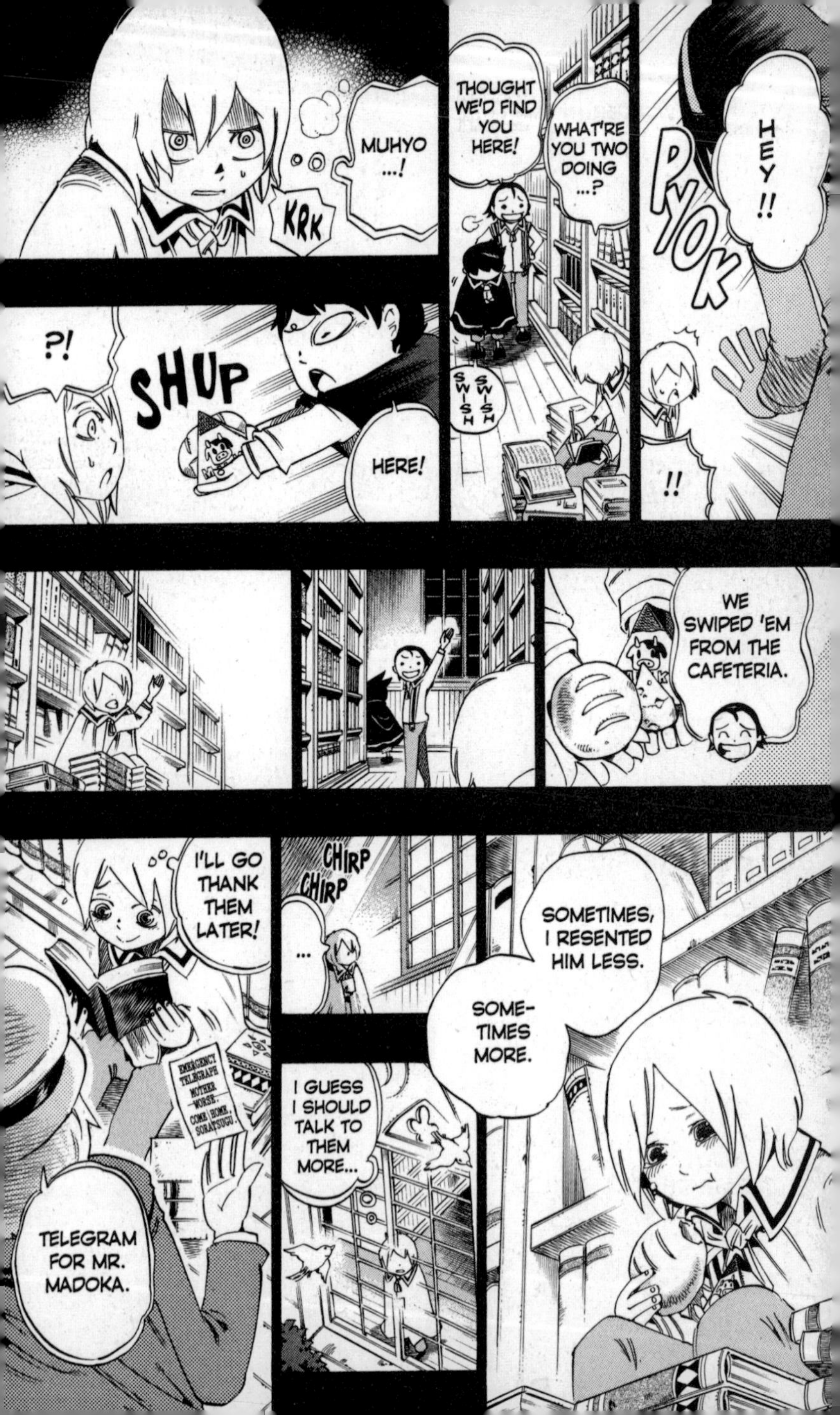
HEY!!
PYOK
!!
WHAT'RE YOU TWO DOING ...?
THOUGHT WE'D FIND YOU HERE!
SWISH SWISH
MUHYO ...!
KRK
?!
SHUP
HERE!
WE SWIPED 'EM FROM THE CAFETERIA.
SOMETIMES, I RESENTED HIM LESS.
SOME-TIMES MORE.
CHIRP
CHIRP
...
I GUESS I SHOULD TALK TO THEM MORE...
I'LL GO THANK THEM LATER!
EMERGENCY TELEGRAPH
MOTHER WORSE.
COME HOME, SORATSUGU.
TELEGRAM FOR MR. MADOKA.

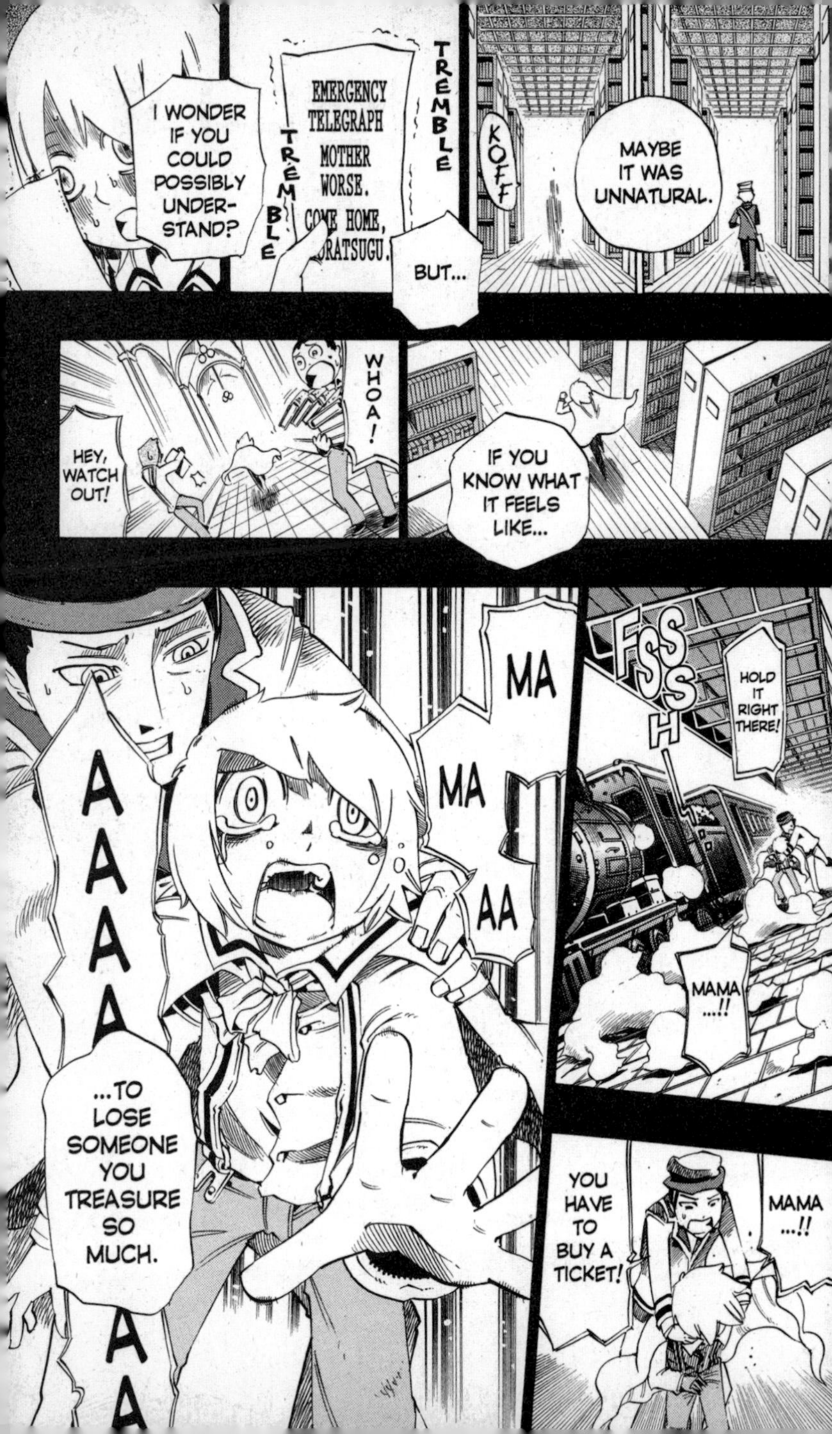
MAYBE IT WAS UNNATURAL.
KOFF
BUT...
TREMBLE
EMERGENCY TELEGRAPH
MOTHER WORSE.
COME HOME,
TREMBLE
I WONDER IF YOU COULD POSSIBLY UNDER-STAND?
IF YOU KNOW WHAT IT FEELS LIKE...
WHOA!
HEY, WATCH OUT!
FSSSH
HOLD IT RIGHT THERE!
MAMA ...!!
MAMA ...!!
YOU HAVE TO BUY A TICKET!
MA MA AA
AAAAAA
...TO LOSE SOMEONE YOU TREASURE SO MUCH.

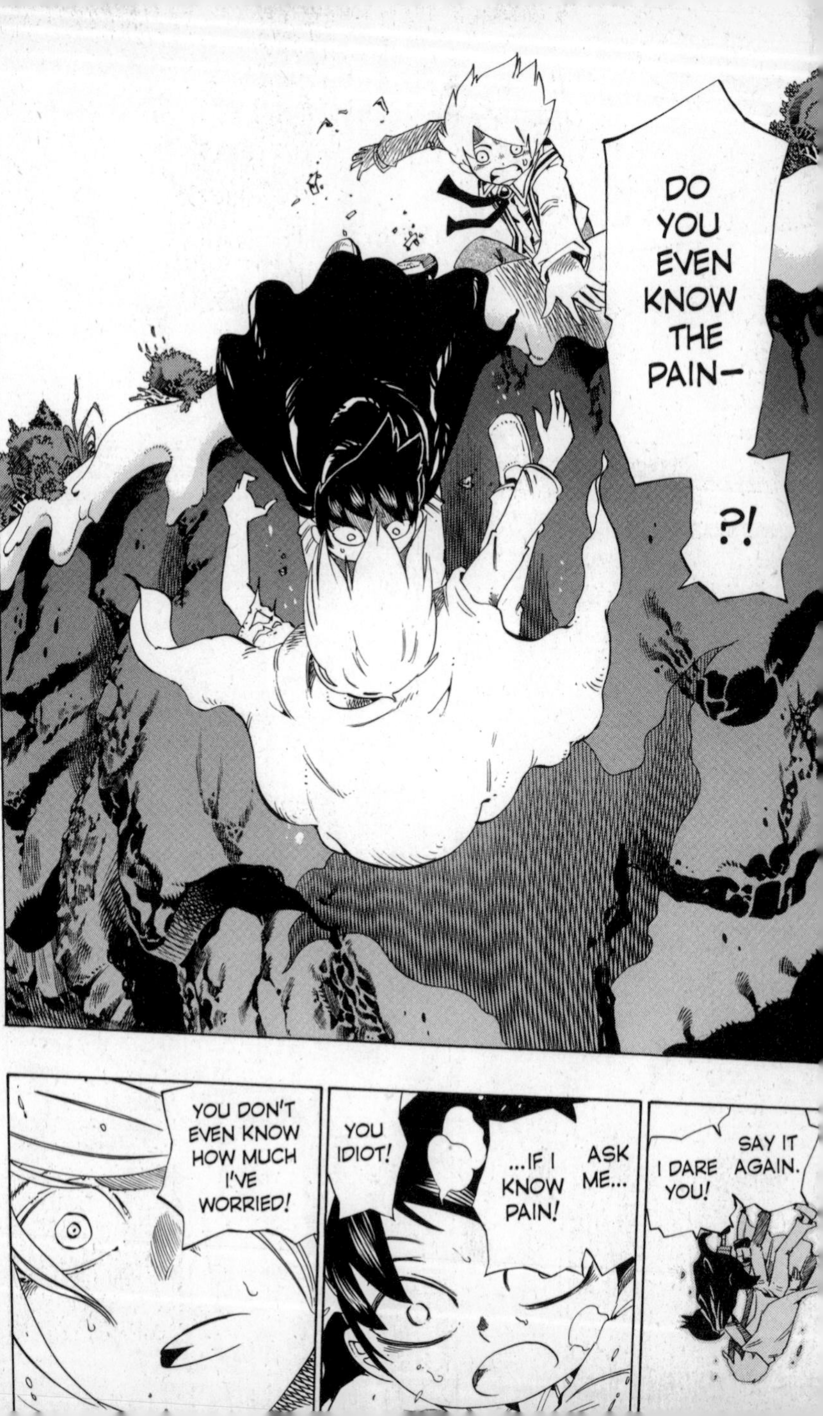
DO YOU EVEN KNOW THE PAIN—
?!
SAY IT AGAIN.
I DARE YOU!
ASK ME...
...IF I KNOW PAIN!
YOU IDIOT!
YOU DON'T EVEN KNOW HOW MUCH I'VE WORRIED!

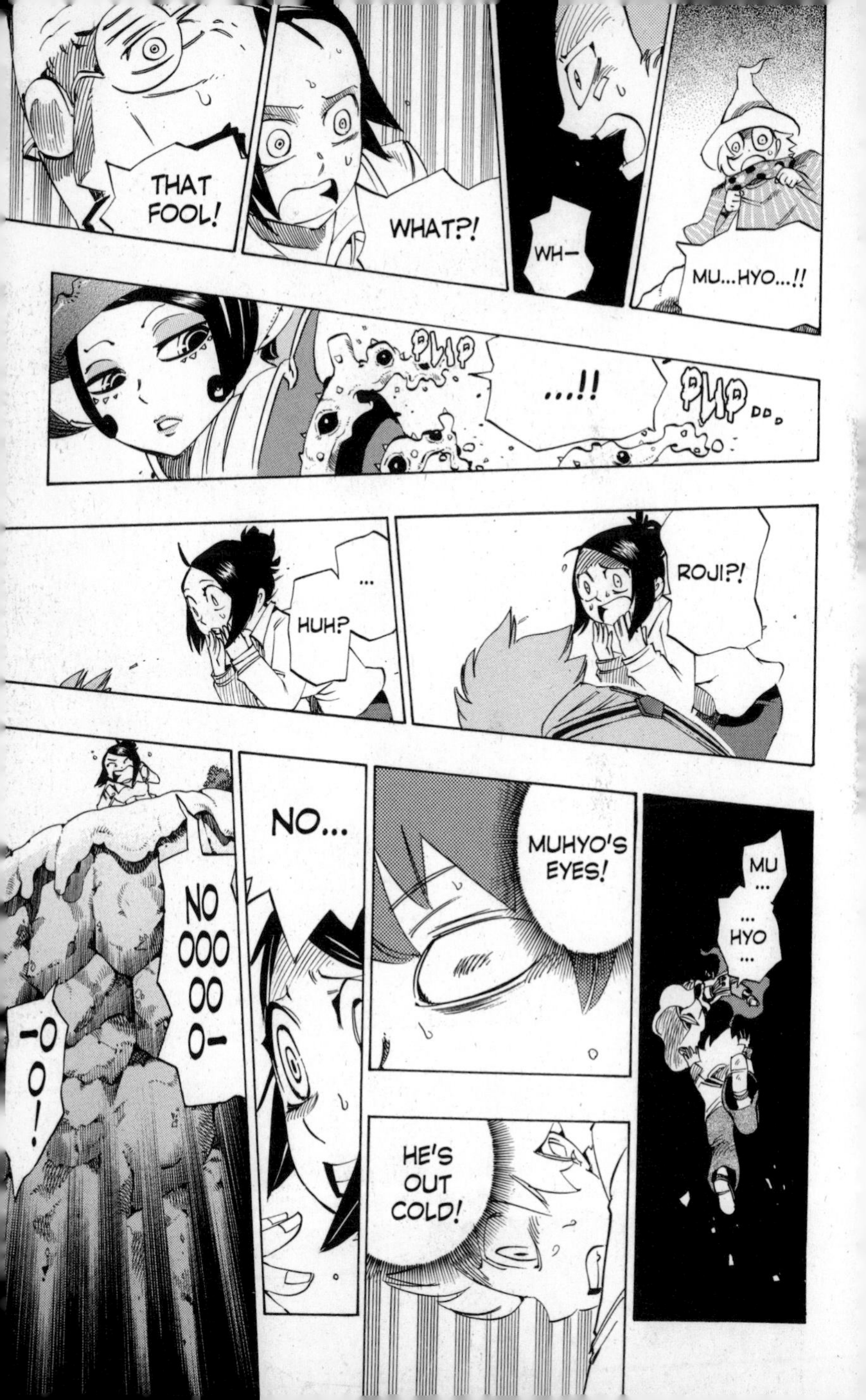
MU...HYO...!!
WH–
WHAT?!
THAT FOOL!
PLIP
...!!
PLIP
ROJI?!
... HUH?
MU ... ... HYO ...
MUHYO'S EYES!
HE'S OUT COLD!
NO...
NOOOOOOOO– –O O!

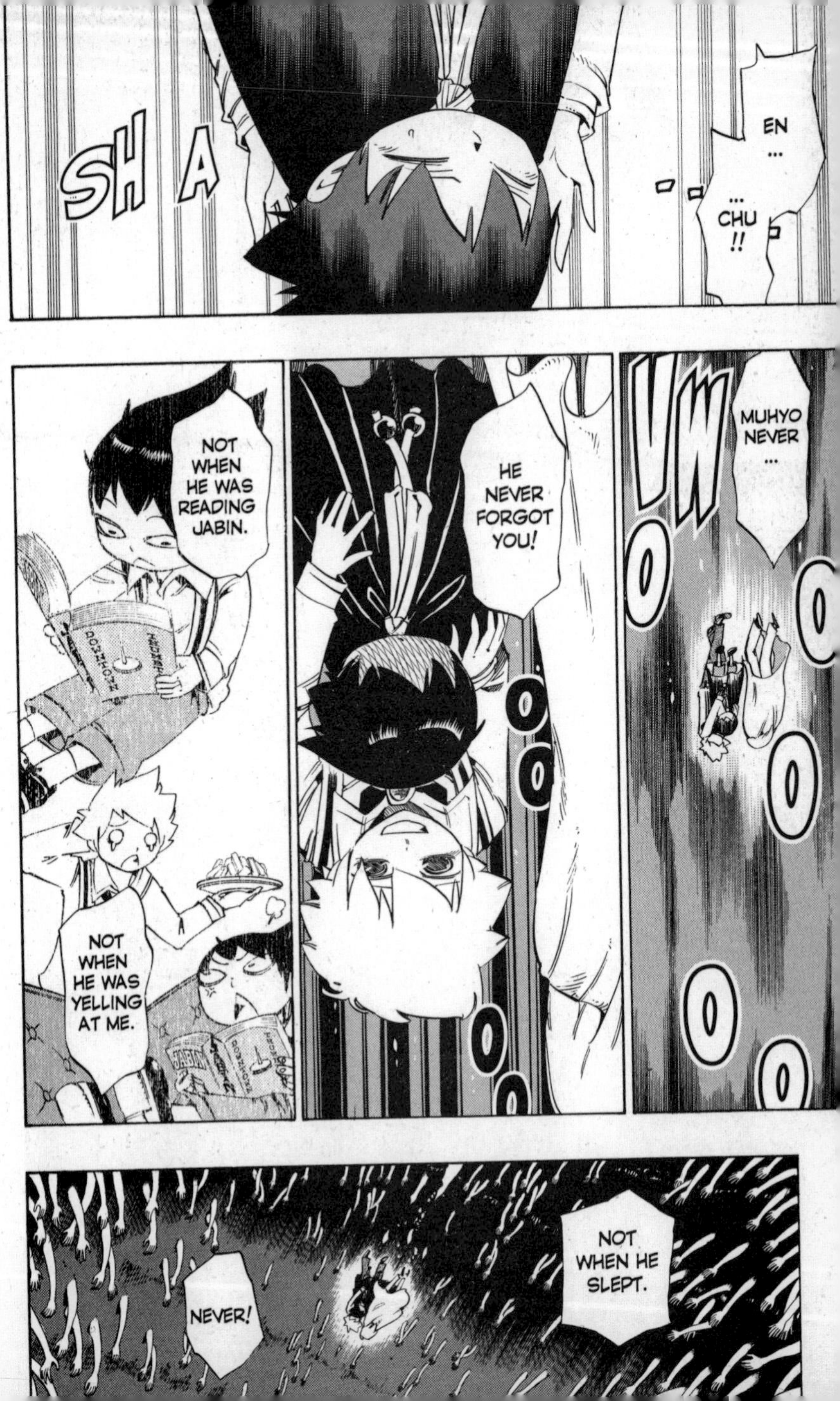
EN ...
... CHU !!
SH A
MUHYO NEVER ...
VWOOOO
HE NEVER FORGOT YOU!
NOT WHEN HE WAS READING JABIN.
NOT WHEN HE WAS YELLING AT ME.
NOT WHEN HE SLEPT.
NEVER!

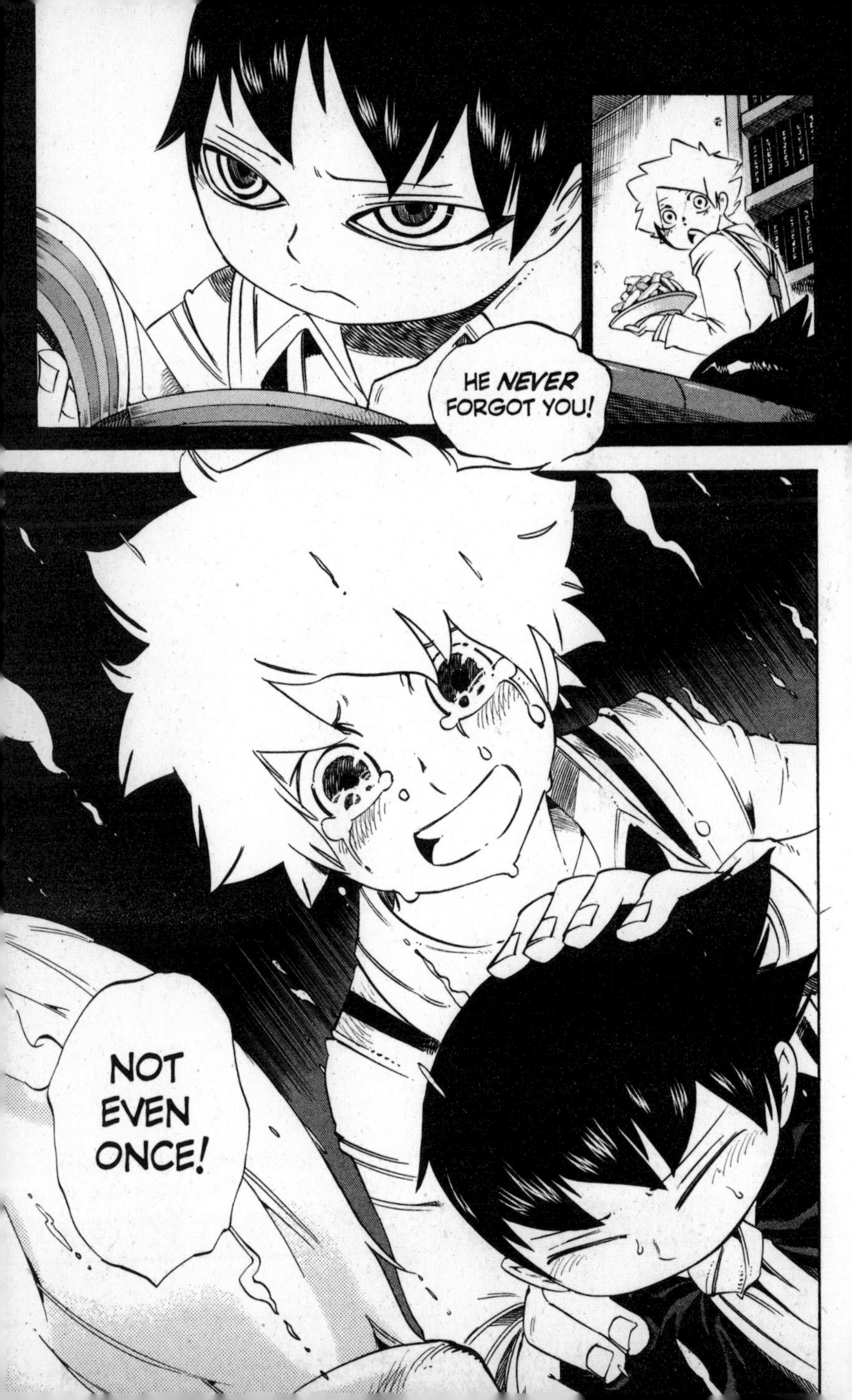
HE *NEVER* FORGOT YOU!
NOT EVEN ONCE!

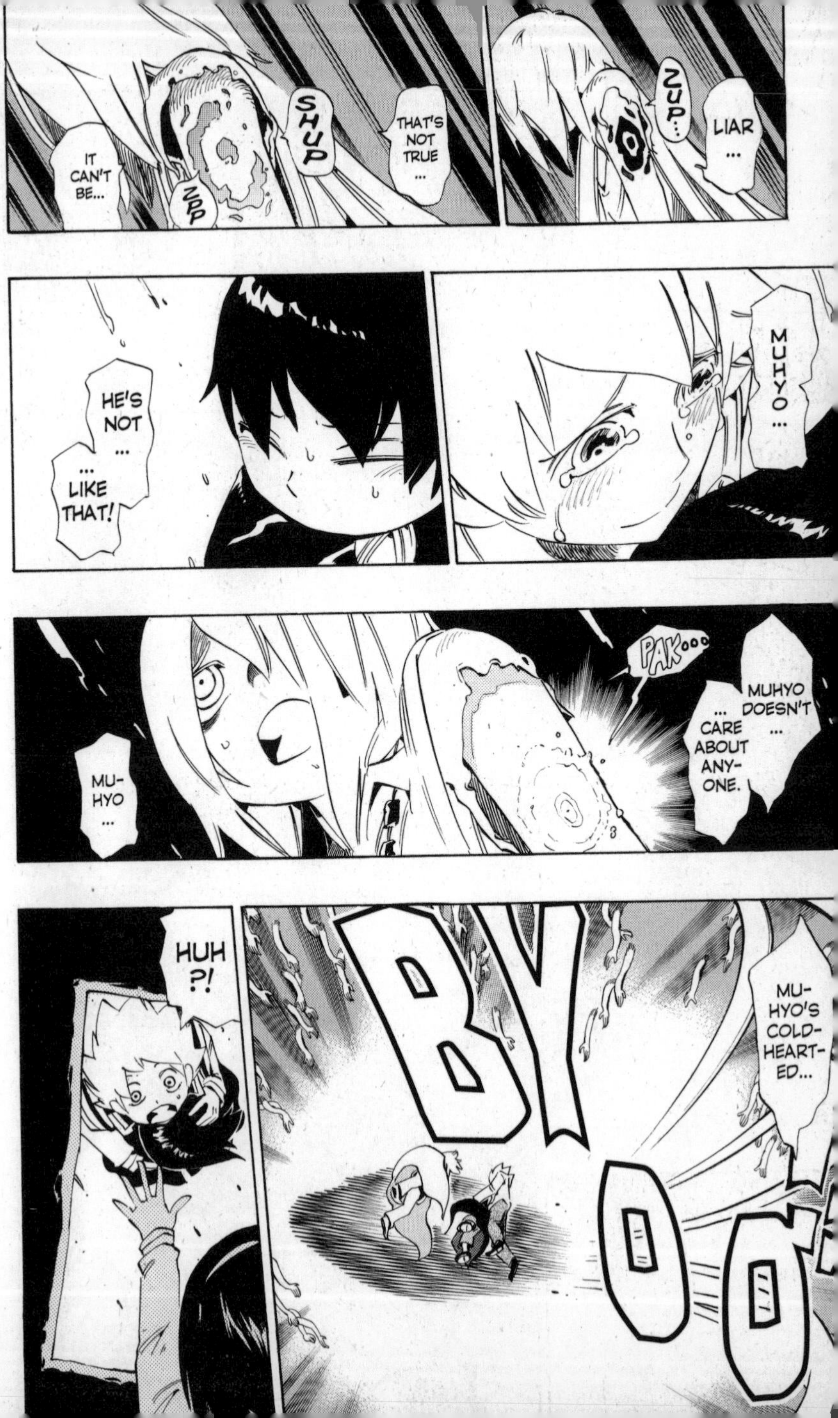
LIAR ...
ZUP...
THAT'S NOT TRUE ...
SHUP
IT CAN'T BE...
ZPP
MUHYO ...
HE'S NOT ...
... LIKE THAT!
MUHYO DOESN'T ...
PAK...
... CARE ABOUT ANY-ONE.
MU-HYO ...
MU-HYO'S COLD-HEART-ED...
BYOOO
HUH?!

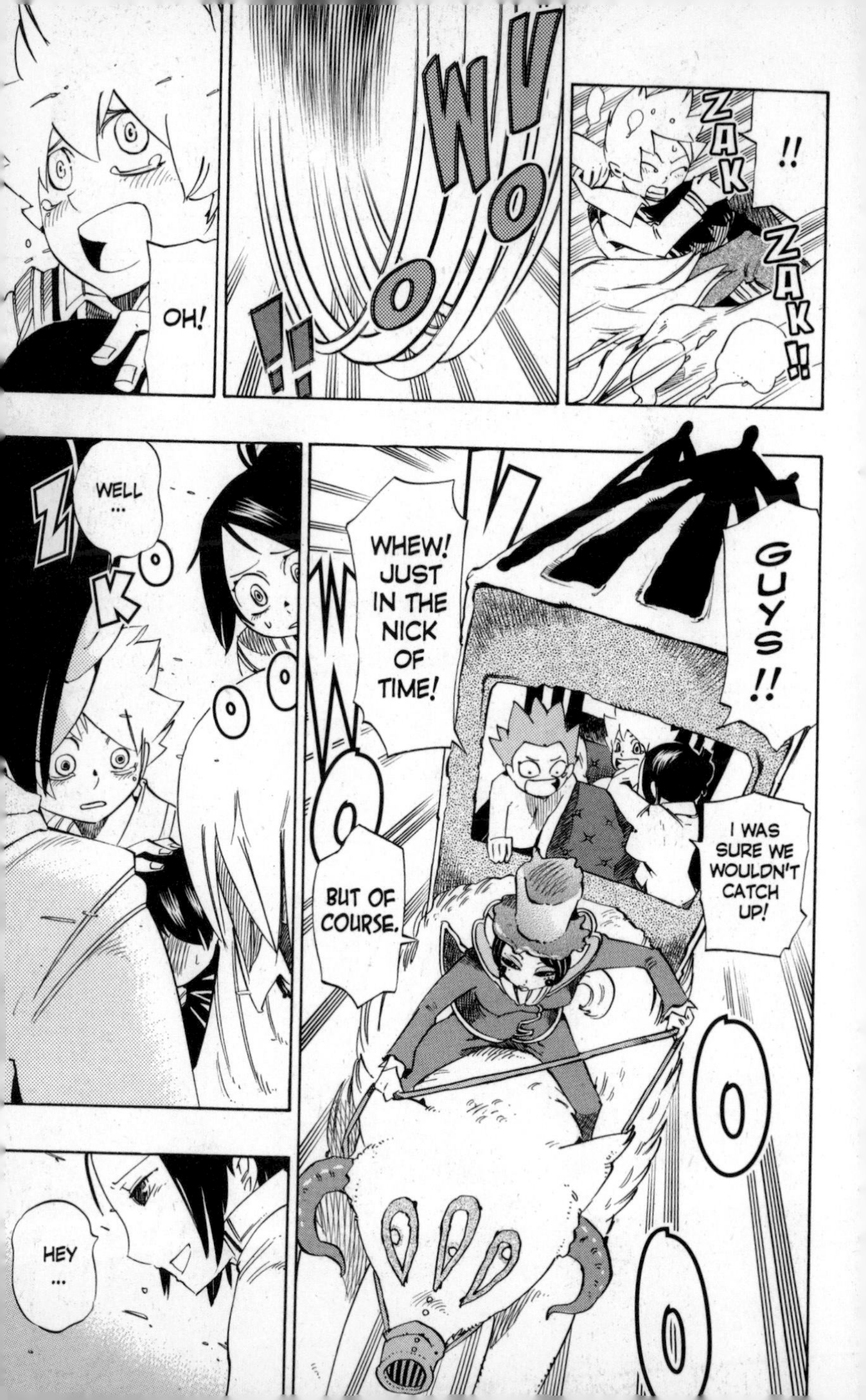
ZAK ZAK!!
!!
WVOOO!!
OH!
GUYS!!
WHEW! JUST IN THE NICK OF TIME!
I WAS SURE WE WOULDN'T CATCH UP!
BUT OF COURSE.
WELL ...
ZK
HEY ...

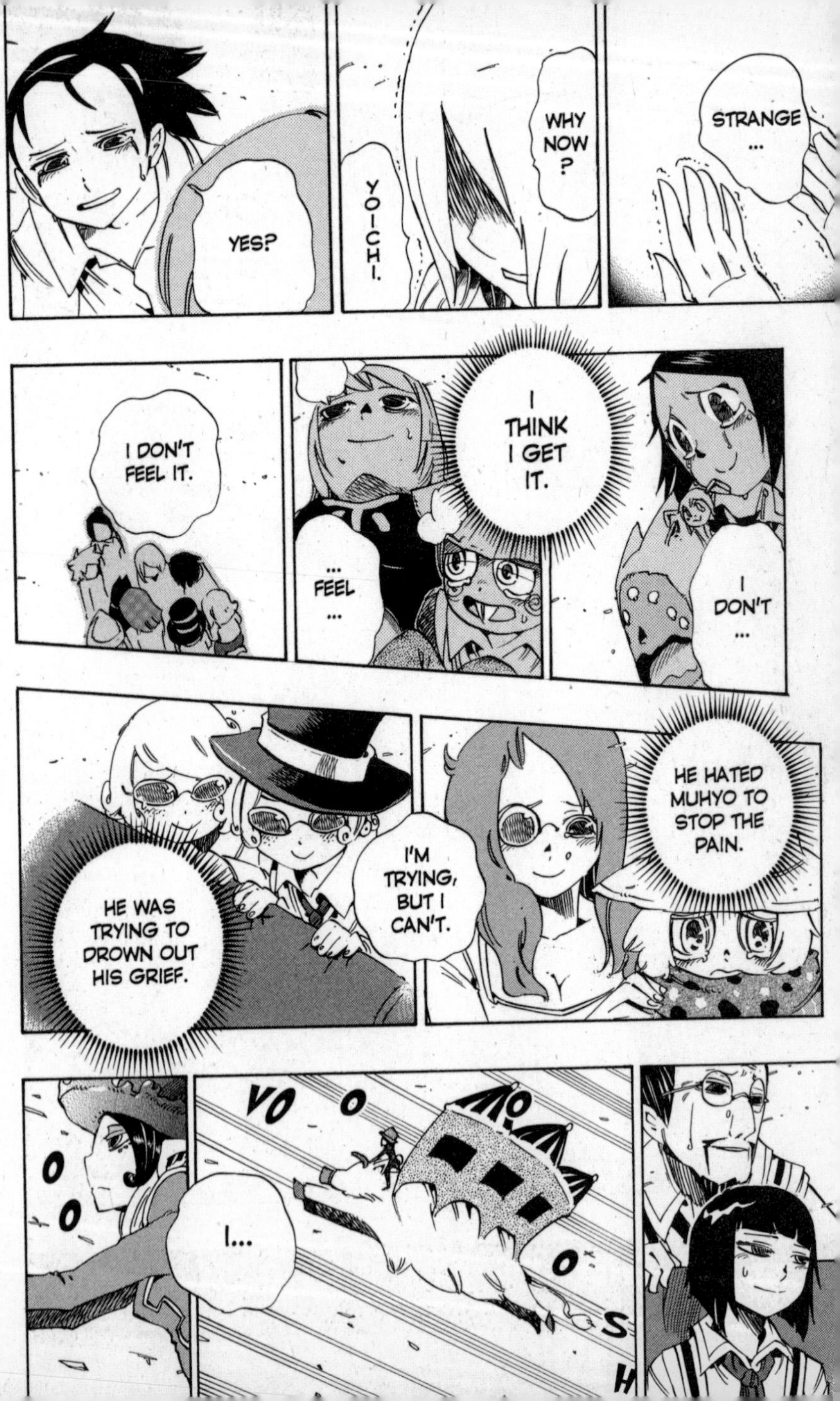

STRANGE ...
WHY NOW ?
YOICHI.
YES?
I DON'T ...
I THINK I GET IT.
... FEEL ...
I DON'T FEEL IT.
HE HATED MUHYO TO STOP THE PAIN.
I'M TRYING, BUT I CAN'T.
HE WAS TRYING TO DROWN OUT HIS GRIEF.
VOOOSH
I...
OO

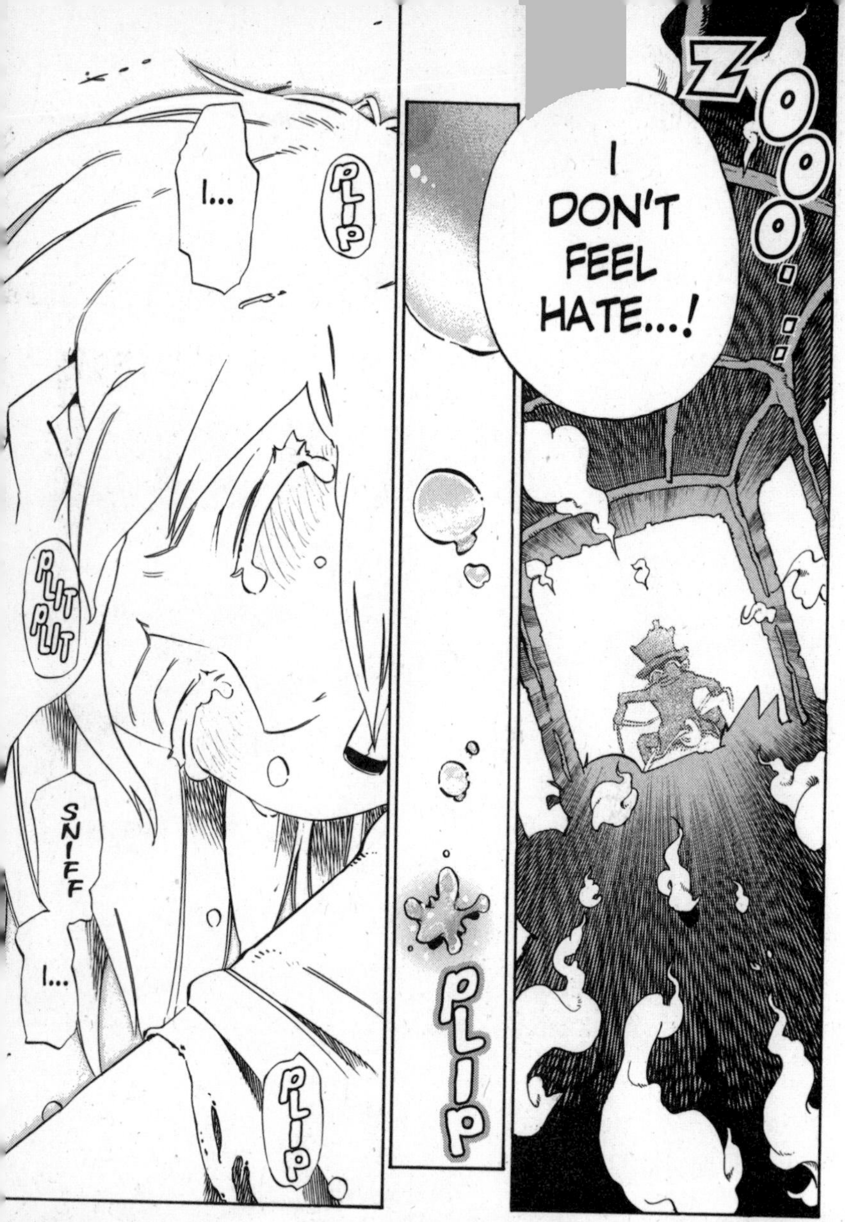
ZOOOO...
I DON'T FEEL HATE...!
PLIP
I...
PLIP
PLIT PLIT
SNIFF
I...
PLIP

EVEN WHEN WE'RE LEFT ALONE, WE'RE NOT ALONE.

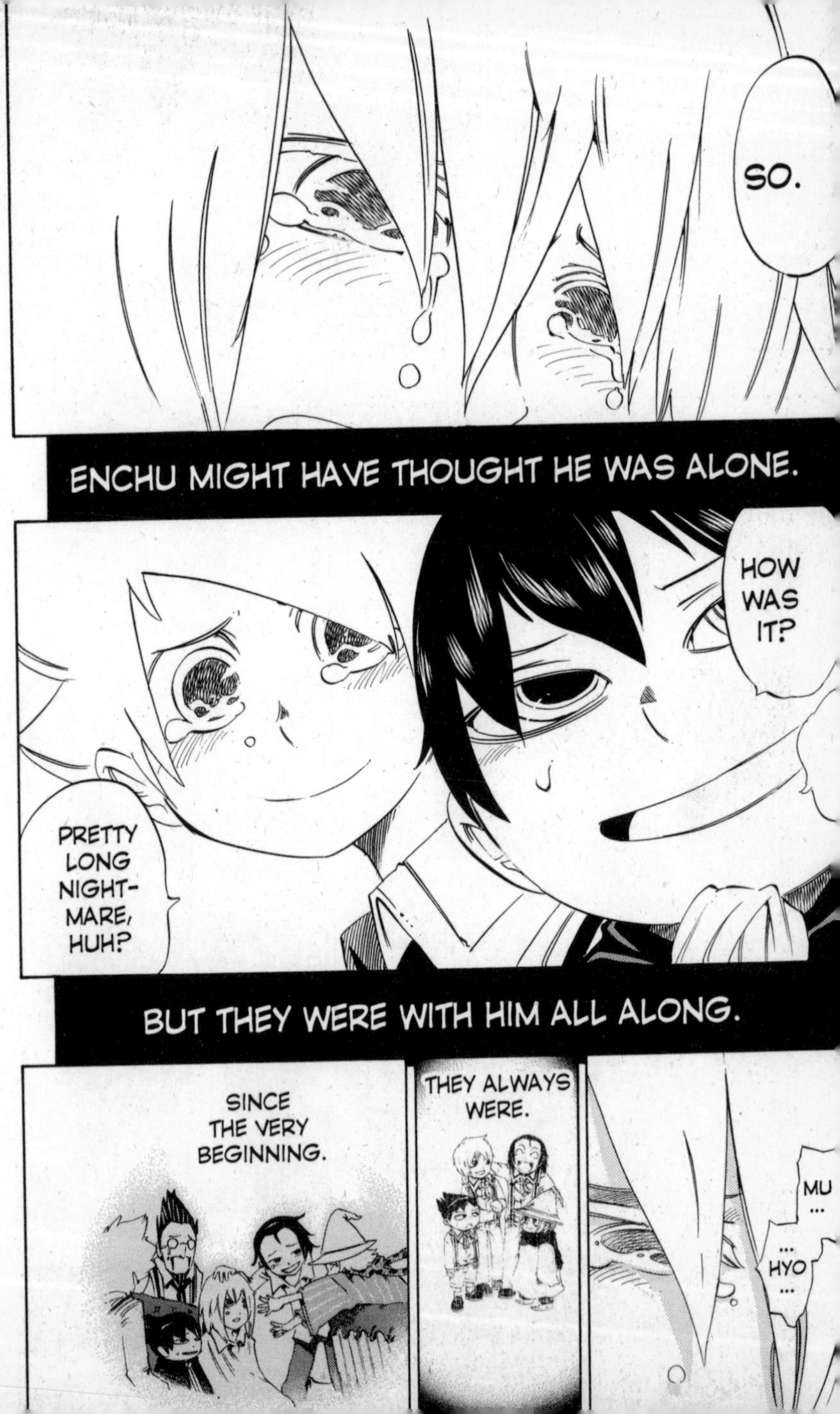
SO.
ENCHU MIGHT HAVE THOUGHT HE WAS ALONE.
HOW WAS IT?
PRETTY LONG NIGHTMARE, HUH?
BUT THEY WERE WITH HIM ALL ALONG.
MU...
...HYO...
THEY ALWAYS WERE.
SINCE THE VERY BEGINNING.

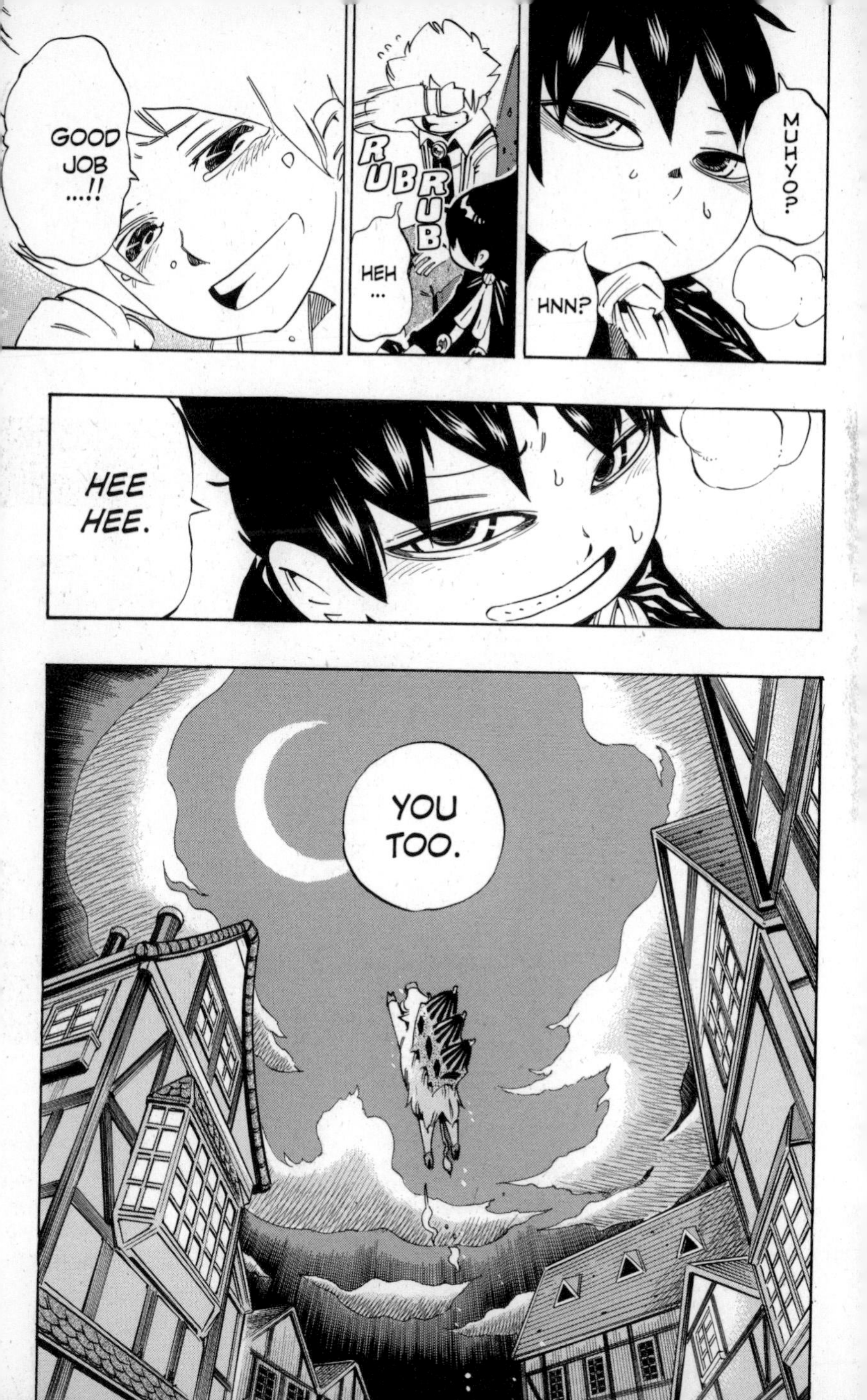
MUHYO?
HNN?
RUB RUB
HEH ...
GOOD JOB ...!!
HEE HEE.
YOU TOO.

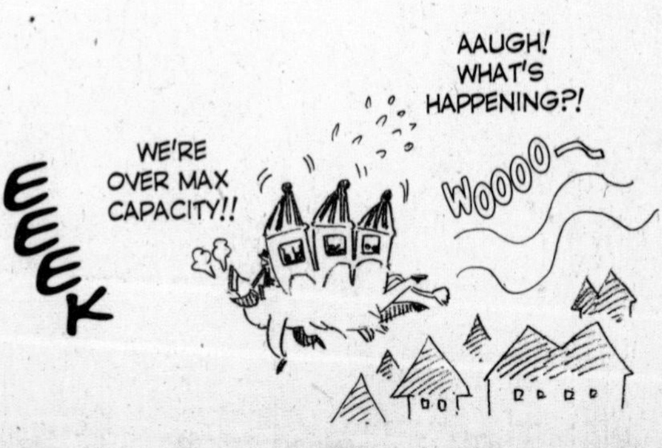
AAUGH! WHAT'S HAPPENING?!
WOOOO~
WE'RE OVER MAX CAPACITY!!
EEEK

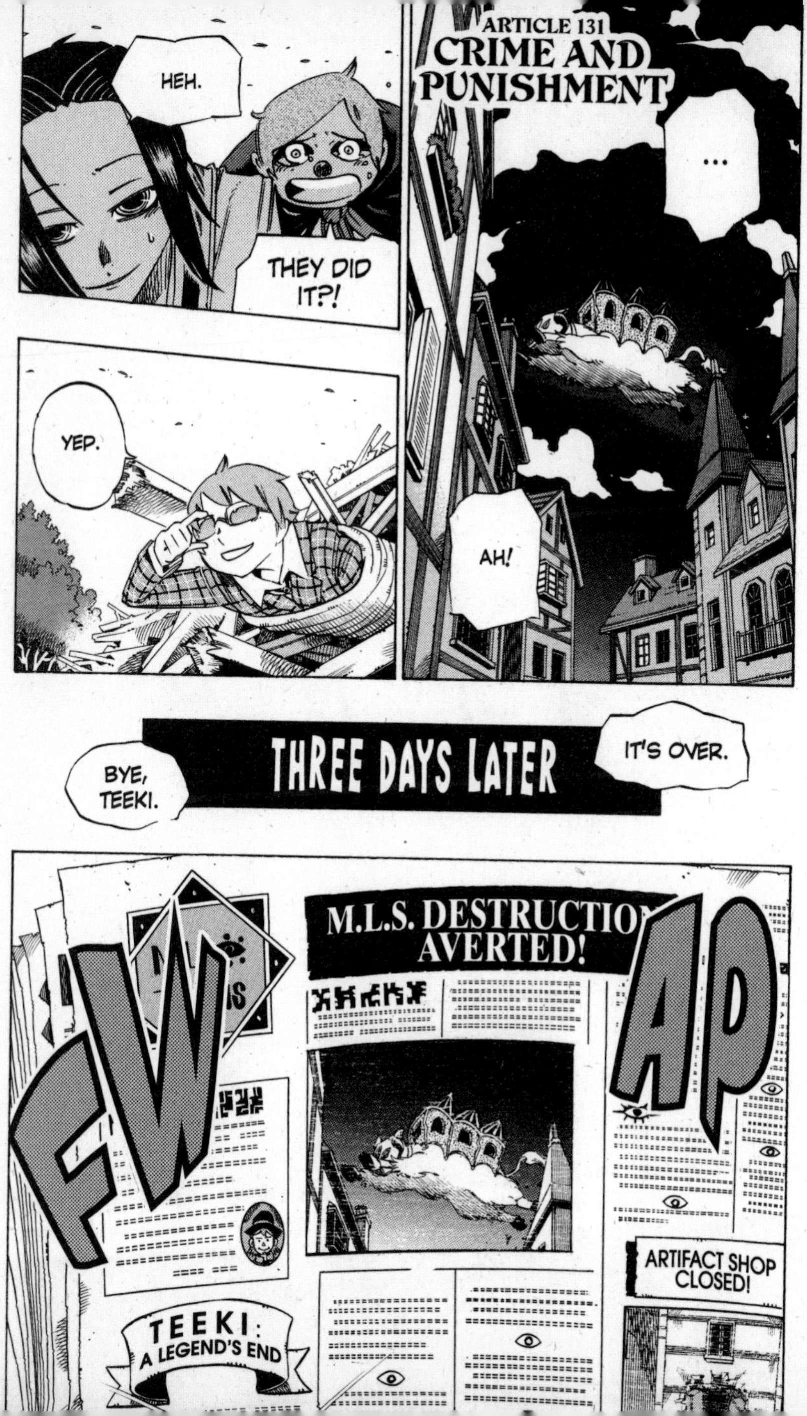
ARTICLE 131
CRIME AND PUNISHMENT
...
AH!
HEH.
THEY DID IT?!
YEP.
IT'S OVER.
THREE DAYS LATER
BYE, TEEKI.
FWAP
M.L.S. DESTRUCTION AVERTED!
ARTIFACT SHOP CLOSED!
TEEKI: A LEGEND'S END

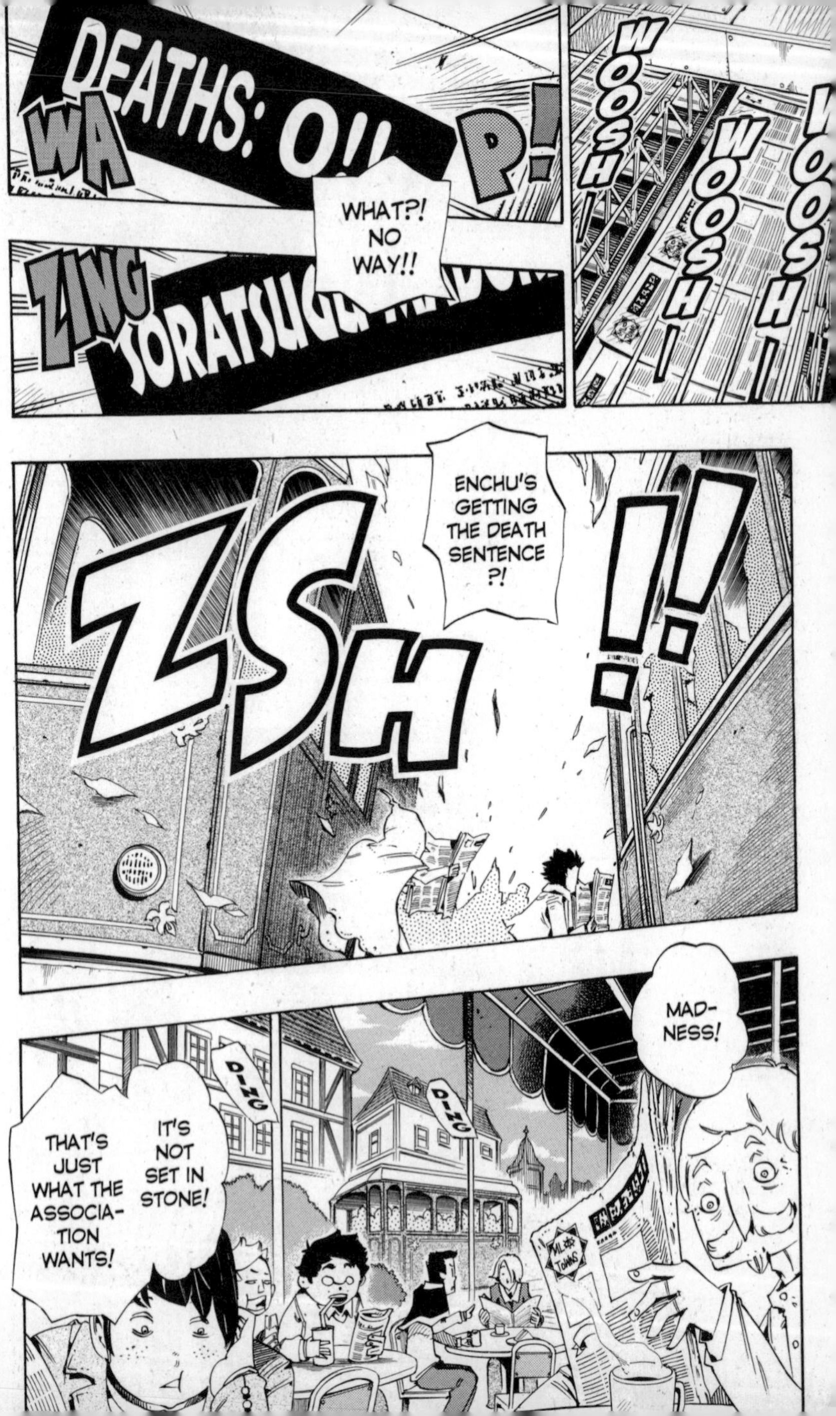

WOOSH
WOOSH
WOOSH
WA
DEATHS: O!!
P!
WHAT?! NO WAY!!
ZING
SORATSUGU
ENCHU'S GETTING THE DEATH SENTENCE ?!
ZSH
!!
MAD-NESS!
DING
DING
IT'S NOT SET IN STONE!
THAT'S JUST WHAT THE ASSOCIA-TION WANTS!

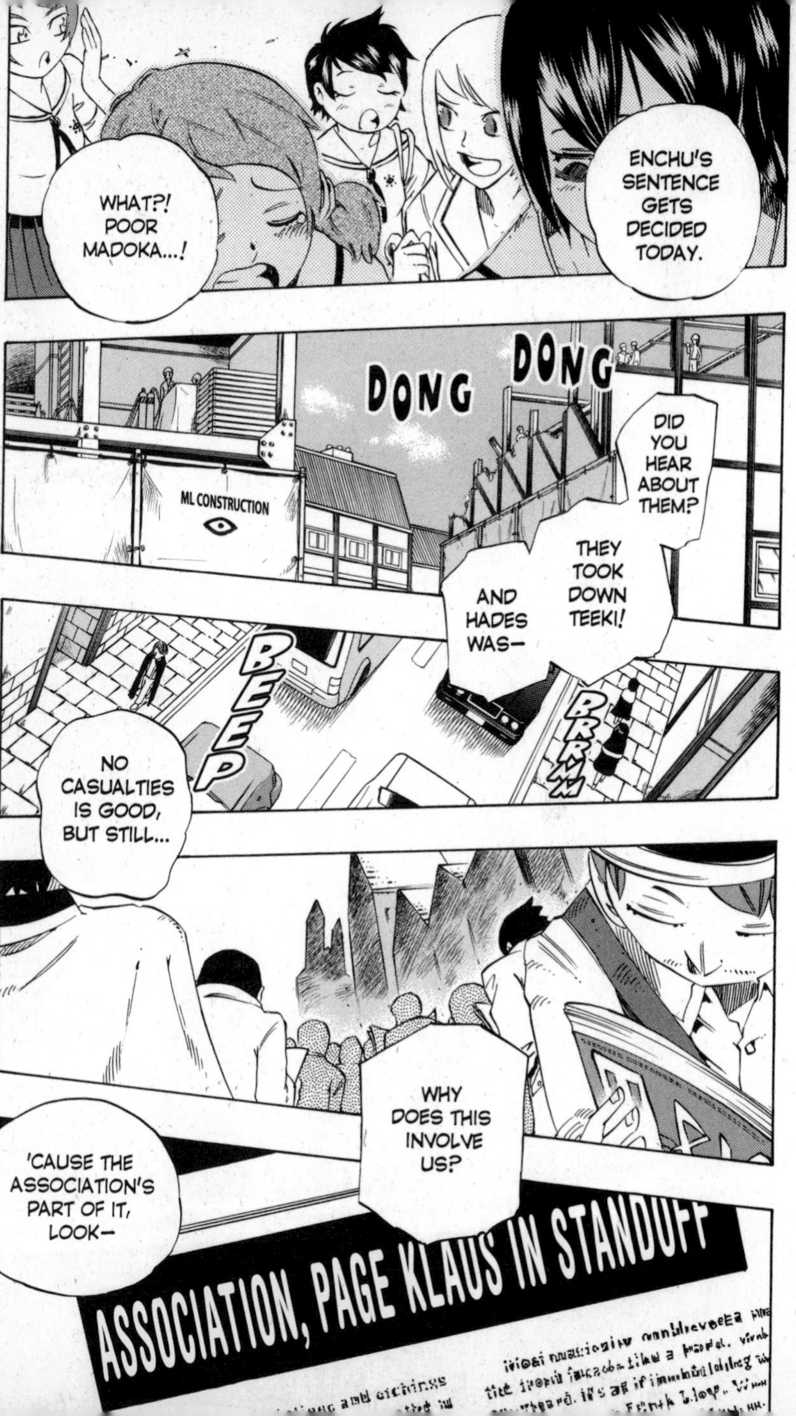
ENCHU'S SENTENCE GETS DECIDED TODAY.
WHAT?! POOR MADOKA...!
DONG
DONG
DID YOU HEAR ABOUT THEM?
THEY TOOK DOWN TEEKI!
AND HADES WAS—
BRRM
BEEP
NO CASUALTIES IS GOOD, BUT STILL...
WHY DOES THIS INVOLVE US?
'CAUSE THE ASSOCIATION'S PART OF IT, LOOK—
ASSOCIATION, PAGE KLAUS IN STANDOFF

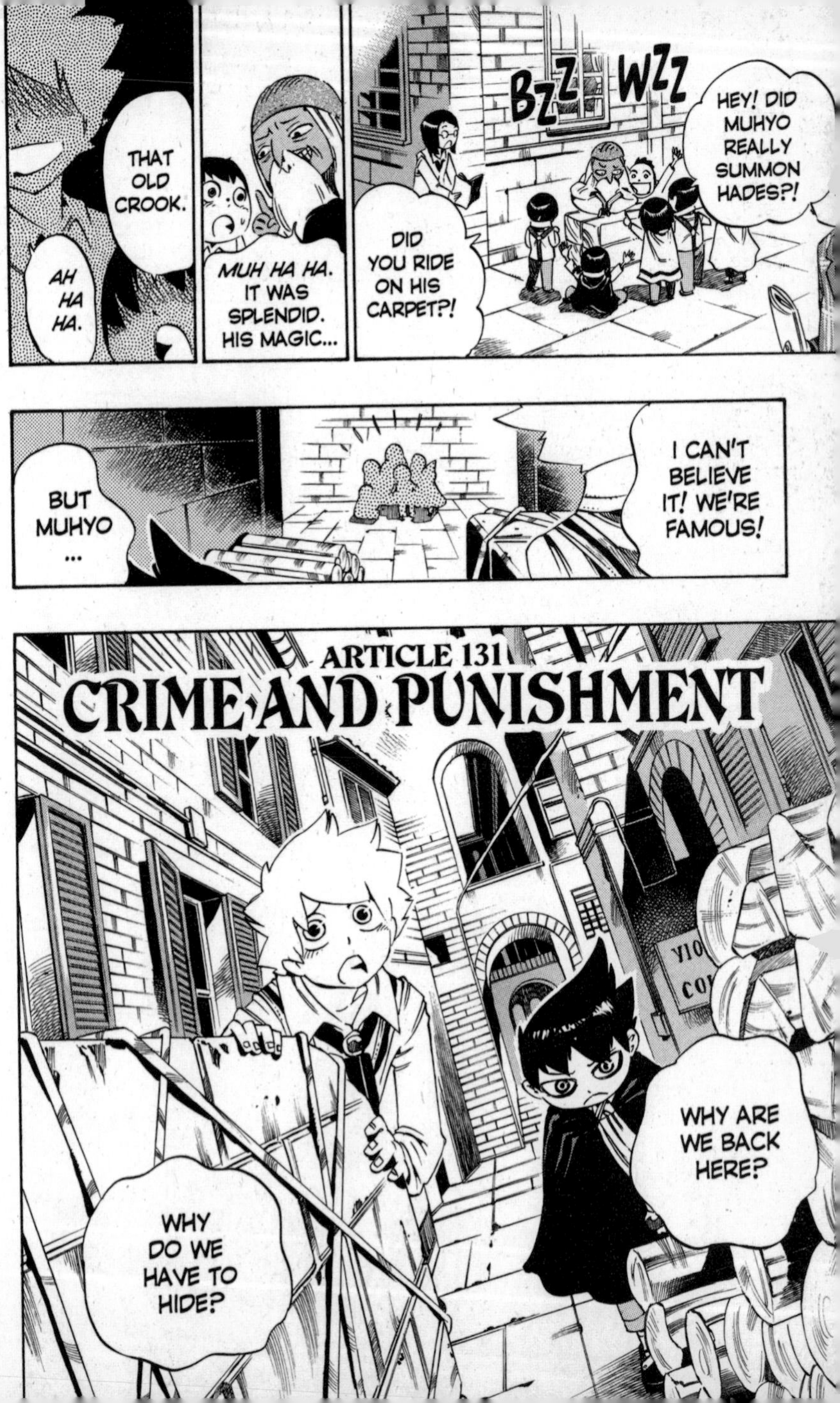
BZZ WZZ
HEY! DID MUHYO REALLY SUMMON HADES?!
DID YOU RIDE ON HIS CARPET?!
MUH HA HA. IT WAS SPLENDID. HIS MAGIC...
THAT OLD CROOK.
AH HA HA.
I CAN'T BELIEVE IT! WE'RE FAMOUS!
BUT MUHYO ...
ARTICLE 131
CRIME AND PUNISHMENT
WHY ARE WE BACK HERE?
WHY DO WE HAVE TO HIDE?

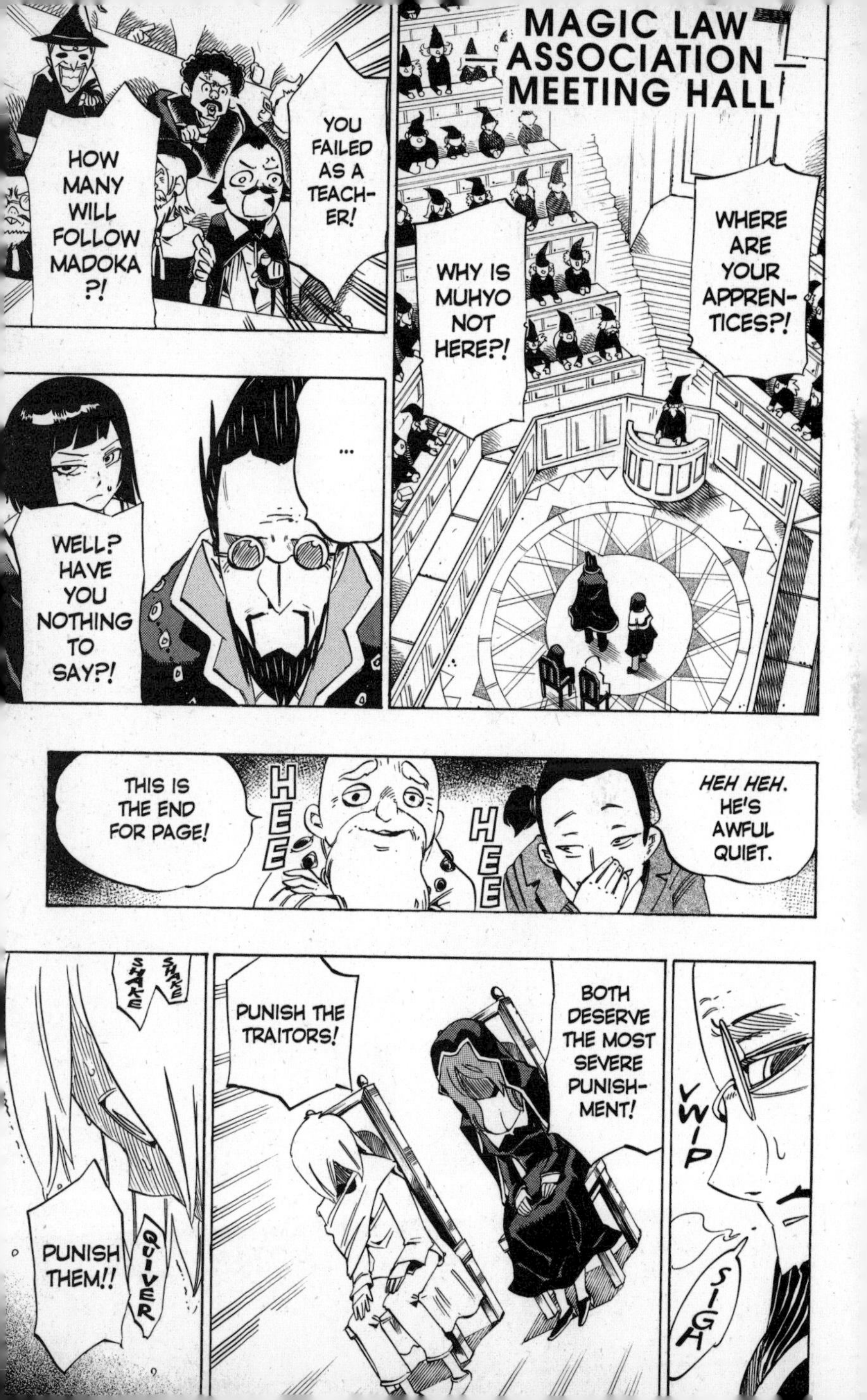
MAGIC LAW ASSOCIATION MEETING HALL
WHERE ARE YOUR APPRENTICES?!
WHY IS MUHYO NOT HERE?!
YOU FAILED AS A TEACHER!
HOW MANY WILL FOLLOW MADOKA?!
...
WELL? HAVE YOU NOTHING TO SAY?!
HEH HEH. HE'S AWFUL QUIET.
HEE
HEE
THIS IS THE END FOR PAGE!
VWIP
SIGH
BOTH DESERVE THE MOST SEVERE PUNISHMENT!
PUNISH THE TRAITORS!
SHAKE
SHAKE
QUIVER
PUNISH THEM!!

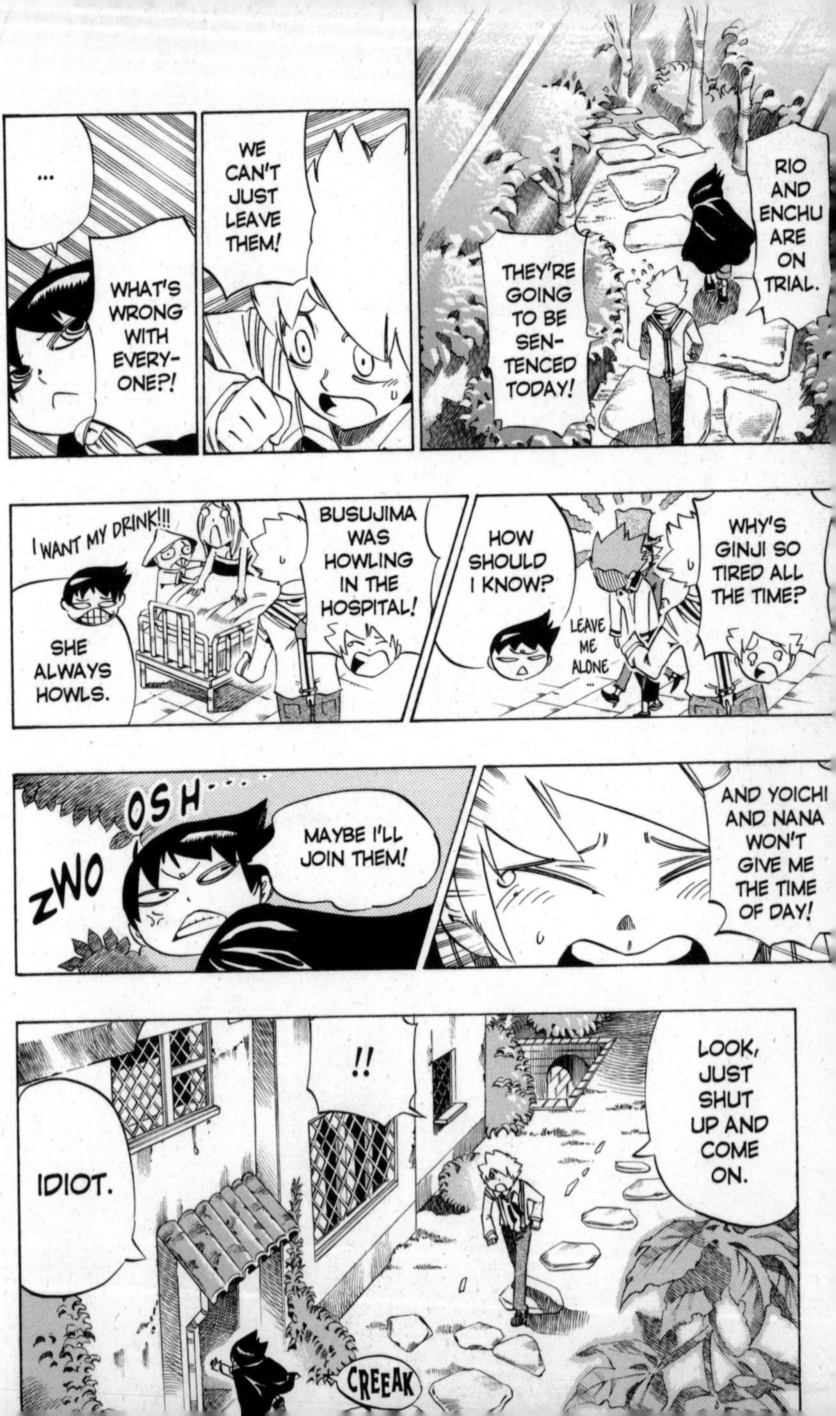

RIO AND ENCHU ARE ON TRIAL.
THEY'RE GOING TO BE SEN-TENCED TODAY!
WE CAN'T JUST LEAVE THEM!
...
WHAT'S WRONG WITH EVERY-ONE?!
WHY'S GINJI SO TIRED ALL THE TIME?
LEAVE ME ALONE ...
HOW SHOULD I KNOW?
BUSUJIMA WAS HOWLING IN THE HOSPITAL!
I WANT MY DRINK!!!
SHE ALWAYS HOWLS.
AND YOICHI AND NANA WON'T GIVE ME THE TIME OF DAY!
MAYBE I'LL JOIN THEM!
OSH
ZWO
LOOK, JUST SHUT UP AND COME ON.
!!
IDIOT.
CREEAK

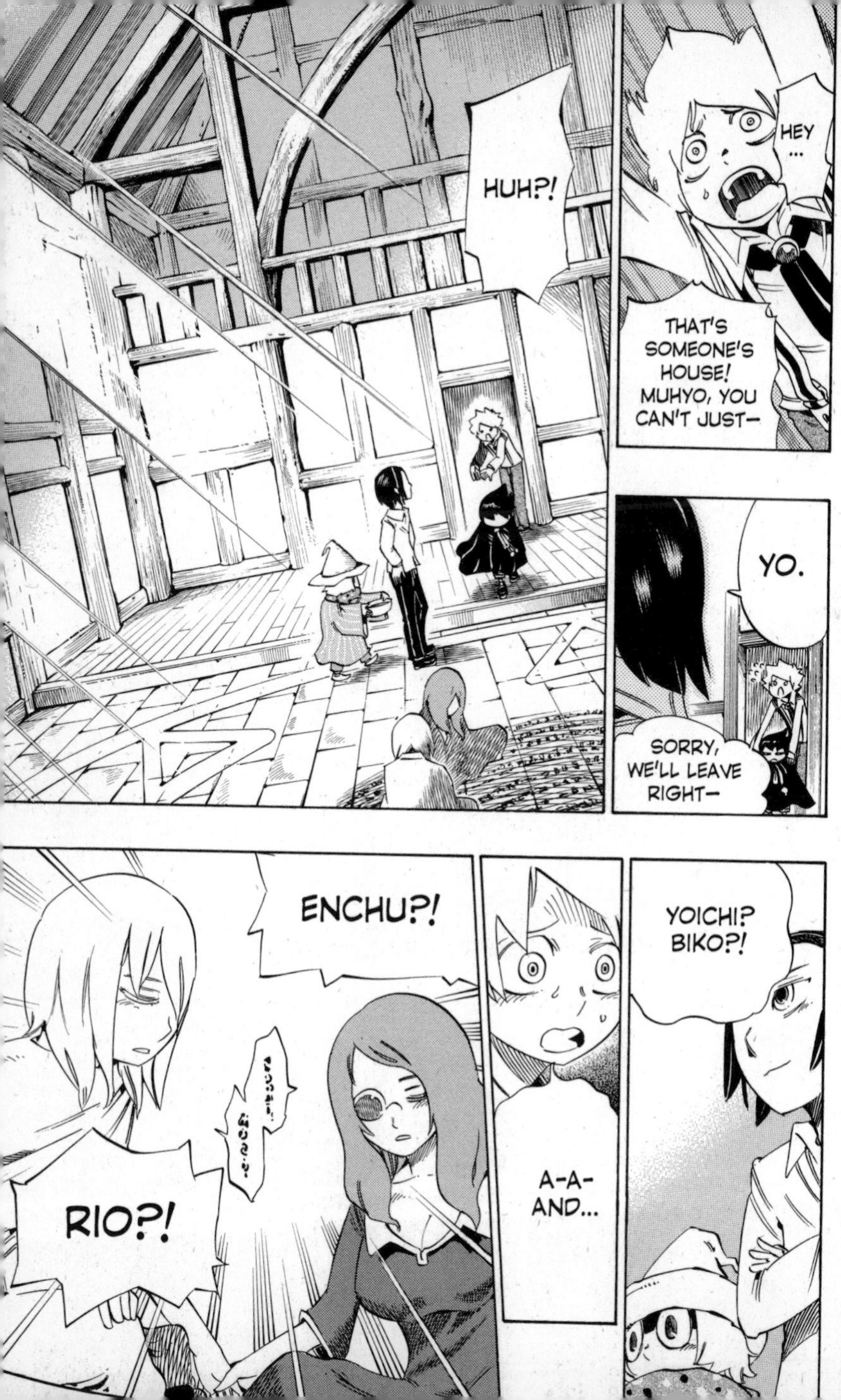
HEY ...
THAT'S SOMEONE'S HOUSE! MUHYO, YOU CAN'T JUST—
YO.
SORRY, WE'LL LEAVE RIGHT—
HUH?!
YOICHI? BIKO?!
A-A-AND...
ENCHU?!
RIO?!

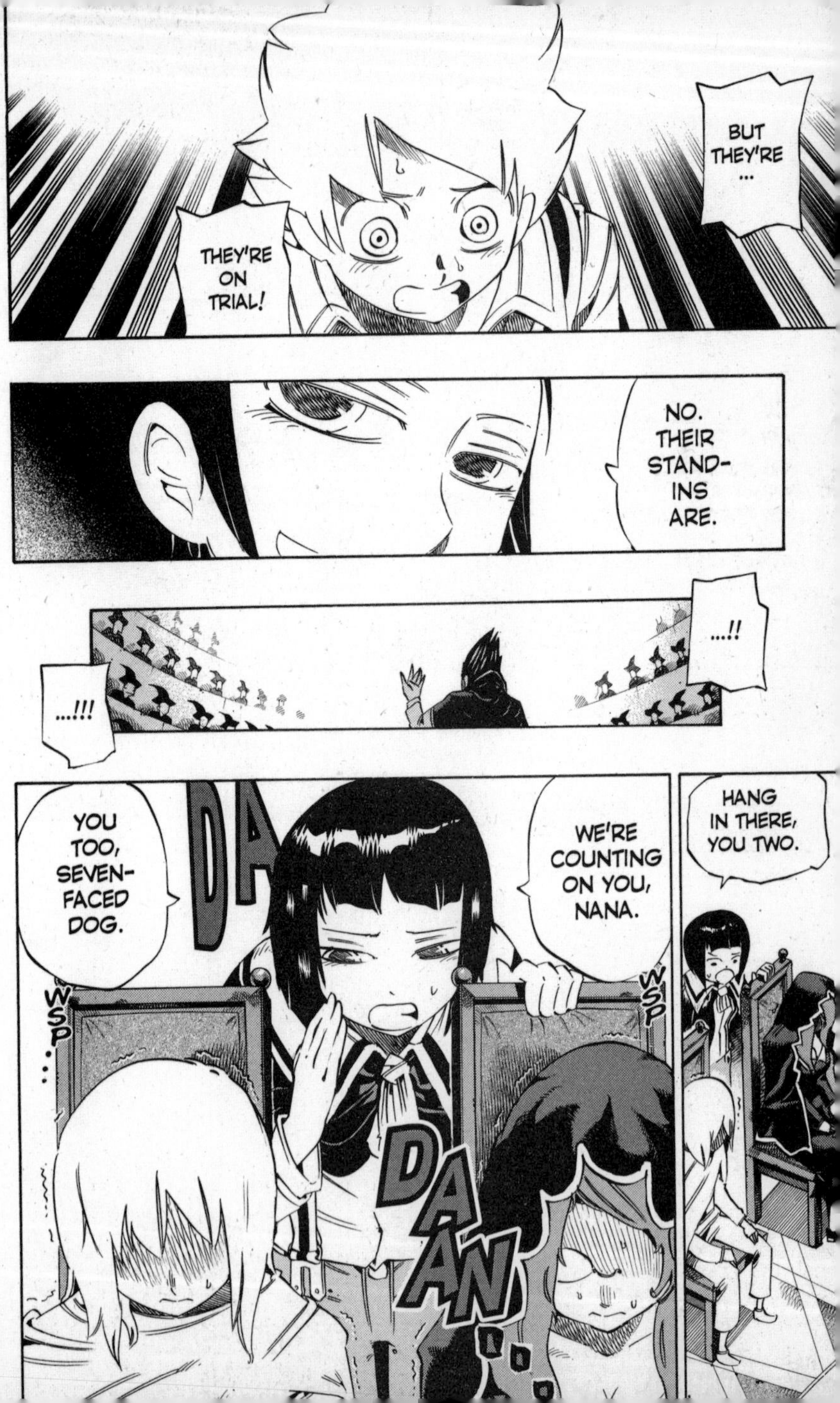
BUT THEY'RE ...
THEY'RE ON TRIAL!
NO. THEIR STAND-INS ARE.
...!!
...!!!
HANG IN THERE, YOU TWO.
WSP
WE'RE COUNTING ON YOU, NANA.
YOU TOO, SEVEN-FACED DOG.
WSP
DA
DADAN

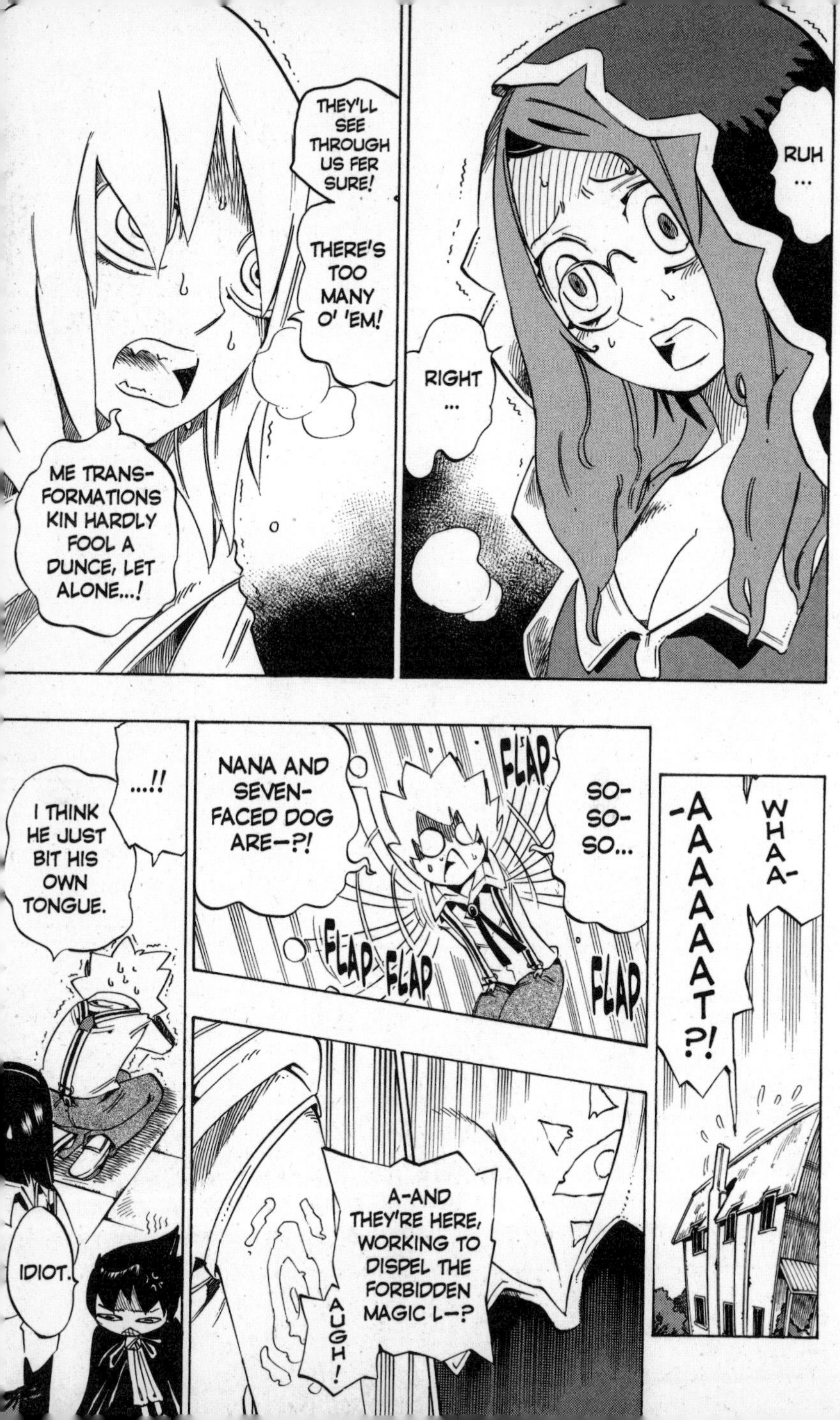
RUH ...
RIGHT ...
THEY'LL SEE THROUGH US FER SURE!
THERE'S TOO MANY O' 'EM!
ME TRANSFORMATIONS KIN HARDLY FOOL A DUNCE, LET ALONE...!
WHAA-
-AAAAAAAT?!
SO-SO-SO...
FLAP
NANA AND SEVEN-FACED DOG ARE--?!
FLAP
FLAP FLAP
A-AND THEY'RE HERE, WORKING TO DISPEL THE FORBIDDEN MAGIC L--?
AUGH!
...!!
I THINK HE JUST BIT HIS OWN TONGUE.
IDIOT.

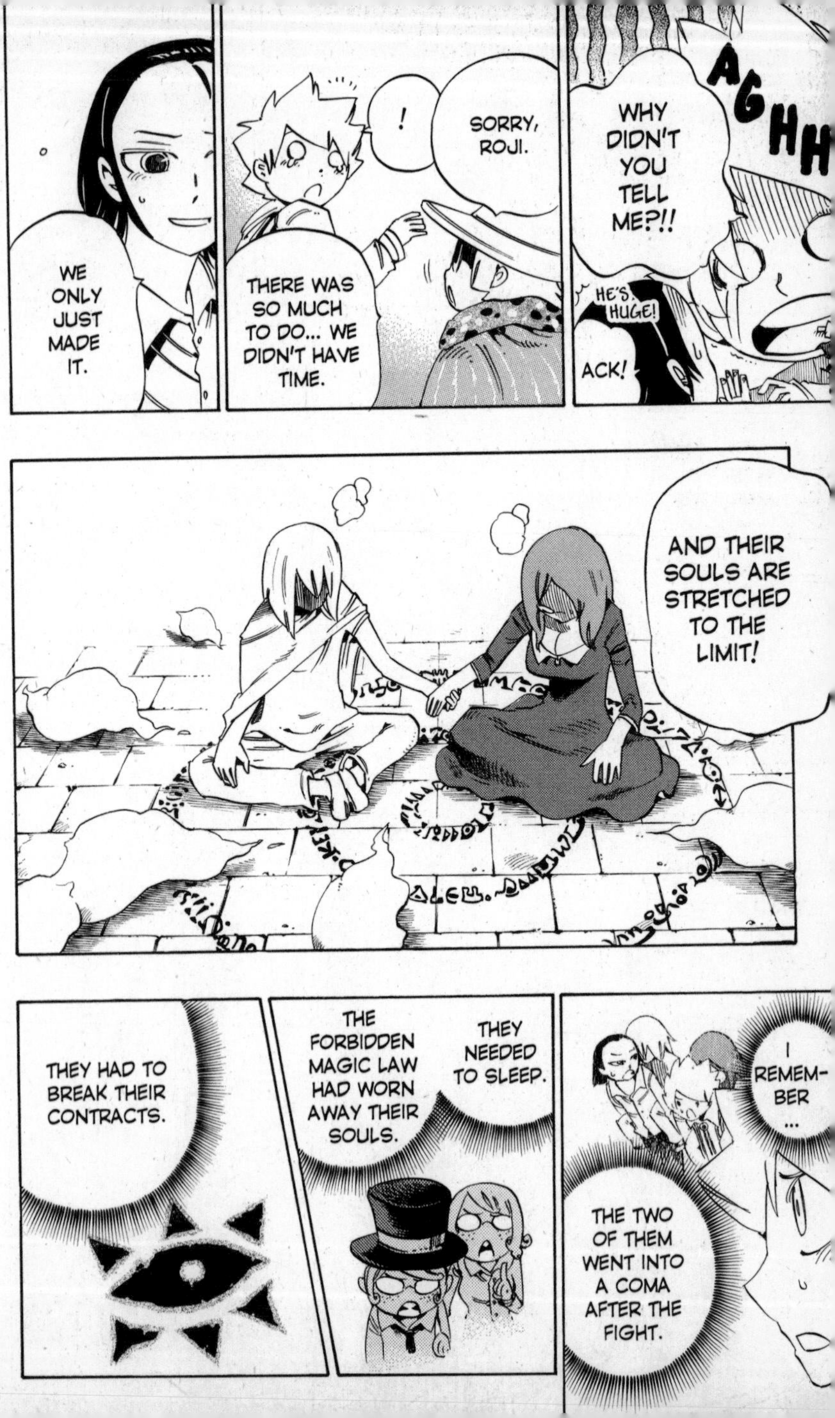
AGHH
WHY DIDN'T YOU TELL ME?!!
HE'S HUGE!
ACK!
SORRY, ROJI.
!
THERE WAS SO MUCH TO DO... WE DIDN'T HAVE TIME.
WE ONLY JUST MADE IT.
AND THEIR SOULS ARE STRETCHED TO THE LIMIT!
I REMEMBER...
THE TWO OF THEM WENT INTO A COMA AFTER THE FIGHT.
THEY NEEDED TO SLEEP.
THE FORBIDDEN MAGIC LAW HAD WORN AWAY THEIR SOULS.
THEY HAD TO BREAK THEIR CONTRACTS.

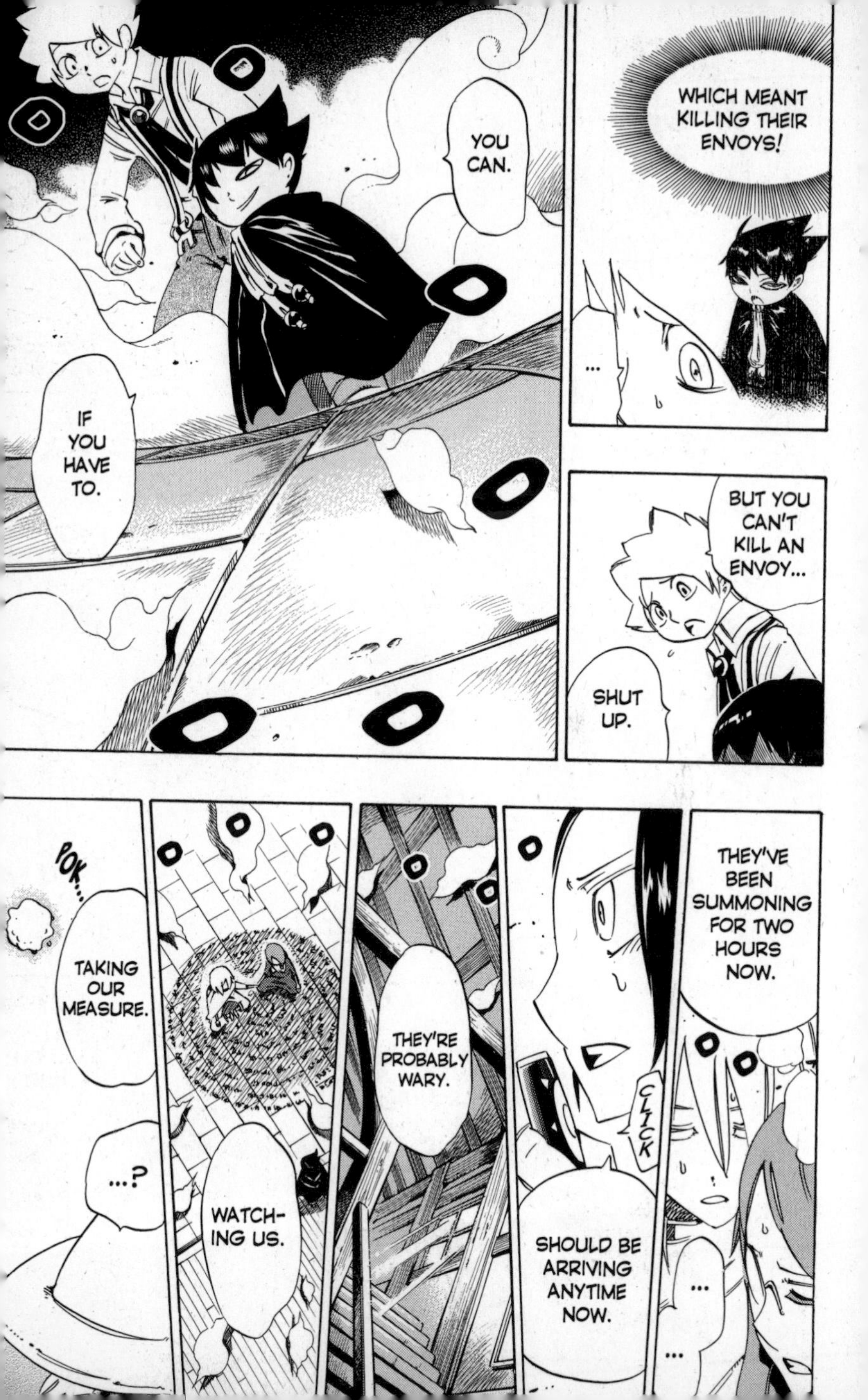
WHICH MEANT KILLING THEIR ENVOYS!
...
BUT YOU CAN'T KILL AN ENVOY...
SHUT UP.
...
YOU CAN.
...
IF YOU HAVE TO.
THEY'VE BEEN SUMMONING FOR TWO HOURS NOW.
...
...
...
CLICK
SHOULD BE ARRIVING ANYTIME NOW.
THEY'RE PROBABLY WARY.
WATCH-ING US.
POK...
TAKING OUR MEASURE.
...?

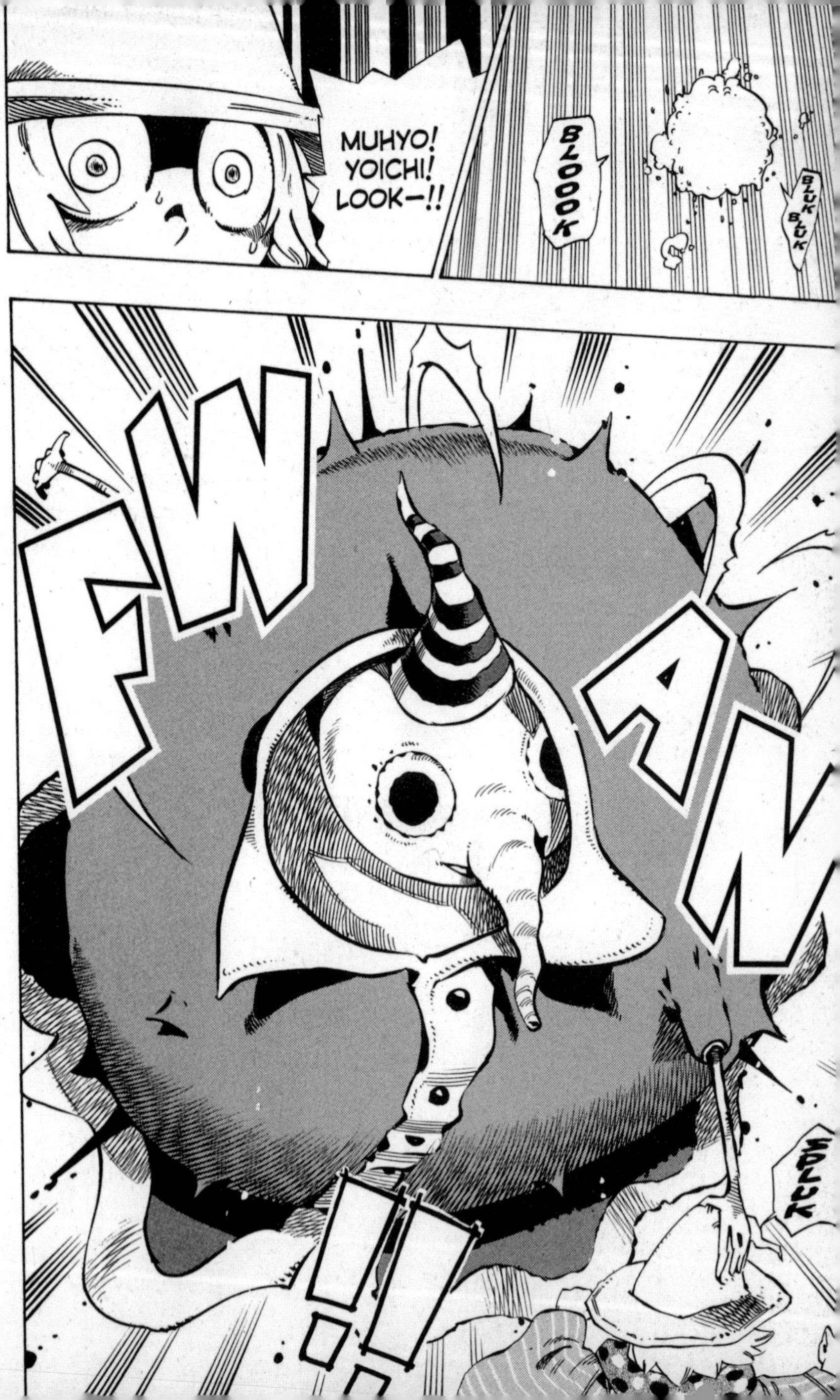

BLOOOK
BLUK BLUK
MUHYO! YOICHI! LOOK—!!
FWAAN
SPLUK
!!

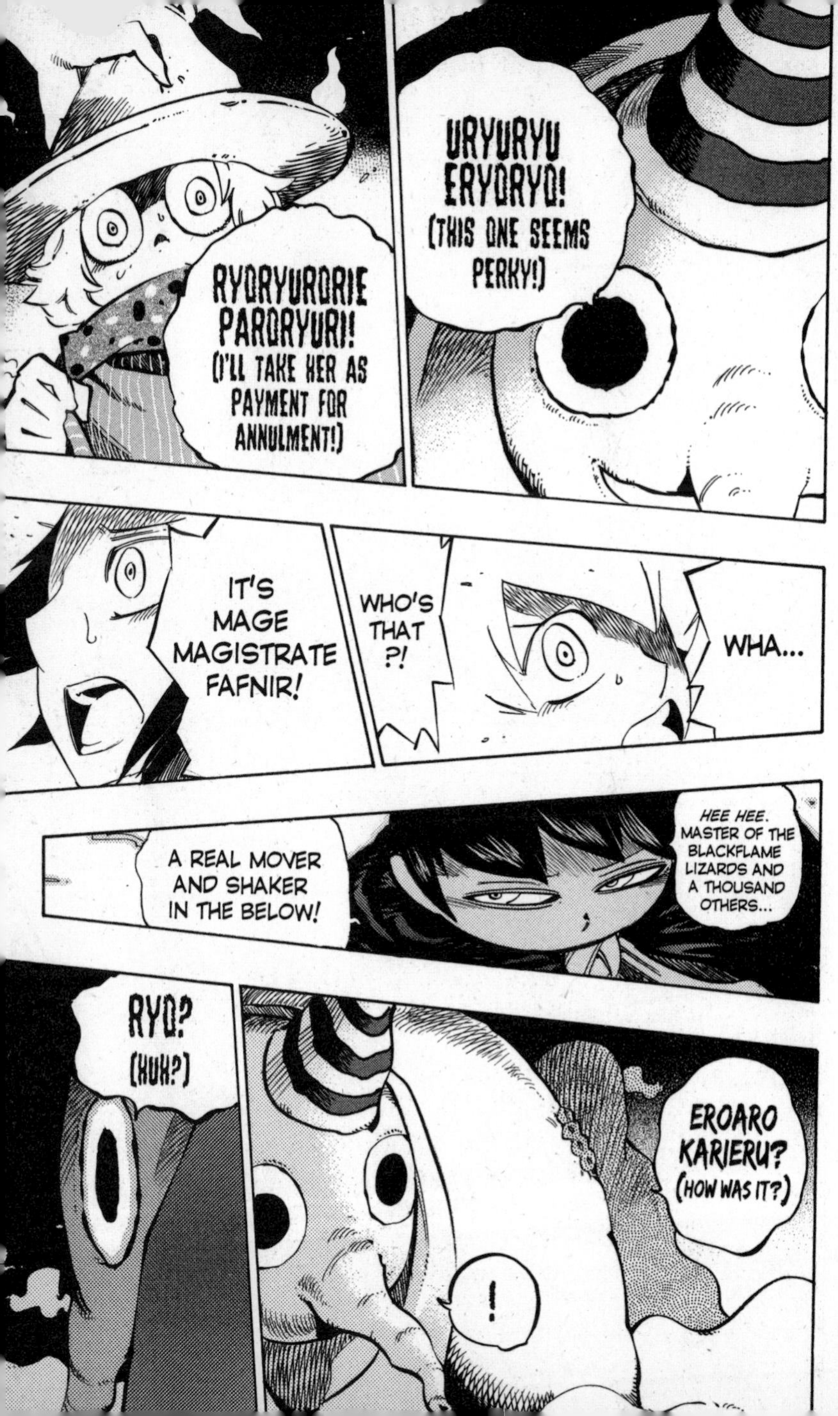
URYURYU ERYORYO! (THIS ONE SEEMS PERKY!)
RYORYURORIE PARORYURI! (I'LL TAKE HER AS PAYMENT FOR ANNULMENT!)
WHA...
WHO'S THAT ?!
IT'S MAGE MAGISTRATE FAFNIR!
HEE HEE. MASTER OF THE BLACKFLAME LIZARDS AND A THOUSAND OTHERS...
A REAL MOVER AND SHAKER IN THE BELOW!
EROARO KARIERU? (HOW WAS IT?)
!
RYO? (HUH?)

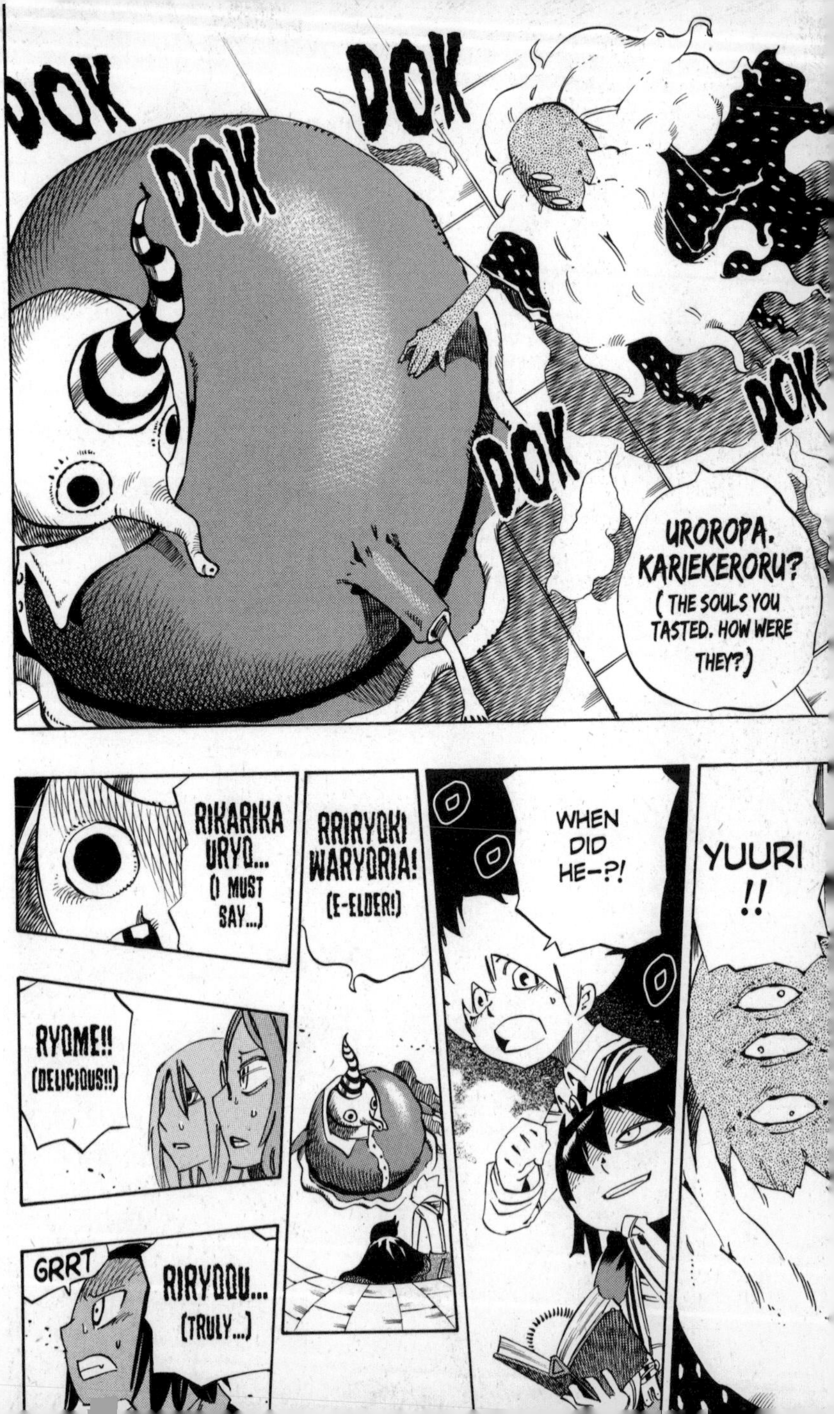
DOK
DOK
DOK
DOK
DOK
UROROPA. KARIEKERORU?
(THE SOULS YOU TASTED. HOW WERE THEY?)
YUURI !!
WHEN DID HE-?!
RRIRYOKI WARYORIA!
(E-ELDER!)
RIKARIKA URYO...
(I MUST SAY...)
RYOME!!
(DELICIOUS!!)
GRRT
RIRYOOU...
(TRULY...)

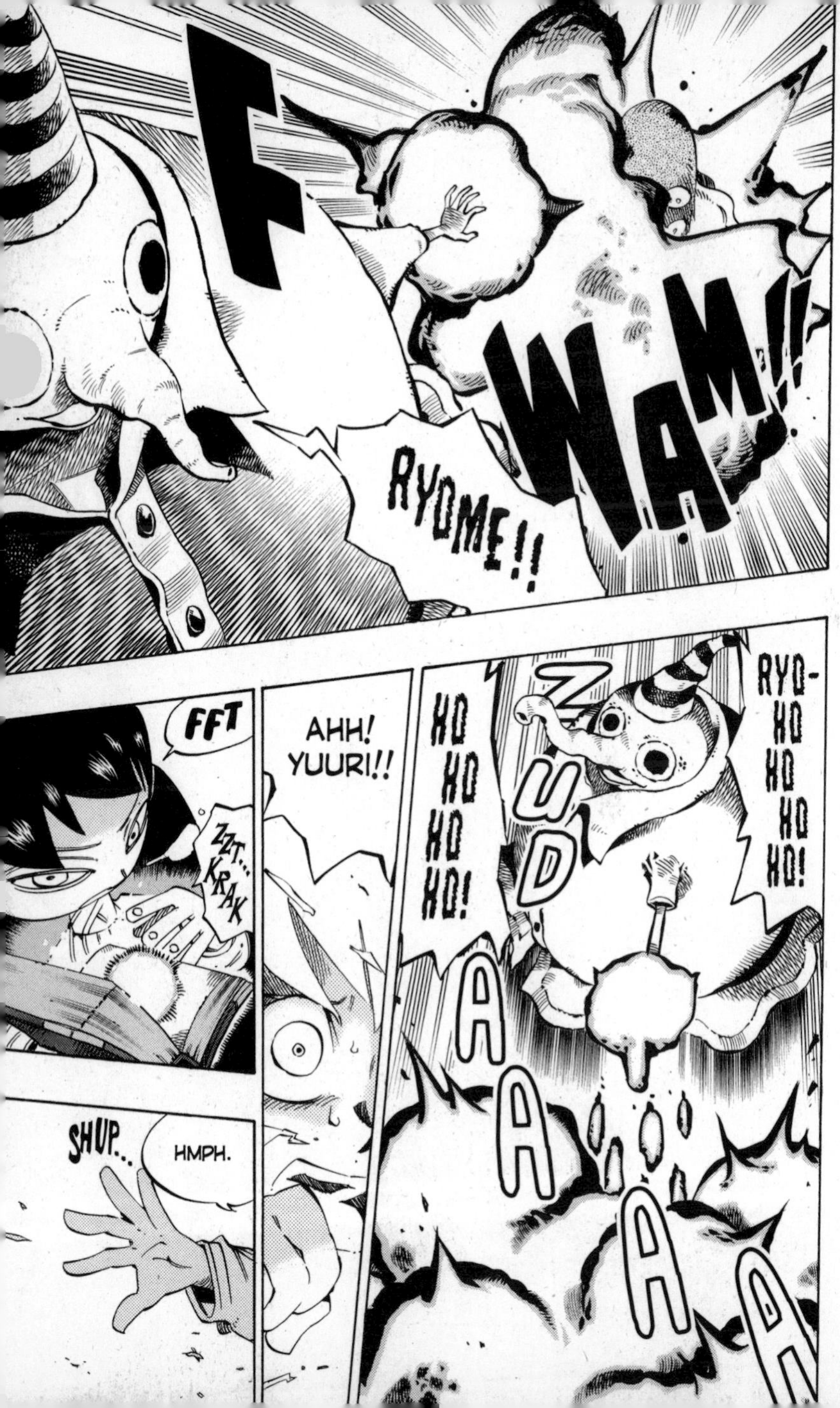
WAM!!
RYOME!!
FF
RYO-HO HO HO HO HO!
ZUUD
HO HO HO HO HO!
AAAAA
AHH! YUURI!!
FFT
ZZT... KRAK
SHUP...
HMPH.

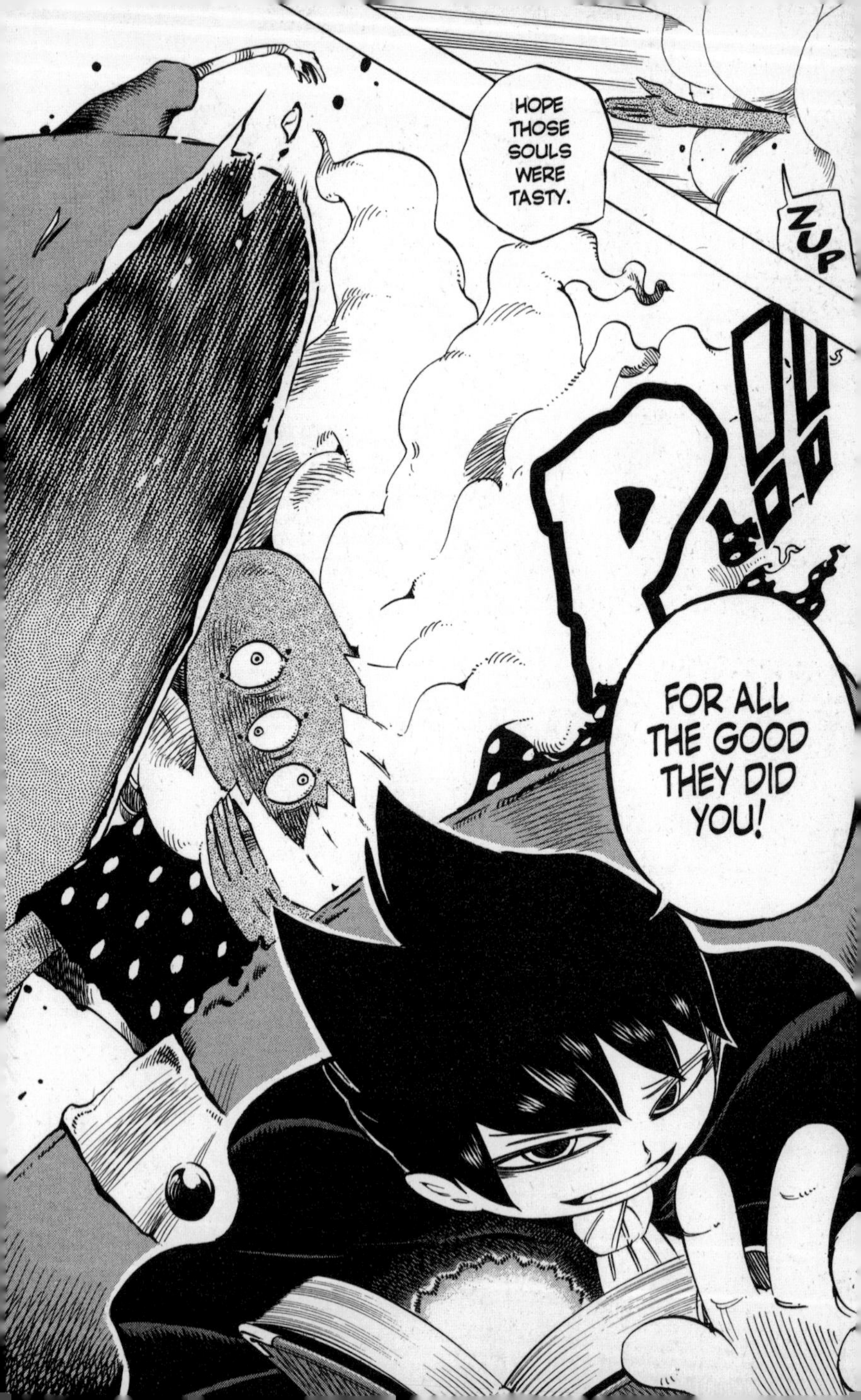
ZUP
HOPE THOSE SOULS WERE TASTY.
DODODOD
FOR ALL THE GOOD THEY DID YOU!

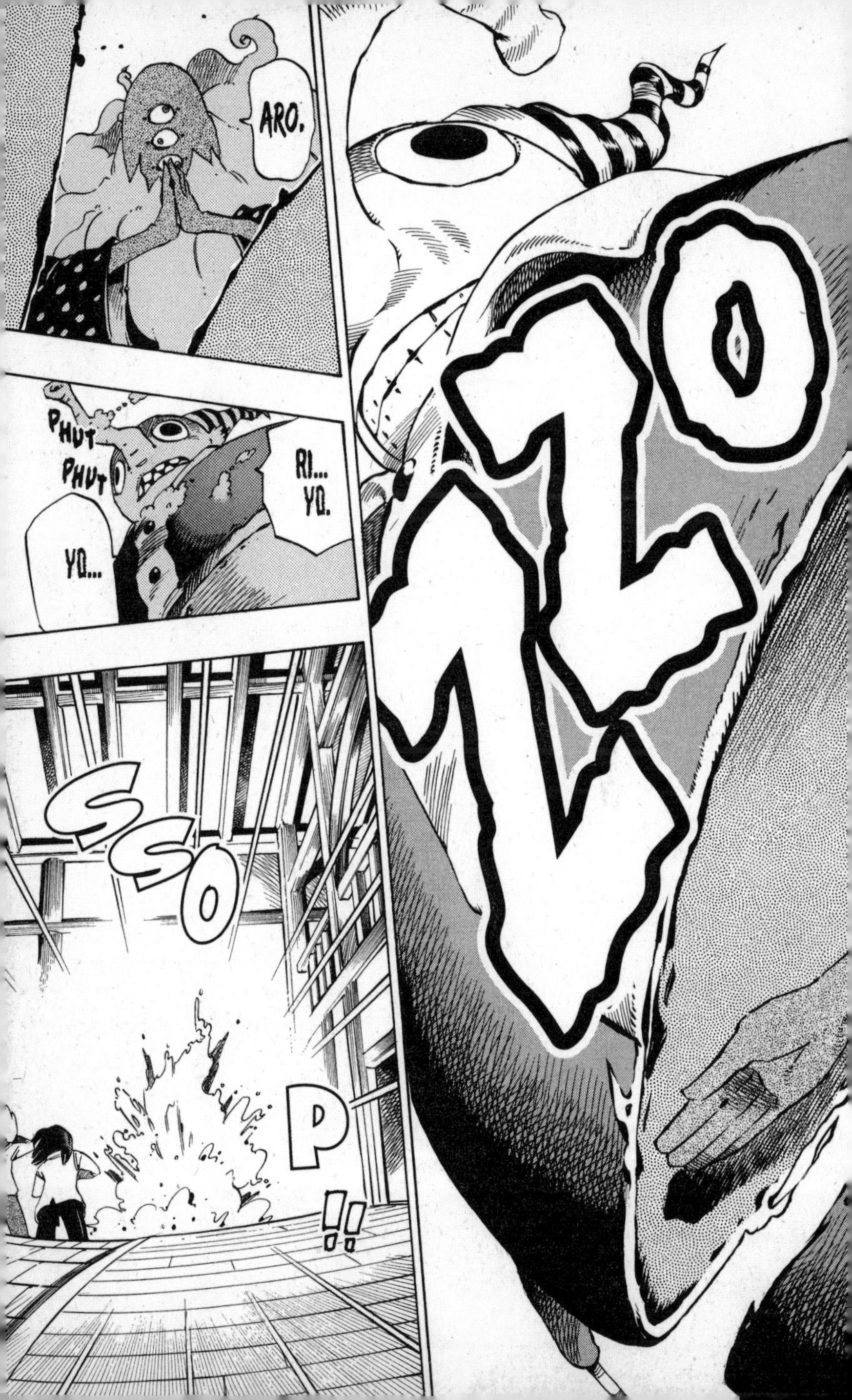
ZO
...
ARO.
RI... YO.
PHUT PHUT
YO...
SSOP
!!

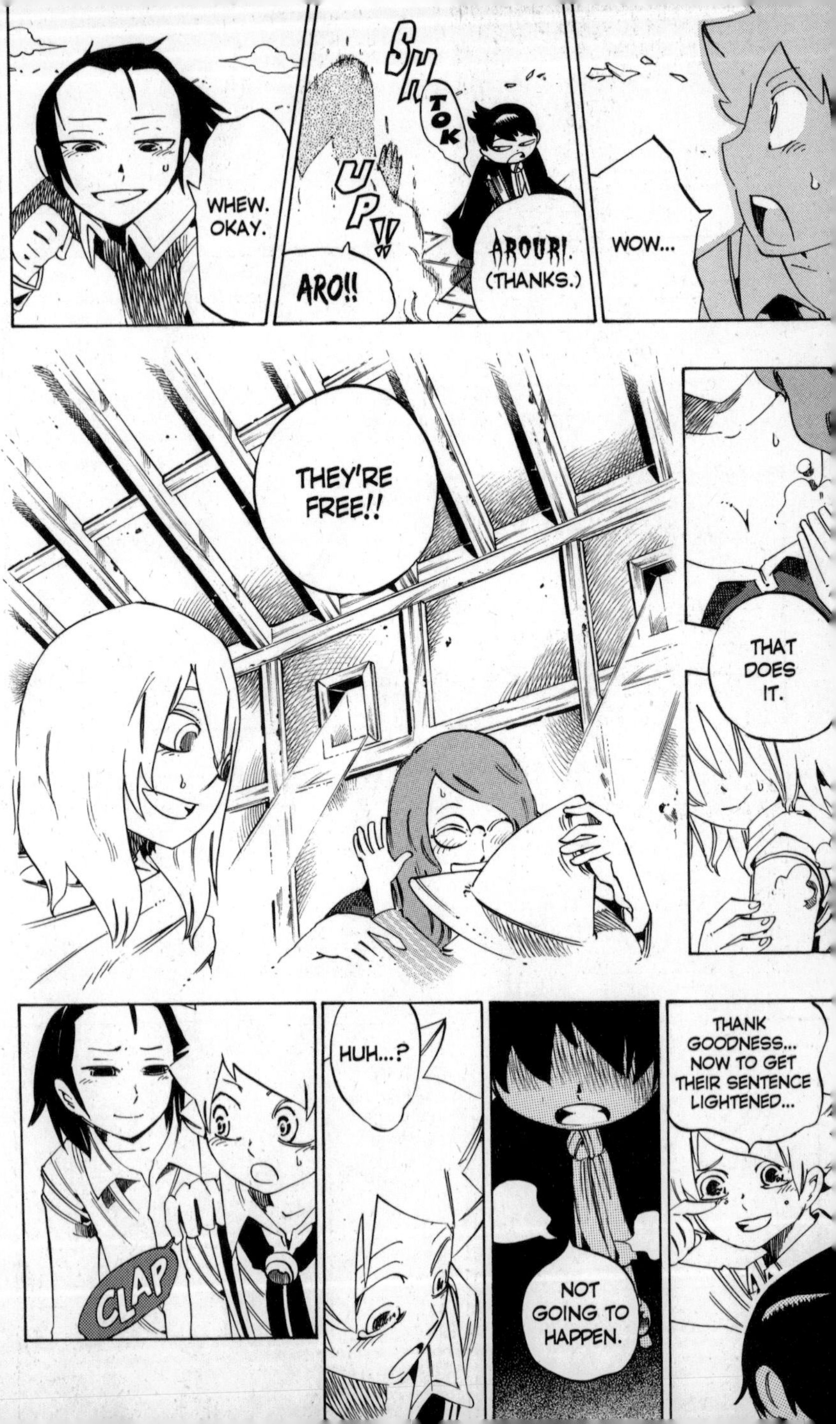
WOW...
SHTOK
AROURI.
(THANKS.)
UP!!
ARO!!
WHEW.
OKAY.
THAT
DOES
IT.
THEY'RE
FREE!!
THANK
GOODNESS...
NOW TO GET
THEIR SENTENCE
LIGHTENED...
NOT
GOING TO
HAPPEN.
HUH...?
CLAP

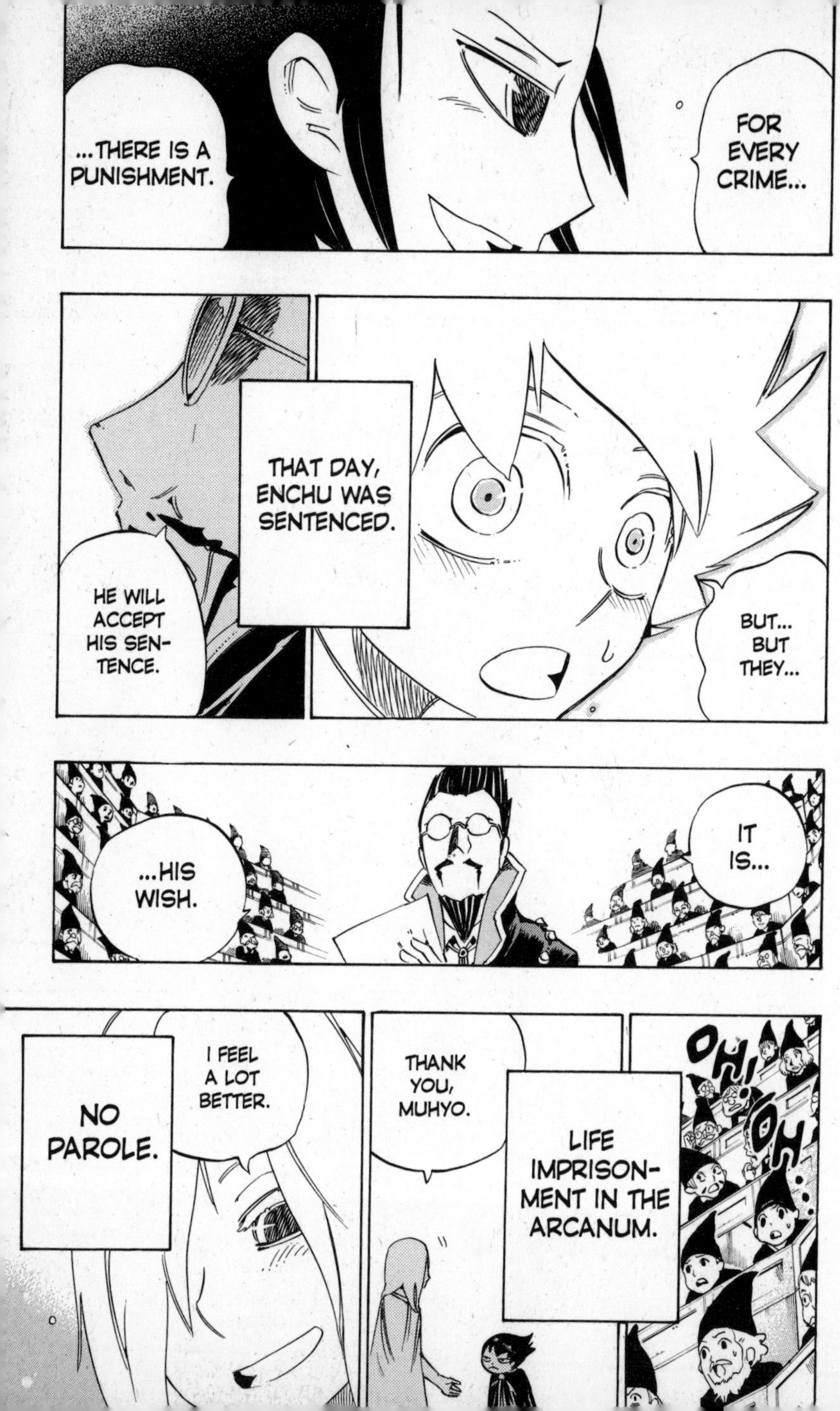

FOR EVERY CRIME...
...THERE IS A PUNISHMENT.
BUT... BUT THEY...
THAT DAY, ENCHU WAS SENTENCED.
HE WILL ACCEPT HIS SEN-TENCE.
IT IS...
...HIS WISH.
OH! OH!
LIFE IMPRISON-MENT IN THE ARCANUM.
THANK YOU, MUHYO.
I FEEL A LOT BETTER.
NO PAROLE.

Inside the carriage

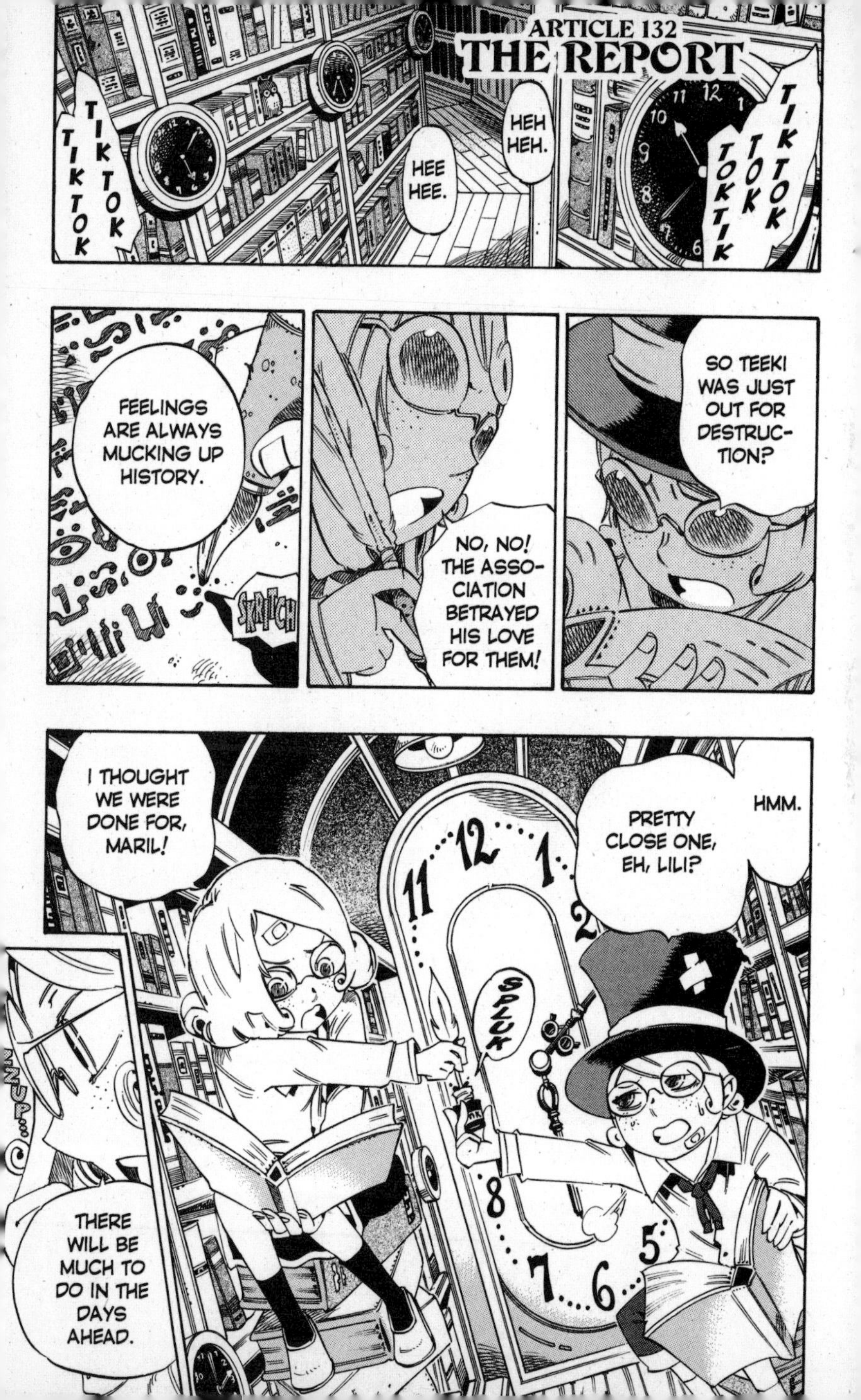

ARTICLE 132
THE REPORT
TIK TOK TOK TIK TIK TOK
HEH HEH.
HEE HEE.
TIK TOK TIK TOK
SO TEEKI WAS JUST OUT FOR DESTRUC-TION?
NO, NO! THE ASSO-CIATION BETRAYED HIS LOVE FOR THEM!
FEELINGS ARE ALWAYS MUCKING UP HISTORY.
SKRITCH
HMM.
PRETTY CLOSE ONE, EH, LILI?
I THOUGHT WE WERE DONE FOR, MARIL!
SPLUK
THERE WILL BE MUCH TO DO IN THE DAYS AHEAD.

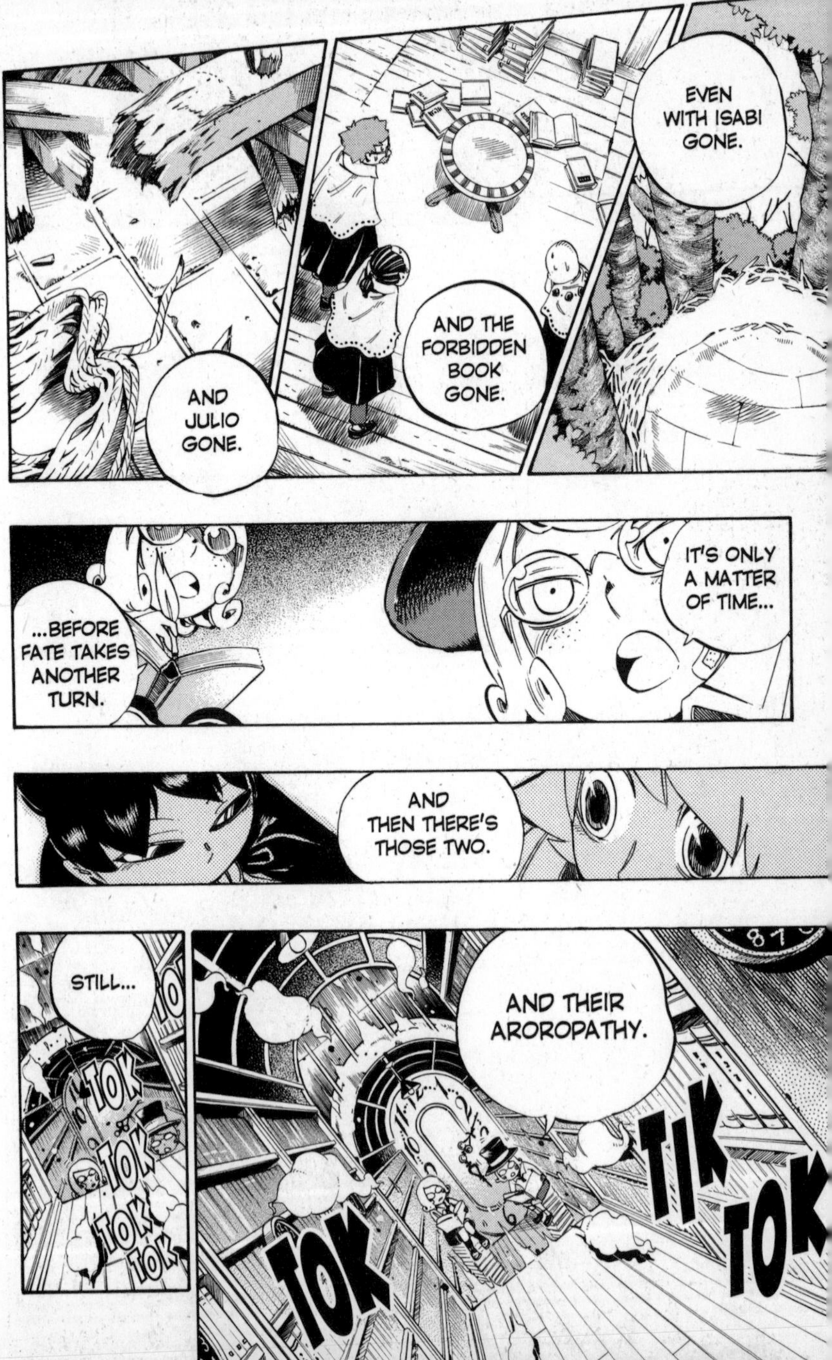
EVEN WITH ISABI GONE.
AND THE FORBIDDEN BOOK GONE.
AND JULIO GONE.
IT'S ONLY A MATTER OF TIME...
...BEFORE FATE TAKES ANOTHER TURN.
AND THEN THERE'S THOSE TWO.
AND THEIR AROROPATHY.
TIK
TOK
TOK
STILL...
TOK
TOK
TOK
TOK

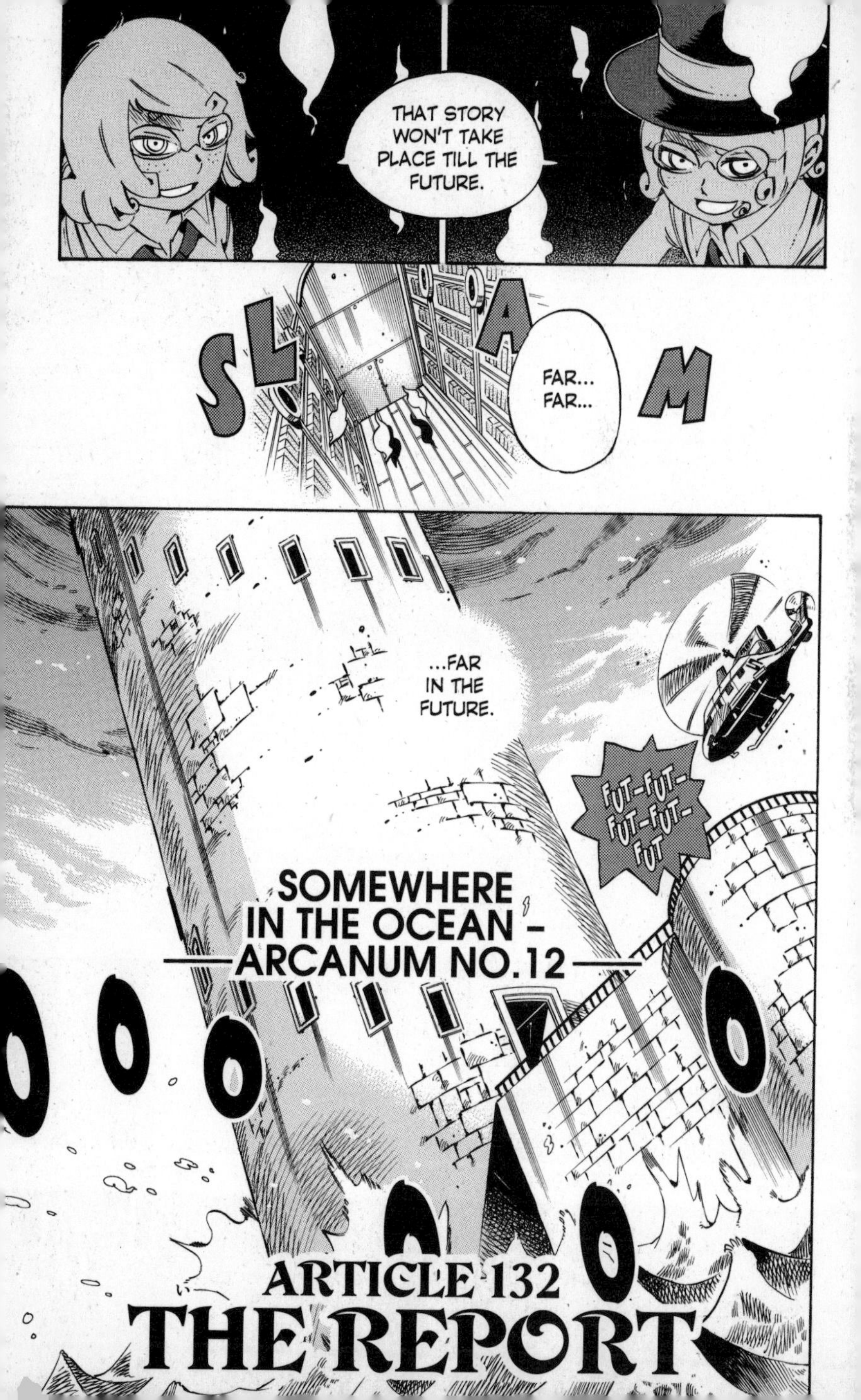
THAT STORY WON'T TAKE PLACE TILL THE FUTURE.
FAR... FAR...
SLAM
...FAR IN THE FUTURE.
FUT-FUT-FUT-FUT-FUT
SOMEWHERE IN THE OCEAN – ARCANUM NO.12
ARTICLE 132
THE REPORT

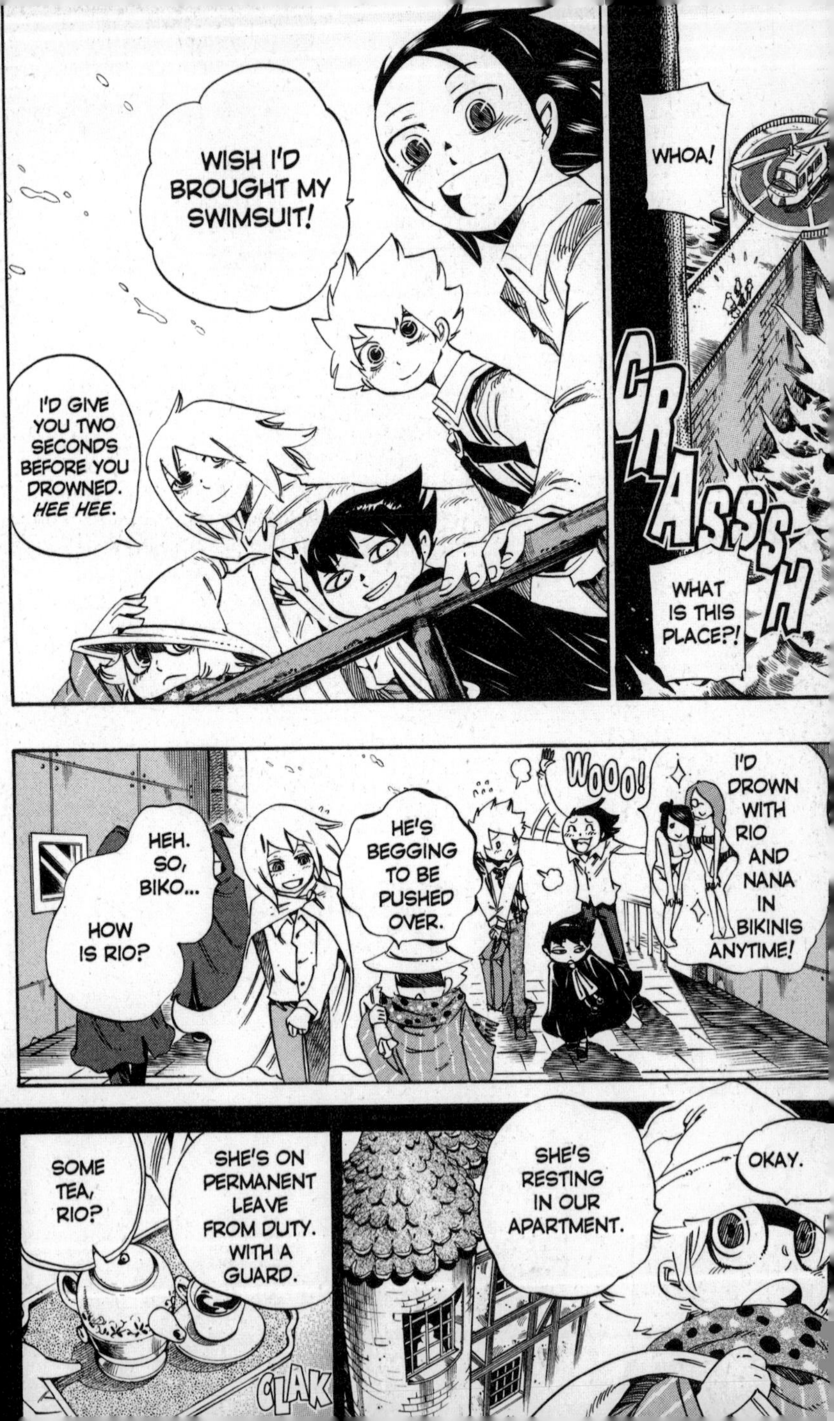
WHOA!
CRASSSH
WHAT IS THIS PLACE?!
WISH I'D BROUGHT MY SWIMSUIT!
I'D GIVE YOU TWO SECONDS BEFORE YOU DROWNED. *HEE HEE.*
I'D DROWN WITH RIO AND NANA IN BIKINIS ANYTIME!
WOOO!
HE'S BEGGING TO BE PUSHED OVER.
HEH. SO, BIKO...
HOW IS RIO?
OKAY.
SHE'S RESTING IN OUR APARTMENT.
SHE'S ON PERMANENT LEAVE FROM DUTY. WITH A GUARD.
SOME TEA, RIO?
CLAK

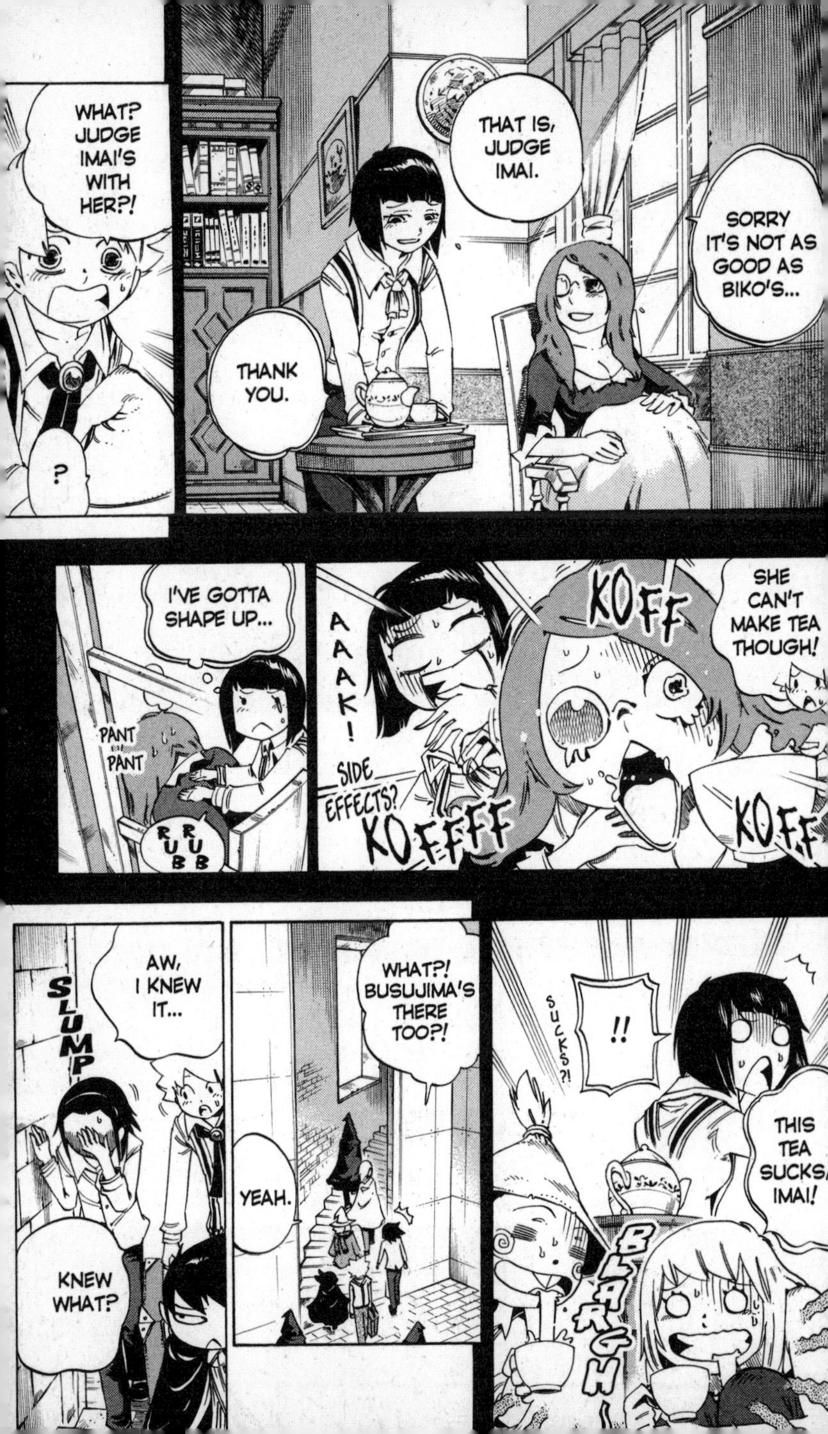
SORRY IT'S NOT AS GOOD AS BIKO'S...
THAT IS, JUDGE IMAI.
THANK YOU.
WHAT? JUDGE IMAI'S WITH HER?!
?
SHE CAN'T MAKE TEA THOUGH!
KOFF
AAAK!
SIDE EFFECTS?
KOFFFF
KOFF
I'VE GOTTA SHAPE UP...
PANT PANT
RUB RUB
!!
SUCKS?!
THIS TEA SUCKS, IMAI!
BLARGH
WHAT?! BUSUJIMA'S THERE TOO?!
YEAH.
AW, I KNEW IT...
SLUMP
KNEW WHAT?

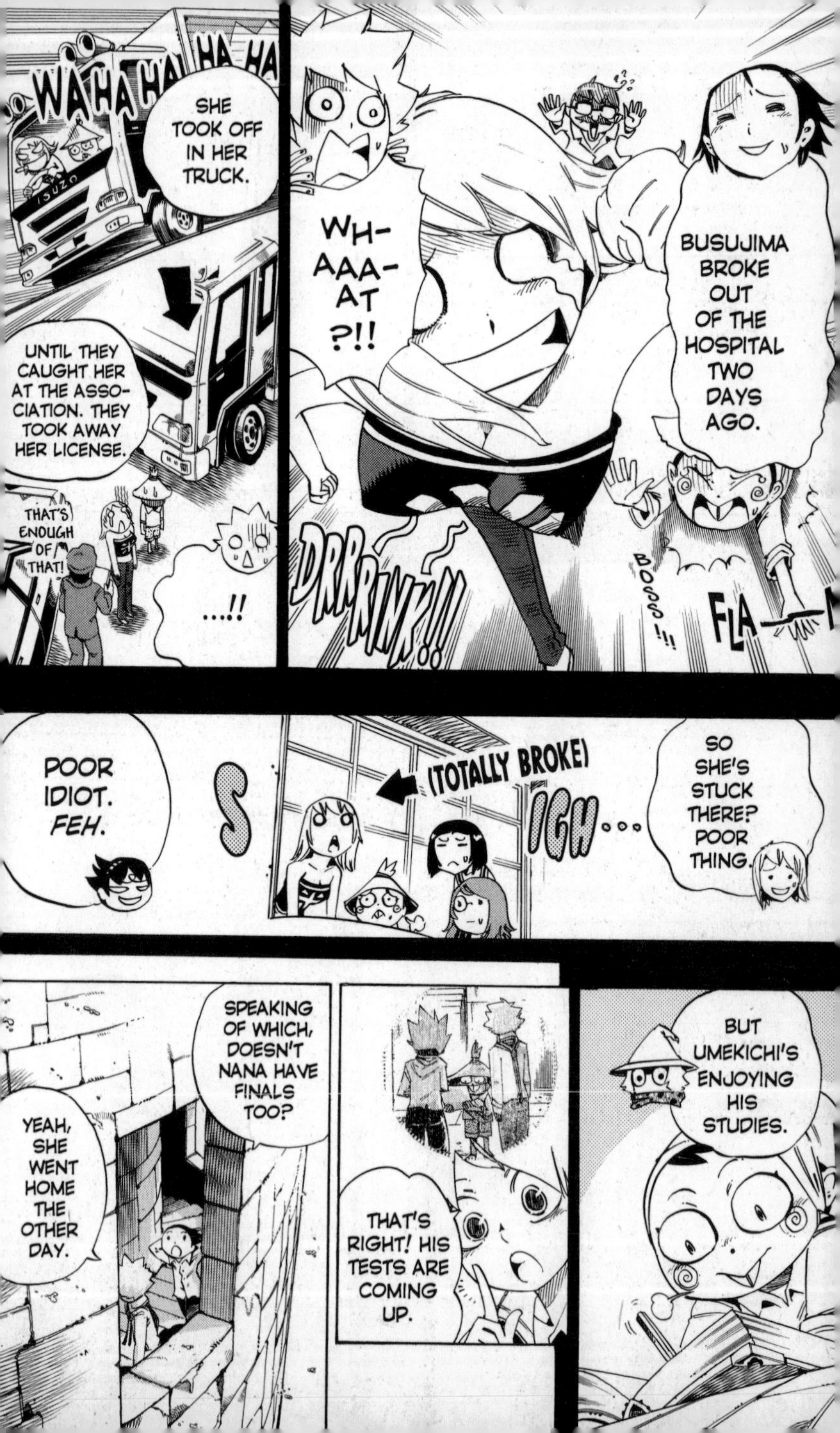
BUSUJIMA BROKE OUT OF THE HOSPITAL TWO DAYS AGO.
BOSS!!!
FLA—M
WH-AAA-AT?!!
DRRRINK!!
WAHAHA HA HA
SHE TOOK OFF IN HER TRUCK.
UNTIL THEY CAUGHT HER AT THE ASSOCIATION. THEY TOOK AWAY HER LICENSE.
THAT'S ENOUGH OF THAT!
...!!
SO SHE'S STUCK THERE? POOR THING.
SIGH...
(TOTALLY BROKE)
POOR IDIOT. FEH.
BUT UMEKICHI'S ENJOYING HIS STUDIES.
THAT'S RIGHT! HIS TESTS ARE COMING UP.
SPEAKING OF WHICH, DOESN'T NANA HAVE FINALS TOO?
YEAH, SHE WENT HOME THE OTHER DAY.

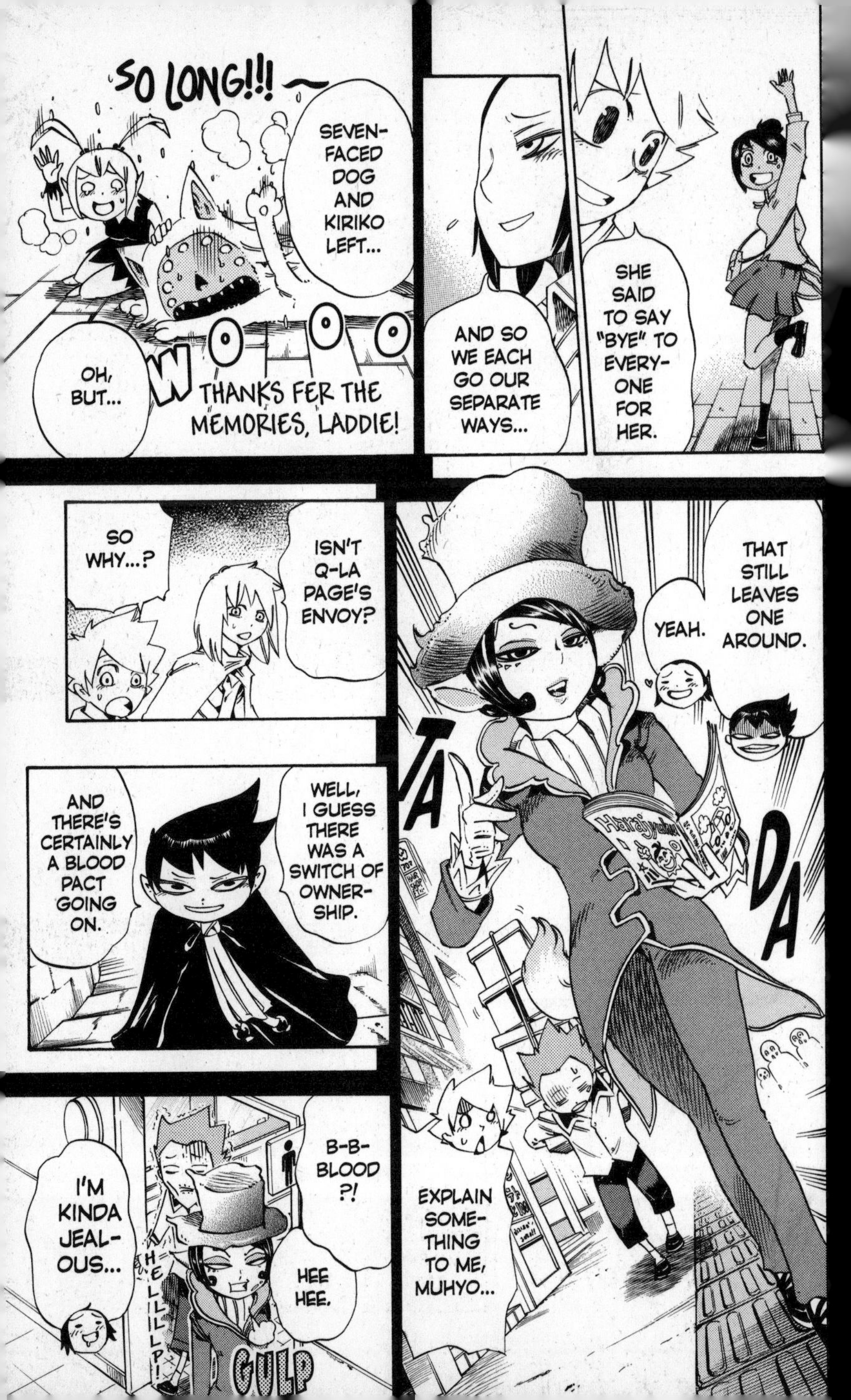
SHE SAID TO SAY "BYE" TO EVERY-ONE FOR HER.
AND SO WE EACH GO OUR SEPARATE WAYS...
SO LONG!!! ~
SEVEN-FACED DOG AND KIRIKO LEFT...
WOOOO
THANKS FER THE MEMORIES, LADDIE!
OH, BUT...
THAT STILL LEAVES ONE AROUND.
YEAH.
TA
DA
EXPLAIN SOME-THING TO ME, MUHYO...
ISN'T Q-LA PAGE'S ENVOY?
SO WHY...?
WELL, I GUESS THERE WAS A SWITCH OF OWNER-SHIP.
AND THERE'S CERTAINLY A BLOOD PACT GOING ON.
B-B-BLOOD ?!
HEE HEE.
HELLLLP!
I'M KINDA JEAL-OUS...
GULP

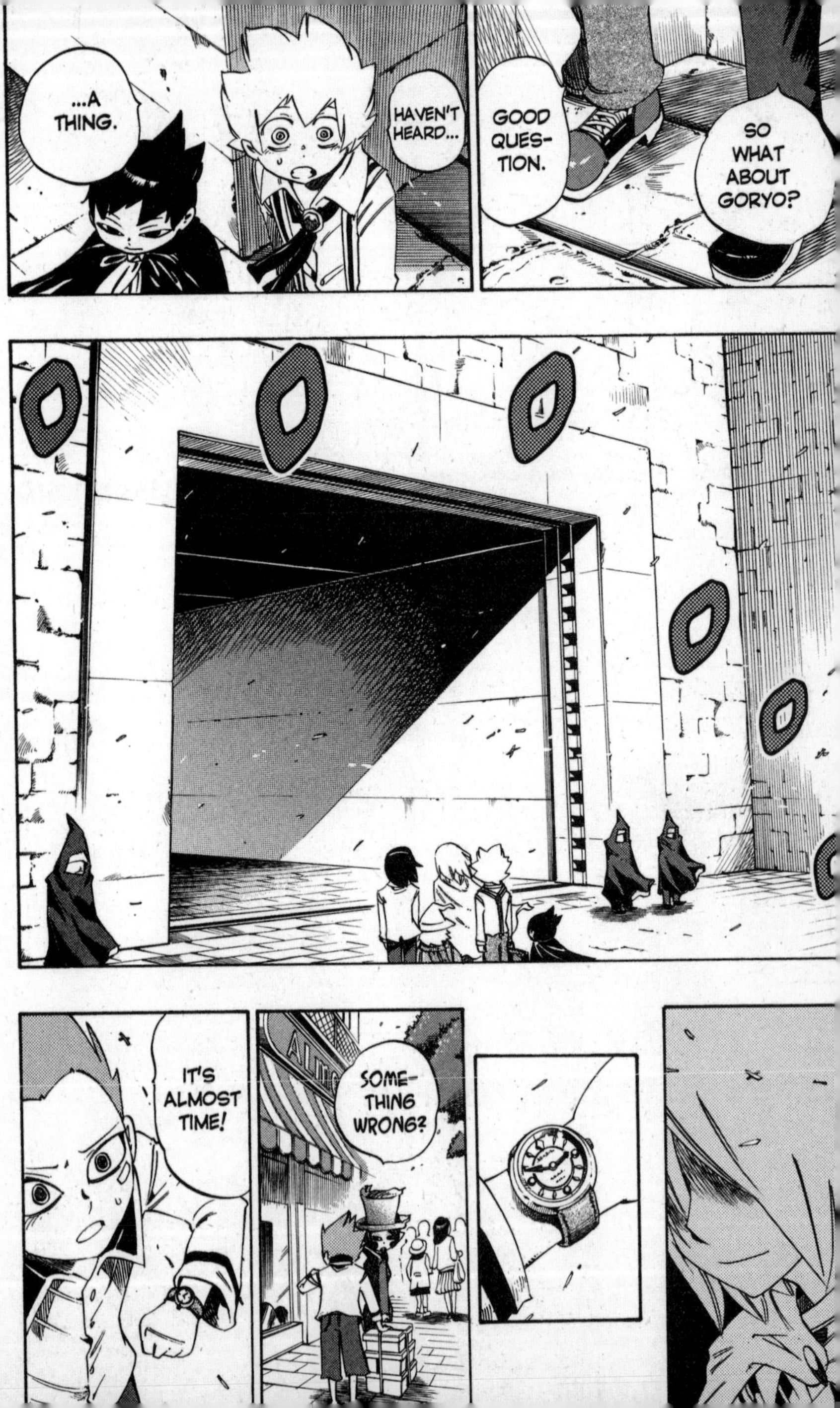
SO WHAT ABOUT GORYO?
GOOD QUESTION.
HAVEN'T HEARD...
...A THING.
SOMETHING WRONG?
IT'S ALMOST TIME!

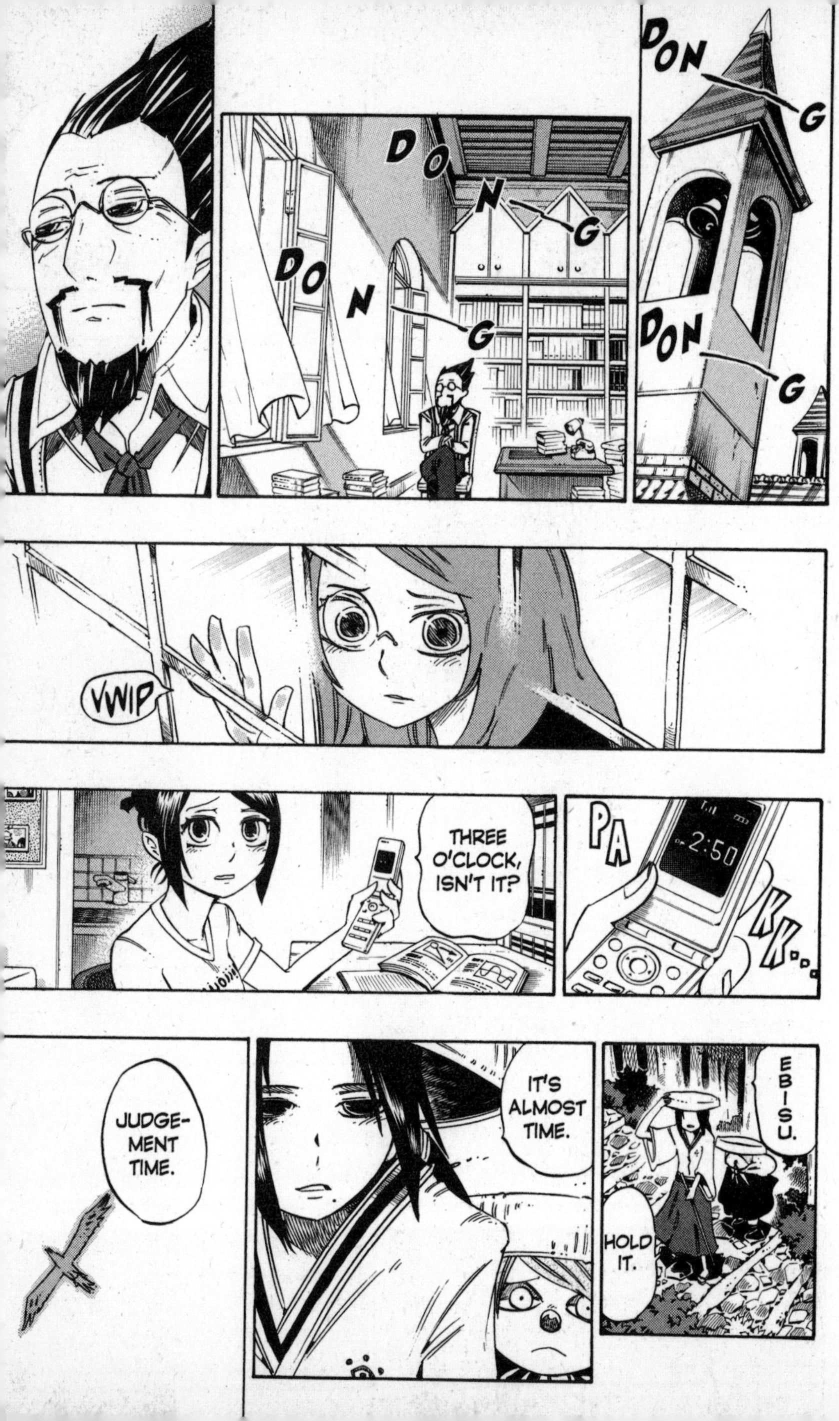
DON-G
DON-G
DON-G
DON-G
VWIP
PAKK...
THREE O'CLOCK, ISN'T IT?
EBISU.
HOLD IT.
IT'S ALMOST TIME.
JUDGE-MENT TIME.

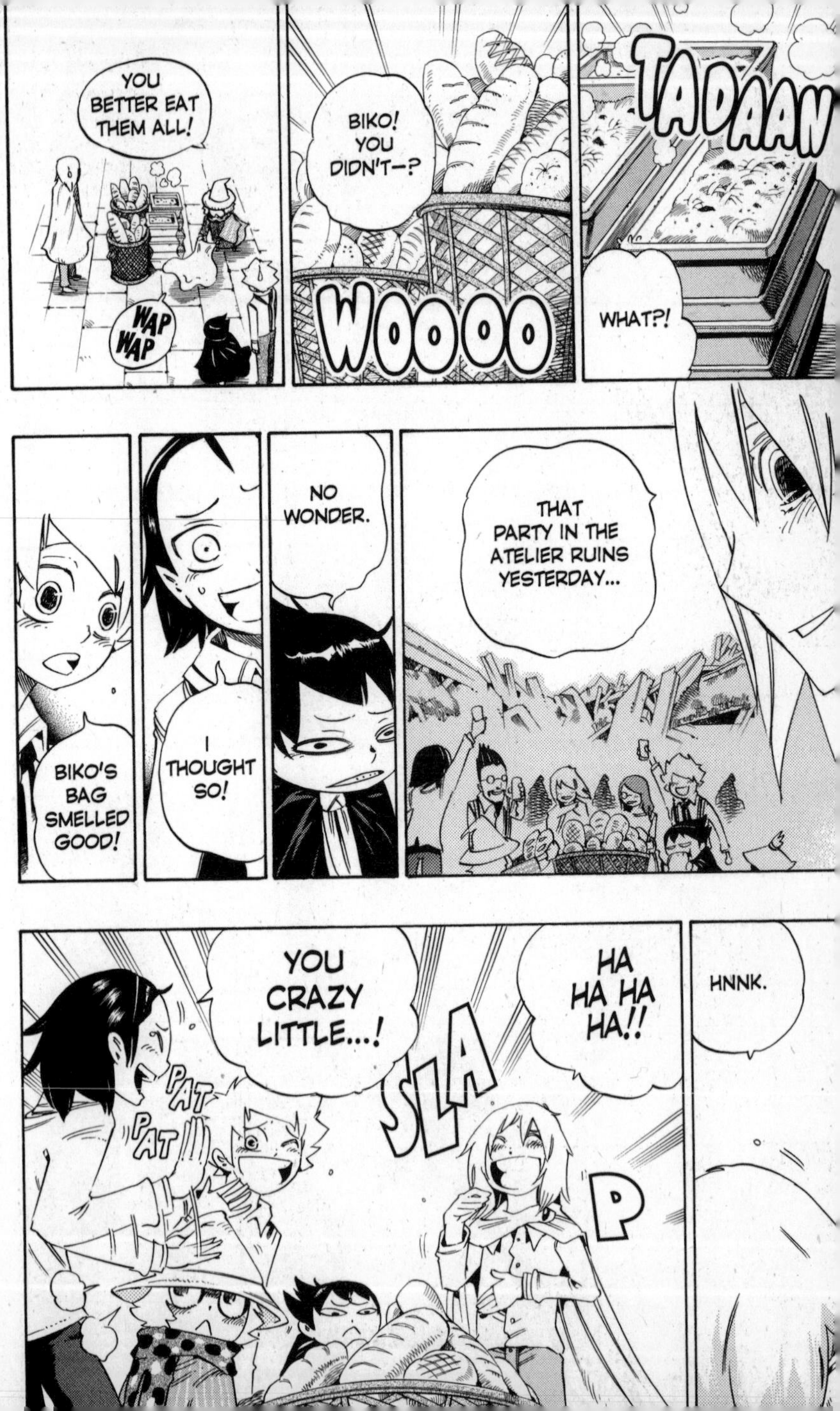

TADAAN
WHAT?!
BIKO! YOU DIDN'T—?
WOOOO
YOU BETTER EAT THEM ALL!
WAP WAP
THAT PARTY IN THE ATELIER RUINS YESTERDAY...
NO WONDER.
I THOUGHT SO!
BIKO'S BAG SMELLED GOOD!
HNNK.
HA HA HA HA!!
YOU CRAZY LITTLE...!
SLAP
PAT PAT

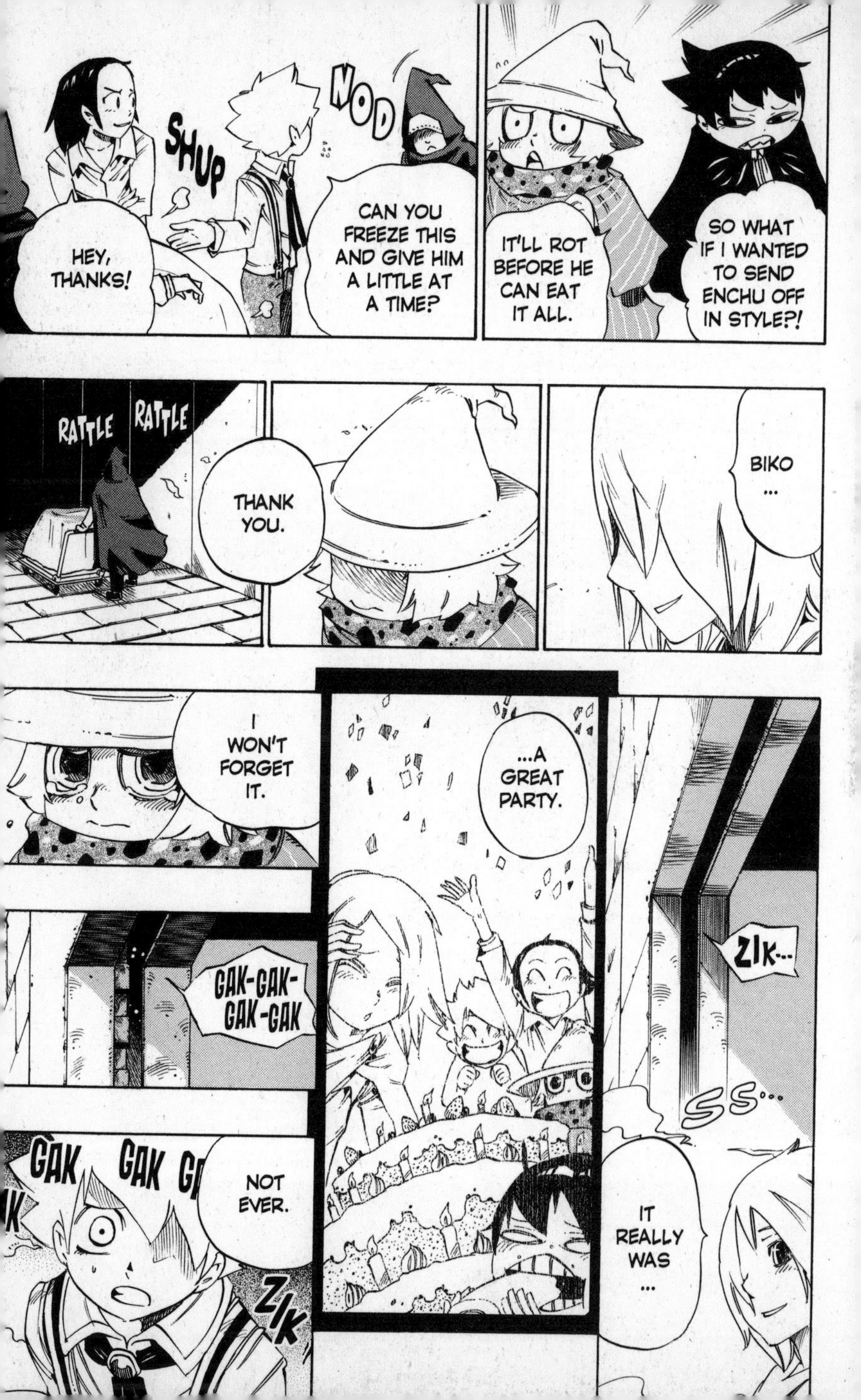
SO WHAT IF I WANTED TO SEND ENCHU OFF IN STYLE?!
IT'LL ROT BEFORE HE CAN EAT IT ALL.
NOD
CAN YOU FREEZE THIS AND GIVE HIM A LITTLE AT A TIME?
SHUP
HEY, THANKS!
BIKO ...
THANK YOU.
RATTLE RATTLE
ZIK...
SS...
IT REALLY WAS ...
...A GREAT PARTY.
I WON'T FORGET IT.
GAK-GAK-GAK-GAK
GAK GAK
NOT EVER.
ZIK

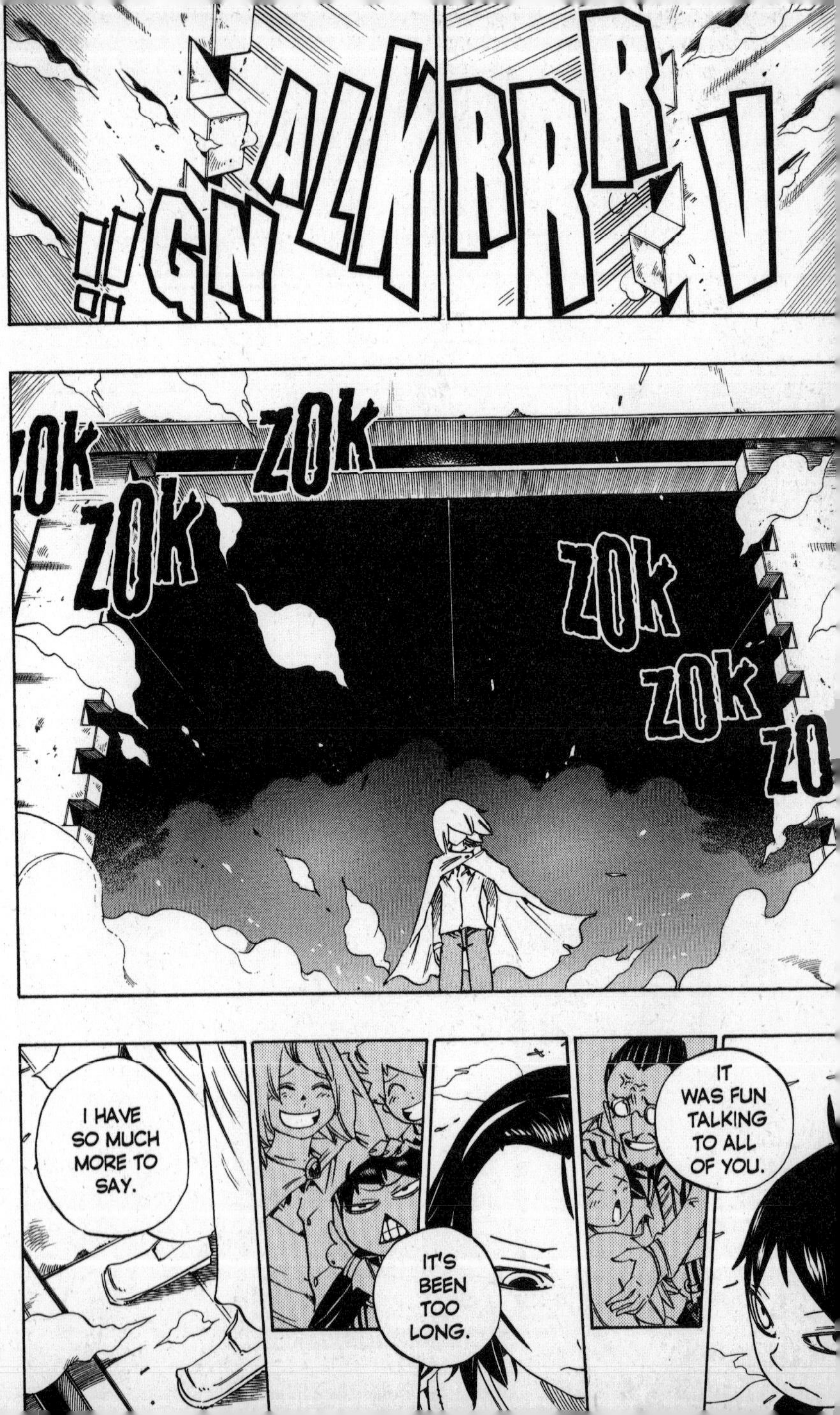
!!GNALKBRRRV
ZOK ZOK ZOK ZOK ZOK ZOK ZO
IT WAS FUN TALKING TO ALL OF YOU.
IT'S BEEN TOO LONG.
I HAVE SO MUCH MORE TO SAY.

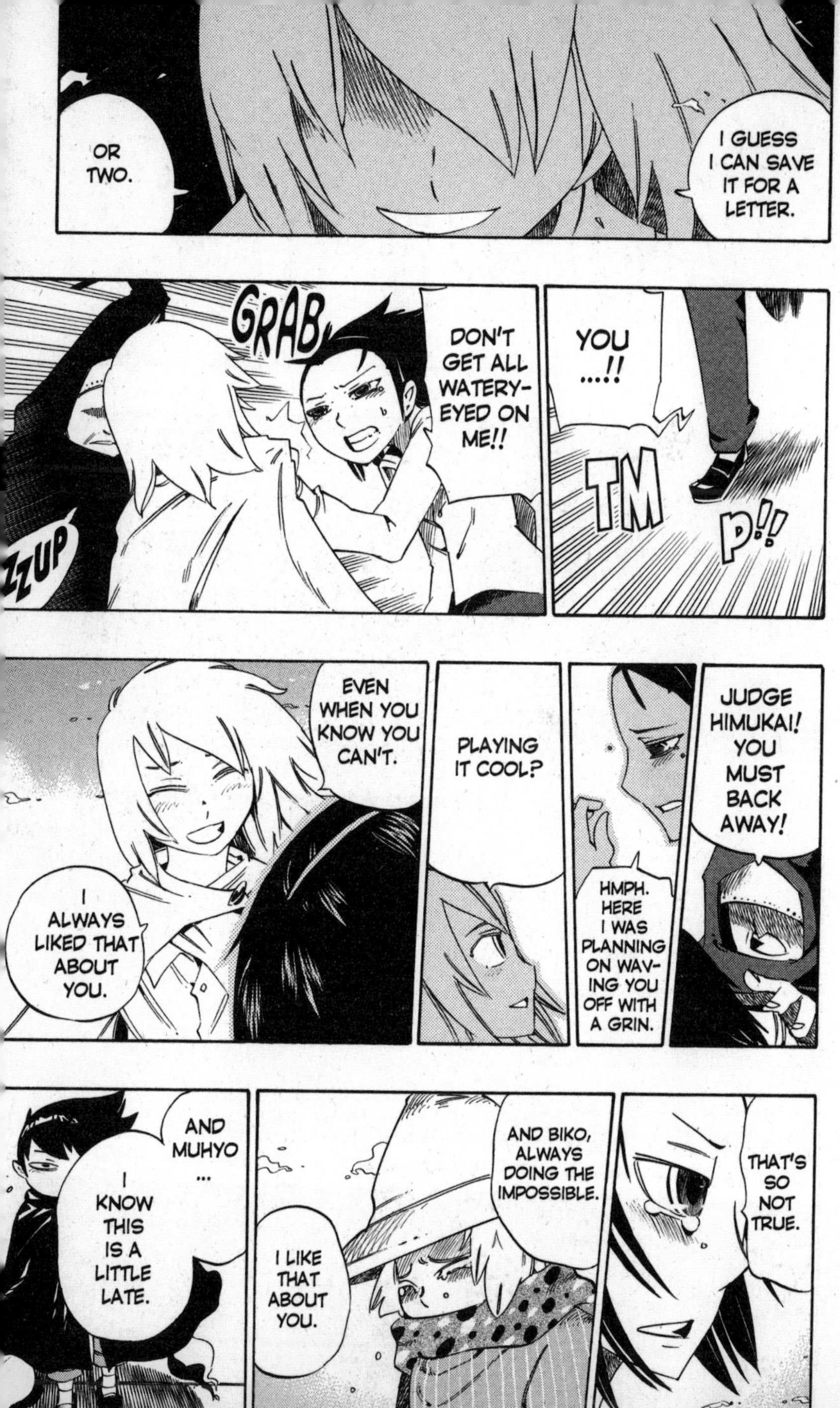
I GUESS I CAN SAVE IT FOR A LETTER.
OR TWO.
YOU ...!!
TMP!!
DON'T GET ALL WATERY-EYED ON ME!!
GRAB
ZZUP
JUDGE HIMUKAI! YOU MUST BACK AWAY!
HMPH. HERE I WAS PLANNING ON WAV-ING YOU OFF WITH A GRIN.
PLAYING IT COOL?
EVEN WHEN YOU KNOW YOU CAN'T.
I ALWAYS LIKED THAT ABOUT YOU.
THAT'S SO NOT TRUE.
AND BIKO, ALWAYS DOING THE IMPOSSIBLE.
I LIKE THAT ABOUT YOU.
AND MUHYO ...
I KNOW THIS IS A LITTLE LATE.

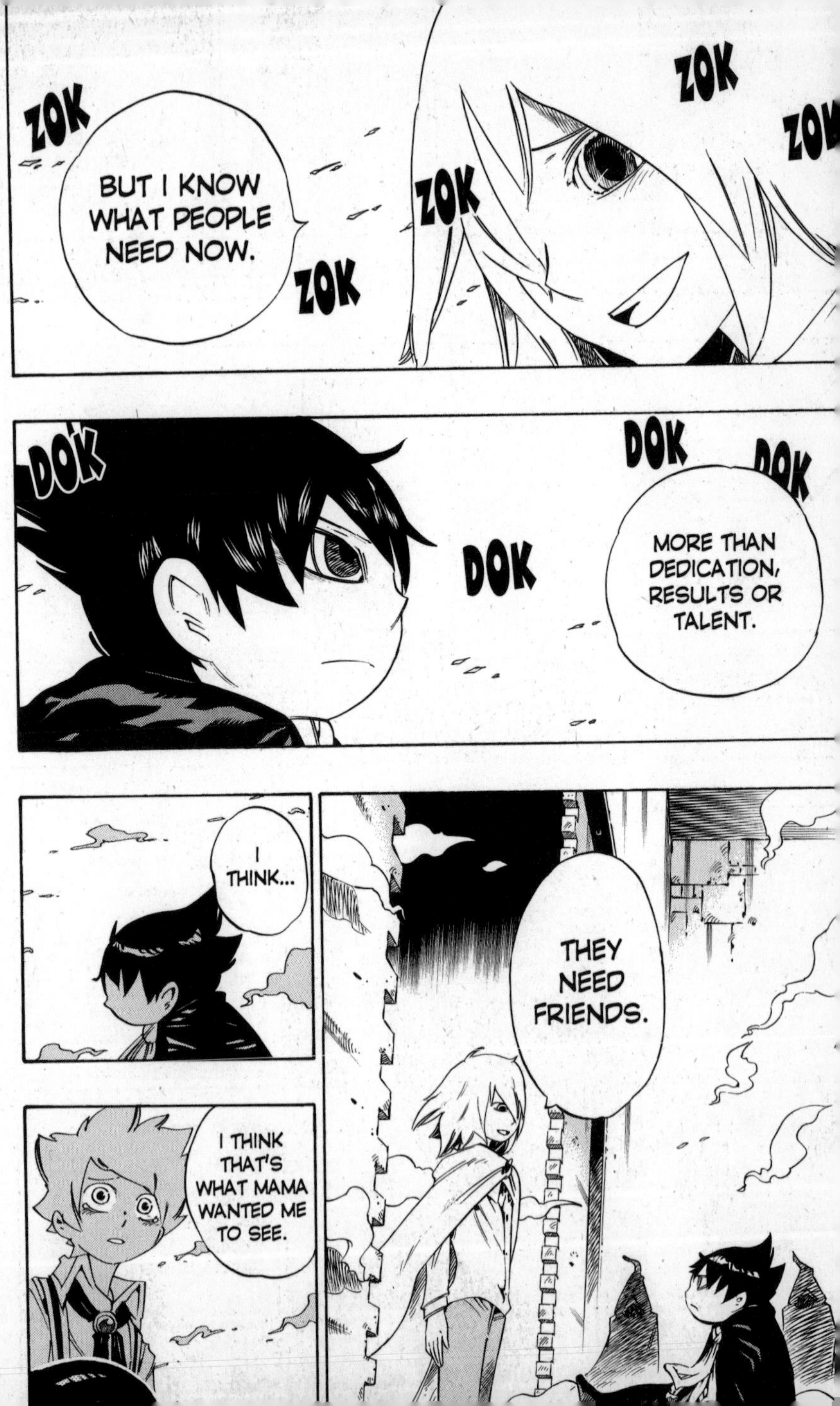
ZOK
ZOK
ZOK
BUT I KNOW WHAT PEOPLE NEED NOW.
ZOK
DOK
DOK
MORE THAN DEDICATION, RESULTS OR TALENT.
DOK
DOK
THEY NEED FRIENDS.
I THINK...
I THINK THAT'S WHAT MAMA WANTED ME TO SEE.

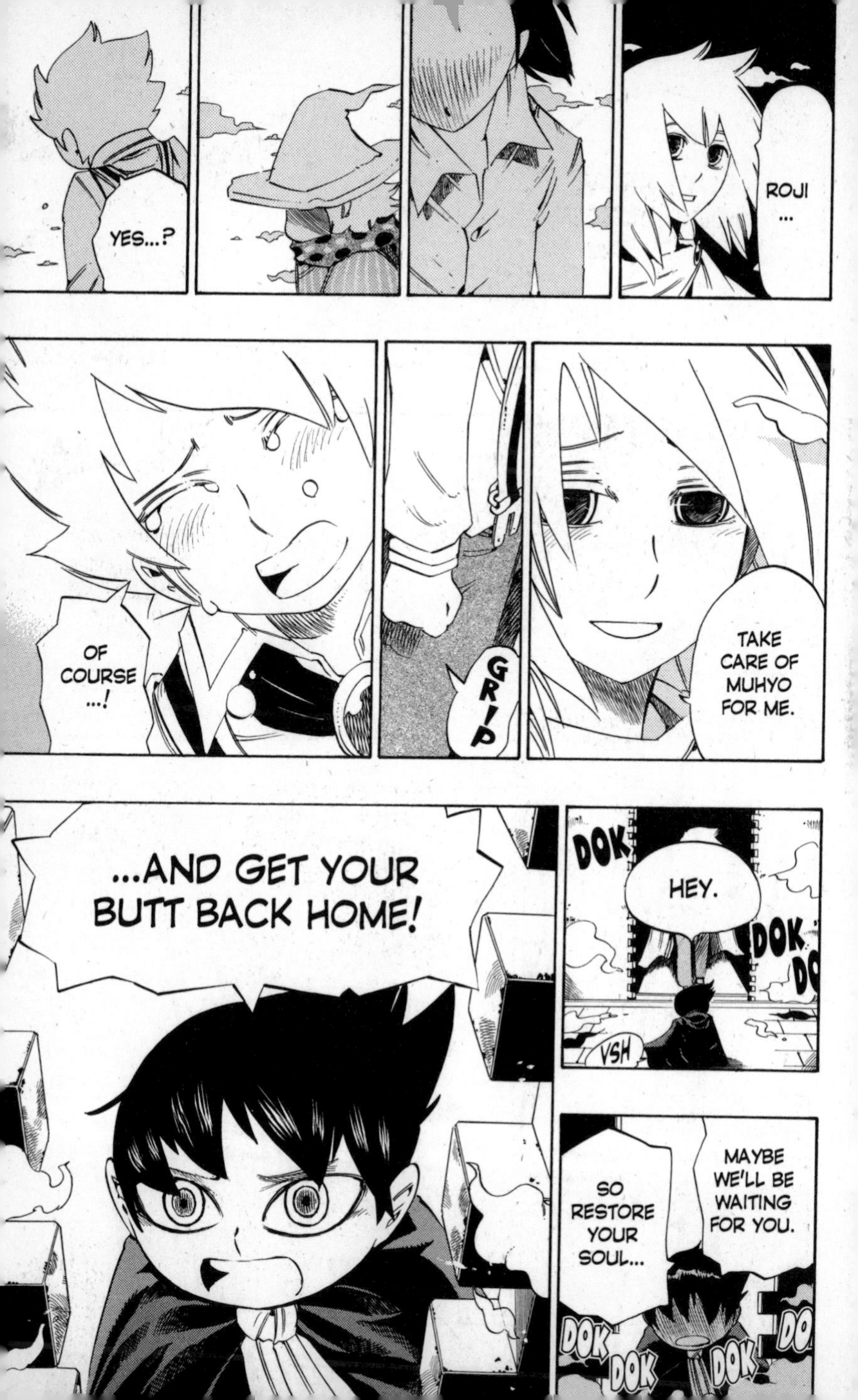
ROJI ...
YES...?
TAKE CARE OF MUHYO FOR ME.
GRIP
OF COURSE ...!
DOK
HEY.
DOK
DO
VSH
MAYBE WE'LL BE WAITING FOR YOU.
SO RESTORE YOUR SOUL...
DOK
DOK
DOK
DO
...AND GET YOUR BUTT BACK HOME!

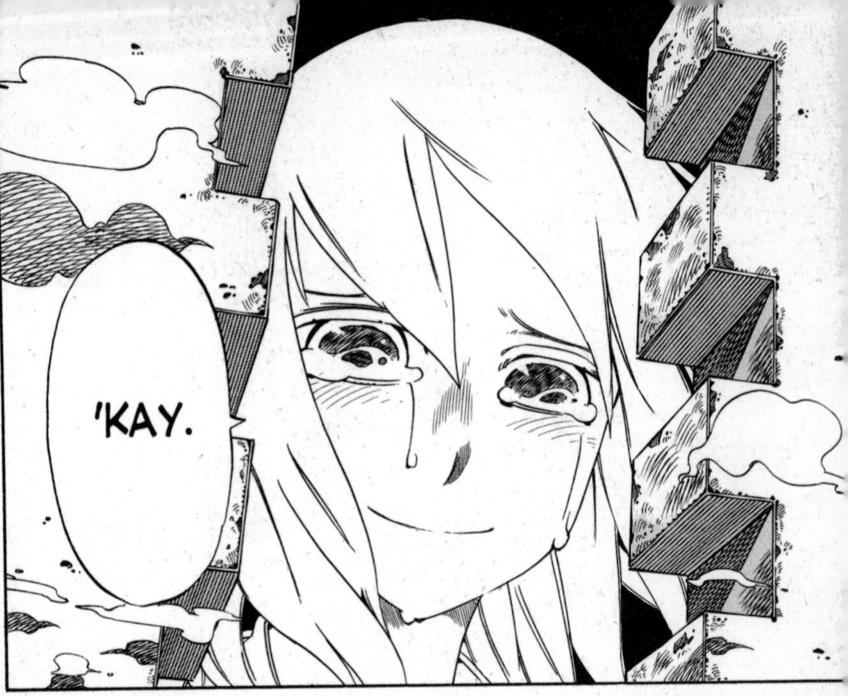
'KAY.
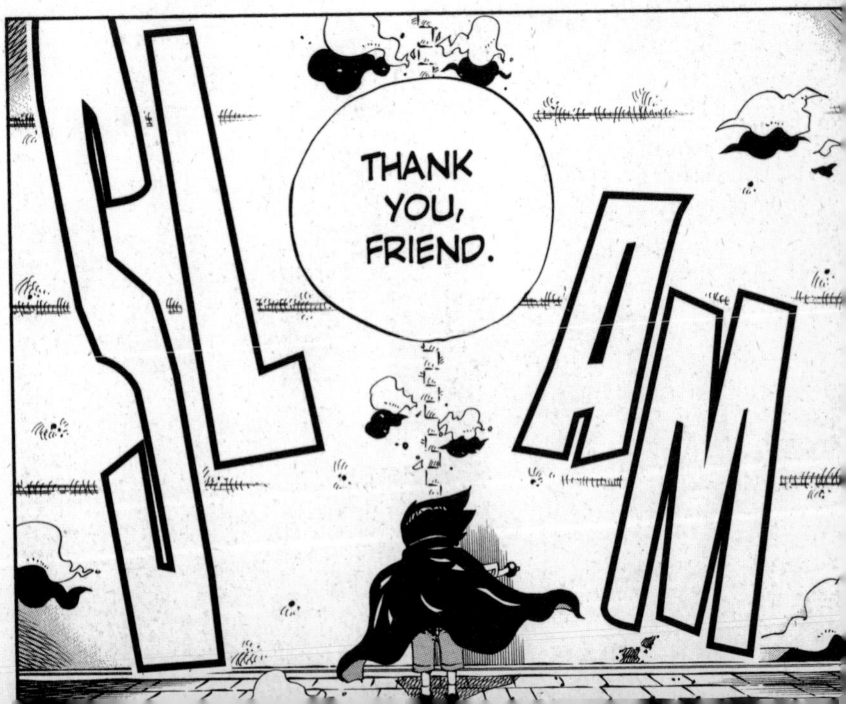
THANK YOU, FRIEND.
SLAM

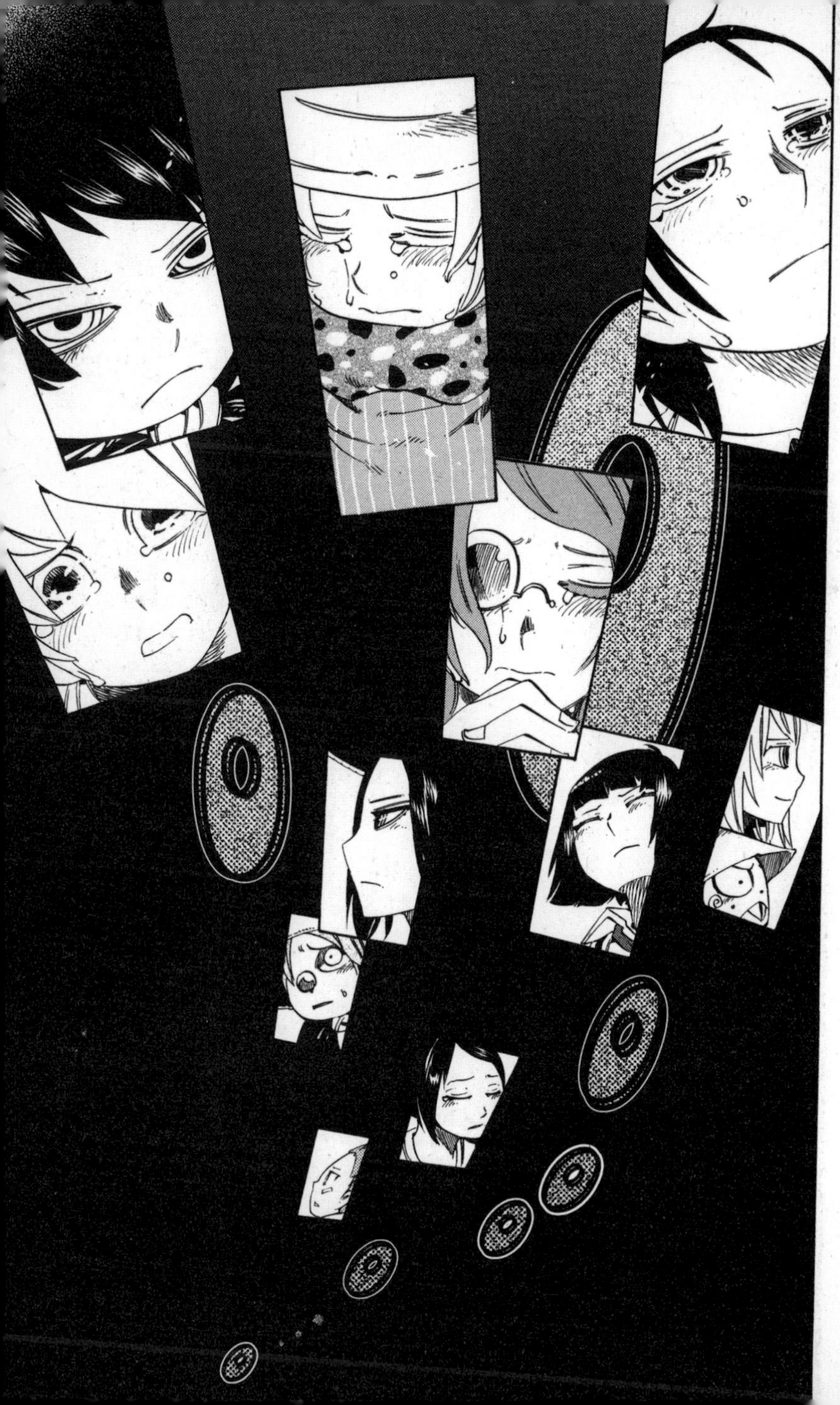

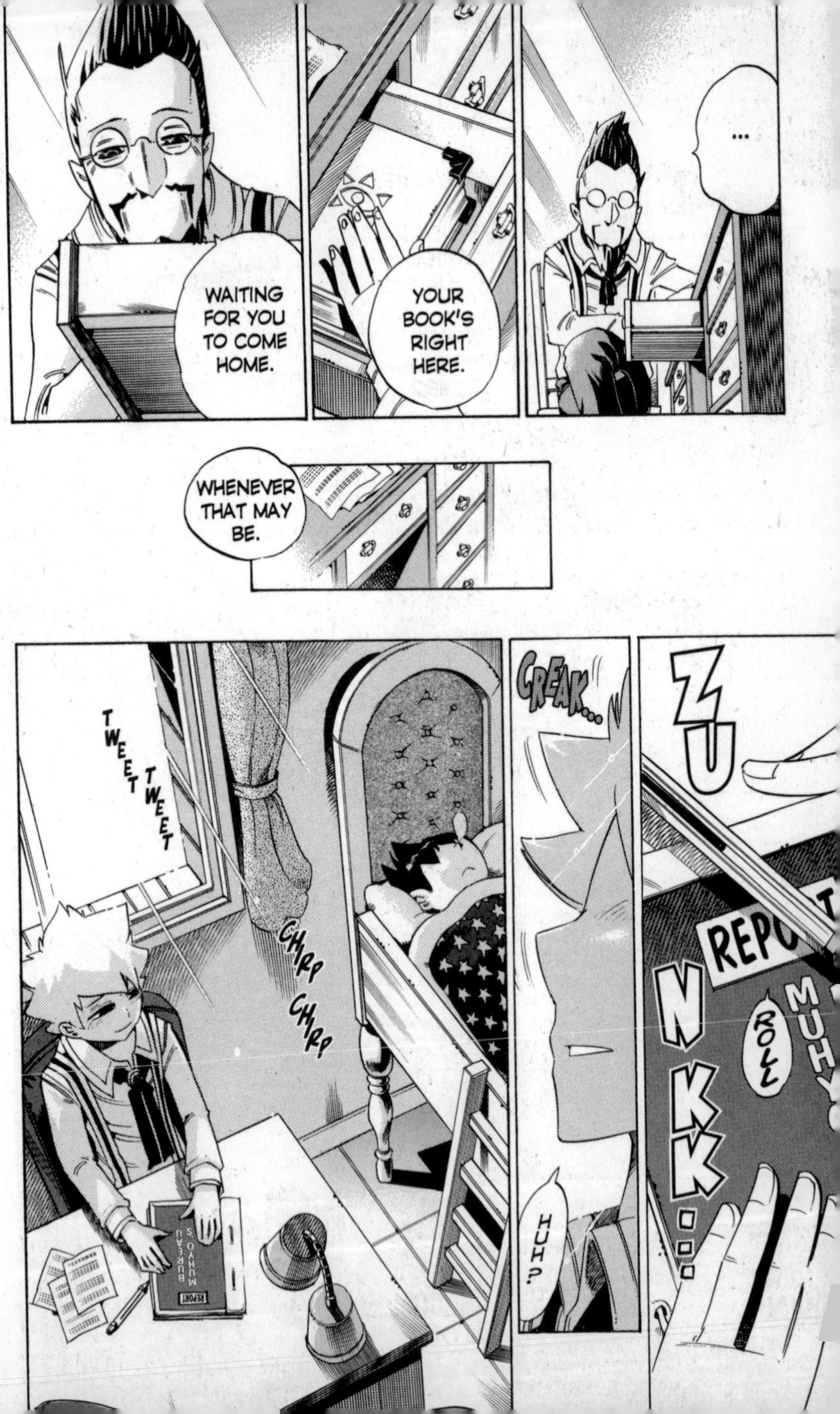
...
YOUR BOOK'S RIGHT HERE.
WAITING FOR YOU TO COME HOME.
WHENEVER THAT MAY BE.
ZU
REPO
MUHY
ROLL
NKK...
CREAK...
HUH?
TWEET TWEET
CHIRP CHIRP

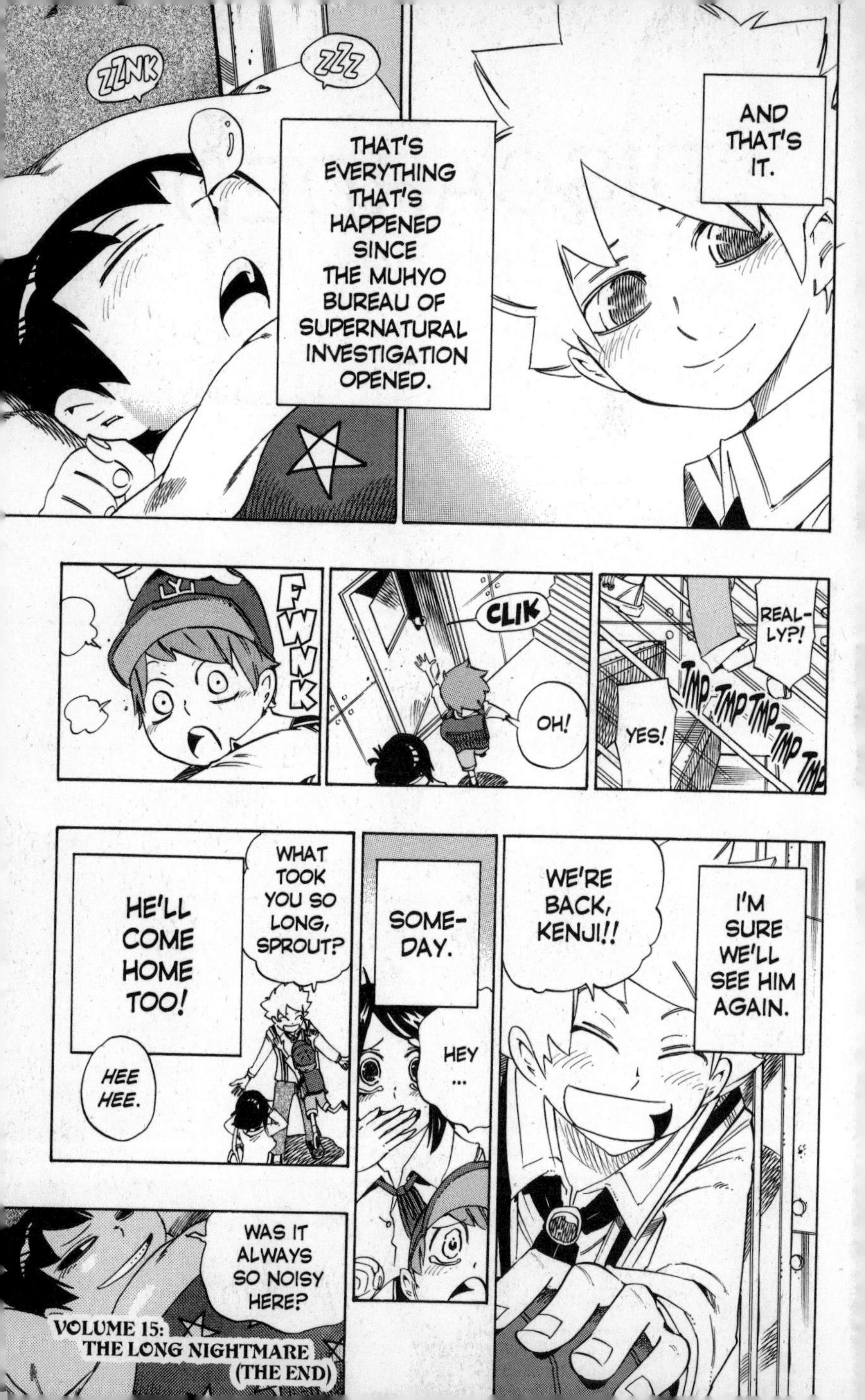
AND THAT'S IT.
ZZZ
ZZNK
THAT'S EVERYTHING THAT'S HAPPENED SINCE THE MUHYO BUREAU OF SUPERNATURAL INVESTIGATION OPENED.
REAL-LY?!
TMP TMP TMP TMP TMP
YES!
CLIK
OH!
FWNK
I'M SURE WE'LL SEE HIM AGAIN.
WE'RE BACK, KENJI!!
SOME-DAY.
HEY ...
WHAT TOOK YOU SO LONG, SPROUT?
HE'LL COME HOME TOO!
HEE HEE.
WAS IT ALWAYS SO NOISY HERE?
VOLUME 15: THE LONG NIGHTMARE (THE END)

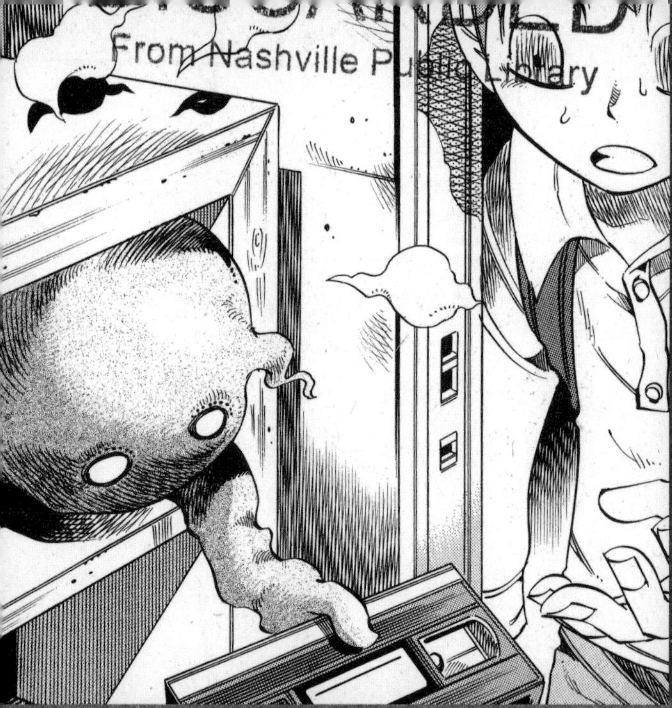

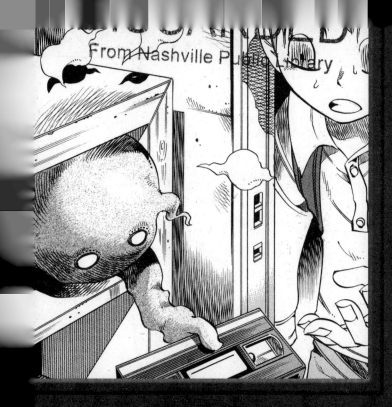

In The Next Volume...

While Muhyo and Roji have been away, the ghosts have been at play!

Available April 2010!